D0848736

The Politics of Continuity

The Politics of Continuity

British Foreign Policy and the Labour Government,
1945–46

JOHN SAVILLE

VERSO
London · New York

First published by Verso 1993
© Verso 1993
All rights reserved

Verso
UK: 6 Meard Street, London W1V 3HR
USA: 29 West 35th Street, New York, NY 10001-2291

Verso is the imprint of New Left Books

ISBN 0–86091–456–9

British Library Cataloguing in Publication Data
A catalogue record for this book is available from the British Library

Library of Congress Cataloging-in-Publication Data
A catalogue record for this book is available from the Library of Congress

Typeset by York House Typographic Ltd, London W13
Printed and bound in Great Britain by
Bookcraft (Bath) Ltd, Midsomer Norton

Contents

Acknowledgements

Historians in their writing and research accumulate many debts to colleagues and friends. I am especially grateful to Professor Ralph Miliband, Dr Tania Rose, Professor Ellen Meiksins Wood and Professor Neal Wood for their careful reading of the penultimate draft of this volume. Dr Dianne Kirby offered me the results of her latest research on the Christian churches and the Cold War; and my colleague Dr C.J. Christie, of the Centre for South-East Asian Studies here at the University of Hull, was kind enough to read my chapter on Vietnam. There have been many others, in the United Kingdom and elsewhere, who have listened and commented on seminar papers I have taken from different parts of my research, and I am grateful for their criticisms and suggestions. To Peter Weiler, of Boston University, I owe a special debt, not only for his published work, from which I have gained much, but also for allowing me to read his unpublished material on Ernest Bevin. To Sir Geoffrey Wilson I am obliged for his comments on what I have written concerning his former colleague in the Foreign Office, Dr Christopher Hill.

I am much indebted to the British Academy for a research grant; and like all who work in libraries and record offices I must acknowledge the general helpfulness that one meets, as a matter of course, so it would seem. My greatest obligation is to the Brynmor Jones Library of my own university, both for its excellent collections and for the never failing assistance of its library staff. Among other institutions I must first mention the Public Record Office at Kew, and I have to acknowledge their permission to reproduce the sources from their papers quoted in my text. I have further to record my appreciation of the staffs of the British Library, in Bloomsbury, Boston Spa and the Newspaper Library at Colindale; the National Library of Scotland, Edinburgh; the university libraries of York, Leeds and Manchester; the Bodleian, Oxford; the Working-Class Movement Library, Salford; the Bibliothèque Nationale, Paris; the Institute of Historical Research and Senate House Library, University of London; and the library of the Institute of Social History, Amsterdam.

I am under particular obligation to Mrs Gill Crag, who put my manuscript on to computer and disk expeditiously and efficiently, and to my friend Irene

Baldwin, the long-serving secretary of the Department of Economic and Social History at the University of Hull, for her general helpfulness. To my wife I am deeply beholden, as I have been for many years, for her constant support and above all for her sympathetic understanding that long hours in one's study and away in other libraries and institutions are an inevitable and necessary part of the historian's vocation.

I have dedicated this volume to Edward Thompson. In the late 1950s and early 1960s he and I were engaged closely in political matters which for both of us were to be of crucial importance in the years that followed. At the time I felt a very close comradeship with both Edward and his wife Dorothy, but I took our intense activity together as a matter of course, a job to be done. It has been in later years that I have come to appreciate the privilege of working with one of the outstanding personalities of our age, and I can but record my gratitude and my affection.

JOHN SAVILLE
University of Hull

Abbreviations

BL   British Library
COS   Chiefs of Staff
DBPO   *Documents on British Policy Overseas*
DLB   *Dictionary of Labour Biography*
DNB   *Dictionary of National Biography*
EAM   Ethnico Apeleftherotiko Metopo ([Greek] National Liberation
          Front)
ELAS   Ethnikos Laikos Apeletherotikos Stratos ([Greek] National
          Liberation Army)
FO   Foreign Office
FRUS   *Foreign Relations of the United States*
JCS   Joint Chiefs of Staff
JSSC   Joint Strategic Survey Committee (US)
NUWM   National Unemployed Workers' Movement
OSS   Office of Strategic Services (US)
OWI   Office of War Information (US)
PLP   Parliamentary Labour Party
PRO   Public Record Office (London)
PUS   Permanent Under-Secretary
SACSEA   Supreme Allied Commander, South-East Asia
SEAC   South-East Asia Command
SOE   Special Operations Executive

Introduction

> The White Rabbit put on his spectacles. 'Where shall I begin, please your Majesty?' he asked. 'Begin at the beginning', the King said gravely, 'and go on till you come to the end: then stop.'
>
> *Alice in Wonderland*

The definition of a beginning in historical analysis is not quite so simple as the King of Hearts suggested, although at least part of the advice offered seems to have been accepted by some writers on the origins of the Cold War. To define a beginning in historical terms involves a complex study of the past and its leverage upon the present. By the summer of 1945 national interests and the political attitudes associated therewith had been affected in diverse ways, and sometimes in dramatic ways, by the years of war; and those interests and attitudes had themselves been influenced and shaped by the decades which went before. Historians who have tried to latch the origins of the Cold War on to some particular event, or episode, or short-term crisis, have greatly simplified, and distorted, the complexities of the real world. It is indeed curious how many attempts there have been.[1]

Historical writing on the Cold War has followed a somewhat jerky pattern. Until the British Public Record Office lowered the age of inspection from fifty years to thirty years most of the writing on the years of troubled peace after the summer of 1945 was American.[2] It was not until the mid 1970s that the public records for the first year of peace became available to scholars in Britain, by which time the vigorous debate between the revisionist school in the United States and their more orthodox brethren had been in progress for at least a decade and a half. Some official histories had been published in the United Kingdom, the most important being the brilliant volume by Margaret Gowing, *Independence and Deterrence: Britain and Atomic Energy. Vol. 1: Policy Making* (1974). An early and highly successful use of both American and British records was the 1978 volume by Christopher Thorne, *Allies of a Kind: The*

1

United States, Britain and the War against Japan, 1941–1945 but this did not go beyond the war years. Since then there has been an increasing flow of published work using government sources on both sides of the Atlantic. Peter Weiler's *British Labour and the Cold War* (1988) is an excellent example of a specialised text based upon a wide-ranging research, but there remains much to be done on the relationships between America and Britain and now, with the new situation in Eastern Europe and what was formerly the Soviet Union, upon the inter-relations of the three wartime Allied Powers, both in war and in the years of peace.

Historians are accustomed to being confronted with generous masses of documentation relating to the subject of their research, but the volume of original materials for the post-1945 years is indeed very large. Britain, like the United States, was involved in every continent of the world during the years of war and their aftermath. This was not true of the Soviet Union, whose geo-politics mostly excluded the countries of Africa, Latin America, India, South-East Asia and Australia. In the immediate post-war years Soviet interests covered most of Asia, the Middle East and above all Europe, and it is in these areas that access to Russian archives should prove highly illuminating. There is no substitute for official documents and despatches, but it is hardly a new thought that analysis of foreign policy decisions cannot be limited to what was said officially, or, even more important, what was being said and written that was not made official. Public opinion, for example, is an ill-defined concept about which political scientists and sociologists have been debating for many years, but we should note the interesting differences in the immediate post-war years between the United States and Britain in the matter of some aspects of public opinion outside the working offices of the decision-makers. In the former, in spite of segments of a radical tradition, anti-communism was already well in place by the end of the war, and it became a populist movement of national significance in the later 1940s and 1950s. In Britain, while the propertied classes had always been consistently anti-communist and anti-Soviet, for the first two years of the Labour Government there was a highly vocal opposition to Ernest Bevin's foreign policy from within the Parliamentary Labour Party, from quite significant sections of the public outside Westminster, and notably from within sections of the trade union movement. Such opposition, it should be emphasised, made no difference to the policies the Labour Government were pursuing in international relations, but it meant that until late 1947 Bevin was a good deal more restrained in his public statements than he otherwise might have been, and he cultivated the impression that he was sincerely concerned to achieve agreement with the Russians. This was not, for the most part, true, but it is still widely believed.

There were other differences between Washington and Whitehall. Decision-making in the British Foreign Office was central to the policies of the Labour Government in foreign affairs, and with Ernest Bevin as the most compelling member of the Cabinet, he and his advisers exercised the most decisive influence. There were exceptions, the most important of which was India. The Indian situation was potentially so explosive that any attempt to maintain British rule could not seriously be considered, although there were some, Bevin certainly could have been included, who might have tried. India was not, however, within the domain of the British Foreign Office, and Clement Attlee became, in effect, the Minister for India during the negotiations which led to independence. In Washington, on the other hand, power was not as centralised as in London, in spite of the particular and special role of the President, and the State Department, which had been by-passed so often by Roosevelt during the war years, had to fight hard to regain its central position among the various decision-making groups.

'History cannot be written unless the historian can achieve some kind of contact with the mind of those about whom he is writing.' These words of E.H. Carr[3] have been mostly disregarded in the contemporary analysis of international politics by British historians of the Cold War; and it is to begin to remedy the discussion of the political consciousness of those involved in global diplomacy that the first, rather long, chapter of the present volume is concerned with 'The Mind of the Foreign Office'. Diplomatic negotiations, and the formulation of policy in international relations, derive broadly from the perception of national interest at any particular time and place. The historian's task is not only the elucidation of perceived interest, and the interpretation of interest by the various groups involved in its application to contemporary problems. The historian must also be concerned with the conflict, if any, between 'perceived' interest and 'real' interest, as the individual historian understands the latter. Perceived interest by any one individual among the decision-making élites is a social construct. In Britain during the first half of the twentieth century the most significant characteristic of those involved in the elaboration of international policies has been their reliance upon traditional modes of thought, and a conservative understanding of what constituted national interest. Empire was always at the centre of their judgements. In January 1907 Eyre Crowe, one of the most influential officials in the Foreign Office in the whole of the twentieth century, defined England's basic interests in imperial terms that remained wholly acceptable to later generations: including the senior members of the Office at the time when the Labour Party came to power in July 1945. Eyre Crowe summed up:

The general character of England's foreign policy is determined by immutable conditions of her geographical situation on the ocean flank of Europe as an island state with vast areas of colonies and dependencies whose existence and survival as an independent community are inseparably bound up with the possession of preponderant sea power.[4]

It has been one of the tragedies of British history in this century that neither Bevin nor his Foreign Office advisers in 1945 had any serious appreciation or understanding that the world in the aftermath of the Second World War was changing rapidly, and that Eyre Crowe's evaluation of 1907 was now no longer appropriate. 'When I say I am not prepared to sacrifice the British Empire what do I mean? I know that if the British Empire fell, the greatest collection of free nations would go into the limbo of the past, or it would be a disaster.' These were Bevin's words in the House of Commons on 21 February 1946.

The stability of the institutional framework at the top levels of government worked in the same direction. Alone among the major powers of Europe during the twentieth century, Britain never experienced either defeat in war or a major upheaval in administrative organisation; and this was matched by continuity in office of members of the ruling groups. In the Foreign Office, for example, Eyre Crowe was an Under-Secretary of State in 1914 and he moved up to Permanent Under-Secretary in 1920. Just before the next world war Sir Alec Cadogan became Permanent Under-Secretary in January 1938, and he remained in post throughout the years of war and for the first six months of the new Labour administration. It was widely assumed that the Labour election victory of July 1945 would be followed by major changes in the administrative machine and among the personnel of the top administrative levels, but this never happened. Continuity in place and position was especially marked within the Foreign Office and throughout the Diplomatic Service. Ernest Bevin made his first speech on foreign affairs in the House of Commons on 20 August 1945, and Halifax, the British Ambassador in Washington, wrote to him a few days later emphasising how much the feared consequences of a Labour victory had now receded. Halifax particularly noted that what had impressed commentators of all sides of public opinion was the stated continuity of British foreign policy in respect of the Empire, and the general lines of agreement with the wartime Coalition Government.[5]

It is not difficult to understand the conservatism of the administrative élites in Whitehall. The social origins of recruitment had remained unchanged. Both Eyre Crowe and Cadogan were surrounded by former Etonians, the school most favoured by Foreign Office entrants. 'Perception' in the Foreign Office, as will be illustrated in the chapters which follow, was conditioned by social class, developed by a traditional upper-class educational system, moulded by departmental traditions, and confirmed throughout life by conservative and affluent life-styles. With Bevin and other Labour ministers analysis is inevitably more complicated since their manifesto for the general election actually mentioned the word 'socialism', and among them many sincerely believed that their social reforms were socialist measures. This could never be said of Bevin's foreign policies, which were probably more anti-Soviet than a Conservative government would have pursued (or have been able to pursue). The chapter devoted to Ernest Bevin is an attempt to begin to understand his motivation as well as his political practices.

This present volume is an inquiry into some of the questions of British international relations after 1945 that either have been too briefly touched upon in the current literature or have been neglected. The argument throughout goes sharply against most of the historical writing on the years when the Cold War was coming to dominate international affairs. The absence of debate and controversy around the direction and the substance of British foreign policy has been quite remarkable, with nothing comparable to the arguments and analysis developed by the revisionist school in the United States. This is not to suggest that the specific contentions of the American revisionist school can today be taken over, but it is to underline the need for a careful re-appraisal of contemporary British writing. In the United States revisionist writing has gone out of fashion with suggestions that a consensus is now emerging between revisionism and orthodoxy.[6] What has also largely disappeared is a critical exegesis of the ever-increasing volume of original materials for the historians' fundamental research. On the British side two examples may be offered. One is the Attlee heresy which forms the subject of Chapter 3 of this book. In the two years following the end of the war and the entry into office of the Labour Party there was only one substantial critic of foreign policy among the top élites of government, politicians, and their administrative and military servants in Whitehall; and that was the Prime Minister. The criticisms that were offered by Clement Attlee remained unremarked upon, in terms of a connected analysis, for something approaching four decades. Kenneth Harris, in his large-scale biography of Attlee published in 1982, insisted on the continuity of British foreign policy and the close relationship between Attlee and Bevin, and yet reprinted Attlee's important memorandum on the 'Future of the Italian Colonies'. Harris noted only that Attlee's critical stand prevented Britain from being 'lumbered' with the trusteeship for Cyrenaica, but his main text emphasised the close partnership between Prime Minister and Foreign Secretary. Alan Bullock, in his massive third volume on Bevin as Foreign Secretary, had a number of comments about Attlee's opposition to some parts of Bevin's policies, but they were not brought together and the general impression followed that of Harris. It was around the mid 1980s that scholars began to document the details of Attlee's critique, but his suggestions for an alternative approach, especially in the Mediterranean and the Middle East, have still not been integrated into a comprehensive survey of these years.[7] The difficulty with any assessment of Attlee is that there is no doubt he agreed with Ernest Bevin on a number of other important issues of foreign policy. At least, that is what the record so far suggests.

In recent years it has been suggested by some historians that Bevin had certain differences with his senior officials in the Foreign Office. Raymond Smith has argued that Bevin had not formed 'a clear view of the unequivocal hostility of the Soviet Union to Britain and the British way of life' and has further surmised that Bevin was possibly 'estranged from both his official advisers and Attlee at the beginning of 1947'.[8] These are matters considered in the text which follows but some preliminary comments may be offered here, since this is not a thesis easily accepted. Oliver Harvey, Private Secretary to Anthony Eden from June 1941 and a close personal friend, reported on several occasions in his *War Diaries* the virulent anti-Soviet attitudes of the Labour leaders in the Cabinet. On the disputed question about the declaration of war on Finland after the attack by Germany on the Soviet Union, Harvey noted (11 November 1941) that

> the opposition came from the Labour leaders. Bevin and Greenwood – shocking! They could only see Communists in the Russians and their hatred of Communism blinded them to any other considerations. A.E. [Eden] had to say that he had been dealing with Soviet Government for years, and knew them better than they did.[9]

There can be no suggestion that Churchill and Eden would have renounced their own anti-communist and anti-Soviet attitudes in the post-war years had they been in government, but they were both pragmatists and in their Conservative way – and this applies even to Churchill – they were never as fervently ideological as Ernest Bevin. There may be something of a parallel here with the replacement of Roosevelt by Truman. Churchill and Eden were certainly very much more experienced negotiators than Bevin ever became in foreign affairs and they might have been expected to exhibit more flexibility in approach than Bevin ever showed. Counter-factual arguments of this or any other kind may be intellectually interesting, but what might have happened is not history for the historian. What these arguments do sometimes offer is an insight into the way certain questions are approached, or solved; and the recognition of Bevin's firm ideological stance with regard to the Soviet Union cannot be neglected in any analysis of his policy decisions. His attitudes were early recognised. When Clark Kerr had his last interview with Stalin on 29 January 1946 – because of his translation to the Embassy in Washington – he asked him if he could make any contribution to improving relations between the Soviet Union and the United Kingdom:

> At this he made a face and said rather sadly that he did not understand your [Ernest Bevin] attitude or that of H M Government. You did not 'treat the Russians as Allies'. . . . You were free to hold any opinion you liked and, if you must, to hate his country, but he wished that you would not express what you feel in such a way as to give pain to him and his people.

This extract comes from the Bevin papers in the PRO (FO 800/501) and those who still hold to the 'uncertainty' thesis should look at the additional documentation in his own private papers as well as the files in the Foreign Office which make it abundantly clear that his hostility never wavered; at Bevin's attitudes during the first Foreign Ministers' Conference in London, September 1945; at the summary of the dinner discussion between Bevin, Senator Vandenberg and Foster Dulles in January 1946 (for which see below, p. 63); and the private discussions between Attlee and Bevin in late December 1946 (for which also see below, pp. 138 ff).

There is a further question to be noted, and it is one of central importance. Many British historians of the early Cold War years have argued directly or implicitly that the Soviet Union was a potential aggressor, straining to march on the Persian Gulf or reach the Channel ports in northern Europe. If they no longer believe that military aggression was the aim, then, in Smith's words, quoted above, 'unequivocal hostility' has always been assumed. Potential aggression and consistent hostility were certainly believed by the members of the British Foreign Office in the years that followed the end of the war. They provided the unquestioned rationale for the consistent anti-Soviet policies that were pursued within a developing relationship with the United States: a relationship that, in spite of many disagreements and frictions, placed Britain firmly in the position of junior partner. The conduct of Soviet foreign policy was at best clumsy and inept, often brutal, and concerned above all else with matters of security along its western borders. Many years ago Isaac Deutscher emphasised both the contradictions in Stalin's international policies and his obsession with 'the thought of future German revenge'.[10] It was not difficult for the former Allies to conflate Stalinist repression inside Russia with potential Soviet aggression abroad, and it certainly suited British interests to work with American support and above all American dollars. There were, however, some questions that have been too easily resolved, not least the material problems of the logistics of military intervention. The physical destruction in large areas of Russia was much greater than Stalin was willing to acknowledge to the world; the rate of demobilisation of the Russian armed forces was more far-reaching than was recognised at the time; and the movement of Russian armed forces into Western Europe or the Middle East was not practicable on a large scale.[11] There were admittedly complicating factors, such as the large communist parties in France and Italy, but if the Soviet Union was overwhelmingly concerned with the problems of security in Eastern Europe, how do we now evaluate Anglo-American policies which were ostensibly based upon the assumptions of far-reaching Soviet aggression? This is not in any way to proffer an apologia for Russian policies, or those who carried them through, but if the thesis of instant aggression is removed, historians will be obliged to examine carefully their own assumptions and hypotheses.

This major issue of Soviet intentions after 1945 is not discussed at any length in this volume, not least because the availability of the Russian archives for research should become possible within a few years, but Appendix 2 offers a brief discussion of Russian military logistics. In wider political terms there has been an important shift of opinion in the past two decades. Denis Healey, in his memoirs of 1989, is only one of the latest of the politicians who lived through the early Cold War years to admit that he no longer believes in the Russian aggression thesis.[12] There has certainly been available for many years in the records of the Western Powers a great deal of material which could have been put together to offer further insights into Russian actions and motives.[13] To look once again at the motivations of the three Great Powers of 1945, and to examine their inter-relationships, is a first requirement; we have to open our minds to new kinds of questions, and to consider the possibilities of different assumptions upon which our research and writing might be based. There is a need for serious debate and informed controversy; and what follows in this volume is in the nature of the prolegomena to certain key questions in the early history of the Cold War. Germany, a central issue of post-war politics, is also omitted from this present discussion. It was during 1946 that the main lines of German policy, from the British side, began to be firmly drawn, and the inter-relationships between the three Great Powers must be considered in extended treatment in a later volume.[14]

The long-term economic decline of Britain – relative to the advanced industrial world – did not intrude upon the consciousness of the policy-makers in Whitehall in the years immediately following 1945; and in general the relationship between foreign policy and national economy remains a neglected theme. The senior members of the British Foreign Office in the post-war years were for the most part innocent of any serious appreciation of economic affairs. They had read the summary accounts of the external position of the United Kingdom that Maynard Keynes had been putting together from the spring of 1945, but neither the Chiefs of Staff, or their planners, nor the leading officials of the Foreign Office appear to have understood the long-term consequences that six years of war had brought about. They were not alone. Analysis of the relative decline of Britain in the economy of the advanced world was not a central consideration of most economists within the United Kingdom. The research findings of Rostas and others concerning relative productivity levels of the major industrial countries were not taken further in the 1950s. The world boom of the third quarter of the century submerged much of the questioning that had begun in the immediate post-war years and it is only the last twenty years – from about the mid 1970s – that critical studies of Britain's long-term decline have come into prominence. It is not easy to discover the views of the Foreign Office in the medium and the long term, but it would appear that since the Empire in 1945 was still in place and was expected to remain, the immediate economic problems could be assumed to be soluble and British superior statecraft would go a long way to compensate for immediate difficulties. Two further points need to be made with regard to the years of the Attlee administrations. The first is that it soon became apparent that American dollars were crucial to the continuation of British commitments overseas, and for Ernest Bevin, in spite of all the difficulties of the American relationship, this remained a central tenet of his general approach; and the second is that the success of the Attlee government in achieving a rapid rate of growth, especially in the export sectors, underwrote the complacency that would appear to have infected many departments in Whitehall. Some of these economic questions are begun to be discussed in Chapter 4 below.

The final chapter is a case study of the earliest military/political intervention undertaken in the name of the newly formed Labour Government; and it underlines the tenacity which the place of Empire occupied within the general strategy of the leading élites. Conservative and imperialist attitudes, as already emphasised, were deeply embedded within the State bureaucracy, and they found active expression within less than a month after the end of the war with Japan by the intervention in French Indo-China, soon to be called Vietnam. British intervention in the first instance was to disarm Japanese troops and to repatriate prisoners of war and civilians who had been in detention. There were, however, further reasons which had long been considered during the years of war. Military intervention by the British against the indigenous nationalist movements of both Vietnam and Indonesia was a striking demonstration of the necessary unity of the imperialist powers. In Vietnam the success of the British allowed the French to return and take over the southern half of the country by Christmas 1945. It was a military action that evoked almost no response within the House of Commons, or outside Westminster. There were some obvious reasons for the silence within Britain even though they do not add up to the whole story. There was almost no reporting from British journalists, and the period of active intervention lasted less than four months. Most of the ground fighting was done by Indian and Gurkha troops, and by Japanese. Indonesia received much more publicity, especially from the world press; but for the British people South-East Asia was far away. Peace had just 'broken out' and life was not easy. Although the political radicalism carried over from the war years was still lively, if the opposition in Britain could make little headway with their criticisms of Bevin's policies towards Greece and Franco Spain, there was scant chance or hope that the people of Britain could be stirred to moral and political revulsion by the killings of Vietnamese or Indonesian peasants. Even in the months immediately after six years of war, when consciences were deeply affected by the revelations of horrors and atrocities, we may recall the words of Disraeli to H.M. Hyndman in 1881: 'It is a very difficult country to move, Mr Hyndman, a very difficult country indeed, and one in which there is more disappointment to be looked for than success.'[15]

The Mind of the Foreign Office

Whitehall

It was 'a curious fact', Gladwyn Jebb wrote in his memoirs, that the Foreign Office in 1939 was dominated by old Etonians, and this was especially true of the senior officials. Jebb did not think that this was 'necessarily a good thing' but equally there were in his view certain advantages. The fact that they all had 'the same start' was undoubtedly a help in personal relationships, and Jebb thought that this promoted efficiency.[1] Tilly and Gaselee in their 1933 study of the Foreign Office had made the same general point:

> Of the clerks on the diplomatic establishment of the Foreign Office whose names appear in the Foreign Office list for 1919, the last before the post-war men appeared, half were Etonians, that is, twenty-two out of forty-four; and that not because any special favour was shown to Eton, but because the sort of people who wanted nominations mostly came from Eton; now the proportion is less than a fourth. Although the Etonian character of the Foreign Office and Diplomatic Service has been a favourite subject for criticism, I think that the critics have been too ready to assume that the Service suffered in consequence.[2]

The First Division of the Foreign Office and the Diplomatic Service were almost completely separate groups before 1914. The nomination of the Foreign Secretary was required for both services before candidates could sit their respective examinations, and a measure of interchangeability was possible between Whitehall and those abroad in the Diplomatic Service. Entrants to the latter were expected to have a minimum private income of £400 a year. This was known as the property qualification, although it was understood rather than a strict formal requirement. In their first two or three years young entrants to the diplomatic world were usually appointed as unpaid attachés, and then followed appointment as a Third Secretary at a salary of £150 a year. Successful entrants to the Foreign Office in Whitehall were paid £200 a year on their first appointment. The social background of the two services was broadly the same, with the Diplomatic Service being somewhat more aristocratic than the Foreign Office clerks; but their education was similar. Almost all were from the better known public schools, with Eton being by far the most important. Examinations had been introduced following the 1853 Northcote–Trevelyan Report, and the academic standards required were raised for the Foreign Office in the 1870s, and after 1890 for the Diplomatic Service. In 1892 the same examination was sat by candidates for both services, although they were evaluated separately. In 1907 a Board of Selection replaced the Secretary of State for the nomination of candidates, but by the beginning of the First World War there had been little change in the social composition of either service, although there was a slow but steady increase in the number of entrants from the higher grades of professional families. This was more true of the Foreign Office than the Diplomatic Service, the latter reflecting the dominating presence of the aristocracy in the chancelleries of Europe. In Britain it was the 'educational homogeneity' of the Foreign Service that provided the marked uniformity of view that characterised both Whitehall and the diplomats abroad, whatever the differences in their appreciation of any one political question.[3]

Criticism of the Foreign Office became increasingly vigorous as 1914 approached. A growing debate developed about the advisability of interchange-ability between Whitehall and the Foreign Service, but there was also much opposition, especially from within the top echelons of both sections. In 1914 the Royal Commission on the Civil Service enquired into the organisation of the Foreign Office, the Diplomatic and Consular Services, and recommended a merger into a single foreign service and the widening of opportunities beyond the existing narrow class selection. The war inevitably delayed change but in 1919 the Foreign Office and the Diplomatic Service were amalgamated. Certainly some permanent change in direction occurred between the wars but by the end of the 1930s it was less than has sometimes been suggested:[4] the result of quite bitter internal disputes among the senior officials. While the examinations demanded a high standard of ability, especially in languages, the interview was still the deciding factor. As Tilly and Gaselee so properly described the situation in their book of 1933:

> The combination of interview by a Selection Board with competitive examination is the best scheme that has yet been devised; benevolent autocracy being ruled out. The greatest difficulty in such cases as ours is not to find the best men, but to keep out the undesirables.[5]

The evidence suggests that since the proportion of Etonians was so high in 1919 and only slowly declined through the following two decades, the Selec-tions Boards were quite successful in this particular aim. The historian of the Foreign Office before 1914 made the point in her concluding remarks that the Office had responded to a changing world only imperfectly – retaining modes of social sensibility and forms of organisation that were already something of a handicap in July 1914. . . . Like many other English institutions, the Foreign Office tended to respond to an uncomely present by taking refuge in the forms of a splendid past.[6]

Tradition and continuity have been the remarkable characteristics of British political life in general throughout the twentieth century. There have been periods of intense unrest and discontent – the huge strike movement of the years immediately before the First World War, with 41 million working days lost in 1912; the General Strike of 1926; the early 1970s, and the winter of discontent of 1978–79 – against a background of two world wars, the major economic crisis of 1929–32 and the rapid decline of the imperialist basis of the British State after 1947; and yet it was not until 1945 that the working-class party, or the party to which the majority of organised workers gave their support, achieved an overwhelming majority in the House of Commons.[7] It is a notable fact that alone among the major nation states in Europe which have been involved in one or more major wars in the twentieth-century Britain has retained its administrative structures more or less intact, without any change of a fundamental kind. Some change there has been, of course, but it has always been change of the traditional British kind: a remodelling here and an amalgamation there, or a new department to meet developing needs; but nothing approximating to a radical upheaval offering new and quite different directions of policy. The Americans, and no doubt the Russians, were sur- prised to see the same advisers to the Labour Government's delegation to Potsdam, after the sensational Labour victory at the general election of July 1945; but this was only the first indication of the conservatism that has been generated by the continuity of political structures in British society and which has been so markedly exhibited in the decades since 1945. The cohesion of the senior civil servants in Whitehall has always remained an important component in the complex of factors encouraging social stability; and certainly in the years after 1945 the top levels of the British civil service have been powerful influences in the carryover of traditional practices into a world which was in the process of rapid transformation.[8]

No department of State has illustrated the processes of continuity in more impressive fashion than the Foreign Office after 1945. Before the Second World War there had been strong, sometimes bitter, differences between the top officials over the strategy and tactics in confrontation with the Fascist Powers; but with victory, and the defeat of Germany and Japan, there deve- loped a notable agreement towards what was now regarded as the central threat of the post-war world – the Soviet Union; and in other areas of policy, such as the crucial importance of the Empire, there was, as indeed there always had been in this matter, complete and thoroughgoing agreement.

The Permanent Under-Secretary during Ernest Bevin's first six months as Foreign Secretary was Sir Alexander Cadogan (1884–1968), seventh son of the 5th Earl of Cadogan by his first wife. There is little doubt that the emotional inhibitions Alec Cadogan displayed in later life – often commented on and certainly exhibited in his *Diaries* – were at least in part the result of the narrow and constrictive regimen imposed upon the Cadogan children.[9] Like all his brothers he went to Eton, and, as Gladwyn Jebb was happy to note, being the son of an Earl, Cadogan 'did not have to worry about his place in the scheme of things'.[10] Cadogan then went on to Balliol (1903–1906), where he evidently worked moderately hard as well as practising the upper-class delights of practical jokes and off-beat adolescent behaviour. He regarded undergraduates who were 'studious' with, it would seem, the customary derision of his set. Cadogan was a member of the Annandale Society, whose aim was to become 'buffy', that is, on the way to drunkenness while still full of high spirits; and he was a great organiser of 'waterfalls', namely, carefully constructed mounds of crockery which were then crashed down steps or staircases.[11]

After graduating, Cadogan spent two years cramming for the Diplomatic Service examinations, which he passed with distinction, and he was then sent to Constantinople, and later to Vienna where he was when the First World War began. He served in the Foreign Office in Whitehall during the war years, and in 1923 was appointed head of the League of Nations section. By this time he was highly regarded by his seniors as both efficient and imperturbable. He remained in London and Geneva until early 1934 when he was posted as Minister to the Legation in Peking. He was in China for over two years when Eden, who had just become Foreign Secretary, brought him home to serve as joint Deputy Under-Secretary with seniority over the other Under-Secretary. His Permanent Under-Secretary was Sir Robert Vansittart whose views on the German question were to become steadily more critical of the Chamberlain policies of appeasement.[12] On 1 January 1938 Vansittart was given the title of Chief Diplomatic Adviser – a move calculated to reduce his influence to zero – and Cadogan became PUS in his place: to remain in that position throughout the war and for the first six months of the Labour Government. In February 1946 he went to the United Nations in New York as the first permanent British representative. He himself would have preferred the Washington Embassy.[13]

Cadogan's reputation with his contemporaries, and with most historians who have written about him, is of a diplomat who was highly experienced, with a calm manner, someone who was a good listener and reasonable in negotiation. Sir Llewellyn Woodward, the official historian of British wartime diplomacy, wrote of Cadogan that he had 'remarkable powers of judgement and lucid expression. His minutes stood out at the time, and are likely to stand out in retrospect, as models of open-mindedness and sound conclusions.'[14] It can, of course, be assumed that all senior civil servants have learned to produce apposite minutes or, in most cases, well-argued memoranda relating to the mass of paper that comes across their desks. Cadogan was, however, a somewhat more complex character than has sometimes been suggested. He emerges from a reading of Foreign Office files and from his diaries as a practised fence-sitter with, however, a marked tendency to agree with his political masters when it really mattered. His attitude to Munich was summed up by the author of his entry in the *DNB* as 'a characteristically middle position. Knowing the Anglo-French weakness in defence (notably the weakness of the French Air Force) he felt that nearly but not absolutely every effort should be made to reach a compromise with Hitler.'[15] 'Nearly but not absolutely every effort' sums up well enough Cadogan's general attitudes to most questions. He knew nothing about economics or international financial matters and he took on trust the analysis offered to him before 1939 by the military; so that with them he greatly exaggerated Germany's military capacity. In mid October 1938 he produced a long review of the European situation which is notable for its lack of intellectual rigour and its general defeatist tone. Although in the last stages of the Munich Crisis Cadogan, according to his diary, was appalled at some parts of the political accommodation Chamberlain was prepared to accept, he himself had taken for many months a position that encouraged the appeasers, as when he wrote, on 18 March 1938: 'F.P.C. [Foreign Policy Committee] unanimous that Czechoslovakia is not worth the bones of a single British Grenadier. And they're quite right too.'[16]

When Cadogan's *Diaries* first appeared in 1971 they seem to have greatly surprised his former colleagues and others who knew him well. In public Cadogan always appeared reserved and calm, while the diaries revealed bouts of considerable irritation, and sometimes anger at individuals or events. Gladwyn Jebb's own memoirs were already in page proof when the Cadogan *Diaries* were first published, and he called them 'astonishing' and added that he had 'no inkling of the volcano that lay beneath that cool and calm exterior'.[17] 'Volcano' is perhaps too strong a word for most people who read Cadogan's thoughts, for while they are moderately informative, and sometimes highly revealing, in bulk they are rather dull and enlivened with only occasional outbursts of spleen. Cadogan emerges from his pages as a somewhat unattractive personality; his diary entries exhibit a man with no serious intellectual interests. He had at times a nice turn of phrase, and his minutes were well-written, although this latter characteristic was not in evidence in the diaries, as his editor notes. What the entries do show is a petty-mindedness towards those outside his own very restricted circle of Whitehall colleagues, and even to some of his close associates, as the comments on Vansittart and Orme Sargent bear witness. Cadogan was stupidly, sometimes malignantly, intolerant of policies opposed to those he was advocating or supporting. On 8 December 1944, a few days after the British military intervention in Athens, an event which aroused anger and opposition round the world, Cadogan wrote in his diary:

B.B.C. gave account of Greek Debate, which seems to have gone all right. What poisonous mischief makers there are. While waiting for dinner, I read . . . article in the 'New Statesman' – a thing I haven't done for 2 years or more. How anyone can write such distorted, biased and dishonest muck passes my comprehension. The 'N.S.' is addressed, I suppose, to more or less educated people. Are there readers really taken in by such dishonest and libellous trash? I suppose so, if the 'Times' readers can swallow the swill dished up to them . . . Barrington Ward is not capable of running a mussel stall. It's a tragedy that he should be, of all things, editor of the 'Times'.[18]

There were occasions when Cadogan could become, verbally, more violent. On this same Greek question, which continued to occupy British public opinion for a long time, Cadogan referred again to *The Times'* criticisms. On 19 January, referring to a speech made by Churchill in the House of Commons the day before, he wrote: 'Read Winston's speech, which was admirable. I am told his attack on the *Times* had terrific success. I hope someone will tie Barrington Ward and Ted Carr together and throw them into the Thames.'[19] Earlier in the previous year Aneurin Bevan, inevitably one of Cadogan's personal aversions, had spoken in the Commons in terms which encouraged Cadogan to write:

> It merely gives Aneurin Bevan the opportunity to sling about libellous charges, for which he would have to pay heavily, were it not for 'privilege'. He and his kidney are mere barnacles on the bottom of the 'ship of state'. In any decent country they'd be bumped off. To that extent am I 'Fascist' – and proud of it![20]

It might be thought that such sentiments belonged to the reactionary core of Tory backwoodsmen on the benches of the House of Commons, and that the supposedly urban sophistication of senior Whitehall officials would be in evidence in private as well as in public. Many of these top-level civil servants, however, notably within the Treasury and the Foreign Office, while fully acknowledging themselves as the élites of the administrative civil service, were often remarkably narrow in their general outlook and decidedly limited in their social contacts. They married within their own social class, and in their daily lives they normally met only their own kind. They lunched together, often within their own clubs. During the years of war they were largely excluded from the rigours endured by ordinary people. John Colville had been Assistant Private Secretary to Neville Chamberlain until the latter's retirement from No. 10 and he then served Winston Churchill. His *Times* obituary described him as a snob (21 November 1987), which he may well have been, but he also had at least the glimmerings of a social awareness, as when he reported in his diary on 6 March 1941 that he lunched with his father at the Turf 'which was full. I am glad to see the sideboard is less groaning with cold meat than when last I was there; but certainly the rich can still feed sumptuously.'[21] It is common for historians of this period to quote the lavish displays of food and drink that the

Russians always provided at conferences in their own country, at a time when the Russian people were suffering appalling hardships. There can be no justification for the Russians, on any count, above all in a country that used the title of socialist. It is, however, necessary to remark that élites everywhere – all that was needed in capitalist countries was money – practised the same kind of good living while their own people suffered, at the minimum, austerity. The United States was the obvious exception in that living standards, because of full employment, improved during the war years for almost everyone. When Colville left Britain to travel to Canada for the Octagon Conference in September 1944, he sailed on the *Queen Mary*; and the menu for dinner on 7 September was:

> Oysters, consommé, turbot, roast turkey, ice with cantaloupe melon, Stilton cheese and a great variety of fruit, petit fours etc; the whole washed down by champagne (Mumm 1929) and a very remarkable Liebfraumilch, followed by some 1870 brandy: all of which made the conversation about a shortage of consumers' goods a shade unreal.[22]

The next in line to Alec Cadogan in the Foreign Office hierarchy was Orme Sargent (1884–1962). He succeeded Cadogan in January 1946. Like Cadogan he had a quite severely restricted childhood, an unhappy one, his parents being 'rather possessive and exacting' (*DNB* entry by Gladwyn Jebb). Orme Sargent was educated at Radley, but did not go to university; instead, he spent quite a long time in Switzerland preparing for the Diplomatic Service, which he entered in 1906. He was sent to Berne in 1907 and then had seven years in Paris. After 1926 he never travelled abroad again, having some kind of neurotic phobia which apparently made foreign travel impossible. As a result his social contacts were more restricted than those of Cadogan, who himself never moved out of the top decision-making élites. Orme Sargent's political attitudes were similar to those of his contemporaries, although during the years of appeasement he took a very strong line in opposition. He was noted for his pessimism and his black moods. Cadogan in his diaries has a number of passages of extreme irritation at Orme Sargent's negative attitude and Bruce Lockhart wrote in his diary for 13 April 1943 that 'For many months now I have noticed signs of antagonism between Moley [Orme Sargent] and Cadogan although, being in the best line of Foreign Office tradition, they never show their feelings, let alone gossip.'[23] It should be added that Bruce Lockhart saw a good deal more of Orme Sargent during the war years than he did of Cadogan, although his comments only confirm what Cadogan was writing in private.

Vansittart had described Orme Sargent as 'a philosopher strayed into Whitehall' and Gladwyn Jebb reproduced the comment in his *DNB* entry; but there was not much of the philosopher in Sargent's remarks at lunch on 26 July 1945 when Labour's electoral victory was assured. Pierson Dixon lunched with

Orme Sargent 'who was in the depths of gloom, prophesying a Communist avalanche over Europe, a weak foreign policy, a private revolution at home and reduction of England to a second class power'.[24] It is interesting that Sargent, who had seen the Labour ministers at work during the Churchill Coalition and who presumably recognised their political moderation, could fall so easily into the attitudes associated at this time with some corner-shop grocers: prejudiced, narrow-minded and politically illiterate. It is an incident that tells us something about the cloistered lives these Whitehall officials lived, as well as their states of mind. Certainly, as was noted in the Introduction, there was a widespread belief among senior civil servants that a Labour government would mean a considerable shake-up inside the corridors of power. Only an understanding of the history of the Labour Party would have allowed them a more perceptive judgement.

It would not be sufficient to leave the discussion of Orme Sargent at this point. By the end of the war he was, like most of his colleagues, tired, and in his case cynical, and he was certainly subject to a pessimistic view of politics which not seldom led him into exaggerated and sometimes absurd statements. The many comments from Sargent which Bruce Lockhart noted in his diaries exhibit, however, a sharpness of intellect that is mostly missing from Cadogan's printed words, although there is no doubt that Cadogan must have been easier to work with. Both were uninterested in administrative change and shared a common dislike for any serious reform or re-organisation of the Foreign Office establishment: although their reasons were almost certainly different. Bruce Lockhart once confronted Orme Sargent with the widely expressed criticisms that were often made in Whitehall about the organisation of the Foreign Office, and Orme Sargent replied in somewhat vehement language:

What's the use of any organisation unless you can get a policy out of ministers. . . . What's been wrong with this country for the last twenty-five years is complete absence of policy. How could you get a policy with a man like Simon Foreign Secretary for four years? You can't get policies out of democratic ministers. Look at the situation today with Anthony [Eden] taking the Leadership of the House. He is away every weekend from 4 p.m. Friday until luncheon-time on Monday; on Tuesday, Wednesday, and Thursday he is fully occupied with Foreign Office work – for F.O. read House of Commons – and for foreign policy and F.O. work he has only Monday afternoon and Friday morning.[25]

These were not opinions that Cadogan would have expressed. Indeed, Sargent might have added Cadogan to his criticism of Eden since Cadogan was also away from the office for quite long periods. The most sustained public argument for drastic reform of the Foreign Office was published in two articles in *The Times* in the first days of January 1943.[26] The analysis centred upon the new functions that had developed during the previous half century and the failure of the Foreign Service to understand their importance and recognise the need for continuous reorganisation to meet the changing conditions of world politics:

> The problem of organisation is urgent and fundamental, and little progress has yet been made towards the solution. The character and organisation of the Foreign Service still bear the imprint of the nineteenth century, when diplomatic relations formed the stuff and essence of foreign policy. The twentieth century complicated these relations by the introduction of economic, financial and social, and, more recently, propaganda relations. Such issues were, however, regarded as extraneous and rather tiresome accretions – the province of 'technical experts' – rather than as an integral part of diplomacy. . . . The real function of the Ambassador is to conduct diplomatic relations: financial, economic, publicity and other relations are subsidiary functions tacked on to his main job and subordinate to it. . . . Right down to the outbreak of war these new instruments of foreign policy were regarded by many British diplomats with a somewhat fastidious disdain.[27]

The years of war, *The Times* continued, have revealed how far behind the realities were the present organisation, and understanding, of the senior members of the Foreign Service; and to meet the needs of the war a number of new departments have had to be created. A multiplicity of departments and ad hoc organisations have had to be established, with the result that the Foreign Office is left with

> only the traditional and somewhat antiquated instrument of diplomacy. The cavalry of foreign policy is still deployed from Downing St: the weightier strategy of tanks and bombers is settled elsewhere, subject to a rather remote control from cavalry headquarters.

Moreover, these developments were not just an abnormal product of the war; they would continue in the years of peace, and the ways of traditional diplomacy would simply not be sufficient. The second article of 4 January argued for a complete modernisation of structure: with a Secretary of State as head of a Department of Foreign Policy overlooking the Foreign Office (now a Ministry of Diplomatic Relations) together with a Ministry of International Economic Relations (corresponding broadly with the existing Ministry of Economic Warfare, the Department of Overseas Trade, the foreign sections of the Board of Trade 'and perhaps of the Treasury'), and a Ministry of Foreign Publicity (the present foreign departments of the Ministry of Information and the Political Warfare Executive). This second article was accompanied by a leader which quoted with approval the Haldane Report on the Machinery of Government of 1918[28] and in general gave sympathetic support to the arguments presented in these two articles. Cadogan's reaction to the first article was predictable – 'A silly, ill-informed and ill-natured article' – and he at first tried to prevent the publication of the second one.[29] It was perhaps not to be expected that there would be much public debate at this stage of the war. In the fortnight after publication there were only three letters in *The Times'* correspondence columns, and rather surprisingly no mention in Bruce Lockhart's diary: surprising because Lockhart had greatly suffered from the problem of too many directing bodies of which the first *Times* article had made so much.[30]

The first *Times* article had noted that in June 1941 Eden had announced in the House of Commons a series of projected reforms for the Foreign Service; but no details were published and it was not until later in the same month of the *Times* articles that a Command paper set out the detail of the proposed changes. Most were concerned with financial matters, conditions of entry and retirement as well as the creation of a single service which now would include the Consular officials.[31] The reforms were mainly carried out after the war by Bevin, who paid especial attention to the appointment of Labour Attachés to the Embassies abroad. What Bevin did not do, contrary to widespread expectations within the Labour Party in the country and the parliamentary Labour backbenchers in the Commons, was to remove the incompetent or the politically reactionary. He favoured the career diplomats when political appointments would have been acceptable and it was not until the early months of 1946 that any significant reshuffle of major posts took place.[32] The 1946 Labour Party Conference at Bournemouth in mid June 1946 produced a highly critical debate on most aspects of Bevin's foreign policy including recruitment to the Foreign Service. A resolution before Conference read:

> This Conference calls upon the Government to undertake a drastic revision of existing methods of recruitment for the Foreign Service. Further, in order to ensure that the execution of a Socialist foreign policy is entrusted to men who believe in it, rather than to those whose whole background and tradition have rendered them incapable of understanding the first principles of such a policy, it calls upon the Government to make the fullest use of its power of retirement, on generous terms and without stigma, of public servants whose capacity for useful work is exhausted and their replacement by persons in accord with the progressive attitude of the British Public as shown in their decision at the last General Election.[33]

There was, of course, no possibility of a resolution of this kind being accepted since the trade union block vote was always in these years at the service of the Labour leaders; and during the whole period of the two Labour governments no alteration of any significance was made to existing practices of recruitment or appointment.

There would be general agreement among most, if not all, of the senior decision-makers within the Foreign Office with regard to certain basic attitudes and political positions. One on which there would be no dissent was the superiority of British diplomacy over all other chancelleries, and certainly when compared with the workings of the State Department in Washington.[34] It seems to have been an article of faith among members of the Foreign Service that their approach in general, as well as in the daily workings of international politics, could always be assumed to be more experienced, more subtle and more persuasive than was to be encountered elsewhere. It was, so it was believed, one of the factors which in the aftermath of war would greatly help to offset the economic and financial weaknesses of the United Kingdom. On 3 April 1945 Churchill presided over an extended War Cabinet at which were present the Dominion Prime Ministers, including Field Marshal Smuts. Churchill delivered an analysis of the current world situation, emphasising the 'position of preponderant power and influence throughout the whole of Europe' of the Soviet Union, and the 'vastly superior' resources of the United States compared with those of Britain. He continued:

> These were the dominating facts in the world situation. How could the British Commonwealth, as the third of the Great Powers, match the Power and influence which would be wielded after the war by Russia and the United States. In material resources we could not hope to equal either of these powers. We could hold our own only by superior statecraft and experience and, above all, by the unity of the British Commonwealth of Nations.[35]

A similar exposition was made by Orme Sargent in a revised version of his 'Stocktaking after VE Day', dated 11 July 1945. He said broadly the same things about Russia and the United States, noting that in the minds of the two Great Powers there was a feeling that Britain was now a secondary power and could be treated as such; and he added that this was especially true of the attitude of the United States. This misconception – of Britain as a secondary Power – must be combated:

> We have many cards in our hands if we choose to use them – our political maturity; our diplomatic experience; the confidence which the solidarity of our democratic institutions inspires in Western Europe; and our incomparable war record. Unlike our two great partners we are not regarded in Western Europe either as gangsters or as go-getters.[36]

The most powerful and the most endurable concept that suffused the collective mind of the Foreign Office as well as other parts of Whitehall was, however, the role and place of Empire. It was the Commonwealth and Empire which enabled Britain to achieve the status of a major power in world politics, and its importance was never questioned.[37] The First World War had been followed by considerable upheavals and disturbances in India, the Middle East and Ireland, but these, even in Ireland, could be immediately attributable to the special circumstances of the war. After 1921–22, and the Irish settlement, the 'troubles' became intense only at certain times, and any sense of a wide-ranging discontent throughout the Empire was no longer at the front of political consciousness in Britain. India, of course, was becoming increasingly prominent in British politics, and at the same time there was a growing recognition of the emerging nationalisms in some other colonies; but new perceptions were mostly limited and among the conservative sections of society there was little if any understanding that the world was changing. It was taken as given that Britain would continue with a world-wide empire. The African colonies, for example, were always assumed by the Colonial Office to be decades away from any real independence[38] and the completion of the naval base at Singapore in 1938 – after many delays – underlined the world role that Britain was supposed to derive from its position at the centre of a very large empire. The principal historian of the evolution of imperialist sentiment in Britain has suggested that 'imperial themes secured greater cultural penetration in the period following the First World War, and indeed prolonged their shelf life until the 1950's.'[39] A minority counter-ideology existed within the labour movement[40] but popular opinion in general, among both working class and middle class, was never in any doubt concerning the importance of Empire to the British way of life.

The Second World War brought major developments of a new kind which greatly exacerbated nationalist tensions in the colonial countries. Moreover, both before and after the United States entered the war, British imperialism came under increasing criticism from influential sections of American opinion, and it was by no means limited to isolationist sentiment.[41] The meeting at Placentia Bay in early August 1941 between Roosevelt and Churchill produced, among other agreed decisions, what became known as the Atlantic Charter. Point three affirmed the right of all peoples to independence and self-government; and it was this paragraph which became the subject of the greatest speculation and debate. Political leaders in India, Burma and Ceylon accepted the words of the declaration as certainly the Americans intended, but Churchill and Cadogan had assented to what was not at all agreeable to most of their senior colleagues in London. Amery, Secretary of State for India and Burma, and Lord Moyne, the Colonial Secretary, asked for a public qualification from Churchill regarding what Amery described as 'dangerous ambiguities'. Churchill met them with a statement in the House of Commons to the effect that point three applied primarily to the conquered nations of Europe and that 'the progressive evolution of self-governing institutions' in the British Empire was a separate problem.[42] What he meant was that self-determination was far from being an automatic consequence of British rule. About a year later Wendell Willkie made his famous world tour, and he was summarising important sections of American public opinion when he said that 'this war must mean an end to the empire of nations over other nations.' When Willkie returned home his speeches received wide press coverage on both sides of the Atlantic;[43] and

Churchill took the opportunity at a Lord Mayor's luncheon at the Mansion House on 10 November 1942 to make the British position clear beyond any doubt. 'We mean', he said, 'to hold our own. I have not become the King's First Minister in order to preside over the liquidation of the British Empire.' Eight days after his Mansion House speech Churchill told the War Cabinet that the American criticisms of British colonial policy, which greatly troubled leading politicians, required 'that a full statement should be drawn up for publication on the development of the British Colonial Empire, vindicating our past and present policy, and indicating the probable trends of future policy.'[44]

There followed considerable comment in the British press on Churchill's Mansion House speech. Margery Perham wrote two articles in *The Times* (20 and 21 November 1942) in which a more liberal gloss was applied to British attitudes and policies for the future; and Lord Lugard further explained what Churchill really meant, namely, that the British control of colonial countries was not a matter of economic exploitation but a trusteeship for the welfare and general progress of the native inhabitants.[45] The liberal conservative arguments were definitively stated by Lord Hailey, who was the leading spirit in the British delegation to the 8th Conference of the Institute of Pacific Relations which met at Mont Tremblant, Quebec between 4 and 14 December 1942. Hailey presented the case for gradualism in the development of joint consultation and the growth of the partnership principle between colonial government and the native populations. The most capable and probably the most persuasive popular statement of the British position was the Penguin Special, *Argument of Empire* (June 1943), by Keith Hancock, who had been Professor of History at the University of Birmingham and who was a close associate of the Royal Institute of International Affairs.[46] In his opening paragraph Hancock wrote:

> It is difficult to conduct an argument across the Atlantic. John Bull wakes up one morning to read newspaper headlines which give him the impression that Americans are making the liquidation of the British Empire one of their war aims. John Bull growls that it's like their cool cheek and that he won't let go. John Bull's growl is cabled across the Atlantic and served up to the American citizen in still bigger headline. The American citizen gets excited and declares that John Bull is a reactionary imperialist and American boys are not fighting for anybody's old empire but for a brave new world. All this is grand newspaper stuff. But it isn't real. The real argument is going on *inside* Britain and *inside* America.

This first chapter heading was 'The Americans Cut In'. Hancock was already accepted as a scholar of distinction when he wrote this *pièce de circonstance*, but it can only be characterised as an apologia which has elements of sophistication interspersed with traditional conservative analysis. His chapter on India is a superficial account of what the realities actually were then, and what was to follow in the aftermath of war; and although it was published in mid 1943 there was no mention of the August 1942 events.[47]

After the Mansion House speech, and the newspaper comments which followed, the House of Commons debated the colonial question on 26 November 1942. Sir Edward Grigg, who had been one of the group round Milner, put down an amendment urging an emphasis on the raising of living standards and regretting that there was no mention of a Colonial Development Board in the King's speech which opened the new session. His main theme was the need to move on from 'trusteeship' to 'partnership' and he especially emphasised the importance of white immigration, and capital, into Africa in order that its great natural resources might be developed. He paid particular respect to the views of Smuts and underlined the contribution of South Africa to the war, expressing the hope – referring to the Boers – that 'we shall not accept the co-operation of our own Europeans in Africa as a distasteful necessity.'[48] Grigg noted the importance of the United States in post-war developments, and he put forward the interesting suggestion that India, the Dominions and the colonies should be a single department, with three subordinate ministers under a senior Cabinet minister. This, among other reasons, would break with what he described as the invidious distinctions between the colonies and other less dependent countries and he went on to argue for the title of Commonwealth to include all types of constitution within what used to be the British Empire. It was an argument that continued throughout the war years, and it was very clearly articulated by Smuts in what became known as the 'explosive speech' of November 1943.[49] Smuts drew a sharp distinction between the sovereign states of the Dominions and the colonial Empire, whose administration was centralised, in the last resort, in London. He argued for larger groupings of colonial territories in which the Dominions might also be involved; but apart from this area of his discussion he several times emphasised the central importance of Empire and Commonwealth which 'remain as one of the greatest things of the world and of history, and nothing can touch that fact.'[50]

Smuts in this speech was developing a comprehensive strategy for the United Kingdom in the post-war world in which links with Europe would be greatly strengthened – to offset the power of the United States and Russia – as well as the necessary re-organisation, indeed integration, of Empire and Commonwealth. Smuts was a sophisticated reactionary who wrapped himself in the mantle of *soi-disant* liberal. Much of the thinking and attitudes towards Empire within Britain were on a more simplistic level, highly emotional and impervious to argument. In the same debate in November 1942 which Edward Grigg opened, a Tory backbencher from Totnes in South Devon enunciated the uncomplicated mythology that provided the inarticulate major premiss of much of British public opinion concerning the Empire. He began by asking whether we could expect the disintegration of the British Empire in the post-war world:

> Is the British Empire likely to liquidate itself? All indications point the other way. Nothing binds so firmly as freedom, and if one moves about the Colonies, one finds the people more fiercely proud of being British than we are ourselves. That remark by the Jamaican negro to the Frenchman who had jostled him, 'I think you forget, sir, that we defeated you at Waterloo' is typical of the spirit we find all over the Colonies. The splendid telegram sent in 1940 by Sir Sikander Hyat Khan, the Prime Minister of the Punjab, to the Government of this country, 'Tell the British people that if there is any trouble in the Middle East, I will raise them a million volunteers without any pressure from the Government or any other Englishman' is also typical of the same spirit. There is the true India, not that imaginary land where chota peg drinking pukka sahibs exploit Indians for British profit. Although the Empire has a few murky pages, it has never been just a convenient capitalist frame for exploitation, as some members sometimes suggest to us in this House.[51]

In practical terms there were no administrative or constitutional changes of any significance within the British Empire during the war years. There was the beginning of a debate during the period when Attlee occupied the position of Dominions Secretary (February 1942 to September 1943) and Cranborne was Colonial Secretary for nine months during 1942,[52] but in spite of Attlee's differences with what he regarded as old fashioned imperialist ideas he defended the Government's handling of the very serious disturbances in the Indian crisis of August 1942.[53] For the remainder of the war and especially as the end of the war with Germany became evident, the Foreign Office, as well as other departments concerned with Empire and Commonwealth, was inevitably increasingly concerned with the politics of the post-war world. What is striking, and remarkable, is that not only did the military plan their strategy upon imperial assumptions which were fundamentally unchanged from those of 1939, but so also did the Foreign Office. The Empire was the bedrock upon which Britain as one of the world's Great Powers rested; and the defence of Empire and the security of its lines of communication were therefore of paramount importance. The simplicities of the military mind are considered below, but their assumptions, and the political consequences derived therefrom, belonged also to the effective decision-makers in Whitehall. There was an internal discussion in March–April 1945 with Attlee as critic, concerning the part which Great Britain could expect to play in the Middle East, and it produced what can be described as a definitive statement of the conservative-imperialist position by the Foreign Secretary, Anthony Eden. He defined the Middle East as Egypt, Palestine, Transjordan, the Levant States, Iraq, Saudi Arabia and the Persian Gulf, with Egypt and the Suez Canal 'as its core'. Eden continued:

It is thus one of the most important strategic areas in the world, and it is an area the defence of which is a matter of life and death to the British Empire since, as the present war and the war of 1914–18 have both proved, it is there that the Empire can be cut in half. Consequently we are bound to give the Middle East an extremely high priority when allotting our available resources to the areas where we have responsibility. . . . Secondly, the Middle East is the sole large source of oil outside America which is available to us. Recent studies indicate that in ten years time neither the British Empire nor even the United States will be able to exert their full war effort in case of need without the oil supplies of the Iraq–Persian Gulf area.[54]

A further exchange of political differences between Eden and Attlee occurred at the Potsdam Conference[55] but no one took any serious notice of Attlee until after the general election results of late July 1945. Then, with Ernest Bevin as Foreign Secretary, the Eden approach to the Empire was resumed. The first major debate on foreign policy expressing the views of the new Labour government took place on 20 August, with a major statement from Bevin. Lord Halifax, the British Ambassador in Washington, wrote to Bevin in his weekly report to London, dated 25 August, that American fears of the radical nature of a Labour government had markedly receded:

> Your own speech of 20 August as already reported (in my telegram 5773) impressed the American public with the continuity and stability of British foreign policy. Many newspapers noting its vigour declared that it was clear that you no more than Churchill would preside over the liquidation of the Empire. Whilst conservative and middle-of-the-road opinion thus commended the speech, there is no denying that it disappointed liberals and left-wing commentators. Some of them admit that in the flush of victory over 'Tory Imperialism' they had no doubt expected – and predicted – too much. Their complaint now is that they have got nothing at all.[56]

This view of Empire as central to Britain's position as a world power was accepted as a major premiss of the Foreign Office attitude towards the outside world. India was, of course, beyond their control, but like the military, they assumed that whatever constitutional developments came about in the future, India would remain associated with the Commonwealth especially in matters of defence. In all these attitudes the Foreign Office were wrong. They appeared incapable of assessing with any degree of realism the world that was emerging from the massive blood-letting of the Second World War; and they seem to have been unable to appreciate the power and the indestructible nature of nationalism among the colonial peoples of the world. Whitehall lacked a sense of history, a recognition that the balance of political forces in the world had changed and was continuing to change. Their attitude towards the white Dominions, for example, assumed that because of their support in two world wars, the future would be one of continued unity and collaboration. The years between the wars had already seen considerable alterations in the power relations between the countries of recent settlement and the United Kingdom, and the war greatly hastened the changes that were under way. The collapse of British power in the Far East, symbolised by the ignominious surrender of Singapore, confirmed the Australians in their recognition of the enfeeblement of the United Kingdom as a world power. Some weeks before Singapore fell to the Japanese the Australian representative in the city informed his government that it was only a matter of weeks before this would occur; and John Curtin, the Australian Prime Minister, published an open letter in the *Melbourne Herald* that was bitterly forthright:

> We refuse to accept the dictum that the Pacific struggle must be treated as a subordinate aspect of the general conflict. . . . The Australian government, therefore, regards the Pacific struggle as primarily one in which the United States and Australia must have the fullest say in the direction of the democracies' fighting plan. Without any inhibitions of any kind, I make it quite clear that Australia looks to America, free of any pangs as to our traditional links or kinship with the United Kingdom. We know the problems the United Kingdom faces. . . . But we know, too, that Australia can go and Britain can still hold on. We are, therefore, determined that Australia shall not go.[57]

In the closing years of the war there began a growing appreciation of the steadily increasing material power of the United States and of the need to keep as close a relationship as possible; but there was in most minds the feeling that Britain would transcend the many problems that developed in the immediate aftermath of the war. What was clearly not understood was the permanent decline in British power, and the idea of an empire in rapid dissolution was wholly absent in the immediate post-war years. The traditions of the past distorted appreciation of the realities of the present, and in no section of the élite decision-makers was this more true than among the military.

Forward planning was not favoured within the Foreign Office; both Sargent and Cadogan were agreed that it was not an acceptable part of the direction of foreign relations. Neither was interested in administration, with the result that the Foreign Office remain understaffed throughout the war, and Cadogan, according to his editor, had to concern himself with the most trivial matters such as what hour the typists should leave in order to get home before the Blitz or which windows should be boarded up.[58] The absence of long- or medium-range planning meant that each event as it came along was approached within the general assumptions, inarticulate as well as explicit, that made up the thinking of the leading officials. The solutions offered were therefore ad hoc but not necessarily arbitrary. They might be, and indeed often were, wrong, but in most cases they would be within the general context of the ideas and attitudes that pervaded Foreign Office calculations. *The Times* critique of early 1943 had listed the absence of planning as one of the many failures that were elaborated upon; and again Bruce Lockhart's diaries during wartime provided a number of comments of a critical kind upon these matters. In the closing years of the war there was some attempt within the Coalition Government to consider external post-war problems. In August 1943 a ministerial committee on Armistice Terms and Civil Administration was established, with Attlee as chairman. Its terms of reference were widened in November 1943, and in April 1944 the Committee was renamed the Armistice and Post-War Committee. It served as a clearing house for the specialised committees of the Chiefs of Staff, the Foreign Office and various inter-departmental committees concerned with international relations.[59]

It was the Chiefs of Staff who possessed the rudimentary structure for the elaboration of post-war strategic planning. A Joint Planning Staff and a Joint Intelligence Sub-Committee were already in existence at the beginning of the war. A Military Sub-Committee was established in 1942 with Foreign Office representatives; a normal practice. Cavendish-Bentinck[60] had become chairman of the Joint Intelligence Sub-Committee in 1940 and remained in place throughout the war. After a great deal of inter-departmental manoeuvring, in August 1943 there was established a new sub-committee of the Chiefs of Staff, to be called the Post-Hostilities Planning Sub-Committee (PHP) whose chairman was Gladwyn Jebb.[61] The purpose of the Foreign Office was clear: it was to influence the definition of military strategy in the post-war world in directions that were considered politically desirable by the Office; and it was upon this rock that the PHP foundered. Jebb, in his memoirs, offers an inadequate account of the internal disagreements and quarrels between the Chiefs of Staff, and their colleagues, and the Foreign Office, which led to his departure from the PHP within a year.[62] One of the main areas of conflict, almost certainly the most contentious of many discordant views, was the insistence of the planning staffs of the Chiefs of Staff to be specific about their future strategic problems and in particular to make it plain that the only potential enemy in the post-war world would be the Soviet Union. There would always be a nod or two in the direction of the projected World Organisation, but it was assumed that it would be ineffective in practice or that it would not serve the strategic interests of the United Kingdom. It was necessary to be realistic, and open, concerning the likely motivation of the power blocs in the aftermath of war. Realism for the military was defined in a Note from the Chiefs of Staff to the Foreign Office on 2 October 1944 (paragraph 8):

> If one looks at the situation which will exist in the world when Germany and Japan have been thoroughly beaten and demilitarised, one finds only two possible menaces to the security of the British Empire, namely the United States and Russia. We eliminate the United States, and are left with Russia, a country of enormous power

and resources which has been cut off for 25 years from contact with the outside world and the trend of whose policy no-one can foretell. Taking a long view, we cannot afford to eliminate from our mind the conception of an expansionist and perhaps eventually aggressive Russia, and this applies whether we are considering the German problem or any other problem which affects our security.[63]

The arguments between the military planners, the Chiefs of Staff and the Foreign Office continued through the summer and autumn months of 1944. The Foreign Office were not of a single mind in opposition to the military but most, including the Foreign Secretary, were vigorously opposed to the apparently unqualified hostility of the military to the Soviet Union. In particular they were against the circulation of documents which elaborated upon this hostility, on the grounds that if the Russians became aware of the various military hypotheses being developed they might take appropriate political action, including a re-alignment with Germany.[64] The military were making their position clear beyond any doubt, and with no qualifications. Alanbrooke, the Chief of Imperial General Staff, was briefed by his planners before a meeting with Anthony Eden, and summarised his own opinions in his diary for 27 July 1944; six weeks or so after the first landings in Normandy:

> Should Germany be dismembered or gradually converted to an ally to meet the Russian threat of twenty years hence? I suggested the latter and feel certain that we must from now on regard Germany in a very different light. Germany is no longer the dominating power in Europe – Russia is. Unfortunately Russia is not entirely European. She has, however, vast resources and cannot fail to become the main threat in fifteen years from now. Therefore, foster Germany, gradually build her up, and bring her into a Federation of Western Europe.[65]

This particular phase of the debate seems to have come to a temporary conclusion in late October 1944 following a meeting between Eden, Orme Sargent and the Chiefs of Staff. The latter had not in any way modified their views on the future hostility of, and towards, Russia, but they agreed on a set of propositions which would restrict quite sharply the circulation of documents which published the thoughts in their minds. Most papers on the subject were to be regarded as drafts but still with a very restricted circulation and in the words agreed: 'any reference to a future threat from Russia should be in polite and circumlocutory terms.' Where it was felt necessary to be more explicit circulation would have to be on a very limited basis.[66]

There the matters of dispute seem to have rested until the spring of 1945 when, with the approaching end of the war, the Foreign Office began to develop a much harder line towards the Soviet Union. That phrase 'a much harder line towards the Soviet Union' can be misunderstood. There have been some British historians who have suggested that certain senior members of the Foreign Office, including the Foreign Secretary, were 'soft' on political issues

28

relating to Soviet Russia during the latter years of the war; and only came to their political senses in the months following the end of the war with Germany.[67] This approach misunderstands the nature of the political problems that confronted the Foreign Office during the war years, centred upon the necessity to maintain the Alliance in as reasonable a working order as possible. It was not at all that Eden and his senior officials such as Orme Sargent had changed their opinions in any way concerning the Soviet Union, or had forgotten what they considered the real interests of Britain were; but the war was not yet won, and there were a multitude of problems which could have been made more difficult if an open hostility to the Soviet Union had been offered. It was one of the curious twists of history that the Russians almost certainly knew about the unfriendly arguments between the British military and the Foreign Office in the summer and autumn of 1944. No doubt the Russians had always been aware of such hostility on historical grounds, but it happened, or it can reasonably be assumed to have happened, that Donald Maclean, who was in Washington during this time, was passing on the main discussions and debates to his Soviet contacts.[68]

The months between the temporary agreements with the military of late October 1944 and the end of the war with Germany in early May 1945 revealed increasing disquiet within the Foreign Office concerning Russian policy. The military, it should be remarked, had continued producing their anti-Soviet appraisals through the Post-Hostilities Planning Staff papers.[69] What was now causing concern to the Foreign Office were the political consequences of the military intervention in Greece from December 1944, the growing difficulties around the future of Poland, and the shape of the post-war world. There were many examples of a developing anti-Sovietism after the Yalta Conference – which for the Foreign Office never produced the euphoria within which Churchill was temporarily enveloped – and no better illustration was a memorandum from Orme Sargent in early April 1945. Sargent had always been clear-cut in his political attitudes. Before the war, for example, he had been Superintending Under-Secretary of the Central Department which included all matters relating to France; and during the Spanish Civil War he was especially concerned to assist all the political forces in France that were working against the communists: to prevent France, he explained 'by hook or by crook from "going Bolshevik" under the influence of the Spanish Civil War'.[70]

In the memorandum of 2 April 1945 Sargent began by suggesting that perhaps the moment had come to reconsider the British approach to the Soviet Union. He then set out the background of wartime attitudes towards the Soviet Union; arguments that he must have used constantly in the angry discussions with the military during 1944:

Till our invasion of France, that is to say till the Second Front had been opened, our

29

attitude was, and indeed had to be, defensive and almost apologetic. Even since then, during the spectacular advances of the Russian armies last year, the Soviet Union seemed in Europe to be establishing a military dominance which would show its full force at the Peace Settlement and which it would be folly to ignore. Indeed it looked until the other day that it would be the Russian armies which would invade and occupy the heart of Germany, including Berlin, before the British and Americans had penetrated the German defences in the West.

In these circumstances it was only prudent that we should in our diplomatic dealings with the Soviet Government set ourselves to propitiate our Russian Ally. On every possible occasion we tried to humour him, and the Prime Minister in particular was at pains to establish a personal friendship with Stalin. The policy was no doubt the right one at the time, and though it produced no spectacular results and indeed very little response from the Soviet Government, who can say that the situation would not have been very much worse if we had during this period asserted our rights on every occasion by the various means of pressure open to us, such as retaliation in kind, denial of material help, and isolated action in those parts of Europe where our interests and those of the Soviet Union appeared to conflict.

But with the sudden, almost unexpected, break-through in the West involving the collapse of the German armies, and the opening of the heart of Germany to invasion by British and American armies, the situation has radically changed. Instead of the Russians being in the position from Berlin to dictate their terms to their Allies, these latter are meeting them on equal terms in Germany, and indeed the terms on which they meet may end by being more favourable to the Western Allies than to the Russians.[71]

Orme Sargent then continued to elaborate the point that the changed situation has been understood by the Russians; hence their 'sudden truculence' and their resistance to all efforts to consider urgently the many problems that were developing as a result of the German defeat. He instanced especially the case of Poland, about which the Allies had been arguing for many months, and ended by suggesting that the 'show-down' he was advocating should concern itself with, first, Germany and Austria, and their administration, and, second, the *cordon sanitaire* of the countries bordering the Soviet Union on its western boundaries. On this latter issue Orme Sargent was emphatic that there should be no bargaining. As a Great Power, he argued, Britain must be involved with the affairs of the whole of Europe. He was, therefore, rejecting clearly and specifically the spheres of influence approach about which there had been intense and diverse discussion, which was to increase in the months and years ahead. As he wrote in this minute:

If, however, we cannot found our policy of co-operation on a system of spheres of influence, we must confine ourselves to making it abundantly clear to the Soviet Government that the policy of Anglo-Soviet co-operation must apply fully to Central and South-Eastern Europe as in the rest of the world, and that indeed we are not prepared to work the policy on any other basis.[72]

Two days later Cadogan appended a minute to Orme Sargent's memorandum which began by saying that he shared 'nearly all' Sargent's suspicions and apprehensions; and that in the case of Poland he fully agreed that the Yalta Agreement must be fully implemented. For the rest, Cadogan was not at all sure that the situation at present required a 'show-down' for the reason that he could not look that far ahead: a typical Cadogan response. Three months later Orme Sargent produced his revised version, 'Stocktaking after VE Day', which has already been referred to. Sargent made three main points which in each case he developed at some length. The first, noted above, was that Britain was still a Great Power and that the current weaknesses could only be overcome by energetic policies related to the building up of Western Europe in conjunction with Great Britain, and closer collaboration within the Empire. The second point, on which he spent most time, was an analysis of the policies of the Soviet Union. Sargent assumed that the Soviet Union was the main enemy, potential or actual, and that it was critical Britain took a stand on important issues immediately rather than wait until the situation possibly or definitely worsened. 'This means', he wrote, 'that we must maintain our interest in Finland, Poland, Czechoslovakia, Austria, Yugoslavia and Bulgaria, even though we may have to acquiesce in Russian domination in Rumania and Hungary.'[73] Further, he developed an early version of what much later came to be known as the 'domino' theory. If Britain did not take action immediately, Orme Sargent argued, the six countries he had listed would come under the control of the Soviet Government and Britain would then be threatened 'further west and south in Germany, Italy, in Greece, and in Turkey'. The Soviet Union had the great advantage of communist parties in every country of Europe, and by itself Britain would not be strong enough to withstand Russian power in Europe. It therefore had to win the support of the United States and this, he suggested, would not be an automatic response:

> But the process of inducing the United States to support a British resistance to Russian penetration in Europe will be a tricky one, and we must contrive to demonstrate to the American public that our challenge is based on upholding the liberal idea in Europe and not upon selfish appreciations as to our own position as a Great Power. Lippman is by no means alone in fearing that British antagonisms with Russia that filled the second half of last century will survive into the coming post-war period and embroil the much less interested United States. We shall therefore be well advised consciously and consistently to enlist American support upon some principle, and perhaps even to exercise some restraint in not pursuing cases where a principle cannot easily be shown. . . . This is not to say that United States policy is always based on principle, far from it; but it is a fact that a British policy is suspect if it is based on anything else, and particularly so at the moment in regard to Russia.[74]

In this memorandum of July 1945 Orme Sargent stated two of the three principal strands of policy inherited by the Labour Government. These were the recognition of the Soviet Union as the main hostile force in the world and the clear understanding of the crucial importance of the United States, and its material strength. In the early months of the Labour Government this appreciation of the role and place of the United States was not always so pronounced as it later became or as it had been stated by Orme Sargent in the 'Stocktaking' memorandum; and some still retained a lingering hope that Britain would be able to overcome the obvious economic weaknesses revealed in the immediate aftermath of war. Such illusions were sustained by the many areas of conflict and disagreement between America and Britain during the first year or so of the Attlee government.

The third component of British foreign policy in the immediate post-war world was the central importance of the Empire, and the lines of communication joining Britain to its imperial possessions, of which the Mediterranean, the Middle East and Suez were the most important. Empire, as discussed already, had always been a pivotal factor in the elaboration of British foreign policy; but its particular significance in the early months of the Labour Government had already begun to be discussed in the spring of 1945, with Attlee acting as the political catalyst. He had become chairman of the Suez Canal Committee and at a meeting of 20 March 1945 had proposed a series of questions which if accepted would have altered in fundamental ways Britain's place in the Middle East. What Attlee's committee was suggesting was a sharing of power on the grounds that 'The time has gone when Great Britain could afford to police the seas of the world for the benefit of others.'[75] This was typical of Attlee's statements which he was to repeat in various forms during the first two years of his government. The Suez Canal Committee's report was answered by Anthony Eden on 13 April 1945[76] in which the Secretary of State provided arguments already familiar to those who had read the various military planning papers and which were to receive considerable elaboration in the months to come. Summed up, the assertions Eden used were those which assumed the Empire would emerge from the war in its 1939 state and that, as the war years had shown, the Middle East and the Suez Canal were obviously crucial to the maintenance of the British Empire in the post-war years. Eden's definition of the strategic importance of the Middle East has been quoted above and his views were to be fully endorsed by both the military and the leading officials within the Foreign Office. They were also to be accepted, without qualification, by Ernest Bevin, but not, as is discussed in detail below in Chapter 3, by Clement Attlee. Bevin's view prevailed.

The defeat of Germany left a great black hole in the middle of Europe and that country's future was inevitably to be one of the major factors in respect of Europe – indeed, it was the outstanding factor in the diplomatic relations between the Allied Powers. There had been agreement at Potsdam on the military occupation of Germany through four zones each controlled by the three Great Powers and France. A measure of autonomy was granted in each zone but major questions were the responsibility of an Allied War Council; and these, so it appeared to be laid down in the Potsdam Agreement, related to the economic and political unity of Germany. It was the interpretation of Potsdam that provided the reasons for the breakdown of Allied unity and the subsequent division of Germany: the reparations issue being especially divisive between Britain and the Soviet Union.[77] What is noticeable about the first months of the Labour Government is the relative unimportance of the German question in British politics compared with the ending of Lend-Lease, the negotiations over the American loan, the situation in Greece and the refusal of Bevin and the Government to sanction any action against Franco Spain. It is these last two issues in particular that illustrate the continuity of policy with Bevin at the Foreign Office and his Tory predecessors.

The military intervention in Greece in early December 1944 generated a notable opposition among wide sections of opinion in Britain.[78] It was *The Times* to which Churchill was referring when he said, on 18 January 1945 in the House of Commons, that:

> there is no case in my experience, certainly not in my wartime experience, where a British government has been so maligned (*loud and prolonged cheers*) and its motives so traduced in our own country by important organs of the press among our own people. That this should be done amid the perils of this war, now at its climax, has filled me with surprise and sorrow.[79]

The violence in Greece began on 3 December and continued thereafter with British troops being used to complete the occupation of Athens by police and military against the EAM/ELAS forces. A Labour Party national conference had been fixed for mid December, to be held at the Central Hall in London; and on 13 December Ernest Bevin spoke for the National Executive in a defence of the action of the Coalition Government in Greece. 'I am here as a member of the War Cabinet', he said, and it was to an audience that was hostile. When Nye Bevan went to the rostrum to reply, he got the loudest applause for a brilliant attack on Bevin's speech, which he characterised as 'garbled and inaccurate when it was not unveracious'. In five minutes he could not answer Bevin as to what was happening in Greece. 'But there is one complete answer. Only three bodies of public opinion in the world have gone on record in his support, namely Fascist Spain, Fascist Portugal and the majority of Tories in the House of Commons.' Bevin, of course, got the decision because of the block vote;[80] but the cause of the Greek resistance and of the Greek republicans continued to be a matter of critical political debate in Britain, as well as elsewhere in the world, and it was to remain one of the main areas of discontent with the Labour Government's foreign policy for the first two years of Bevin's tenure as Secretary of State. In the first major debate of foreign policy in the

House of Commons after the Labour victory, it was striking how many of the Labour backbenchers spoke on the Greek question: all in varying degree hostile to Bevin's continued support for the right-wing factions in Greek politics.[81]

What was perhaps even more surprising to many Labour supporters was the refusal of Bevin and the Labour Cabinet to take action against Fascist Spain. In the case of Greece, the population had been overwhelmingly anti-fascist during the war years and had developed a considerable national resistance movement which at the time of the German withdrawal controlled about three-quarters of the whole country. Military intervention by Churchill, with agreement by those in Whitehall specifically concerned with foreign policy, was motivated by the recognition of the strategic importance of Greece for Britain, the assumed danger of communism, and, in Churchill's case, the additional factor of his absurd romanticism for the return of the monarchy. Now Spain was quite different, except for its strategic occupation of the entrance to the Mediterranean; but during the war there had been no doubt which side of the struggle Franco was on, even though he was not formally at war with Britain or America. In July 1944 the Union of Democratic Control published a sixteen-page pamphlet entitled *Franco's 'Neutrality' and British Policy*. It was a soberly written, well-documented account of the many ways in which Franco had assisted and supported the Fascist Powers during the war. The Blue Division was sent to fight on the Eastern front: German submarines were allowed to refuel in Spanish harbours; the *Falange Exterior* worked closely with Nazi organisations outside Spain, and in the Philippines assisted the Japanese landings; and the Spanish press and radio consistently exalted Nazi victories. Anti-British propaganda was especially virulent during the years 1940–41. And so on;[82] the list of material and political assistance afforded by Franco to Germany and Italy could be considerably extended, and there is abundant evidence from other sources.[83] This was not, however, how Churchill or the Cabinet or the Foreign Office looked upon the fascist regime in Spain.

The story begins in the months preceding the outbreak of the Civil War in Spain during the summer of 1936. The Foreign Office had been anxious about radical developments in Spanish politics following the overthrow of the Spanish monarchy in April 1931 by a bloodless republican revolution, but it was the victory of the newly established Popular Front grouping in the February 1936 elections that began the development of a more comprehensive anti-communist analysis in Whitehall. Widespread strikes and rioting confirmed their deepening fears, and on 26 March Sir Henry Chilton, the British Ambassador, wrote to Vansittart that 'The communist leader, Largo Caballero, will kick out the President of the Republic, and set up a Soviet Republic, in which case the lives and property of no one will be safe.'[84] Britain's oldest ally, Portugal, most of whose communists were either in exile or in jail at home, warned the Foreign Office of the spectre that was looming over the Iberian peninsula; the British Embassy in Paris confirmed their fears with accounts of the success of the Popular Front coalition, led by Blum, in the elections of 3 May; and it was not difficult for the politically aware as well as the politically illiterate to conjure up the threats to established order as a result of developments on both sides of the Pyrenees. There were important business interests in Spain owned by British companies, of which the Rio Tinto mines were among the best known. Thomas Jones, Deputy Secretary to the Cabinet, wrote in his diary of 25 May in terms which illustrate the fevered imagination of these days among the policy-makers in Whitehall. Jones had supported the Munich decisions:

> Dined at the Astors. Bullitt, the USA Ambassador at Moscow, there, and made our flesh creep with his Bolshevik stories. . . . He corroborated all von Ribbentrop has told me of the amazing efficiency and widespread penetration of the Communist propaganda, and described the training through which the Spanish contingent had been put before they were sent back to Spain, loaded with money, to stir up strife. This was the real danger to the world, not the military preparations of Russia. Says Moscow foretells a Communist government in Spain in three months.[85]

'Moscow foretells a Communist government in Spain in three months': an apposite introduction to the discussions which followed the military rebellion against the elected republican government of Spain. It was on the night of 17 July 1936 that military officers, recognising the authority of General Francisco Franco, seized garrisons throughout Morocco; and the Civil War began. It was an outcome that Whitehall had believed to be inevitable. While Italian and German arms and technicians moved into support of Franco, Anthony Eden and the British Foreign Office devised the formula which led to the Non-Intervention Committee, the consequences of which were gravely to disadvantage the republican government.

> The Western democracies failed Republican Spain! Fear of a general war, Chamberlain's desire for Italian friendship, and the Conservative government's distaste for 'Red' Spain committed England to non-intervention and brought pressure on Blum, sympathetic to Republican Spain, to adopt a similar course.[86]

What Raymond Carr, whose words these are, does not fully elaborate is the ascendancy of ideology over the strategic requirements of an imperialist Britain. Only Lawrence Collier, head of the Northern Department of the Foreign Office, had the wit to comprehend the advantages which would accrue to Germany of a victory for Franco; among the senior officials as well as the more junior such as Gladwyn Jebb the communist menace dominated their thinking.[87] Basil Liddell Hart, military correspondent for *The Times* and a lecturer to the Staff College, was consistent throughout the years of the Civil

War with the general argument that a victory for Franco, supported materially as he was by Germany and Italy, would be a strategic defeat of major proportions for both Britain and France; and after the war was over the Chiefs of Staff were asked to produce an assessment of the new situation that followed the defeat of the Spanish republic. Their report dated 10 May 1939 made sombre reading.[88]

It is understandable that Britain should follow a compromising policy towards Franco Spain in the first years of the 1939 war. There was always the danger of a formal adherence to the Axis Powers by Spain as against the widespread informal collaboration remarked on above. From the latter part of 1942, however, it was becoming very clear that Germany was unlikely to win the war – as Franco had repeatedly declaimed, in public as well as privately – and what is interesting is the caution with which the British proceeded in their relations with Franco. Always in their minds were the fears of what kind of regime would follow any overthrow of the fascist dictatorship. In a foreign policy review in the House of Commons on 24 May 1944 Churchill made a series of statements about Spain that aroused considerable controversy. He commended Spain for keeping out of the war and he had especial praise for its actions at the time of the North African landings of November 1942 'when the Spaniards remained absolutely friendly and tranquil. They asked no questions, they raised no inconveniences.' Churchill went on to say that he had no sympathy with those who took every occasion to insult and abuse the Spanish government, and he hoped that Spain would be a strong influence for peace in the Mediterranean after the war. Moreover, and this was to be the crucial element in future British policy, he regarded Spanish internal political problems as matters for the Spanish people themselves.

Considerable comment appeared in the left-wing and liberal press in Britain over these references to Spain, and there was similar and widespread unfavourable criticism in the American press. Churchill wrote to Roosevelt on 4 June:

> I see some of your newspapers are upset at my references in the House of Commons to Spain. This is very unfair, as all I have done is to repeat my declaration of October 1940. I only mentioned Franco's name to show how silly it was to identify Spain with him or him with Spain by means of caricatures. I do not care about Franco, but I do not wish to have the Iberian peninsula hostile to the British after the war. I do not know how I can depend on a de Gaullist France. Germany would have to be held down by main force, and we have a 20-years alliance with Russia. . . . We should not be able to agree with her in attacking countries which have not molested us because we dislike their totalitarian form of government. I do not know whether there is more freedom in Stalin's Russia than in Franco's Spain. I have no intention to seek a quarrel with either.[89]

Towards the end of 1944 both British and American ambassadors were recalled, to be replaced by diplomats considered less sympathetic to the Franco regime; and a British Embassy's despatch from Washington noted that American opinion assumed

> the imminent fall of Franco, who cannot be expected to last long without Allied support which is now expected to be denied him. . . . If and when Franco falls, United States opinion may be expected to watch for divergences between British and American policy under the impression that we are more likely to plump for a more conservative regime than is likely to be desired by the American Government and public.[90]

A month before Roosevelt died, on 10 March 1945, he wrote to the new American ambassador in Madrid in very different terms from those accepted by Churchill. 'As you know', Roosevelt said:

> it is not our practice in normal circumstances to interfere in the internal affairs of other countries unless there exists a threat to international peace. The form of government in Spain and the policies pursued by that Government are quite properly the concern of the Spanish people. I should be lacking in candor, however, if I did not tell you that I can see no place in the community of nations for governments founded on fascist principles.[91]

These were precisely the assumptions that the labour movement in Britain expected its own government would adopt after the overwhelming victory of July 1945; and certainly among the émigré Spanish republicans there was the same fervent belief that at last the Franco regime would be overthrown. In his first major speech on foreign affairs, that of 20 August 1945, Bevin introduced his comments on Spain with the words: 'May I now turn to a very popular subject – Spain?'; and after noting that Potsdam had excluded Spain from the United Nations, he insisted that there could be no intervention in the internal affairs of Spain, and that any proposed intervention would have the effect of strengthening General Franco.[92] What the United Kingdom would not do was to promote or encourage civil war and it was this argument that reverberated round the political and trade union conferences of the months to follow. The Labour Party Conference at Bournemouth in June 1946 debated the Spanish question with Bevin summing up the Government's policy at some length. 'I have been in the closest possible touch with the Spanish people and my experience is that they dread civil war. They dread it and so would you. They lost more people in that civil war than Great Britain lost in the last war.'[93] It was a typical piece of Bevin rhetoric, but it was only repeating in his own words what the Foreign Office had been deciding upon long before the Labour Government came to office.

Relations between Britain and Spain are considered in some detail by

Woodward in the official history of British foreign policy.[94] We may begin with Franco's letter to the Duke of Alba, the Spanish Ambassador in London. The subject was relations with the United Kingdom and was especially directed 'to our good friend, the British Prime Minister'. The letter, which was a long one, was dated 18 October 1944 and was passed on to the Foreign Office. Woodward provides a quite inadequate short summary, suggesting that it concerned mainly complaints about British policy, among them the wartime activities of the British secret service in Spain. What Woodward omitted was Franco's emphasis upon the potential dangers in the current European situation and his central concern with the menace of Bolshevism: 'with a Germany annihilated, and a Russia that has consolidated her ascendency in Europe and Asia, and a USA similarly dominant in the Atlantic and Pacific oceans'. Spain itself, unlike France and Italy, was not in a state of disintegration. What Woodward also failed to emphasise was the confidence, indeed arrogance, that Franco displayed throughout the closing period of the war and in the years which followed. R.J. Bowker, Counsellor at the Madrid Embassy, wrote a major report on the Spanish situation dated 12 June 1945 and received in London a week later. Bowker discussed the various options that were at least being talked about in Spanish diplomatic circles relating to modifications of the regime, but he remained sceptical about change of any significance. He emphasised how confident Franco seemed to be that no external intervention would compel any serious reorganisation, and certainly not transformation, of his regime:

> The attitude of Great Britain and the United States is still officially one of cold reserve. General Franco knows that neither Power is going to use force to turn him out. Meanwhile commercial exchanges with both Powers proceed on a substantial scale and there are good prospects of building up post-war economic relations of benefit to all three parties. For the present Spain cannot hope to get much in the way of armaments, but meanwhile only British and American supply considerations limit the possibility of her industrial re-equipment.[95]

Bowker went on to note that Franco's confidence was buttressed by his firm belief – to be reiterated on many occasions in the future – that the Western Allies and Soviet Russia would soon be at war with one another; and also by the confidence which he believed he was receiving from the United States – a matter which puzzled Bowker somewhat. He summed up:

> If, for the reasons given above, the external situation gives General Franco no cause for concern, he is equally unperturbed by the possibilities of dangerous developments from within. The Monarchists are divided among themselves, and with a few exceptions are quite indisposed to risk anything in order to bring about a return of the King. Spanish politicians in exile are equally, or more, divided and present police vigilance is such that it is extremely difficult for any political opposition

movement in the country to attain formidable size without being discovered or broken up.

Officials in the Foreign Office comforted themselves with the general belief that the end of fascism in Italy and Germany would assist internal changes, and this line of approach was especially emphasised after the election victory of the British Labour Party. F.R. Hoyer Millar, for example, who had returned from Washington to Whitehall in June 1945, minuted on 14 August 'that the British elections, coming after the Potsdam declaration, have had a profound effect on Spain and on Franco. There is therefore a real chance now of a radical change in the regime in Spain and of the disappearance of Franco'; but what must not be done was to try to accelerate change by foreign intervention. What was important was to leave things to develop on their own; allow the Spanish people time to work matters out, and to encourage the force of public opinion abroad to convince Franco 'that the time has come for him voluntarily to withdraw'.[96]

These illusions continued to circulate among the officials of the Foreign Office and provided the basis of Bevin's policy towards Spain. Franco's policy inside Spain did not change; he went on killing his opponents and putting many more in prison, and gradually he worked his way back into the anti-communist front of America and Britain. The United States military began to be increasingly interested in the establishment of bases in Spain and from about 1948 began to take active steps to ensure this.[97] At the same time the collapse of the Left opposition within the British Labour Party meant that Spain became an issue of minority concern, especially associated with the Communist Party.[98] Political consciences dimmed and by the end of the 1940s Spain moved out of British politics, to come back in somewhat different style with the beginnings of mass tourism at the end of the next decade.

Greece and Spain were at opposite ends of the Mediterranean. Greece was subjected to military intervention by the British in 1944 in order to save the country from communist 'bandits': the description commonly used by Churchill and others, including Macmillan.[99] Spain suffered non-intervention in two main periods of its mid-century history: the first, during the Civil War years, in order not to favour the Republic, behind which, it was fervently believed, stood the threat of communism; and the second, once Italy and Germany had been defeated, to ensure that the continuation of its fascist order would also keep away the communist threat. Greece, after the Soviet Union, suffered most in economic and social terms during the years of war; it remained desperately poor, and the colonels' regime, which succeeded years of repression against all progressive forces well beyond those who accepted the title of communist, ended only in 1974. At the further end of the Mediterranean Franco died in 1975.[100] The long years of suffering of the Greek and Spanish peoples were a tribute to the policies of Ernest Bevin and his officials in Whitehall, and the

Cabinet of Clement Attlee who supported them. They were not alone, of course, but of the burden of their responsibility there can be no doubt.

Moscow

Political fears of communism in general, and its embodiment in the Soviet Union in particular, began with the Bolshevik Revolution of October 1917. In the decades before 1914 the ruling classes of Europe had become inured to the spread of various kinds of socialism, syndicalism and anarchism, and to the practice of political terrorism, but the hysteria generated by the 1917 Revolution went beyond the apprehensions of the years before the First World War. The processes of peace-making were profoundly influenced by the Bolshevik threat. Arno Mayer, in his study of Versailles, wrote that:

> Russia did not withdraw from the European system; she was excluded from it. This exclusion was ideologically and politically motivated, particularly with statesmen and generals who otherwise advertised their unswerving allegiance to the canons of the balance of power. The further to the right they stood on the political spectrum, the greater the opposition to any diplomatic *rapprochement* with Lenin. In the last analysis, then, Russia was ostracised and quarantined because of her revolutionary transgression, and this transgression became both cause and excuse for treating Russia as if she were a decaying empire.[101]

In Britain the anti-Bolshevik fervour was pervasive, with *The Times*, *Daily Mail* and *Morning Post* the most vehement in their denunciations of this newly arisen monster. Winston Churchill's statements about Russia in the early days of the Soviet State are well known, and he was the most ardent interventionist in the Cabinet;[102] but hostility among the propertied classes was world-wide. Herbert Hoover, head of the American Relief Organisation, explained to the editor of the New York *Nation* on 17 August 1921, that 'the whole of American policies during the liquidation of the Armistice was to contribute everything it could to prevent Europe from going Bolshevik or being overrun by their armies.'[103] The British Foreign Office included some senior officials who were virulent in their anti-Soviet attitudes. J.D. Gregory was one, and the general temper of the Office was well illustrated during the Zinoviev Letter episode of the autumn of 1924 when Eyre Crowe, the Permanent Under-Secretary, released the letter on the grounds, so he averred, that it was in the political interest of the Labour Government: five days before election day. Even Ramsay MacDonald, who defended the actions of his civil servants before his Cabinet colleagues, wrote in his diary, after the election campaign was over: 'In my absence the anti-Russian mentality of Sir Eyre Crowe was uncontrolled. He was apparently hot.'[104] The Arcos raid, and the TUC break with the Soviet trade unions after 1926[105] coming after the Zinoviev Letter, helped to keep the anti-communist and anti-Soviet temperature 'hot' for the remainder of the decade.

In the 1930s the situation began to change in that the Soviet Union began to move once again into the politics of Europe. The catastrophic economic crisis in the capitalist world, the emergence of fascism in Germany, the entry of the Soviet Union into the League of Nations in 1934, the outbreak of civil war in Spain in July 1936, all helped to encourage sharp divergence of opinions among all social classes in Europe, and elsewhere in the world. Suspicion and mistrust towards Russia among propertied groups did not abate, and the growth of communist parties in some countries of Western Europe intensified fears and hostility. Moreover, such opposition was not always limited to the wealthy groups in society as revelations of gross violations of justice, and the harshness of the Stalinist regime, began to be appreciated in parts of the organised labour movements, although there was a marked difference in these matters between different countries. For most of the politically organised working people, the threat of fascism overshadowed all other consid-erations.[106] It was now not possible to ignore the Soviet Union although neither France nor Britain, in their attempts to come to terms with the new Europe of German and Italian fascism, ever seriously contemplated a re-alignment with the East.

An example of ruling-class attitudes in Britain was exhibited in late July 1936 when Stanley Baldwin, then Prime Minister, received a deputation on defence matters. Churchill had become the leader of a quite small Tory faction who argued for rearmament in face of the increasing threat of Nazi aggression and it was he who introduced the deputation. After listening to their case Baldwin then answered with an illuminating statement which did not quite fit the popular image of honest 'John Bull' that the pipe-smoking Baldwin presented so often to the British public. After quoting, and agreeing with, Neville Chamberlain that rearmament would damage the British economy, Churchill's historian, who described the interview, continued:

> Baldwin had another reason for rejecting the Deputation's sense of urgency. Hitler, he said 'wanted to move East, and if he should move East, I should not break my heart'. But he did not believe that Germany wanted to move West because, as he expressed it, 'West would be a difficult programme for her'. He was not, he added, going to get Britain into a war with anybody 'for the League of Nations or anybody else, or for anything else'. If there were to be any fighting in Europe, Baldwin declared, 'I should like to see the Bolshies and Nazis doing it.'[107]

It was the British government that put such strong pressure upon Léon Blum to accept non-intervention in the Spanish Civil War, and which caused F.L. Lucas, literary critic and poet and not identified with any specific Left grouping, to write to the *Manchester Guardian* on 16 February 1937 about the hypocrisy of the non-intervention policy:

> As over Ethiopia, our policy is palsied over by one fundamental thing. More and more it stands out above every other factor. A large section of British public opinion is obsessed with a *delirium tremens* which sees everywhere the red rat of Bolshevism gnawing its way into the bank cellars. Hitler may arm to the teeth, bestride our trade routes, yell for colonies; no matter, this agony about their beloved bank balances blinds these people to all else. . . . Nothing will get done till we are cured of this ignoble paranoia.

F.L. Lucas was not exaggerating. This polarisation of political opinion was growing with increasing bitterness on both sides of the main argument. Harold Nicholson noted in his diary for 18 May 1938: 'On my way I stop at Pratts' where I find three young Peers who state that they would prefer to see Hitler in London than a Socialist administration.'[108]

Political attitudes towards the Soviet Union inevitably became even more embittered after the signing of the Nazi–Soviet Pact; and at the time of the attack on Finland, there was an important minority opinion among ruling circles, in both France and Britain, in favour of switching the war.[109] The turning point was, of course, the invasion of Russia by Germany in June 1941. There were still indications that influential sections of conservative opinion would be content to see the Germans and the Russians cut each other's throats. Truman, who was a Senator, said this in the United States as did the British Minister of Aircraft Production, Moore-Brabazon, who was later retired from office after country-wide protests.[110] Most in Whitehall, however, kept their own counsels; in any case very few expected the Russians to last out through the first winter. The general political attitudes of the administrative élites did not alter in any fundamental way; what did change was the recognition that the failure of Germany to achieve a quick victory, together with the growing strength of the Soviet armed forces from the later months of 1942, was beginning to alter in radically different ways the power relations within Europe; hence the acceptance by the Foreign Office of the crucial importance of war-time co-operation in order that their bargaining position in the aftermath of war should not be compromised. It was this that the uncluttered minds of the military could not appreciate, from which followed the quarrels of 1943–44 that have been briefly touched upon above.[111]

It was in the last year of the war that perceptions of Russia within the Foreign Office began to move back into their traditional forms and thereby to come steadily closer to the Chiefs of Staff's appreciation of global strategy. Some members of the senior group – Cavendish-Bentinck for example – had never altered their basic position; but now there was developing a remarkable consensus within the Office of the threat to Britain's position, not so much from

Germany, but rather to the lines of communication to the British Empire. It was the eastern Mediterranean and the Middle East in particular that were now central to their anxieties; and from the spring of 1945, through the Potsdam Conference to the coming together of all the heads of missions in the Middle East in September 1945, the fear of Russian expansion increasingly dominated the minds of senior officials in Whitehall. It was during these months that the 'vacuum' theory was brought into their calculations: namely, that if for any reason Britain moved out of a given area or region, Russia would take its place; and the same would be true if Britain reduced its traditional control or power in any country. The only critic of importance within Whitehall whose views could not be dismissed out of hand was the Prime Minister himself, and for some two years from the spring of 1945 until the spring of 1947 Attlee developed serious objections to the acceptance of traditional ideas of policy and strategy in Egypt, the Suez Canal and the Middle East as a whole. These are matters considered in detail in Chapter 3 below.

The year the war ended had seen, then, a marked hardening of official opinion in respect of the Soviet Union: a general view that the new Foreign Secretary found wholly compatible with his own personal and private opinions. It was during the early months of 1946 – some six months after Labour had taken office – that the anti-Sovietism pervasive throughout the Foreign Office was provided with a more sophisticated ideological thrust. Within the American administration, which was always more open than its counterparts in Whitehall, there had always been some of its leading personalities who had never concealed their anti-communism and their total distrust of the Soviet Union. In the same month as Roosevelt's death, at a meeting of the top-level decision-makers presided over by Truman — the main subject for discussion being the Soviet Union and Poland – James V. Forrestal, Secretary of the Navy, was quoted as saying that it was 'his profound conviction that if the Russians were to be rigid in their attitude we had better have a showdown with them now than later'.[112] Forrestal remained convinced in his anti-communism, and at the end of 1945 he commissioned Professor Edward Willett, of Smith College, to provide an analysis of the 'enigma of Russia' and to offer possible solutions to the political problems of relationships with the Soviet Union. Willett produced his paper in mid January 1946 with the title 'Dialectical Materialism and Russian Objectives' in which he stated categorically that the Soviet leaders remained committed to a global revolution against the capitalist order, so that 'violence between Soviet Russia and the United States would seem to be inevitable'.[113] Forrestal then circulated copies of Willett's paper around Washington.

There was a backcloth of crisis to these months of late 1945 and early 1946. There had been a number of disputed matters between the major powers since the failure of the Foreign Ministers' Conference in September 1945 – Poland, Trieste, the Italian colonies – but it was the Iranian question which now came to dominate Anglo-American–Soviet relations. The British and the Russians had invaded Iran in August 1941 in order to ensure the safety of the supply lines to the Soviet Union from the Persian Gulf; and by the terms of a Tripartite Agreement of 1942 all Allied occupation forces would be withdrawn within six months of the ending of hostilities with Germany and its associates. The Americans and the British withdrew their troops within the agreed limit but the Russians delayed and from the beginning of the year a critical situation began to develop with the Anglo-Americans insisting upon Russian withdrawal. The British had the enormously profitable Anglo-Iranian Oil Company to protect while the Americans had almost no oil interests at this time; both, for different reasons, came to regard the Iranian situation as a crisis issue.[114] The United States was certainly not being discouraged by the reports being sent from its missions overseas. George Kennan in a despatch dated 17 March 1946, from Moscow, was expressing with his usual vigour a series of statements about Russian intentions which were to be proved, mostly, wrong. He began by suggesting as 'almost a foregone conclusion' that the Russians would work for the establishment in Iran of a government subservient to themselves and in order that such a government would grant Soviet demands for the continuation of Soviet forces in the country and for an oil concession. Kennan then proceeded to justify these statements by insisting that the Russian government 'has no intention of withdrawing its troops from Iran. On the contrary, reinforcements, even though not on a large scale, have been sent in.'[115] In London Bevin was assuming the same outcome of the Iranian question. Dalton reported meeting him at the end of March and finding him 'in a great state, saying that the Russians were advancing in full force on Teheran, that "this meant war" and that the US were going to send a battle fleet to the Mediterranean'.[116] Truman was also talking about the possibility of war.[117]

What the Russians were primarily interested in was the oil concession, and this they achieved in early April, although instead of a concession there was to be a Soviet–Iranian oil company. At the same time Soviet troops were to be withdrawn within a six-week period that began on 24 March. There was never the likelihood of war, and Truman's claim that he sent Stalin an ultimatum is untrue.[118] The standard version of the Iranian crisis has much simplified the motivation and objectives of the three Great Powers involved. Britain, for example, would have been willing to accept a Soviet sphere of influence in the northern sector of Iran, at the same time as Britain was ambiguous about a greater American commitment in the region. When the newly elected *majlis* overwhelmingly rejected the Soviet–Iran oil agreement in October 1947 it was because of their confidence that the United States would provide support in the event of Soviet counter-action. Rejection of the oil agreement was a major defeat for the Russians, but the principles invoked were to be used against Britain half a decade later; and it is from the period of the 1946 Iranian crisis that we may date the decline of British power in the region and the enhancement of American influence.[119]

Within three weeks of Edward Willett's paper on the Soviet Union Stalin made an election speech on 9 February 1946 which aroused extraordinary interest, and a great deal of hostility, in the United States. Its impact upon British opinion was a good deal more muted. Kennan had been reporting to the State Department on the election campaign in Russia, and upon the speeches of the Soviet leaders in particular. He summarised Stalin's speech in five main points. Stalin began with a

> Straight marxist interpretation of World War One and Two as products of crises inherent in monopoly capitalism. This was coupled, however, with the statement that World War Two bore anti-fascist liberating character from the very outset – an interesting deviation from the recently revived 1939–41 line that was purely 'imperialist' in pre-Soviet phase.

The other four points, according to Kennan's summary, were all concerned with the superiority of the Soviet system over capitalism, and the material targets for the forthcoming Five Year Plans. Stalin's speech, it needs to be emphasised, was a good deal less aggressive than others quoted, such as those by Kaganovitch and Maienkov, but inevitably it was Stalin's words which called for widespread comment. Interest was not confined to the media, for the State Department seem to have taken the speech very seriously.[120] The growing anti-communist hysteria in the United States undoubtedly affected judgement on international issues, and episodes such as the defection of Louis Budenz, the editor of the *Daily Worker*, in the autumn of 1945 was one of the many examples of this period which contributed to the public anxiety and disquiet. When Budenz was brought before the House Un-American Committee in the early spring of 1946 he offered testimony to the effect that 'the Communist Party in the United States is a direct arm of the Soviet Foreign Department' and he went further with the statement that every American Communist 'is a potential spy against the United States'.[121] The 'Great Fear' was beginning to penetrate American consciousness well before Joe McCarthy began to move to the centre of the anti-communist stage.

George Kennan was asked by the State Department, in response to his analysis of the Russian election campaign and in particular of Stalin's speech, to provide 'an interpretative analysis of what we may expect in the way of future implementation of these announced policies'[122] and the result was the 'Long Telegram' of 22 February 1946: a document of seminal importance in the definition of the assumptions of American policy in the aftermath of the Second World War. What Kennan was saying to the leaders of the American people was that they were confronted with a world conspiracy whose central purpose was 'to undermine the general political and strategical potential of major western powers'. Kennan centred his analysis upon the ideology that was driving the Russian leaders to extend their military power in the world in order to guarantee external security to hide the internal weaknesses of their regime:

> In summary, we have here a political force committed fanatically to the belief that with US there can be no permanent *modus vivendi*, that it is desirable and necessary that the internal harmony of our society be disrupted, our traditional way of life be destroyed, the international authority of our state be broken, if Soviet power is to be secure. This political force has complete power of disposition over energies of one of the world's greatest peoples and resources of world's richest national territory, and is borne along by deep and powerful currents of Russian nationalism. In addition, it has an elaborate and far flung apparatus for exertion of its influence in other countries, an apparatus of amazing flexibility and versatility, managed by people whose experience and skill in underground methods are presumably without parallel in history. Finally, it is seemingly inaccessible to consideration of reality in its basic reactions. For it, the vast fund of objective fact about human society is not, as with us, the measure against which outlook is constantly being tested and re-formed, but a grab bag from which individual items are selected arbitrarily and tendentiously to bolster an outlook already preconceived.[123]

He ended this section by insisting that the post-war diplomatic situation could only be successfully managed by the same kind of care and thoroughness which characterised the General Staff work of the war years; and he then listed what he described as observations 'of a more encouraging nature'. He had made the point that his own conviction was that the problems the United States would face could be solved without recourse to military conflict. While the Soviet Union was 'Impervious to logic of reason' it was at the same time 'highly sensitive to logic of force'; and it would withdraw when sufficiently strong resistance was encountered. Moreover, compared with the Western Powers, the Soviet Union was still 'by far' the weaker force; and the future was uncertain. We could not know what would happen in the event of Stalin's death, and there would be longer term problems: including those of the nationalisms of the newly annexed regions. In a prescient final paragraph he wrote:

> the greatest danger that can befall us in coping with this problem of Soviet Communism, is that we shall allow ourselves to become like those with whom we are coping.[124]

Kennan in later years has spent much time arguing that his approach was misunderstood and that in particular his analysis did not lead directly to an acceptance of a hard, Cold War response to the Soviet Union. There were certainly ambiguities and subtleties in the original Long Telegram and in the subsequent article in *Foreign Affairs* a year later,[125] but in the climate of political opinion in the United States in the early spring of 1946 it was naive of Kennan to believe his argument would not be used to support a hard-line approach towards the USSR. The receipt of the Long Telegram in Washington was stunning. Everyone, including Byrnes, Secretary of State, praised it for its lucidity and the cogency of its analysis. Forestal had hundreds of copies made to be distributed round Washington; and it was leaked to some members of the press corps – *Time* had a full page in the edition of 1 April 1946.[126]

Yet the Long Telegram was a deeply flawed document. The comment that objective fact meant nothing to the Russians could equally be applied to a large part of Kennan's own exposition. His approach bordered at times on the manic; it took little account of the world that had emerged from six years of war; and his reasoning was an a priori analysis of a model of world communism, with Soviet Russia at its centre, that developed out of his own imagination. Above all, and like many who came after, he wholly omitted from his analysis the massive devastation in those regions of the Soviet Union which before 1939 had produced a large part of its food production and a high proportion of its industrial output. In terms of industrial capital investment, the consequences of war had been more serious for Russia than for Germany. Kennan was apparently unable to accept that the Soviet Union might have an interest in stability, in order to undertake post-war reconstruction, and that this would have to include a willingness to compromise on international issues with her former allies. He failed to understand the deep-seated fear of a resurgent Germany. As Stalin said just before the Yalta Conference: 'It would be naive to think that Germany will not attempt to restore her might and launch new aggression. . . . History shows that a short period – some twenty or thirty years – is enough for Germany to recover from defeat and re-establish her might.'[127] Kennan failed also to appreciate the political caution that Stalin exhibited in respect of the Italian and French communist parties, and that his territorial objectives were strictly limited to the establishment of a security zone along Russia's western borders, as some Western commentators such as E.H. Carr recognised as historically inevitable. Daniel Yergin summed up: 'The contradiction in his portrait of the Soviet Union and its leaders – the rational fanatic, the devastated aggressor – went unrecognised.'[128]

Just about a month after the Kennan Long Telegram Frank Roberts, in temporary charge of the British Embassy in Moscow following the departure of Clark Kerr to Washington, sent three long despatches to London which provided a similar overview of Soviet attitudes. Roberts, in his late thirties at this time, had served in Cairo, was proficient in Arabic, and went to Moscow in January 1945 and served three years. He returned in January 1948 to become Private Secretary to Ernest Bevin. When the Labour Party delegation visited Moscow in July–August 1946 Harold Laski picked out Roberts as a very bright young man, in marked contrast, so Laski wrote to his wife, to Sir Maurice Peterson, who had recently been appointed Ambassador.[129] Inevitably, Roberts had come on close terms with Kennan in Moscow; 'a happy relationship' he described it over forty years later.[130] At the beginning of March 1946 Roberts provided Christopher Warner, Superintending Under-Secretary of the Northern Department, with a summary of the Long Telegram, having first obtained Kennan's agreement. There were some interesting differences in the abridgement that Roberts made. One was the introduction of the phrase 'a social democratic Britain' which Kennan never used but which was at this time just coming into the thinking of the Foreign Office in London[131] and a second was the impression Roberts gave that Kennan suggested, in spite of the Soviet Union's hostility to America and the outside world, that, 'provided we put our own house in order and maintained our strength there was no reason why we should not live in peace in the same world with the Soviet Union.'[132] This was not quite a fair summary of Kennan, whose approach was more unbending, but it did represent Roberts' general approach, in contrast with his colleagues in London.

All three despatches from Roberts were printed after they reached London; the normal practice when a paper was thought to be worthy of a wider circulation than usual. Roberts' first despatch was dated 14 March, and addressed to the Foreign Secretary.[133] He introduced it by describing his account as 'a sombre picture'; and wondered whether the vehemence of Soviet attacks on the United Kingdom might not represent:

> a certain fear of our inherent strength, which may have been increased by the recent London meeting of the UNO at which the Soviet delegates found the whole world, with few exceptions, ranged on our side under your own moral leadership. The rulers of Russia already realised when Labour was returned to power at the general election of last July that there was now a progressive force in the world of equal and possibly greater attraction than their own Communist system . . . and behind the UK is the USA, for whose material strength there is the most pronounced respect here.

Roberts later speculated whether the world was not now to be faced with 'the equivalent of the religious wars of the 16th century, in which Soviet Communism will struggle with Western democracy and the American version of capitalism for domination of the world'.

His second despatch was dated 17 March. His account of the Soviet Union was preceded by a long historical analysis of the beginnings of the Muscovite State and a brief summary of the subsequent history of Anglo-Russian relations. Then he came to the present situation and here his approach was hostile on most issues with rather interesting qualifications at some points of the analysis. He insisted that the Soviet Union was making every effort to develop the country into the most powerful military state in the world, and that at a time when others were demobilising and reducing their armed forces the Soviet Union was maintaining a very large military establishment, modernising

48

its equipment and industrial base. All these were largely Roberts' a priori deductions, as was his statement of the 'domino theory' of Russian strategy:

> The search for security is a constantly expanding process. The establishment of the Soviet frontier on the Curzon line has meant that a puppet Polish state must have its frontiers on the Oder and the Neisse. This, in turn, leads to Soviet control of the eastern zone of Germany through a faithful Communist Party and the encourage-ment of Communist influence in the rest of Germany and even in France. To take another example, the domination of Persian Azerbaijan to protect the oil in Baku leads on naturally to the domination of Persia as a whole, to encouragement of a puppet Kurdistan republic, to the isolation of Turkey and eventually to infiltration into the whole Arab world. A legitimate demand for a large say in the control of the Dardanelles is at once followed by demands for bases in the Dodecanese and Tripolitania. In fact Soviet security has become hard to distinguish from Soviet imperialism and it is becoming uncertain whether there is, in fact, any limit to Soviet expansion.

Roberts had set out in this second.despatch the assumptions on which British policy should be based and in the third despatch, of 18 May, he continued with specific proposals. The first was a reiteration of a general point that Kennan had made, namely, that it would be necessary to treat Anglo-Soviet relations 'as major military problems were treated during the war': with close co-ordination of political strategy on all fronts. Then Roberts, again echoing Kennan, laid emphasis upon the need to establish Britain as a dynamic and progressive society which could appeal to the world as a counter to communist propaganda; but he ended on a note of sober caution, in a rather remarkable passage which was at variance with many of his earlier statements:

> British relations with Russia were for three centuries maintained not unsuccessfully on such a basis of distant realism between Governments. If we do not aim too high, we shall at least avoid constant irritations and disappointments. The many important interests we have in common, and much of our joint determination that no other one Power shall ever become a menace to us both, should remain a solid bond, despite the deep gulf between our social systems.

The response in London to Roberts was friendly, with Warner using the word 'magnificent' and emphasising the importance of the contact with Kennan and the American Embassy. An earlier minute from Warner sug-gested, however, that the third despatch was not quite so successful as the first two, mainly, it may be assumed, because Roberts was not wholly uncom-promising in his anti-Soviet attitudes. Roberts continued to adopt a more independent position than the majority of his colleagues throughout 1946. For example, he wrote an important despatch to Bevin on 4 September 1946 in which he recognised the appalling problems of reconstruction in the USSR –

as he had not in his March despatches – and he also criticised the proceedings of the Peace Conference in Paris during the summer.[134] Australia was especially picked out as being unhelpful. This long memorandum was a statement rarely to be found in Foreign Office papers in the post-war years for Roberts actually suggested that diplomatic dealings between the two worlds 'call not only for patience and firmness, but also for external correctness, courtesy and discretion, which have not recently been apparent in for example the Australian approach nor in the present American handling of the USSR': admonitions that could certainly be applied to his own Foreign Secretary. His despatch was widely circulated. Brimelow,[135] in a longish typed minute, more nearly reflected the common view:

> His general conclusion is that the Soviet and the non-Soviet world can live together without head-on conflict, though there must inevitably be friction where their frontiers meet.
> In my minute on the telegram referred to above, I set out the reasons for my belief that this general conclusion of Mr Roberts' is too optimistic and that we must expect a general deterioration of relations as time goes on.

The Foreign Office took what they wanted from Roberts, and there followed from the three March despatches what was probably the most important single document in 1946 in its characterisation of Russian policy and its emphasis upon the urgency of countervailing measures. The author was Christopher Warner and the title of his memorandum 'The Soviet Campaign against This Country and Our Response to It'. Warner, from Winchester and Oxford, had been head of the Northern Department in the later years of the war (1943–45) and was now Superintending Under-Secretary of both the Northern and the Southern Departments.[136] Like most of his colleagues in the Northern Department, he was not a Russian speaker. His typed document, with twenty-eight paragraphs covering seven pages of somewhat greater length than normal foolscap, was a remarkable testimony to the thinking of the Foreign Office in these years.

It might be expected that an examination of Soviet policy, less than a year after the defeat of Germany, would begin with an estimate of the 'weight' of the Soviet Union in world politics; what its 'real' strength was compared with the front that it presented in diplomatic negotiations; the extent to which Russian policy was dictated or affected by the changing geo-politics of the post-war world; how the tribulations of its wartime experience had impaired its industrial power, and future potential, and in which ways this was relevant to military capabilities; what the estimated motivations were of the Soviet leadership and above all of Stalin; and whether there were any conclusions that might be drawn from the wartime experiences of the relations between the Allies. Warner, however, was not concerned with questions of this kind. In particular he made no serious reference to the two outstanding questions that were at the centre of the formulation of Russian foreign policy in the post-war years: one was the massive destruction and devastation that the western regions of Russia had suffered during the German occupation and retreat, and the enormous loss of life in the armed forces and among civilians;[137] and the second – and here there was a partial reference only – was the overriding concern for security on its western borders following the experiences of two world wars. Instead, like Kennan, it was the ideology of the Soviet leaders that provided his starting, and finishing, point of reference, and from the alleged fixed and unswerving dogma of the Soviet leadership Warner then made a series of deductions about the course of Russian policy. His text was not a serious analysis but a disquisition on the assumed provocative and aggressive tendencies that flowed inexorably from the omniscient intellectual and emotional faith that suffused the Soviet leadership.

Warner began by listing the three main points in the policy currently being pursued by the Soviet Union:

1. The return to the pure doctrine of Marx-Lenin-Stalinism.
2. The intense concentration upon building up the industrial and military strength of the Soviet Union.
3. The revival of the bogey of external danger to the Soviet Union.

It was the return to the dogma of Marx-Lenin-Stalinism that propelled Russia, and its allies in other countries, to pursue aggressive policies, at all levels, against the non-communist world. The 'tremendous reaction' to Winston Churchill's Fulton speech was evidence enough to underline the general argument. Warner then followed with what must be judged as among the most insensitive statements in modern diplomatic history. Of course, he wrote, 'The Soviet Union is no doubt war-weary.' Here is the paragraph in full:

> The Soviet Union is no doubt war-weary, and, as the Soviet leaders have pro-claimed, wants a prolonged peace to build up her strength. But she is practising the most vicious power politics, in the political, economic and propaganda spheres and seems determined to stick at nothing, short of war, to obtain her objectives. Having regard to the declarations of policy referred to above, it would be very rash to assume that her present political strategy and tactics are short-term only.

His next paragraph discussed the argument that Russia's concern for security was founded upon genuine suspicion, although he offered no examples of why the Soviet Union should argue in this way; and he noted that the Soviet authorities were currently intensifying these suspicions among their own people:

Can it be, in reality, a convenient excuse for an aggressive policy; after all, at the end of the war, the only two countries that could threaten Russia were her allies, Great Britain and America, and these, as any good Soviet observers must have reported, were only too anxious to relax and demobilise? Or again, are anxiety about the internal situation in Russia and the need to supply the spur to their own people the principal motives? Whichever of these explanations be correct, the fact remains that Russian aggressiveness threatens British interests all over the world. The Soviet Government are carrying on an intensive campaign to weaken, depreciate and harry this country in every possible way.

This central theme, that the Soviet Union was conducting an implacable war against Britain – the weaker of the two liberal democracies – was repeated in different ways throughout Warner's memorandum. His last main section, from paragraphs 17 to 28, set down various suggestions of a political and administrative nature by which the Soviet offensive could be countered. He especially emphasised Russia's 'clever trick' of establishing international federations and groupings of various kinds, and arranging for their control by communists of various nationalities. The World Federation of Trade Unions was the obvious example. In his biography of Bevin as Foreign Secretary, Bullock does not mention the Warner memorandum, but in a letter Bevin wrote to Attlee on 10 April 1946 he used – or whoever drafted his letter used – exactly the arguments developed by Warner: 'The Russians have decided upon an aggressive policy based upon militant Communism and Russian chauvinism'; and he went on to make the point that Britain, as the leader of social democracy in Europe, was their especial target together with the fact that 'we appear the less formidable of Russia's only two rivals as Great Powers.'[138]

The advice that both Kennan and Roberts had proposed in respect of the urgent and necessary co-ordination of policy against the Soviet Union's machinations was acted upon in Whitehall with the establishment of the 'Committee on Policy Towards Russia' or, as it commonly became known, the Russia Committee. The first meeting of the Committee was on 2 April, and its terms of reference were drafted by Christopher Warner and Sir Nigel Bruce Ronald, also, like Warner, from Winchester and Magdalen College, Oxford. Ronald was the Superintending Under-Secretary of the Economic Intelligence Department, the General Department, the Reconstruction Department and the Research Department. The main aims of the Russia Committee were set down as a weekly review of all aspects of Soviet policy; with an especial emphasis upon propaganda campaigns against Britain; to ensure 'a unified Interpretation' throughout the Foreign Office; to consider what action was needed 'with particular reference to the probable degree of support to be looked for from the United States and to a lesser degree from France and others'; and to make a brief report each week to Orme Sargent, now the Permanent Under-Secretary. Members of the Committee included Oliver

Harvey, Superintending Under-Secretary of the German Department, and Robin Hankey, who was the successor to Warner as head of the Northern Department. It was, then, at its beginning, a powerful committee, and chairmanship seems to have rotated. Their discussions, following the terms of reference, included everything relating to Russia. There were some interesting matters to come before the Committee in the first year of its existence and it continued through 1947 into 1948 when Gladwyn Jebb became chairman. Attendance had begun slowly to fall away, and while it was a useful stage post for the collection of information it was considered steadily less important; and only when the Information Research Department was established at the beginning of 1948 did effective practical action really get under way.[139]

There were, nevertheless, some matters deserving of comment. The suggestion by Lord Addison[140] in a letter to Attlee that the Catholic Church might be made use of in the anti-communist struggle was discussed by the Russia Committee on 14 May 1946. Foreign Office minutes exhibited varied reactions. Brimelow thought it 'a most dangerous suggestion' (23 April); Hankey (24 April) wrote: 'Let's keep clear of the Vatican. Their ways are not ours, and they are rather in disgrace all over Europe for trimming during the war.' On the other hand there were some suggestions that opportunities might occur in the future for using the influence of the Vatican on specific matters. After reviewing the arguments:

> The Committee was of the opinion, however, that as the Roman Catholic Church was one of the most powerful anti-Communist influences it might be of advantage, without directly seeking the co-operation of the Vatican, to assist the Church in deploying its influence by facilitating the movements of its emissaries, or by other inconspicuous means. It was recommended that His Majesty's Minister at the Vatican should be furnished with information regarding Communist activities for use in his contacts with members of the Papal entourage, Catholic bishops visiting Rome, or other influential members of the ecclesiastical hierarchy. It was further recommended that in the circular despatch to Heads of Missions abroad, their attention should be drawn to the potential importance of organised religion in combating the spread of Communism.[141]

Early in its existence the Russia Committee took note of what was common knowledge about the differing political attitudes to Russia within the Cabinet. A memorandum from R.G. Howe, Superintending Under-Secretary for the Eastern Department and for the Egyptian Department, to Orme Sargent quoted Hall-Patch[142] as saying that 'some Ministers took the line that it would be wrong to consider Russia to be "hostile" to this country, that we should not treat the Soviet Union as an "enemy" and so on.' Howe continued by noting that Warner's memorandum 'The Soviet Campaign Against this Country' had been approved by the Prime Minister for circulation to those ministers who would be in discussion with the Dominion Prime Ministers at their London conference, and that the document

> is, of course, based on the premise that Russia *is* at present 'hostile' to us in almost every possible way and has in fact launched an offensive against this country. Action is, as you know, being taken, under the general supervision of the Russia Committee, to put into effect a counter-offensive designed to protect us from Russian aggressive tactics. It is, in the Committee's view, essential that this policy should have the full backing of the Cabinet. . . .
>
> It is possible that the Prime Minister and the Secretary of State may find it undesirable to discuss too openly with certain of their colleagues this aspect of our official policy.

To this memorandum Orme Sargent was re-assuring, and he replied that the Committee was covered by the Foreign Secretary's approval, endorsed by the Prime Minister, and assuming that the Committee did not go beyond the proposals set out in the definition of its purposes, it had nothing to worry about. It should be added that the distribution of Warner's memorandum left out all of the Cabinet ministers who might possibly have raised objections to its tone as well as its contents; these included Hugh Dalton, Stafford Cripps, Aneurin Bevan and Manny Shinwell.[143] For the rest of 1946 the files of the Russia Committee are not very interesting. They looked into organisations like the International Student Congress which met in Prague in August, and they set in motion inquiries into the management of the British National Union of Students; they analysed the replies from British missions abroad to the Warner memorandum; and they decided that Stalin's denial of the possibility of war in the Werth interview published in *The Sunday Times* was a 'purely tactical move'.[144]

The general impression from the Foreign Office papers through 1946 is of a consistent and apparently unanimous agreement concerning the aggressive character of Russian foreign policy and of its particular virulence against Britain. Ronald produced a memorandum dated 7 November 1946 in which he underlined the urgency of effective counter-action against the Russian threat:

> Given the formidable differences between our western and their essentially oriental backgrounds and modes of thought, it is not to be hoped that we can, anyhow for some years to come, reach a collaboration with the Soviet Union closer than that of a 'modus vivendi' which may indeed from time to time have to take on all the outward appearances of a 'modus pugnadi'.[145]

Ronald hoped for a degree of collaboration, and most of the senior officials seem to have believed that the best that could be expected was an agreement over the peace treaties with certain very large questions, especially concerning Germany, being left open for the present. Warner always in this year took an 'impossibilist' position, although even he did not believe in a 'hot' war.[146] The Chiefs of Staff who were producing their estimates of the future regularly throughout the year, working their way to a comprehensive approved Defence Strategy – which was to appear in May 1947 – assumed that the Soviet Union would not engage in armed conflict for at least five years. Warner, who accepted this, nevertheless continued to insist upon the subversive politics of the Soviet Union, on a global scale and within countries and regions.[147]

Indications were not wholly absent that serious negotiations, undertaken with goodwill and patience, could provide understanding and perhaps positive results. The last interview that Clark Kerr had with Stalin has already been mentioned. It took place on the eve of Clark Kerr's move to the Washington Embassy and he reported to London that it was conducted on a very friendly basis. The date was late January 1946. As noted above, Stalin was apparently mainly concerned with Bevin's antipathy towards the Soviet Union; and when Clark Kerr suggested that the recent Moscow conference had dispelled much of the ill-feeling, Stalin disagreed. Clark Kerr had remarked that Bevin's sincerity had impressed everybody, including Stalin and Molotov:

> Stalin laughed and said this had not been so. The impression of Bevin on the Russians had not been good. He did not understand why it had not been possible to arrive at a good official and personal relationship with yourself. He had achieved it with the late government.

Clark Kerr wrote in his report that he gave as good as he got and that he had spoken to Stalin of the many things that were 'incomprehensible to us'. Stalin replied that he would do his part to remove suspicions, if Bevin did his.[148]

There were new ambassadors to Moscow from the United States and Britain during 1946 and both had important meetings with Stalin. General Walter Bedell Smith met Stalin at the beginning of April 1946 and Roberts provided an interesting summary of the matters he considered important. He empha-sised that it was a 'perfectly friendly' discussion and that Bedell Smith came away with the clear impression that 'Stalin was not pushing an aggressive line.' It was a frank exchange with Stalin making it very plain that Churchill's Fulton speech was taken as a very hostile act. The American President should never have allowed such a speech to be made in the United States, but Stalin went on to insist that in his view 'Churchill was speaking with authority, and also that he regarded a close Anglo-American understanding as already existing.' Roberts ended his report with the hope that Maurice Peterson, Britain's new Ambassa-dor, would have a similar frank exchange when he arrived in Moscow towards the end of April.[149]

Peterson did not leave England until May. He had a meeting with Bevin on the 15th, and the minute of the discussion was written by Pierson Dixon, read and approved by Bevin, and then sent to Peterson. The main points began with the Middle East followed by the need for greater freedom of trade in Central Europe; the offer of the fifty-year alliance with Russia; Trieste and the Italian colonies; and Greece. The last was not mentioned at all in the interview and the main part of Stalin's comments centred on the subject of the Russian bases in the Middle East. Stalin's reported answers to Peterson on the Middle East were highly interesting:

> he said that Russia fully recognised the importance of our position in the Middle East and did not seek to dispute it. If there had been no British troops in Egypt that country would have collapsed into the arms of the Axis, and this would have been bad for 'all of us'. At the Crimean Conference Stalin himself had favoured the retention of British bases in the Mediterranean. At San Francisco Molotov had suggested that all the principal powers should be allowed strategic bases no matter where these might be situated. This proposal had not been accepted because there was a general desire that Russia should not have bases. It was this which had really disrupted allied Front.

Stalin then came back later in the interview to this general matter, pointing out that Churchill had promised to welcome the appearance of a Russian fleet in the Mediterranean but that the Labour Government were not giving effect to this suggestion, and he asked what use would the Suez Canal be to Britain if it had no bases from which to defend? In this same telegram summarising his meeting with Stalin, Peterson also had a comment to the effect that 'American demands for bases, however comprehensible, do seem to offer an unfortunate precedent for the Soviet Government.' It was a comparison that was continually to be made, mostly from the Russian side, in the early years after the war.[150] A later letter from Peterson to Orme Sargent, to be found in the same file, commented that Stalin looked far from well and was possibly suffering from high blood pressure. However:

> There is nothing wrong with his mind. He hardly bothered to consult Molotov during our long talk. He made his own notes while I was speaking, interspersed with luxuriant doodles in red ink.

Two months later the British Labour Party sent a goodwill mission to Russia. The delegation consisted of Alice Bacon, MP, Harold Clay, Harold Laski and Morgan Phillips, who acted as secretary. The details of their visit and the personalities and organisations visited are set down in an Appendix to the Annual Conference Report of 1947; and Roberts provided Warner with a long report after the delegation had left Moscow.[151] The letter from Roberts was dated 23 August 1946. He had a long talk with the delegation at the beginning of their visit and found them well-informed on most Soviet issues, but ignorant of the 'bitter anti-British press campaign'. Roberts noted that Stalin had a serious discussion with the delegates about the different roads to socialism and he admitted that he had not expected a Labour victory in 1945. The Foreign Office files also contain the report which the delegation made to the National Executive Committee of the Labour Party, the most interesting section being the discussion with Stalin in the evening of 7 August, in particular the acknowledgement by Stalin of some of the problems Russia confronted. He mentioned the need to speed up demobilisation 'but care must be taken to ensure that there was no further danger of aggression', and he then proceeded to offer a most interesting comment on some of their other difficulties:

> The level of culture was one of deep concern and this was having their urgent attention. They had also a large peasant population whose approach to Socialism and its implications was different from that of the industrial workers. . . . We [i.e. the British] had not a substantial peasant problem but we had a highly organised working class and a higher level of culture. We had, of course, other problems and difficulties; for example, our business men were wealthier, much more clever and experienced than the Russian business man. He nevertheless felt that we had the opportunity in Britain of a more peaceful approach to socialist construction than they had in Russia.[152]

There were many questions on both sides, and the report notes that at the end of this interview one of the delegates 'got the impression that there was still a fear in Russia about the possible strength of reaction in Britain'.

Morgan Phillips published three articles in the *Daily Herald*, on 20, 21 and 22 August 1946. Their tenor was positive. He described the Russian people that they had met as 'a vigorous, healthy people, tremendously busy on reconstruction; consumer goods were in very short supply; great progress in education but still a great deal to be done, with 20,000 schools having been destroyed; no collective bargaining in industry.' His last article, on 22 August, was devoted to a summary of the two-hour interview the delegates had with Stalin: 'he warned us that our "clever and experienced bourgeoisie" might prove more of a problem than was the case in Russia, where the old ruling class was "merely silly".' He ended his article on a favourable note.

There are other examples that could be enumerated which would suggest that the inflexibility and single-mindedness assumed of Soviet policy by the Foreign Office was not as instinctive or as inevitable as commonly believed. Above all other considerations, it was the terrible and hideous experience of the years of war that barred the possibility of another conflict coming from the Russian side. Large parts of their country were in ruins, and the pall of twenty million dead – or was it twenty-five million? – spread over those who survived.[153] There was never the possibility of Russian miscalculation that would lead to war, as was so often referred to in the Foreign Office papers.[154] What is so striking about Foreign Office thinking in the first eighteen months of peace is the absence of any serious attempt to analyse the complexities of the world situation and emerging geo-politics of the war's aftermath. The Americans, for example, could understand the new Arab nationalisms that within the first post-war decade were going to transform the Middle East; but not the British, whose perceptions were narrowly encapsulated within an imperialist consciousness. With the exception of Poland, whose political problems were discussed at different levels throughout the war, the first serious delineation of British anti-communism of the post-war era was to be found in respect of the countries of the Middle East and what was called the Northern Tier of Greece, Turkey and Iran.[155] It was in these regions that the Russian threat was first expected and it was here that the belief in the inexorable drive of Soviet communism became an inescapable premiss of the decision-making élites of Whitehall.

There is no simple formula, of course, to explain the ways in which the idea of an aggressive communism hardened into an undeviating dogma. One factor was indisputably the conduct of Russian foreign policy, the main responsibility for which, in the capitals of the world, lay with Molotov. It could be expected that the media in the capitalist world would display a hostile picture of what the Soviet Union was about; but in large and small ways the Russians presented themselves as impossibly obdurate and intransigent. There were populist issues such as the Russian wives – Russian women who had married Britons and who were not allowed to join their husbands[156] – and there were innumerable matters of human rights and civil liberties. It was not that inhumanity was absent from British and American actions, but the Russians were especially vulnerable as a result of the trials of 1936 to 1938, the Katyn Graves massacre and the political attitudes of the Stalinist communist parties which were moving into power in Eastern Europe. It was, however, not these questions that were the central reasons for the quite remarkable change in public attitudes towards the Soviet Union in the first two years after the end of the war in August 1945. Britain in particular was markedly skilful in the manipulation of public opinion and the fact that it was a Labour Government which was implementing a series of welfare schemes, as well as nationalisation, made it easier for the anti-Soviet line of the Government to be increasingly accepted by the population. The British government, in the immediate aftermath of war, were guilty of serious malefaction: the military interventions in Greece, Indo-China and Indonesia, and the refusal to undertake any resolute action against fascist Spain were the most obvious examples. A more subtle and astute direction of Russian foreign policy would not have altered the basic anti-communism of the Western Powers, but it would undoubtedly have made it more difficult to achieve the isolation of the Soviet Union that was to come about. This was widely appreciated in both Washington and Whitehall. J.C. Donnelly noted on 14 October 1945 how Russian 'intransigence' was greatly helping the British attempts to bring the United States into the ways of British thinking, and he hoped that the Russians would not see the path of 'wisdom'.[157]

A few days later N.M. Butler, Superintending Under-Secretary of the American Department, was minuting that 'The Russians are giving us unexpected help.'[158] Of all the comments of this kind, which were quite numerous, that of the former American Ambassador to Moscow is probably the most telling since Joseph E. Davies was among the Soviet Union's most sympathetic interpreters. On 8 January 1946 he wrote in a private letter: 'I know of no institution that needs a high pressure "public relations" organisation as much as the USSR. They do not seem to get their case across, even when, as it happens sometimes, they have a good case.'[159] Anthony Eden made the point in his 1960 volume of memoirs, *Full Circle*:

> These immediate post-war years would have presented the Western nations, and the Labour Government in the United Kingdom in particular, with infinitely greater difficulties if the Soviets had played their hand with skill. They were improvident and careless. They squandered their goodwill, and there was then so much of it that it almost seemed as if they did not care. I was perplexed at this aspect of Soviet policy, for I knew Stalin to be a prudent if ruthless man. Perhaps the answer is to be found in this conversation. In Moscow one evening during the war, Mr Churchill and I were invited after our work to supper in Stalin's flat. In the course of conversation we spoke of the diplomatic methods of a number of countries. We came last to Russia and Stalin remarked, 'Perhaps we Russians are not as simple as you think'. I replied that we had never thought them that, but rather as skilful and therefore formidable. Stalin rejoined that the truth probably lay between the two, that they were neither as simple as some thought nor as skilful as others believed.[160]

There is one final matter in this general discussion of anti-communism within the Foreign Office that must be considered. It has been suggested that in the period before the announcement of what became known as the Marshall Plan Bevin showed a degree of equivocation with regard to the policy to be adopted towards the Soviet Union. The argument is largely deduced from what Bevin said in public, and his decisions on the internal circulation of memoranda which were hostile to the Soviet Union. Certainly in the latter case he did refuse to allow some papers to be circulated as widely as some of his advisers wished. There are two arguments here. One is the nature of Bevin's approach to the Soviet Union from his earliest days in office: in other words what were his ideas in August 1945 and did they change over time; and the second is what were the particular circumstances in which Bevin would refuse to allow the distribution of papers or memoranda hostile to Soviet Russia.[161]

It is necessary to make clear the sharp division of opinion between the Prime Minister and his Foreign Secretary with regard to policy in the Middle East from the very early days of the Labour Government. The issue arose because of the need for a decision about the future of the former Italian colonies but it then broadened into a more general consideration of imperial strategy. The details are set out in Chapter 3 below; let it just be observed that the conflict of opinion between Attlee and Bevin, the latter fully supported by his permanent officials, continued into the spring of 1947. It was not completely, but almost nearly, a private matter between Attlee and Bevin and the latter's Private Office; and the dissent between the two leading members of the Government was not carried into the meetings of the Cabinet. The problem that historians have with Bevin is that his public pronouncements quite often do not agree with his own personal views or with the policy he is pursuing at any one particular time. For politicians of any rank that is hardly a novel proposition. No one achieves high office in parliamentary democracies without having travelled a road of lies, deceit, double-talk, hypocrisy and ruthlessness. The balance within the mixture will naturally vary with individuals and with circumstance. In the case of authoritarian societies terrorism, mayhem and murder will be normal accompaniments of the highway to power, and in the twentieth century this has been on a frightening scale.

Let us return to Bevin, who for the first years of office had two major problems to contend with in addition to the normal (sic) processes of diplomacy in the aftermath of a horrendous war. The first was domestic and concerned his own political party and large groups of the trade union movement in Britain. There was, as Anthony Eden noted in the quotation give above, a considerable reservoir of goodwill towards the Soviet Union. Most people with any political understanding recognised that without the enormous sacrifices of the Russian people, and their skill and heroism in battle, the war with Nazi Germany would have ended quite differently. Moreover, the Labour Party was widely assumed to have been elected upon a socialist platform and would therefore, so it was expected, exhibit a natural sympathy with the Russian people and their leaders; but from the very beginning of the Labour Government taking office this was not at all how international politics worked out. Until the summer and autumn of 1947 the opposition within the labour movement in Britain to Bevin's foreign policy was vigorous, and widespread. Among the more intense moments were the foreign policy debates at the 1946 and 1947 annual conferences of the Labour Party, and the formation of Keep Left group in the spring of 1947. Even though Bevin had a considerable personal triumph at the 1946 Conference – the first to be held since the Labour Party took office – his temporary success over his critics did not stem the flow of adverse comment. The *New Statesman* through the latter part of August and into the whole month of September 1946 published a series of articles calling for a thorough re-orientation of British foreign policy which would match British commitments with its financial and economic resources. In particular it argued that the attempt to maintain the pre-war Empire was 'foolhardy'.[162] Towards the end of this month the interview between Alexander Werth, Moscow correspondent of *The Sunday Times*, and Stalin was published, and on 24 September *Tass* issued the text of the answers to Werth's questions. The tone as well as the content of this interview was warmly welcomed in the international press as an important and welcome contribution to current world politics, with Stalin insistent upon the possibilities of peaceful co-operation. It was this speech, as noted above, that was dismissed by the Russia Committee as a 'purely tactical move'.[163] Within two months, there developed within the Parliamentary Labour Party a serious confrontation with the policies of the Foreign Office that the Government was supporting; and on 13 November a meeting of the PLP discussed an amendment to the King's Speech criticising the Government's foreign policies. Attlee and his other ministers were not able to persuade the critics to withdraw their motion of censure, which had been signed by 58 Labour MPs, but it was agreed not to press for a division. The debate took place in the Commons on 18 November, with Attlee summing up because Bevin was in New York. No one supported the amendment but there were 130 abstentions, a figure which, although it included the sick or members absent with good cause, was a demonstration within the Party that clearly went beyond the well-known critics within the PLP. In the following May (1947) the pamphlet *Keep Left* was published by a group of fifteen members of the Parliamentary back-bench. It was written by Crossman, Foot and Mikardo, and did not include the identified members of the extreme Left of the Party in matters of foreign policy, such as Zilliacus, Platts Mills and others who were later to be expelled.[164] However, the pamphlet was countered by one published in the name of the International Department of the Party: this was *Cards on the Table*, written by Denis Healey; and the 1947 Conference was the last time an effective opposition to Bevin came from the floor of the Conference.[165]

For two years, then, Bevin and his ministerial colleagues were subject to intense disapproval by quite significant sections of the movement, both on the political and on the trade union side. In all his public statements, therefore, he had to abstain as far as possible from giving his critics further material for their opposition; and it was this important factor of domestic politics that some of his own officials in the Foreign Office, and certain of the historians who have commented on these matters, quite failed to understand. Gladwyn Jebb commented on the *Keep Left* pamphlet at the time of its publication:

> Much of what Crossman says would have appeared sensible two years or even eighteen months ago. Indeed all our papers were then based on the assumption that there should in no circumstances be any Anglo-U.S. line up against the U.S.S.R. or indeed against Communism, until such time at any rate as the Soviets should have made it abundantly clear that they did not intend to co-operate with the West. It will be recalled with what passionate conviction the F.O. represented this thesis to the Chiefs of Staff and what care was taken to prevent even the smallest whispering getting round that we favoured the Americans rather than the Russians.[166]

Jebb was being disingenuous, as well as inaccurate in his chronology. It was 1943 and especially 1944 that the conflict between the Chiefs of Staff and the

Foreign Office was at its most concentrated, and by the time the Labour Government came into office the anti-communism of the administration was already settled along the lines that later developed. It was, however, always recognised, even in the 1943–44 years, that the United States would have to be brought in to share the global burden of anti-Sovietism; and that understanding grew rapidly once the war had finished, and the financial and material weaknesses of the United Kingdom became steadily more evident. For the Russia Committee to expect Bevin to agree to make public their suggested 'defensive-offensive' policy against the Soviet Union in 1946 was to ignore or be ignorant of the political situation he confronted within Britain;[167] and it was the highly vocal opposition from his back benches in the House of Commons as well as outside Westminster that explains the gap between his public statements, or those communications that could possibly be leaked – as at the Dominion Prime Ministers' Conference in the spring of 1946 – and his personal views and antipathies. There is no basis for any argument that Bevin was 'estranged' from his senior officials during 1946, or that from the day he took office he was seriously seeking accommodation with Soviet Russia. His judgement was based upon what he regarded as politically practicable at a given point in time; and for the whole of 1946 he was in part hemmed in, certainly in terms of public pronouncements, by the contours of his own domestic situation. This was why Denis Healey's *Cards on the Table* was so important; it said in forthright language what Bevin himself had always believed about the Soviet Union.[168]

There was a second constraint upon Bevin in these first years of office which required more delicate timing even than his own domestic problems. It was central to Bevin's strategy that the United States should become integrally involved in the struggle against communism and the Soviet Union. Without American support, Britain's global commitments would of necessity have to be sharply reduced. In this context Bevin had two problems which on occasion would conflict with each other. On the one hand, Britain could not pursue too independent a line from that being developed by the United States even though there were a number of important issues on which there were serious differences; and on the other, Britain must not be seen to be too anxious for American support because of the large segments of American opinion who were Anglo-phobe and always ready to assume that Britain was using American strength to buttress its imperial positions. That was true, of course, although in the medium and long run it was the United States which came to dominate; but in the early years of Bevin's tenure of office his diplomacy was directed towards committing America to a general and particular support of the various positions the United Kingdom was adopting in respect of its policies towards the Soviet Union. Since the American President and the State Department had their own lines of policy we come back to the intermesh of these two approaches and the difficulties they caused the Foreign Secretary and his senior advisers.

On 24 January 1946, just under six months from the assumption of office, Ernest Bevin had dinner with Senator Vandenberg and Foster Dulles.[169] The political background was the growing crisis in Iran. A summary of their conversations was made by Pierson Dixon, marked 'Top Secret' and limited to circulation within the Foreign Office. Vandenberg asked 'How was Moscow?', referring to the recent meeting of Foreign Ministers:

The Secretary of State began by saying that he thought Mr Byrnes had done very well in Moscow. It was true that he (Mr Bevin) had at first considered that the meeting in Moscow, which had been arranged on Mr Byrnes' initiative, was a mistake.[170] But in the event the meeting had not turned out badly and we (by which the Secretary of State meant the Americans and ourselves) had lost nothing. The Secretary of State went on to voice his fears of Russian aims. He used the figure of the 'two arms of the bear'[171] and explained to his hosts what he meant on a map. He showed them how the Russians were trying to wrap one arm to the West around the Straits and the other arm round the eastern end of Turkey by acquiring the provinces of Kars and Ardahan. The cession of these two provinces to Russia furthermore would mean that the Turks would have a considerably greater length of frontier to defend. Coming to the present Soviet policy towards Persia the Secretary of State explained that, in his view, after undermining the Persian province of Azerbaijan the Russians hoped to be able to penetrate through Kurdistan and so further wrap the arm of the bear round the eastern end of Turkey, as well as imperilling the oilfields of Mosul.

Senator Vandenberg and Mr Dulles were greatly interested by this exposition and pored for a long time over the map.

The Secretary of State said that the moral was that over the Persian issue it was vital to stand up to Russia. The Russian technique, which was precisely the same as that followed with such success by Hitler, consisted in taking one position at a time. Appeasement must be avoided at all costs. If the Russians were rebuffed over their designs on Persia Turkey could be saved. Let there be no mistake: if the Turks were attacked, they would fight. Could America stand aloof? Would not another world war be inevitable? So he begged America to weigh the importance of opposing the present designs of Persia.

Senator Vandenberg asked the Secretary of State why he had been so rough with Mr Stettinius the night before last [concerning the appointment of a Secretary-General for the UN].

. . . The Secretary of State explained that his advice to Mr Stettinius was based on the following: the Russian technique allowed of no give and take. If the British and Americans had a difference of opinion, they usually could find a middle way out and reach agreement by concessions by both sides. But with the Russians there was no question of concessions. They insisted on their point of view at all stages, and if the other parties did not like their point of view they imposed their veto.

These are the words and thoughts of Ernest Bevin at the beginning of his years as Foreign Secretary. He believed them on his first day of office and there is no evidence that he changed his ideas in any fundamental way in the years that followed. As far as the printed record goes there were no dissenters from among the officials of the Foreign Office. There were always areas of tactical disagreement, matters sometimes of serious dispute, but in the years after the end of the Second World War there were no differences of the kind that scarred the history of the period of appeasement. On all basic questions the Foreign Secretary and his officials were at one with each other, a working partnership based upon a genuine respect, a recognition that the political head of their Office was the strongest man in the Labour Government; and he was their man.

Washington

If all diplomatic records from the end of the war in August 1945 to the beginning of the Korean War in the summer of 1950 had subsequently been destroyed, it would have been a difficult exercise to reconstruct the way the relations between the Great Powers had evolved during these five years. The evidence of the war years would have recorded the steadily growing anti-communism within the ruling circles of both Britain and America, but they would also have chronicled bitter differences between the two English-speaking nations. The wartime Anglo-American alliance had been constantly strained by sharp differences and acerbic debates, sometimes concerned with fundamental questions both of war and of the peace to come; and inevitably there developed degrees of personal animosities. Roosevelt and Churchill did not wholly trust each other nor were they always as frank in their communications as has sometimes been assumed.[172] Important matters such as the conditions attached to Lend-Lease, the post-war development of civil aviation, the American critique of colonialism, atomic energy, Argentina – the list could be extended – as well as the issues of military strategy central to the conduct of the war itself, such as the Mediterranean strategy of the British in contrast with the more direct approach of the Americans – all were areas of dispute and disagreement.[173] Some of these questions are considered in this volume, but all contributed to the formation of distinctive national attitudes. At the same time, during the years of war, there was a remarkable partnership between the two countries in many different areas of the war effort. The innovation of Lend-Lease, regardless of the conditions attached; the decision of the Americans to retain the Europe-first strategy following Pearl Harbor; the acceptance of unitary military commands – these were only the vital parts of a major collaboration, especially on the military level, that covered an enormous range of activities and worked efficiently and effectively. The outstanding exception was the Far East.

The arguments and differences on policy issues, military and civil, were naturally played out against the backdrop of past historical relations between the two countries. Anglo-American relations had deteriorated sharply during the inter-war years. The rejection of the League of Nations by the American Senate; the repudiation of war debts by Britain; the development of the Ottawa agreements in the 1930s as a response to the world economic crisis; the strong areas of isolationism in America and the highly critical appraisal of Britain's imperial role in the world – all combined to encourage censorious attitudes on both sides of the Atlantic that constantly resurfaced during the war years. Without the personal relationship that developed between Roosevelt and Churchill, in spite of the reservations on both sides, the succession of wartime crises would have made collaboration much more difficult. As it was, working together was often fraught with misunderstandings, both personal and political, that could easily have slid into unmanageable strains and tribulations.

There were, to begin with, many stereotypes on both sides that seriously handicapped co-operation, and some were never overcome. The Foreign Office in Whitehall believed as an article of unshakeable faith in the superiority of their diplomacy over the Americans and they also had the curious belief that the Americans did not have any serious ideas about their own future in the world once war came to an end. This is somewhat surprising in that the weekly despatches they received from the Washington Embassy were stating quite emphatically that the Americans were increasingly aware of their material and military strength and were referring to themselves and the Soviet Union as the two major powers. Writing of a recent speech by Henry Wallace, for example, a despatch commented: 'His theme falls into the now all prevalent Big Two rather than the Big Three pattern.'[174] The date was 26 May 1945. There was every reason for American optimism about their material future. Between 1939 and 1944 GNP had risen from $91 billion to $210 billion, and by 1945 the industrial capacity of the United States was nearly twice as great as 1939. For the average citizen of the United States it was butter as well as guns.[175] Moran, Churchill's physician, quoted him as saying: 'Up to July 1944 England had a considerable say in things; after that I was conscious that it was America who made the big decisions.'[176] As could only be expected, many groups within the American administration, the military complex and the business world fully appreciated the growth in their own economic power, and the growing contrast with the position of Britain. Stanley Troutbeck, an important State Department Official, wrote to Cordell Hull early in January 1944 that the United States was now 'in a position to get from the British agreement to and co-operation in any reasonable course of action upon which we may choose to insist.'[177] The two questions in this statement are the definition of 'reasonable' and the matter of choice 'upon which we may choose to insist'. From the time of the signing of the Atlantic Charter – which was before the Americans came into the war – the help the United States gave to Britain was usually controlled by financial or other kinds of leverage. Lend-Lease, for example, was manipulated in order to prevent the United Kingdom's currency reserves from rising to levels which would make the British economy independent or at least less amenable to the American advice.[178] Among the more important matters that had emerged during the years of wartime discussion of the future world economy were the system of imperial preference that Britain operated, the mounting problem of the sterling balances, and their discriminatory aspects.[179] American attempts to move towards a more open multilateral world order and the end to discrimination belong to the financial history of the immediate post-war years. Traditional conservatism in Britain, for example, was highly conscious of what was involved in the Loan agreement of December 1945. As L.S. Amery wrote: 'The British Empire is the oyster which this loan is to prise open.'[180] A truth, of course, but not the whole truth.

The officials in the Foreign Office in Whitehall showed a remarkable reluctance to appreciate the fundamental changes in the world's power relationships that had come about through six years of war. There was a recognition of America's economic and financial strength but, as mentioned above, a striking lack of understanding about America's own appreciation of the new position it occupied in world politics. In the spring of 1944 there had been produced within the Foreign Office a report on 'The Essentials of an American Policy' in anticipation of a visit by Stettinius, the American Under-Secretary of State. The author, Alan Dudley, was quite a low level member of the Office, and he had prepared his paper under the direction of Richard Law who was Minister of State at the Foreign Office.[181] Law approved of the paper and wrote to Eden that he would like it circulated to the Cabinet: 'so many of our colleagues are quite haywire on the subject of the United States . . . I think it very good; and contains much food for thought.' This was on 22 March 1944 and Eden replied on 2 April that he thought it better not to spread it too far; Cadogan agreed to circulate only within the Foreign Office. The memorandum was printed, no doubt one of the reasons why it has been quoted, or partly quoted, by a number of historians. More important is the insight it offers into the mind of Whitehall. After some platitudinous comments to the effect that a common language between the two countries does not automatically guarantee 'immediate unity or solidarity', paragraphs 3 and 4 continued:

> Nevertheless, in the long run, the nature of the relationship does compel national collaboration between ourselves and the Americans, no matter what friction may occur. And it should be noted that more often than not this means that the Americans follow our lead rather than we follow theirs. Fortunately, we are not confronted with the alternatives of pleasing them or standing up to them; we also have the opportunity and the capacity to guide and influence them. They have enormous power, but it is the power of the reservoir behind the dam, which may overflow uselessly, or be run through pipes to drive turbines. The transmission of

their power into useful forms, and its direction into advantageous channels, is our concern.

Many Americans are now thinking for the first time about taking part in world affairs, and to most of them this means collaborating with us. It must be our purpose not to balance our power against America, but to make use of American power for purposes which we regard as good. The process of calling in the New World to redress the balance of the Old is still incomplete, and the ability to evoke the New World's immense resources is stronger in these islands than elsewhere. We should be throwing away one of our greatest assets if we failed to evoke it, or if we were to credit the people of the United States with having developed their own ideas of the world's future to such a point of clarity that they were uninfluenced by ours. If we go about our business in the right way we can help to steer this great unwieldy barge, the United States of America, into the right harbour. If we don't, it is likely to continue to wallow in the ocean, an isolated menace to navigation.[182]

A later paragraph included the comment that 'commercial rivalries' were likely to be the most serious disturbers of Anglo-American harmony. It would be difficult to find a more illiterate statement of the relations between Britain and America; and it could be thought to be a chance aberration were it not for the repetition of the apparently widespread belief that the Americans really were novices in the Great Game and that they would have to come to accept the greater sophistication and diplomatic experience of their British cousins in the Foreign Office. Within a year of the Labour Party taking power reality had begun to break through into the Foreign Office mind, not least because their colleagues in other parts of Whitehall, who dealt with the world as it was in all its gritty unpleasantness, had never been wholly subject to the illusions of the diplomats. Those involved in the administration of Lend-Lease, or who were concerned with the politics of oil in Saudi Arabia and elsewhere in the Middle East, could never have subscribed to the 'unwieldy barge' image.

Foreign Office attitudes seem, however, to have pervaded all levels of the senior officials. John Balfour in Washington, with the rank of Under-Secretary of State, wrote a long letter to London dated 11 January 1946 concerned with Anglo-American attitudes arising out of the changed economic positions of the two countries. One of his later paragraphs illustrated the common approach to the analysis of relationships between Britain and America:

America, it might be added, is herself troubled in spirit: conscious that she has attained greatness but ruefully aware that she is inadequately equipped with gifts of leadership in many fields and confronted with serious domestic problems of her own. Here in itself is an opportunity for Britain to set an example of greater steadiness and sanity to the English speaking world.[183]

These presumptions with regard to the conduct of American foreign policies need to be emphasised further, for they provide additional illustration of the misunderstandings by the British of their own position in the new world order which was emerging from six years of global war. The young man whose political views are briefly described below has been selected not because he had much or any influence upon policy from Whitehall but rather as offering a demonstration of the ideas of a junior official who articulated sharply and clearly the assumptions of his seniors; and who, it may be not unreasonably assumed, could be expected to be on the way up the Foreign Office ladder.

John Cyril Donnelly was born on 2 April 1912 and educated at Trinity College, Dublin. He was appointed a probationer Vice-Consul in October 1935 and a month later took up duties in New York, where he stayed two years, moving to Boston in July 1937. Just after a year in New England, he was moved to Chicago and stayed there until he came to London in early May 1943. In September 1945 he was promoted to Consul and continued working in the American Department of the Foreign Office in Whitehall until he was transferred to Lima in August 1946. He died in post on 29 June 1948 at the age of 36.[184]

Donnelly was a very bright young man; thoroughly reactionary, with a considerable knowledge of American affairs and politics; and possessing a coruscating turn of phrase that would have gone down well in the Oxford Union debates. His comments were often to the point but their intellectual and political substance always remained with the traditional ways of Foreign Office thinking. He assumed that many Americans in leading positions were fairly or completely stupid, and that they were mixed and uncertain in their aims and objectives in marked contrast with the luminous statements of policy that came forth from Whitehall. Donnelly, it should be noted, has not infrequently been quoted in evidence by some American historians without reference to his junior status within the North American department.[185]

By the middle of 1945 Donnelly was providing the first minute on the weekly despatches from Washington, the procedure normally followed in Whitehall whereby the comments on papers and memoranda received would be made in ascending order of seniority. Donnelly took his position seriously, as the first, that is the most junior, commentator, and produced on occasion typewritten minutes on two sides of the foolscap sheets that were in circulation. For 1945 and the early part of 1946 the comments of his seniors were usually approving and it was only in his last six months in London that there appears the hint of an occasional suggestion that this young man was possibly getting ahead of himself. It was all done in the usual gentlemanly manner.

It would make an enjoyable anthology to be able to quote Donnelly at length. In early September 1945 he referred to the simple-minded American public and their 'illogical prejudice against secret diplomacy'; on the same Washington despatch he picked upon General MacArthur's reference to 'a spiritual recrudescence' pointing out that 'The General, who is devoid of humour, would certainly have not said "recrudescence" if he had known what the term usually conveys.' And he continued:

It is however not ill-chosen because there is always a tendency for a rather crude kind of American nationalism, or even imperialism, to drape itself in robes of distinctly Pharisaic virtue. Perhaps it is not unfair to cite the American attitude towards Argentina as an example. We must use our not inconsiderable influence to keep the tendency as far as possible within bounds.[186]

Donnelly welcomed the decline of the anti-Franco attitude among the American public; like everyone else who had the opportunity to comment, Harold Laski was his especial symbol for the ill-advised and irresponsible positions taken up by the Left: 'He has become a permanent thorn in the flesh of H.M. Representatives abroad';[187] and Donnelly always said exactly the right words about the Foreign Secretary, touching at times on sycophancy. On a number of occasions he started his weekly minute on the Washington letter by noting that it was too long and diffuse in its analysis. This was hardly likely to encourage his reputation with Washington; and he could also be condescending and patronising, as when he wrote, at the end of 1945, of the summary of the American press: 'This is much more interesting than last week's summary. Although it still seems too long perhaps this is justified by the special volume of interesting material. I have, however, marked what seem the passages of most immediate interest.'[188]

Donnelly, however much he polished his phrases and rehearsed his barbed commentaries, never strayed from the path of Foreign Office righteousness. When sixty-four American educationalists came together to argue the case for the sharing of the atomic bomb with the rest of the world, Donnelly was ready with his put-down technique for such a foolish idea: 'The Chicago educators were, I believe, headed by Dr Hutchins, who can usually be relied upon not to espouse a cause unless it is an unpopular one.'[189] While he was often contemptuous of American ignorance, as demonstrated so often by public opinion polls, and of the American administration in Washington, he was always clear that the hope of the Western world was that the United States would in time see that the way to salvation lay in the coming together of the United States and the United Kingdom; and he was hopeful that America would, in the end, understand how necessary it was to appreciate the more sophisticated understanding of the world's problems that emanated from London. On 5 March 1946, following tougher anti-Soviet speeches by Senator Vandenberg and Byrnes, the Secretary of State, Donnelly welcomed their statements as embodying a shift of opinion 'of enormous importance to the world':

It would be wrong, of course, to expect that the United States will live up to Mr

Byrne's declarations immediately and in a firm and consistent manner. With Mr Truman and Mr Byrnes at the helm that would be far too much to hope. The ineffective attitude towards the Persian question already shows the divergence which there can be between American generalities and the more practical side of American diplomacy. In any case, the Americans and their system of government being what they are, it is unlikely that even the most ideal American administration imaginable would achieve what we should regard as a high standard in clarity of thought and consistency. We must as always take things as they are and allow for human nature. But the immensely important fact remains that once again the fundamental oneness not only of British and American aims but also of British and American interests has come to the surface of the American mind. This is powerful reinforcement for the belief that whenever confronted with a clear choice the overwhelming sentiment of the United States is to go almost any distance to prevent a serious collapse of Britain. In 1940 and 1941 I was able to see how true this is even in the theoretically most isolationist parts of the Midwest. It seems to me that the issue may today be even plainer to Americans than it was either then or in 1916 because of the apparent fact that a Russia unbalanced by Britain and Western Europe would be an even more formidable menace to the United States than a victorious Germany would have been in the pre-atomic era.[190]

Donnelly was 34 when he wrote these words, and obviously a candidate for a senior position in the Foreign Office. Unless he was already being nurtured as a specialist in American affairs, there would have been better locations than Lima to place him. He had high intelligence, a forthright style, and a concentration of the prejudices of his superiors that must have been found attractive. There was no stirring of new ideas among the mandarins at the top levels of the Foreign Office. Donnelly would not have betrayed their trust.

Late in 1942 Roosevelt requested a survey of bases throughout the world which would serve as locations for air facilities for a post-war international police force. Three months earlier, in September 1942, A.A. Berle had produced a memorandum – which he sent to Cordell Hull – on the importance of aviation in the post-war world, comparable he insisted with that of sea-power in the past. In January 1943 there was established what later became known as the Interdepartmental Committee on International Aviation, and at its first meeting Robert Lovett, Assistant Secretary for Air, emphasised the importance of civil and military air bases, and went on to explain that in the Caribbean and Latin America there was a general sentiment among the military that no foreign-owned or foreign-operated line should operate in these areas.[191]

It was, then, early in the American war that the inter-relationship between civil and military air routes and bases became clearly appreciated. When the Joint Strategic Survey Committee (JSSC) made its first report on the bases survey in the spring of 1943 it stressed the international police role that Roosevelt had talked about, but went on to note that an international police force might never be established, and therefore the United States must first look to its own national security. The Joint Chiefs of Staff, in their comments on the JSSC report, were obviously sceptical about any international police force, and instructed the JSSC to reconsider the problem, with national security as the central matter to be analysed. Throughout 1943, in all the discussions of this kind, it was national defence that emerged as the primary concern and it was during 1943 and 1944 that the first clear statements were enunciated of what constituted American strategic and economic interests in the aftermath of war. American domination over the Pacific and Atlantic oceans was always assumed, and to ensure American hegemony an extensive system of bases would be required. In the Pacific this meant a defensive ring of bases which would include the Aleutians, the Philippines and the former Japanese mandated islands; and in the Atlantic, apart from the Caribbean, where the Americans already had bases from the fifty destroyer deal before the United States entered the war, some American planners envisaged not only the Azores or Canary islands, but even bases on the mainland of West Africa. It was the theory and practice of defence in depth, an obvious by-product of Pearl Harbor.[192]

Several points should be noticed from this brief introduction. The first is that American security, as it was defined on the defence in depth principle in 1944, was related to the defence of the United States and did not involve strategic relationships or obvious conflict with the Soviet Union. There were no bases seriously planned for Europe, the Middle East or South Asia by the spring of 1944, although the situation was going to change rapidly thereafter, at least among the military planners. The second point to remark upon is that recognition of the symbiotic relationship between civil and military air bases round the world was inevitably going to involve Great Britain, whose own plans for post-war aviation development were already being seriously considered. The bargaining between the two countries was often rancorous, especially over the so-called 'fifth' freedom.[193]

The definition of national security on the part of the American military planners began to widen significantly from early 1944, much encouraged by the growing appreciation of Russia as the next potential enemy, but until early 1946 there was not majority agreement between the different groups of the top decision-makers. The military were divided. On the one hand their planners were becoming increasingly insistent about Russian expansionism, which they suggested had no limits. In July 1945 a G–2 paper entitled 'Soviet Intentions' argued that the time had come to offer a firm opposition to Soviet aggression,[194] and similar arguments were being heard in other military groups. At the same time, however, the war with Japan was not yet over and there were mounting casualties. The totals of dead, wounded and missing on Okinawa and its surrounding waters between 1 April and 22 June 1945 added up to 75,000. In the first year of the war after Pearl Harbor the United States had 2,300 killed in action; for the three months from 30 December 1944 to 31 March 1945 the Army suffered 802,000 casualties of whom 159,000 were killed. There were estimates of one million casualties for the planned invasion of Japan.[195] It was crucial, therefore, that the Soviet Union should fulfil its pledge to enter the war against Japan within three months of the conclusion of war with Germany. There were problems, too, with the British. Churchill's belligerency over Trieste was not to the American's liking although the episode confirmed many in their anti-communism; but in this summer of 1945 the American Secretary of State for War and his staff were vocal in their opposition to joining with the British in an anti-Russian crusade. The Mediterranean strategy which the British had so assiduously fostered during 1943 and 1944 was regarded by many groups in Washington as integrally connected with British imperialist interests.

There were many incidents and episodes – large, sometimes thought to be large, and small – which inexorably worsened the relations between the United States and the Soviet Union. The Warsaw rising, when American planes were not allowed to develop a shuttle service;[196] the indictment of General John Deane, in the much publicised letter to Marshall in early December 1944; Trieste; and then the Foreign Ministers' Conference in London in September 1945 – all contributed, against the domestic background of rising anti-communism, to a perception of the enemy now threatening American values as well as its security. During the immediate months after the ending of the war there was, however, nothing comparable with the anti-Soviet unanimity to be found in the British Foreign Office in Whitehall, and Byrnes was not as single-minded as Ernest Bevin. In London there were no alternative strategies to the basic anti-Soviet diplomacy which, whatever was offered at the negotiating table, was never qualified in principle. Public opinion, as represented on the back benches of the Parliamentary Labour Party and in a substantial part of the daily and weekly press, was much more divided on the Russian question. *The Times* was highly critical of certain aspects of Bevin's handling of foreign issues[197] and it was not until mid and late 1947 that the volume of opposition to Labour's foreign policy began to diminish sharply within the political and industrial sections of the Labour Party. Whitehall was different, and the Foreign Office in particular was unvarying in its hostility to the Soviet Union. Matters were more complicated in Washington and while top-level opinion was steadily hardening, the processes of intellectual and political change were longer drawn out, and critical appraisals of Russian actions were more sophisticated as well as more adequately factually based than was the case in London.

The example to be given below had no influence upon American policy but it is offered as an illustration of the recognition within the State Department of the different options that were on the diplomatic table in the months immediately following the ending of the war with Japan. On 24 October 1945 the Chief of the Division of Southern Affairs, Cloyce C. Huston, produced a memorandum which proposed a redefinition of American policies in Eastern Europe. Huston was a long-serving career diplomat, having been for nearly a decade in East European countries before coming to the State Department in 1941. He was, therefore, someone to be reckoned with. His paper, it should be noted, was a response to the failure of the Foreign Ministers' Conference in London. He began by reminding his readers of what in the chancelleries of Europe was often forgotten, namely that following the Versailles Treaty there was established along Russia's western borders 'a great invisible wall . . . built of hate, fear, mistrust and suspicion'.[198] This was later to be Arno Mayer's thesis.[199] Huston then continued to insist that it was inevitable the Soviet Union, having shattered this fascist and semi-fascist *cordon sanitaire*,[200] could not be expected to permit its renewal. Soviet control, Huston agreed, could and would be repressive, above all if there was suspicion that the Western Powers had any intention of encouraging anti-Soviet elements. It was necessary therefore that the United States should make it clear that it supported Russia's objectives in Eastern Europe and that by so doing – and this was Huston's crucial assumption – Russia would adhere to democratic procedures in those countries within its political control. The assumption was, of course, critical, although, as was occasionally noted in diplomatic papers and memoranda on both sides of the Atlantic, Panama and Latin America for the Americans, and Egypt and the Middle East, Hong Kong and India for the British were not good examples to argue from in matters such as these. Huston did not, however, make these points. His memorandum was not dismissed out of hand but was accepted as one of the diverse trends of thought concerning American policies towards Russia. Dean Acheson, Under-Secretary of State, in an attempt to achieve a broad measure of agreement, decided to require the Department to complete a survey of Russian affairs. The title was to be 'The Capabilities and Intentions of the Soviet Union as Affected by American Policy'. The main specialist responsible for the final report was Charles E. Bohlen, whose credentials were highly impressive.[201] He had two tours in Moscow before returning to Washington in 1942 and he became Roosevelt's personal interpreter at all the major wartime conferences with the Russians. Bohlen's main collaborator, although he also called upon a number of specialists in the State Department, was Dr Geroid T. Robinson, an academic on leave from Columbia University. Robinson was head of the USSR Division of the State Department where he presided over a staff of sixty specialists in Soviet affairs: historians, economists, political scientists. He himself was a distinguished historian. It may be noted in passing that the specialist knowledge and expertise available to the Foreign Office in Whitehall was pitiful by comparison. At the beginning of 1945 only two members of the Northern Department could actually speak and read Russian, and both were temporary appointments. There were, of course,

Russian speakers in the Embassy at Moscow and in the Foreign Office Research Department, but they were few.

A first draft of 'The Capabilities and Intentions of the Soviet Union . . .', a subtle, sophisticated document, was ready by early December 1945.[202] Some main points may be noted here.

It began, inevitably, with the consequences of the atomic bomb. The memorandum assumed that there would be no sharing of knowledge and that it might be five, perhaps ten years before the USSR had atomic bombs in sufficient quantities, or, and this was a point often overlooked, would be able to prevent their delivery on Russian targets.

It was not inconceivable that warfare would be conducted on a non-atomic basis and that therefore it was necessary to analyse the comparative capabilities of Russia and the USA. The authors assumed that the Russians would be able to maintain a 'relatively high tempo of industrial expansion', but with one-fourth of Russia's fixed capital lost and its population weakened by severe wartime privations, Russia would be able to produce an annual national income (in the American sense) of not more than 25 billion dollars, or $150 per capita, in 1945. (The comparable figure for the United States was about $1,000 per capita.) Leaving the atomic bomb out of account, the Western Powers might have been expected to have, for some years, an advantage over Russia in terms of total material capabilities. Yet this is a statement respecting capabilities in the abstract, without regard to possible areas of military operation: in a conflict on the continent of Europe, the logistical advantage would be heavily with the Russians, especially after current American and British withdrawals and demobilisation; in the Far East, on the other hand, American and British shipping and air transport could easily outmatch the Trans-Siberian Railroad plus Soviet air transport.

While ideology would remain, it was itself in process of change; and 'It is by no means to be expected that in the future the foreign policy of the Soviet leaders will be determined entirely by Marxian theory.' The matter was left undecided, in sharp contrast to the dogmatic and unyielding approach adopted by George Kennan. The report further suggested that the popularity of the USSR, and of local communist leaders, had declined since the end of the war:

> Eastern Europe. Here the disorders of Russian soldiers, the conspicuousness and crudity of Russian political intervention in several countries, and the weight of Russian economic exactions, have led to a weakening of pro-Russian and pro-Communist elements and a growth of opposition movements, except in Finland and Yugoslavia and, to a lesser extent, in Czechoslovakia.

The authors of the report derived two basic options from their analysis. The first, policy A, was pivoted on the recognition of American military superiority, including the atomic bomb, in order to achieve compromise and agreement with the Soviet Union by which amicable relations could be continued in the second phase of the post-war years when the Soviet Union had manufactured the Bomb itself. This was their first option, which they considered at some length. Their second, policy B, they stated in succinct terms:

> To withhold all knowledge and assistance that would contribute to the development of Soviet capabilities, and to exert all the pressure short of war that American capabilities will permit, in attempting to build up, at home and abroad, a balance of power so strong that the USSR will be held in check in Period II regardless of what Soviet intentions may be at that time.

The final draft of the Bohlen–Robinson report, which did not differ in any fundamental way from that described above, was produced about a week before Kennan's Long Telegram was received in Moscow. Bohlen and Robinson had agreed that there were problems and risks in their advocacy of a reasoned and reasonable approach towards the Soviet Union; but their arguments, which asked for intelligence, subtlety, patience and hard-headedness, could not withstand Kennan's precise, definite and unequivocal depiction of the Soviet Union as an aggressive and expansionist nation. The Bohlen–Robinson report was submerged beneath the acclamation given to Kennan; and it was forgotten even by Bohlen himself, who, in his own *Witness to History*, published in 1973, provided an inaccurate account of his own conversion to a hard-line Kennan approach.[203]

Kennan himself later noted that the reception of his Long Telegram 'was nothing less than sensational'. To understand this extraordinary response involves analysis of a complicated set of domestic and foreign events that came together in the months before March 1946. On 19 January Iran had filed its complaint against the Soviet Union, with American support; and the American press responded accordingly. There was no reason why negotiations would not have yielded positive results, as the Secretary-General of the United Nations argued,[204] but American public opinion was beginning to equate negotiations with appeasement, and the continuing swell of anti-communism had begun to touch the State Department over alleged communist sympathy and disloyalty. Stalin's election speech of 9 February was probably the most immediate factor in encouraging the welcome that was given to Kennan's analysis, for the hostile reception in the United States was quite remarkable. In the last resort, given that the national vibrations were sympathetic, it was the vigour of Kennan's writing, the directness of his exposition and the clear lead he was now providing that ensured the understanding for which he sought.[205]

The years following Kennan's Long Telegram saw a continued hardening of American opinion and political attitudes towards the Soviet Union. This included the growing involvement of America in Europe, which would certainly have been strenuously opposed in the immediate aftermath of war, but which was now symbolised by the merging of the British and American zones in Germany, formally agreed in January 1947.[206] However, 1946 had not been a period of calm and growing appreciation of world problems between Britain and America. The harsh realities of Britain's economic position and its sharp decline in the world power structure made even Foreign Office officials – whose sense of global questions was often somewhat hazy – recognise with increasing urgency the crucial necessity of American support. That recognition had always been present, but was not as pressing as it became during the first two years of peace. The military, in their post-war assessments during the later years of the war, had always written into their appraisals the assumption of American involvement in any open conflict with the only potential enemy, the Soviet Union; and the same was true of most Foreign Office documents relating to the post-war world. It was, however, the bitter facts of the 1945–47 years that made Whitehall aware of the central significance of American support, and especially of American dollars. However, while there was complete agreement within the Foreign Office on the Soviet threat as the main problem that confronted the United Kingdom and its Empire, this was not always true of other departments in Whitehall, notably the Treasury, and it was often obscured in Anglo-American relations during 1946 by many disagreements and areas of discord. The United States and the United Kingdom were often drawn together against Russia at the many conferences of this year,[207] but outside the conference chambers there were many seriously disputed questions. Palestine was the most wounding and Ernest Bevin's notable heavy handedness only exacerbated an exceedingly complex situation.[208] Among the many other issues that plagued the Atlantic relationship were the American Loan, which it can be argued only passed Congress under the anti-communist banner – a demonstration of the much quoted comment by Halifax[209] – the atomic controversies and what was believed to be American duplicity,[210] and a range of economic questions with which the financial and commercial departments were deeply concerned. The questioning also went on within the Foreign Office on the part of those sections which were specifically concerned with the economic world; and in the first two months of 1947 an important controversy took place of which those involved in analysing diplomatic politics seem to have taken little or no notice: an unfortunate omission since the matters discussed were about the real world. In the second half of January 1947 E.L. Hall-Patch, who had been transferred from the Treasury in June 1944 and promoted to Under-Secretary of State, circulated a draft of a document on the effects of the UK's external financial position on foreign policy.[211] He noted that the balance of trade in 1946 had been better than anticipated; that dollar reserves were being expended at a faster rate than planned; that the cost of the British occupation of Germany greatly exceeded the original planned forecast; and that it would seem difficult if not impossible to curtail significantly

Britain's dollar imports or to reduce its overseas military, and political, expenditure. As for the country's longer term industrial future Hall-Patch was gloomy. He expected a 'permanent worsening of our industrial position' largely because of the stimulus the war had given to industrial production in the United States and Canada and also because of the more general industrial growth round the world. Oil was a matter of importance; in a few years the United States would have to begin to import oil from the Middle East, the largest potential supplier, and it was therefore of great importance to the United Kingdom to broaden its own interests in the region as quickly as possible. His general conclusion emphasised the importance of exerting British diplomatic influence 'to the full' in order that Britain's present authority should be maintained but that it could not live beyond its means, and that involved, so Hall-Patch believed, a recognition that there were many steps that could not be taken 'unaided'. He summed up this part of the argument:

> Our financial weakness has necessarily increased dependence of our foreign policy on that of the only country which is able effectively to wield extensive economic influence – namely the United States. Not only do we have to draw many of our more essential supplies from U.S. sources, but we also have to trust to the U.S. providing substantial help to countries on whose stability and welfare we have a particular interest. This is a state of affairs to which we must condition ourselves whether we like it or not if Anglo-American collaboration is to be as fruitful and effective in the future as in the past.

There were a large number of comments on this first draft. One, from E.A. Radice, who was head of the Economic Intelligence Department, attacked the idea of industrialisation in other parts of the world being to the disadvantage of Britain. He referred to a recent League of Nations publication[212] which argued that continued industrialisation was a stimulus to world trade, and Radice insisted that the opposite view, as stated by Hall-Patch, was commonly held among Foreign Service Officers, and needed to be rebutted. 'I should much prefer', he wrote, 'that it should be stated positively that industrialisation should be welcomed as it affords a great opportunity for British exports.' It was a point of view acceptable to professional economic historians.

Radice was involved in further controversy on matters relating to world economic issues. A draft by a member of the Economic Relations Department of the Foreign Office entitled 'Major Economic and Financial Questions Affecting Anglo-U.S.' Relations' was circulated as a background document to a forthcoming conference.[213] The most trenchant comment, dated 20 February 1947, was from Radice, who stated at the outset that his view of Anglo-American relations was somewhat more pessimistic then the authors. Radice wrote that what impressed him were the many examples of serious conflict of interests between Britain and America 'all over the world':

We have regretfully come to the conclusion that these conflicts are at the root of everything else and that they are the inevitable outcome of the expansion of United States economic power into the vacuum caused by the contraction of the economic power of the countries of Western Europe. Except in the Russian sphere we are the rivals of the United States. One need only cite such instances as competition in armaments in South America, in Civil Aviation in Italy and the Middle East, and in economic matters generally in the Far East. . . .

I think we should be absolutely frank and realistic about this. Only if we think in terms of economic power rather than of ideologies or economic doctrines are we likely to arrive at satisfactory settlements. . . .

While we are perfectly well aware (your paragraph 3) that the American dislike of controls is not much more than affectation, we are frequently in danger of granting the Americans their case by admitting that their economic ideology is more 'liberal' (and therefore more moral) than our own. Fundamentally their dislike of imperial preference is due to their suspicion that it hinders American economic penetration into the British Commonwealth; their dislike of bulk purchase agreements, State trading etc. is due to their unconscious fear that these modern forms of economic organisation will prove cheaper and more efficient than their own competitive methods (which they frequently abandon when it suits them!). The truth is, surely, that American business knows that a publicly owned U.K. concern can, at best, be subjected to political blackmail. It cannot be bought out or browbeaten.

Radice then went on to suggest that a reading of *The Economist* would help to make clear some of the Americans' economic malpractices, among which he included tied loans, restrictive agreements in agricultural products, and the political pressure groups associated with cotton, tobacco and the Farm Bloc in general. His critique did not go unchallenged from some of his fellow economists in the Foreign Office, and in any case it was the diplomatic side of the Office that required to be impressed. Their view was different, and it continued so.

At the same time as the discussions noted above were taking place within the Office a circular letter was being prepared to all embassies and missions abroad. It used some of the material in the Hall-Patch memorandum referred to above, but it was wide in scope and followed the pattern of earlier surveys of 1945 and 1946. The printed circular on 'External Financial Position of the United Kingdom and Effects on Foreign Policy', dated 12 February 1947, was in two parts: a general introduction of three pages and then the memorandum proper. The introduction emphasised the importance of conserving dollars, of maintaining good relations with those countries which held substantial accumulations of sterling (not least in order to try to persuade them to scale down British indebtedness as payment for the British war effort, and, finally, the over-riding importance of good relations with the United States.[214] By this time, in the months before the Truman Doctrine and the Marshall Plan, with dollar reserves rapidly declining and the shut-down in industry because of the

'Great Freeze', Britain was at the low point of its immediate post-war years. The choice was a radical alteration in its general position in the world and in particular a very sharp retrenchment in its financial obligations overseas, with a massive increase in domestic industrial investment and training, or a continuation of its traditional role which it could now only afford if American dollars became available. The choice had been made before the Labour Government came to power, and apart from Attlee there was no one who challenged the basic postulates of a declining imperialist power maintaining the semblance of a Great Power by the equivalent of the receipt of alms: with conditions. Already in the summer of 1946 Spaatz, who was head of the newly created US Strategic Air Command (SAC), had visited England in order to obtain an agreement whereby British bases could be used by American bombers on atomic bomb missions. This was in June–July 1946 and negotiations were conducted through Air Chief Marshal Tedder. It was agreed that five RAF bases should be allocated and be made ready for the B 29 bombers. The next month Col. E.E. Patrick arrived to supervise the construction of assembly buildings and loading facilities at the five chosen RAF bases: Lakenheath, Mildenhall, Scampton, Marham and Bassingbourn. Whether the politicians or the civil servants in Whitehall were informed is not yet clear, but it must be expected that the Prime Minister and Ernest Bevin were told what was going on. This was the beginning of the American bases in Britain which by the middle 1980s had reached a total of about 135, of which 25 were major operational bases or military headquarters; there were also at least five confirmed US nuclear weapon stores.[215]

To return to the memorandum of 12 February 1947. As noted above, it followed the Hall-Patch thesis that we drew many of our essential supplies from the United States and had also to depend upon the US providing substantial help to countries whose general stability Britain wished to maintain. And then there was enunciated the recognition of what reliance upon the United States involved:

If the corollary of United States intervention and strength is that we find ourselves at times irked at the role of junior partner, we must recognise, nevertheless, that the partnership is worth the price. Nor is this partnership as unequal as might appear at first sight. We have much to contribute in political experience and worldly wisdom. Despite occasional evidence to the contrary, our contribution is on the whole appreciated; and in many issues the underlying strategic or political interests of the United States operate to bring her down on our side. We cannot complain by and large that our advice is unheeded or our objectives frustrated, particularly when we consider, on the one hand, the domestic criticism to which a Democratic Administration, faced with a Republican Congress, is frequently exposed, and, on the other, our relative financial weakness. But it remains to be seen how long the position will remain in this respect even as reasonably satisfactory as it is today. With a Republican majority in the present Congress, and with the prospect of a Republican Administration in 1949, the divergence between our political philosophy and that of the United States will be intensified; and we must expect that our nationalisation programme and the controls which we choose or find it necessary to maintain may prove a constant source of future friction. But it must surely be our aim to keep the partnership in being on terms not less favourable than those which prevail at present. Only if we were to find ourselves alone with our political objectives widely divergent from those of the United States would our financial nakedness be fully apparent to the world.

There can be few more explicit statements of the condition of Britain in the diplomatic history of the United Kingdom during the aftermath of the Second World War or of the character of what became known at 'the special relationship'. *Leonina societas*.

2

Ernest Bevin as Foreign Secretary: Attitudes, Work Patterns, Health

Ernest Bevin was born in 1881 but his political career came only in the last ten years of his life. It was his trade union experience that shaped him irreversibly, and even here he developed slowly. Not until the years between 1905 and 1908 did he begin to shift his main interests from chapel to politics and trade unionism. As a young man he was an active member of a Baptist mission, took a lively part in discussion classes, and began reading widely. By the early 1900s he was beginning to attend socialist meetings, and the experience gained in local preaching was now turned to effective use when he joined the British Socialist Society.[1] It had been a good training. Bevin had a powerful voice, a directness and a fluency of speech that was impressive, and he was capable of a vehemence that remained with him all his life. At the beginning of 1908 he became secretary of the local Right-to Work Committee, and in the autumn of the following year he stood, unsuccessfully, as a Socialist candidate in the local elections.

For most of these years he was earning his living as a vanman, delivering mineral waters in Bristol and the surrounding countryside, but it was not until 1910 that he began his career as a trade unionist. In June of that year Bevin began to co-ordinate relief efforts for Avonmouth dockers who were on strike; and shortly afterwards Harry Orbell, one of the leaders of the Dock, Wharf, Riverside and General Labourers' Union, asked him to organise the local carters into a branch of the Dockers' Union. In August 1910 Bevin called a meeting at which the carters formally established themselves as a branch of the Union. It had a phenomenal success: within a year membership was around 2000, the Union had been recognised by the employers and there had been an improved wage agreement. In the spring of 1911 Bevin became a full-time organiser of the Dockers' Union in the Bristol region at a wage of two pounds a week.

His long apprenticeship in the Baptist chapel and the adult school movement marked him intellectually for life. He was self-taught with the weaknesses and strength of that tradition. His recognition of social injustice was a loitering conversion from the politically ignorant 'commonsense' of the ordinary working man[2] to some degree of appreciation of the class nature of society: a matter of political comprehension that owed little to theoretical insights and almost everything to the assimilation of political experience. The British Socialist Society at the time that Bevin became a member was affiliated to the Social-Democratic Federation and for a few years Bevin used class-conscious phraseology. From his early days as a trade union official, however, he began to move into the labour-socialism of twentieth-century opposition politics.[3] For the rest of his life he wanted a reformed capitalism that would provide the opportunities for the control of workplace conditions by trade unions against a background of rising standards of living. He was to look to the State as the third partner in a new tripartite grouping that would regulate industry and eliminate the injustices that he had been born into. Bevin never believed that the changes he wanted in society would come about easily; and he always assumed that the unions must always be prepared for tough negotiations. Political and social changes, however, were practicable and possible within the existing system, and it was parliamentary democracy that offered these possibilities. This was the central labourist creed inherited from the nineteenth century, and while it was to a degree modified by socialist rhetoric during Bevin's lifetime, the Fabian belief that the State and State power were at the command of those with a parliamentary majority was central to the convictions of the leaderships of both the Trades Union Congress and the Labour Party. There were, it was appreciated, immensely powerful vested interests to be overcome; narrow-minded individuals to be convinced; the inertia of the system to be mastered. With the continued extension of political democracy the opportunities for social reform would begin to widen. The political strength of the conservative groups in society encouraged a reciprocal toughness of stance among working people, and especially among those who were trade unionists, for it was they upon whom the struggle largely devolved. All these things Bevin believed, and they shaped his attitudes throughout his public life.

Bevin would seem to have adopted a moderate political position in British trade unionism from early in his career. In his younger days he had attended the Baptist chapel whose pastor, the Rev. James Moffat Logan, took a courageous stand against British involvement in the Boer War; but what Bevin's attitude was on this issue does not seem to be clear. In the first world war he adopted what may be described as a trade union approach: one which was neither jingoistic nor in political opposition. He was certainly contemptuous of the political pacifism of the Independent Labour Party as represented by Ramsay MacDonald and Snowden; although in the period immediately after the war he took a stance of militant opposition to the military intervention against the young Soviet Republic, but then so did almost all his colleagues, regardless of their customary moderation. Direct action, in any situation, was not part of

Bevin's normal responses, and during the inter-war years he does not appear to have been radicalised in political terms: rather the contrary. The failure of the General Strike[4] pushed him into more moderate positions, as it did, of course, all his contemporaries in the top echelons of the TUC. The aftermath of the Strike also meant that power within the TUC moved steadily towards Walter Citrine and Bevin, not least because of the disintegration of the Left in the TUC General Council.[5] The collapse of the Labour Government in 1931 further strengthened the position of the trade unions within the Labour Party, and Henry Pelling accurately described the situation within the 1930s as 'The General Council's Party'.[6] By the end of the decade Bevin was the strongest personality in the labour movement. In foreign affairs he had remained outside the tradition which became increasingly radicalised alongside the growing menace of the Fascist Powers in Europe. Bevin was never, for example, passionately interested in the Spanish Civil War as were so many of his contemporaries. He defended non-intervention at the TUC in September 1936, and the block vote gave him an overwhelming majority. He was probably the only leading figure of the British labour movement who never spoke on a Spanish Aid platform.[7] It is not unreasonable to argue that the communist influence, both within Spain and in the international movement outside, was an important factor inhibiting Bevin from all-out support. Certainly by the mid 1930s Bevin was vigorously anti-communist, and both he and Citrine were a good deal more sceptical about the internal situation in the Soviet Union than many of their colleagues: a scepticism underlined by the trials of 1936–38.

Typical of Bevin and the labourist tradition he represented was the offer he and Citrine made in February 1937 to Baldwin, then Prime Minister, to help with the difficulties of the rearmament programme in return for an official inquiry into holidays with pay. The Amulree Committee, on which Bevin served, recommended one week's paid holiday instead of the two weeks the TUC had asked for; and this passed into law in 1938.[8] The importance of paid holidays for working people is not denied; but rearmament was a political issue of major importance, and to trade it off for the paid holidays issue was typical of the economistic view of their responsibilities adopted by both Bevin and Citrine. In this decade Bevin was a firm advocate of consultation with employers and government: a policy which had developed consciously after the General Strike and which continued and expanded thereafter. Soon after he became chairman of the General Council of the TUC in 1936, Bevin noted the differences between the statements and reports of the 1920s and those of the present. The striking thing for him was the growth in responsibilities accepted by the TUC, and their involvement with both employers and government. 'Most of these things', he commented to his own Executive Council, 'were to them [in the 1920s] propaganda points. Those were the days of advocacy. Ours is the day of administration.'[9] A year later, at the 1937 TUC, Bevin was telling Congress that the TUC 'has now virtually become an integral part of the State and its views and voice upon every subject, international and domestic, heard and heeded'.[10] Bevin was, of course, exaggerating, although the differences between the first decade after the war and the 1930s were certainly considerable. It was the experience of the Second World War that confirmed Bevin in this understanding of the working of corporate bias in British society.

At the beginning of the war Bevin was probably at the height of his powers. He had had the first intimations of the heart trouble that was to remain for the rest of his life during his year of office as chairman of the General Council, 1936–37, but in 1938 he was four months away from England, on a visit to Australasia, and he returned refreshed, and physically in better shape. He was now more than ever confident of his considerable abilities. John Horner, in an unpublished memoir, relates a story that helps to illustrate what sort of a trade union leader Bevin was. Horner had just become general secretary of the Fire Brigades Union, and a Joint Trade Union Civil Defence Committee had been established in 1940 to assist the co-ordination of the many different union members involved. Arthur Deakin, assistant general secretary of Bevin's union, was chairman. His request for government recognition was not accepted and Deakin asked Bevin to help. So a meeting with Sir John Anderson was arranged. Horner continued:

> But that afternoon Sir John was busy elsewhere. We would have to make do with the Deputy Under-Secretary, who conveyed Sir John's apologies. These were grave times, the Secretary put to a disgruntled Bevin, and he hoped that we would understand. Mollified, Ernie put our case for recognition. In his reply the civil servant emphasised Sir John's misgivings. If recognition were granted to trade union officials, not all of whom might be full time, these individuals would seek access to ARP depots, report centres, fire stations and so on. In times of war no Home Secretary could be expected to lightly agree that such sensitive establishments should be open to all and sundry, particularly trade union officers whose political affiliations might be 'widely spread'. Mr Bevin was asked to take a note of the recent occupation of Norway by the Nazis. That country's administration had been easily taken over by the enemy since it had already been undermined by Quisling groups in public administration. In the Home Secretary's view, these matters were relevant to Mr Bevin's request. At the mention of Quisling, I saw Bevin's great neck redden and as the civil servant expanded on this theme, Bevin exploded.
>
> 'Don't dare mention Quisling and trade unionists in the same breath when you talk to me', he growled. 'Tell Sir John that it wasn't our lot that sold Germany to the Nazis. Tell him', he went on, 'that it was *his* lot – just as they would dig the ground from under our feet in this country and sell it abroad if they could get two and a half per cent profit.'
>
> 'And tell him this too', he added. 'Tell him to tell his friend, Chamberlain, that if he wants to win this war, he will only do it with the help of the trade unions. So he had better make up his mind.'
>
> And hefting his great bulk from his chair, he turned with: 'Let's get out. I won't sit here and be insulted anymore.'[11]

A week later he was Minster of Labour. He accepted this position in the Churchill Coalition Government because he appreciated, as many others did not at the time, its very considerable potentialities, not only for the war years but in the years after the war.[12] Here he showed great prescience. His highly successful tenure of the Ministry, and his substantial contribution to the planning of national resources, placed the Ministry of Labour at the centre of decision-making on the home front. Much, of course, was the product of Bevin's forceful and powerful personality allied to his wide-ranging knowledge of the problems involved. His personal contribution to the success of the Ministry of Labour was central to the adaptation of the whole labour force to the requirements of the war economy; and he was strong enough within Whitehall to ensure that conservative recalcitrants were effectively put down.[13] There were many mistakes, inevitably, but comparison with either Germany or the United States stands up well. For Bevin, the experience of the wartime Coalition Government confirmed the central proposition of labourism: the achievement of national recognition for the workers' movement and their acceptance within the national interest. When the Labour Party took office in July 1945 as the constitutional government of the country, this for Bevin meant that the Party's interest was now the national interest.[14] And what did Bevin understand by 'national interest'? 'In general terms', Bullock explained,

> the security of the United Kingdom and its overseas possessions against external attack; the continued financial and economic as well as political independence of Britain; the right of people to trade freely with the rest of the world, their right to maintain a policy of full employment and a decent standard of living.[15]

These were sentiments which any progressively minded Tory in 1945 would accept. It is necessary once again to emphasise how much the business of wartime administration had deepened Bevin's predilection towards the corporate relationship between government, business and labour, for now the obvious manifestations of class conflict had been muted, and the sharp cleavages of the inter-war years had been blunted and softened. It was Bevin's practical experience of the workings of the State machine that confirmed his already firm belief in the neutrality of the institutions of the State and its acceptance of any constitutionally elected government.

There has been much speculation about Bevin's appointment as Foreign Secretary. Until Labour's victory in the general election of July 1945 it was generally assumed that Hugh Dalton would go to the Foreign Office, and indeed the day after the election results were declared Attlee himself told Dalton that 'almost certainly' it would be the Foreign Office. This was just before lunch on 27 July, but by 4 p.m. on the same day Attlee phoned Dalton to tell him that on reconsideration Bevin would go to the Foreign Office and

Dalton to the Treasury. According to Dalton's memoirs, from which these details are taken, Attlee added that one reason for the change was to keep Morrison and Bevin apart.[16] Wheeler-Bennett, in his biography of George VI, suggests that the King's preference for Bevin over Dalton may have been a factor in the decision; but while there is no doubt that the King did offer his advice in these terms, it is improbable that it made much impact on Attlee. The latter specifically denied the emphasis which Wheeler-Bennett placed upon the conversation in an article in *The Observer* in 1959.[17] The Foreign Office itself was against Dalton, not least because of his well-known opinion of their incompetence. The most convincing story was given by Douglas Jay, in his memoirs of 1980, who had been told by Joe Burke, then second Private Secretary at No. 10, that it was Edward Bridges – Secretary to the Cabinet and head of the civil service – who persuaded Attlee that to put Bevin on the domestic front would mean continuous conflict with Morrison. The feud between them was well-known among the top civil servants.[18]

It had been assumed by many, inside and outside Whitehall, that the Labour victory of 1945 would result in considerable changes in the organisation and personnel of the Whitehall élites, and most certainly in the Foreign Office. Bruce Lockhart told Dalton in late February 1946 – the incident is recorded in Dalton's Diary, 22 February 1946 – that a number of people inside the Labour Party had preferred Bevin to Dalton because they thought he would make considerable changes in the Office and clear out the 'old gang'. As it turned out, Lockhart went on, after only two months Bevin became devoted to the Office 'so that all the old nags were going back to the old stables, even Brian Newton' (who had been Minister at Prague during the Munich crisis). In Bevin's first week, according again to Lockhart, 'Cadogan and Orme Sargent both thought they were out'.[19]

Bruce Lockhart may not have been entirely accurate in all his details, but there is no doubt that many thought change was inevitable. It is possible that Bevin himself may have felt somewhat awkward in the early days of his new position. Bullock comments on his uncertainty, and certainly the story that Henderson records in his account of the first night at Potsdam suggests a degree of unease. Bevin was talking to Cadogan and other senior officials at supper, and he suddenly turned to Cadogan and said: 'Ever been to the Communist Club in Maiden Lane?' It was an extraordinary question to put to an aristocratic Permanent Under-Secretary at the Foreign Office, among other reasons because Bevin himself had not been to Maiden Lane on political business for at least a quarter of a century, and in any case there was never a communist 'Club' in that street. The office of the British Socialist Party in 1919 was in Maiden Lane, and when the Communist Party was formed it took over the BSP headquarters until it moved to its own permanent offices in King Street, just round the corner.[20]

While Bevin may have arrived at the Foreign Office somewhat unsure of his relations with the permanent officials, Cadogan himself was soon writing in warm terms about his new master. On Tuesday, 31 July 1945, while still at Potsdam, he wrote to his wife:

> Bevin will, I think, do well. He knows a good deal, is prepared to read any amount, seems to take in what he does read, and is capable of making up his own mind and sticking up for his (or our) point of view against anyone. I think he's the best we could have had.[21]

William Ridsdale, head of the Foreign Office News Department, came back from Potsdam impressed with Bevin's handling of the many difficult problems that he was encountering for the first time; and Ridsdale went on to say – this was in late August 1945 – that 'Bevin likes the Foreign Office and thinks there is nothing wrong with it except that the staff is too small and too badly paid.'[22]

Bevin, wrote Gladwyn Jebb in his memoirs, was a great man, and for most people he was 'a very loveable man'. Of course, Jebb went on to say 'he had terrible faults'[23] and some are commented on below. Jebb was wholly correct in respect of the attitudes towards Bevin by his Foreign Office officials. What they appreciated above all was his complete loyalty and support in their daily work. This had been true of Bevin's period as Minister of Labour; but for the Foreign Office it was especially important. For the first time for many years the Foreign Office was restored to the position in Whitehall that all who worked within the Office thought right and proper. During the days of Neville Chamberlain, before the Second World War, there had been a considerable current of dissent from the policy of appeasement towards the Fascist Powers, and there were considerable differences of opinion concerning the attitudes to be taken towards Italy as against Germany.[24] Moreover, Chamberlain had created his own power base in the conduct of foreign affairs. During the war years the Foreign Office often found itself again pushed to the margins of decision-making although now for different reasons. It was not so much a matter of fundamental differences of political strategy as in the days of appeasement, although there were issues of bitter division between the Office and Churchill: the attitudes towards de Gaulle being well-known.[25] It was rather that Churchill was not only Prime Minister and Minister of Defence but also, in part, his own Foreign Secretary; and this was above all true of his relationships with Roosevelt. Many of Churchill's letters to Roosevelt, for example, were sent through the American Embassy in London and not through normal diplomatic channels. It is a well-known story that needs no elaboration,[26] and which was paralleled on the other side of the Atlantic by Roosevelt's much more cavalier treatment of his own State Department.[27]

All this changed immediately when Bevin became Foreign Secretary, and his senior officials were quick to appreciate the new regime. For one thing Bevin was the most powerful man in the Cabinet, and the one on the closest terms with the Prime Minister. Then, as in his days at the Ministry of Labour, he could always be relied on to defend the Department against all comers, either in the Cabinet or in the corridors of Whitehall. His officials in the Foreign Office soon discovered that there were no basic disagreements in policy terms: there were naturally many arguments, but nothing fundamental. It was the quality of loyalty to the Office that was a central feature of the total support that Bevin received from his officials throughout his tenure as Foreign Secretary; and it accounts for the toleration he was accorded for the many tiresome and sometimes unpleasant ways of which he was capable. For 'Uncle Ernie' to clean his fingernails with a knife during international conferences; to tell his unfunny, somewhat salacious jokes and expect them to be translated; to listen for hours to his interminable stories of himself and his past career; to humour his dreary, demanding wife when she accompanied him on visits abroad[28] – all these tedious and often wearisome matters were accepted with resigned patience and often a remarkable good humour by members of Bevin's Private Office and by other officials of the Foreign Office. No doubt they were dismissed as just the 'quaint' habits of their great minister on whom they could so solidly rely. 'Uncle Ernie' had his faults, of course, but what a man! Rock-like integrity and so thoroughly dependable. No senior civil servant ever felt more safe than did members of the Foreign Office during Bevin's tenure of office; and in their private diaries and memoirs there is a remarkable unanimity in their warm appreciation of Bevin as a great Foreign Secretary.

Bevin's intelligence and executive ability had never been in doubt throughout his career, although there are certain qualifications that must be made after 1945. Nor is there any doubt about his faults. Most outstanding men have large weaknesses, and certainly Bevin was a personality of great strength and determination. In the quotation given above from Gladwyn Jebb that Bevin was for most people 'a very loveable man', Jebb continued:

> Of course he had terrible faults. He was rather vindictive; he was very vain; he was often prejudiced – against Jews, Catholics and the lower middle class for example. . . . Once when I got to know him better he even confided to me his views on class distinctions. 'You know, Gladwyn', he observed in a meditative way, 'I don't *mind* the upper class. As a matter of fact I even rather like the upper class.' (I think that by 'upper class' he meant anybody who had been to a 'good public school', not only Dukes or Earls). 'They may be an abuse but they are often, as like as not, intelligent and amusing. Of course I love the lower class. It's my class and it's the backbone of the country. But Gladwyn, what I can't abide is the *middle* class. For I find them self-righteous and narrow minded'. . . . I think the reason for this prejudice was that he was a little jealous of people whose origins had perhaps not been much more noble than his own but who had somehow or other managed to become better educated in a conventional way. This no doubt accounted for the special aversion which he had for Herbert Morrison.[29]

Bevin's attitude towards Morrison is the best known example of his unreasoning hatred of those whom he had come to mistrust or dislike. He called Morrison 'a scheming little bastard', and during their years together in the War Cabinet (Morrison became a member in November 1942) Bevin constantly behaved in an extremely unpleasant way when Morrison was speaking: with 'a stream of sneers and jibes' which greatly embarrassed Eden who often sat next to Bevin at the Cabinet table. Soon after the new Labour Government took office in 1945 Bevin told Francis Williams, Attlee's adviser on public relations, to 'keep an eye on 'Erbert when I'm not 'ere, Francis. Let me know if he gets up to any of his tricks. I wouldn't trust the little bugger any further than I could throw him.'[30]

It was in keeping with these attitudes that Bevin's reactions to criticism had always been so violent. 'He was sometimes impatient of opposition', Attlee wrote in 1952.[31] He was indeed. 'Treachery' was a word he often used against those who thought it fit to comment adversely on his policies, and the 'stab in the back' was a familiar phrase from much earlier in his career. His instincts, and his practice, were always to bludgeon the opposition. In the spring of 1944 Bevin made a vigorous attack upon the critics of the Coalition Government and especially upon its Labour representatives, and Harold Laski answered him in an article in *Tribune*, 5 May 1944. Laski, Nye Bevan and Sydney Silverman had been specifically named:

> Mr Bevin is in many ways a man of big ideas, and, as Minister of Labour, he has done a remarkable piece of organisation with energy and determination. But Mr Bevin has never, ever since he emerged as a trade union leader of importance, liked criticism, still less opposition. It has been the unstated assumption of all his activities that to doubt the wisdom of the policy he supports is a kind of political blasphemy. He must not be asked to discuss; he must be permitted to lay down the law. He does not want colleagues but followers.
>
> He is always certain that he is right; and he is unwilling to admit that any other view than his is legitimate. Masterful in temper, obstinate in disposition, accustomed, over long years, to give orders which must be obeyed without question, he has come to regard the measures he recommends as good because he recommends them. And it follows that he has become able, as a consequence, to regard a doubt of those measures as the proof that his critics are wrong.
>
> They lack experience; they are disloyal; they are hostile to trade unionism; and perhaps, worst of all, they are 'intellectuals' who have not come into the Labour movement through the gateway of trade unionism in general, not by the special road, in particular, which Mr Bevin believes that the Labour movement should tread. It does not occur to him to consider that there are occasions when it is at least possible that he is mistaken.[32]

The most serious public criticism of Bevin's foreign policy from within the Parliamentary Labour Party came in November 1946 at a time when Bevin was in New York. R.H.S. Crossman opened the debate in the House of Commons with Attlee himself standing in for Bevin. Hector McNeil, at the time Minister of State in the Foreign Office, telephoned Bevin in New York to give him an account of the debate, and Nicholas Henderson, who was Principal Private Secretary in Bevin's Private Office, listened to the conversation, and recorded it in a memoir. Bevin asked McNeil who were his critics, and the latter went through the list one by one. 'Well', said McNeil, 'there's X.' 'I'll break him', said Bevin; and so on through the list. There was no one who was not to be broken.[33]

A different, but no doubt psychologically related attitude, was his vanity. Everyone remarked on this. John Colville noted in his diary that Bevin liked to take credit for most things around him, even though he had, in fact, little or nothing to do with their organisation or result.[34] To Christopher Mayhew, at the time his Parliamentary Private Secretary, Bevin said of the Indian settlement that he had been 'much responsible for the whole policy' when it is widely accepted that it was largely Attlee's doing, at least from the Whitehall end. Kenneth Harris, author of the most detailed biography we have of Attlee to date, noted that if Bevin had been Prime Minister or closely responsible for the Indian policy, independence for that country would not have come as early as it did.[35] The Foreign Office was not involved nor were the Chiefs of Staff consulted in any serious way. There is not one reference to Bevin in the Indian section of Ziegler's official biography of Mountbatten;[36] and the statement that broadly speaking Attlee was his own Minister for India remains acceptable.

In the closing years of the war and during the first years of peace the London *Times* was a serious critic of many aspects of British foreign policy, especially in the area of Anglo-Soviet relations. Barrington-Ward had become editor in 1941 and E.H. Carr joined the staff as leader-writer.[37] Both were agreed that the post-war settlement, if it was to lead to a durable peace, must be based upon the full co-operation of the three big powers of the war years. Barrington-Ward first met Bevin on 9 October 1945, after the first London conference of Foreign Ministers, and he was impressed, as he communicated to his diary, with Bevin's frankness and general friendliness. 'I am sure', he wrote, 'we have a good man for the job.' Two months later they met again at a luncheon party, and Barrington-Ward was not quite so enthusiastic: 'I can't help thinking some of Bevin's views a bit naif, for immediate purposes at least, but he is without doubt a big man.' Their third meeting, in early March 1946, in the description of *The Times*' historian, was 'calamitous'. The meeting took place six days after Churchill's Iron Curtain speech at Fulton, to which *The Times* had responded with two leading articles, moderate in tone, but asking for a patient dialogue with the Russians. Barrington-Ward had gone to the Foreign Office by appointment, and Bevin attacked him in the most violent language for *The Times*' refusal to support an anti-Soviet line. It was a tirade which evidently greatly astonished, and disquieted, Barrington-Ward, and his diary records first his indignation and then a more philosophical opinion:

> In truth, I suppose, some allowance should be made for a harassed Minister in an admittedly awkward situation. But my opinion of Bevin is not what it was. Vain men are always limited. He was a fool to try to tackle the *Times* in this way. It would do me no good nor him either.[38]

One of the most revealing stories of Bevin's egotism and vanity was given in Jebb's *Memoirs*. Jebb's first meeting with Bevin was after their return from Potsdam. Jebb had seen him there but they had not talked together, and Bevin sent over for him:

> The initial reception was a little formidable. In fact he said nothing for a few moments after I had sat down and simply looked me over in my chair. Finally he observed, 'Must be kinda queer for a chap like you to see a chap like me sitting in a chair like this?' Slightly nonplussed, I thought it better not to take up the challenge. So I just shrugged my shoulders and smiled. Bevin was rather nettled. 'Ain't never 'appened before in 'istory, he remarked, scowling ferociously.

Jebb wrote that he could not let that one go so he told Bevin the story of Cardinal Wolsey who had been a butcher's boy in Ipswich, 'and he became the Foreign Secretary of one of our greatest kings'. Bevin, Jebb continued, was 'visibly impressed'; and the exchange did no harm to Jebb in his future dealings with the Foreign Secretary.[39]

The insistence that during his years in the Foreign Office Bevin was 'his own man' has been constantly reiterated in the decades since he died. The suggestion that he was malleable in the hands of his senior officials has been vehemently denied in the diaries and memoirs of his former colleagues, and historians of this period seem to have agreed with their assessment of Bevin's independence in the making of decisions. Sir Roderick Barclay, a former member of the Private Office, wrote that the idea that Bevin was 'in the hands of his Foreign Office officials' showed a complete misunderstanding of his character, for he was a man of very strong will who knew, normally, just what he wanted.'[40] There does not appear to be in print any denial of these basic propositions. It was Attlee who was perhaps the most important witness to Bevin's independent role as the conductor of British foreign policy. In his testimony to Francis Williams in 1961 he insisted that:

> foreign affairs are the province of the Foreign Secretary. It is in my view a mistake for the Prime Minister to intervene personally except in the most exceptional circumstances [and he added in the typically banal way he so often expressed himself] There is a lot in the proverb 'If you've got a good dog you don't bark yourself.'[41]

Attlee was adumbrating only half the story. His own role in the achievement of Indian independence brought with it profound changes in the position of Britain in world politics, and altered in fundamental ways the strategic priorities of the armed forces. Moreover, as discussed in Chapter 3 below, Attlee disagreed sharply with Bevin over Middle East policies for the first two years or so of the Labour Government's term of office, although their differences were never made public and even a majority of the Cabinet were unaware of how wide their disagreements were. Attlee, however, for his own reasons, did not push matters to anything approaching a matter of crisis, and after the spring of 1947 other areas of the world, especially Europe, became of much greater importance. What has come down to our own day as received wisdom is Bevin's wide-ranging knowledge of foreign affairs and 'a definite vision in broad terms of the policy he wanted to pursue'.[42]

The relationship between a Foreign Secretary and his officials is, of course, crucial, and Bevin lacked two qualities the absence of which was to be of inestimable value to the conduct of affairs by the senior members of the Foreign Office. The first was that Bevin had little practical experience of foreign affairs. He had been a member of the War Cabinet and had therefore taken part in decisions affecting the global struggle Britain was engaged in; but being the departmental minister responsible was quite different. He did not have the long years of experience and the background of knowledge that made him such an effective Minister of Labour during the war years. Industrial problems had become his second nature and he had spent his whole trade union career in negotiations, with employers, other unions and his own members. For matters concerning labour and industry Bevin had instinct, flair, intuition, and these were aptitudes he now had to acquire. The man who arrived at Potsdam for the resumed Conference after Labour's victory with the words 'I'm not going to have Britain barged about'[43] had much to learn about the differences between the diplomatic and the trade union worlds. Bevin lacked a second quality for the position he now occupied. There was a vacuum in his mind of what a Labour, let alone a socialist, foreign policy would or should involve. None of his pre-war or wartime statements offered any suggestion that his approach to foreign affairs differed from his Tory colleagues in the War Cabinet; and from the earliest days of his office as Foreign Secretary he underlined the continuity of policy with that of the Churchill Coalition Government. During the war years he had developed close relations with Anthony Eden, and these continued during the years of the Labour Government. The evidence for their close association throughout the years that Bevin was in office is abundant. C.L. Sulzberger, the American journalist, recorded an interview with Eden on 14 November 1949:

> Eden said that, although there was no formal evidence of bi-partisan foreign policy in England, actually a good situation prevails. It is not generally known – and he does

not want it to be known – but Bevin has remained very friendly with Eden, and calls him in from time to time to talk things over. He has also offered Eden access to the telegrams of the Foreign Office, on any subject in which he is interested, and Eden feels the Labour Party in that respect, chiefly because of Bevin, has played the game very straight.[44]

Frank Roberts, who retired from the Diplomatic Service in 1968, underlined 'the close post-war understanding with Eden, which resulted in major matters to what amounted to a bi-partisan foreign policy. I had worked under Eden throughout the war and was often used by Bevin as an intermediary to keep Eden informed or to get his reactions.'[45] Eden himself confirmed the relationship with Bevin in the last volume of his memoirs by noting that although he would have no doubt handled some matters differently:

> I was in agreement with the aims of his foreign policy and with most that he did, and we met quite frequently. He would invite me to his room in the House of Commons where we discussed events informally. In Parliament I usually followed him in debate and I would publicly have agreed with him more, if I had not been anxious to embarrass him less.[46]

The earliest days of Bevin's tenure of office exhibited the agreement between the two front benches over foreign affairs. The first important debate of the new government on foreign policies took place on 20 August 1945 when Bevin made a broad sweeping review of the many questions that confronted Britain in the immediate aftermath of war; and Eden intervened with a long speech in the debate which followed. He remarked that he and Bevin had taken part in many discussions of foreign affairs, in the War Cabinet:

> but I cannot recall one single occasion when there was a difference between us. I hope I do not embarrass the Foreign Secretary by saying that.
> Mr Bevin: No.
> Mr Eden: There were no differences on any important issue of foreign policy. My right hon. Friend helped me during those critical war years and, in the same spirit, I should like to help him now. . . .[47]

Bevin's mind was already closed to new ideas by the time he reached the Foreign Office at the end of July 1945. His views on international relations had been confirmed during his years in the War Cabinet and the major premisses of his political reasoning were not thereafter to be altered in any fundamental way. Some parts of his thinking had undoubtedly been strengthened during the war years. His anti-communism was already a well-established attitude; his anti-

Sovietism was reinforced through the discussions in Cabinet; and of his positive ideas, they were those of the traditional right-wing of the British labour movement, above all a belief in the beneficent influence of the British Empire in world affairs, and the crucial part which the Empire contributed to the status of Britain as a world power. In these matters he was wholly at one with his officials in the Foreign Office. For them, as for him, the national interest was founded upon the United Kingdom as the largest imperial power in the world. The radical wing of the labour movement in Britain – represented at its most generous by H.N. Brailsford, the outstanding socialist journalist of the inter-war years[48] – had developed a critique of imperialism, above all around the case of India, that achieved wide currency before the Second World War; and this had encouraged a genuine sense of internationalism among a minority of working people and intellectuals, above all among the political activists. It was a tradition that went a long way back in British radical history and it only became infused with a socialist component in the later nineteenth century. Between the wars, and after the 1917 Revolution, there was inevitably a contributory influence from the communist position.[49] None of this affected Bevin in any way that can be discerned except in the recognition that it was in the interests of all that living standards were raised. His views on colonial empires and international economic problems were explicitly defined in the years immediately before the Second World War. He spoke in 1937 to the Labour Party Conference on world economic problems[50] and at the beginning of 1938 he developed his ideas in his union journal:

> The great colonial powers of Europe should pool their colonial territories and link them up with a European Commonwealth, instead of being limited British, French, Dutch or Belgian concessions as is now the case. Such a European Commonwealth, established on an economic foundation, would give us greater security than we get by trying to maintain the old balance of Power.[51]

By the time Bevin wrote these words the ideas he was expressing were commonplace among Liberal thinkers. The 'colonial problem' had become a major subject of international discussion against the background of Italian aggression against Abyssinia, and Germany's threatening preparations for war; and the question of colonial 'revision' was fully supported by the leaders of the labour movement in Britain. In September 1935 the Trades Union Congress had accepted a resolution, drafted by the National Council of Labour, and later also adopted by the Labour Party Conference of the same year:

> We call upon the British Government to urge the League of Nations to summon a World Economic Conference and to place upon its agenda the international control of the sources of supply of raw materials with the application of the principle of equality of opportunity to all nations in the undeveloped regions of the world.[52]

Bevin, as shown by the article of January 1938 – in part quoted above – was as deluded as the other commentators at this time who were suggesting that the world's colonial powers would seriously consider divesting themselves of their sovereignty over those parts of the world acquired by past imperialist expansion, although he had his own particular gloss on the argument, and he never suggested the removal of territory from British sovereignty. His ideas were greatly strengthened by his attendance in 1938 at an unofficial Commonwealth Conference in Australia, convened by Chatham House of London and the Australian Institute of International Affairs. The leader of the British delegation was Lord Lothian, a vigorous supporter of appeasement, and among the other British delegates was Lionel Curtis, the most intellectually woolly of all the 'high-minded imperialists' associated with the Round Table, and the one with the most grossly inflated reputation.[53] The delegates to the Conference came from the four older white Dominions as well as India, Ireland and the United Kingdom. Bevin and his wife sailed from Canada across the Pacific, and the weeks of the journey were spent in the company of some of the leading delegates: Keith Hancock, Sir Alfred Zimmern, Lord Lothian and Lionel Curtis. It must have been an educative journey for Bevin. The Conference, held in the Blue Mountains about forty miles from Sydney, lasted a fortnight, and there is no doubt about its powerful impact upon Bevin's ideas of Empire and the colonial problem. He returned with his mind excited with a new enthusiasm and political zest. His ideas were not in any fundamental way altered but he now talked of the problems of Empire and the colonies with vehemence and excitement. In a speech to Chatham House[54] his most serious proposal was the suggestion that the Ottawa agreements should be extended to bring in other countries who would agree to renounce aggressive intentions, and lower their tariffs; and such a proposal, he argued, would be enormously helped if the other colonial powers, such as the Netherlands and Belgium, would join the consortium, ready to open their territories for access to raw materials and markets. Colonial exploitation, as such, did not seem to exist for Bevin. 'Our crime', one of his early biographers reported him as saying, 'isn't exploitation, it's neglect.'[55]

Bevin had been in Australia at the time of Munich, and since then the Chamberlain Government had recognised Franco and the Spanish Civil War had ended in March; what remained of Czechoslovakia was occupied by the Germans on 15 March 1939; Italy had invaded Albania in April, and the inevitability of war with the Fascist powers was now accepted. The British Government decided to double the size of the Territorial Army and to introduce conscription. As a result of decisions made in 1937, the Labour Party Conference of this year (1939) was held at Whitsuntide, at Southport, and the debate on foreign affairs was at the centre of political concerns. Bevin's contribution to what was an exceedingly depressing and unconstructive conference was a restatement of his ideas on the need to extend the Commonwealth in order to pool the resources of the colonial empires. The appeal should be made to Russia as to the United States and together with the European powers 'they would in fact be controlling 90 per cent of the essential raw materials of the world':

> The real trouble which is disturbing the world rests primarily in Europe and Japan. Having pooled our arms, resources and economic power, cannot we then say, and mean, to the people of these countries: 'Put away your weapons, discard them as a means of bettering your conditions of life and you can come in on the ground floor with the rest of us. . . .
>
> In addition, here is a chance now to settle the problem of the colonies on a different basis. Transference of territory from one Great Power to another will not solve any economic problem. The right method of approach is to deal with the great resources of the world. Then we can say to the peoples I have referred to – 'We have something better to offer than war can win.' Show to the peoples of the world that, whilst we are determined to resist aggression, the policy we are advocating gives them all a chance for 'a place in the sun' and a right to develop their standard of living.[56]

Alan Bullock, in his first volume of the Bevin biography, suggested that this speech by Bevin was the only one to arouse the enthusiasm of the audience at Southport, but this is not how it has appeared to other historians.[57] No doubt Bevin's considerable powers of oratory helped to clothe his simple, naive and illusory ideas with a degree of power and sophistication that encouraged at least some of his listeners. Bevin was, however, speaking within a few months of the outbreak of war, and nothing he said at Southport was relevant to the menacing situation the world was facing. It will be remarked that Bevin made no reference in his speeches at this time to the inhabitants of the colonial territories who already had 'their place in the sun' – because that was where they lived; nor did he have any serious appreciation of the bitter poverty which the colonial peoples endured. He was certainly always talking about the problem of living standards, but it was an academic understanding that wholly failed to comprehend the economic relationships involved between the metropolitan powers and their colonial dependencies.

There was one area, however, with which Bevin and his senior colleagues in the TUC were already intimately connected before 1939, and that was a working partnership with the British Colonial Office to help guide the rising nationalist sentiment into safe paths, and in particular to ensure that moderate counsels prevailed among the emerging trade unions. The details of this relationship have only become fully documented in recent years.[58] The Colonial Office had been slow to appreciate the part which the emerging labour movements, often built around the trade unions, would play in the development of anti-imperialist consciousness in the colonial world. It was a series of explosions of discontent – notably Northern Rhodesia in 1935 and Trinidad and Jamaica in 1937–38 – that forced the Colonial Office in Whitehall to recognise the emergence of labour issues as political questions. As the Colonial Secretary somewhat belatedly recognised in 1938, there were now 'revolutionary changes in native opinions regarding social conditions'.[59] Major Granville St John Orde Browne was appointed Labour Adviser to the Secretary of State for the Colonies in 1939, and this more or less coincided with changing attitudes within the Colonial Office and the beginnings of a new approach. The TUC had already begun to recognise the problem. Bevin, president of the TUC in 1937, had called attention to colonial labour questions, and in December of the same year the General Council – which by now had concentrated almost all dealings with the Government in its own control – established a Colonial Advisory Committee, and began pressing the Colonial Office for positive action. The next year Sir Walter Citrine – he had been knighted in 1935 – served on the West Indies Royal Commission and was greatly shocked at the living and social conditions that were revealed by the Commission's inquiries.[60] Malcolm Macdonald became Colonial Secretary in May 1938 and there was now a growing recognition of the need to develop 'responsible' trade unions in order to contain the demagogues and wild men. In 1942 the Colonial Office created the Colonial Labour Advisory Committee (CLAC) which, in addition to civil servants, included representatives of the TUC and overseas employers' federations. One of the key personalities in this close relationship between the senior officials and the General Council and Whitehall was Frederick Leggett, the Ministry of Labour's Chief Industrial Advisor from 1940 to 1942 (later Deputy Secretary) and a man in whom Bevin had great confidence. Leggett was clear that with sensible guidance 'the politically motivated union' could be curbed and contained; or, as Leggett suggested in a later discussion, with a proper approach 'West Indians could be persuaded to want things which people in this country thought they ought to want.'[61] The Colonial Labour Advisory Committee was an important stage in the incorporation of the higher echelons of the trade union movement in Britain with the State apparatus, and it was to lead to the important developments in the post-war world which included the break-up of the World Federation of Trade Unions.[62]

Bevin always assumed that the British Empire, official and unofficial, was crucial for the economic well-being of Britain itself, and that the Empire was a major component of the general political position of Britain in the world. Such assumptions were clearly implicit in his pre-1939 thinking; they became unadorned and explicit during the years when he was Foreign Secretary, and thereby matched the intellectual premises of his senior officials at the Foreign Office. The theme of 'neglect' rather than 'exploitation' was woven into his general attitudes towards imperial questions. He took for granted the continued existence of the British Empire after the Second World War, and he assumed, as a general proposition, that it was right and proper for all the traditional imperialist powers to assume once again their territorial sovereignty over their previous colonies, once the war had ended in victory. We have an early statement which defined his uncomplicated approach to the problem of colonialism in general. In the extract given below, Bevin was writing to the British Ambassador in Chungking, reporting on a discussion which he recently had with T.V. Soong and the Chinese Ambassador in London. The date of the letter was 17 September 1945, less than two months after Labour had assumed office:

> I said that we naturally assumed that Indo-China would return to France, and that being the case, the safeguarding of Chinese interests in Indo-China would be a matter for direct negotiations between China and France. Dr Soong did not react to this, but I got the impression that he would have welcomed a less unequivocal assertion of our support of French rights in regard to Indo-China.[63]

The preservation of British territorial interests was central to Bevin's approach. At the London conference and in the Commons, he spoke of the Russian demand for a place in the Mediterranean as coming across 'the throat of the British Commonwealth'. He later assured Fitzroy Maclean it was 'the intention of HMG to safeguard British interests in whatever part of the world they may be found'.[64] This was not the approach of many of the ordinary members of the Labour Party. The Party had gone into the general election of 1945 with a manifesto entitled *Let Us Face the Future* which was largely concerned with home policy; but statements during the war years had considered colonial problems in general and the question of India in particular. There was indeed no issue more important than India among Labour activists when colonial questions were being debated. An interim Labour Party report in 1942, *The Old World and the New Society*, was cautious about India's future, emphasising that while self-government was desirable, it must wait upon the agreement between the Indian parties themselves. At the same time the report underlined the duty of British governments to take every possible step towards that agreement. In September 1944 a conference of British and Dominion Labour Parties published an important statement under the title of *From a People's War to a People's Peace* in which it was recognised that India had the right to 'full self-government', and expressing the hope that 'a free India will decide to remain a partner in the British Commonwealth of Nations'. Attlee was known to be deeply interested in and concerned with the problem of India; and from the beginning of his government Indian affairs were never pushed to the margin of political decisions.[65]

None of this appeared to have penetrated the minds of the senior members of the Foreign Office – or of most parts of Whitehall it can be added – and they approached the strategic and political problems along the road to India with the simple assumption that the geo-politics of British power remained unchanged.

During the early months of the Labour Government there was no suggestion in Foreign Office policy documents that it was likely there would be any significant shift in power relations within the Middle East, and throughout the years of the Attlee administration the opinions of Bevin and his advisers were not, in this context, modified in any fundamental way. As discussed in the following chapter, there was only one critic of weight within the Cabinet of the traditional policies towards the Middle East, and that was Attlee himself; but as late as August 1949, when Britain's Middle East strategies were in rags and tatters, and two years after the independence of the Indian sub-continent, Bevin was still propounding unchanged views in a paper circulated to the Cabinet:

> In peace and war, the Middle East is an area of cardinal importance to the U.K., second only to the U.K. itself. Strategically the Middle East is a focal point of communications, a source of oil, a shield to Africa and the Indian Ocean, and an irreplaceable offensive base. Economically it is, owing to oil and cotton, essential to United Kingdom recovery.[66]

For Bevin, then, the Empire was integrally linked with his constant insistence that Britain was still a Great Power alongside the USA and the Soviet Union. Just as important in his thinking was his attitude towards the Soviet Union and his implacable hostility towards communism in all its forms. During the inter-war years he had been consistent in his political appreciation of Russia. As noted above, he had played a part in the opposition to military intervention against the young Soviet Republic in 1920, but so had every other trade union leader. He was against the Arcos raid[67] but again so were most of the leaders of the labour movement, on both political and industrial sides. On all the major political issues in the years between the wars, however, Bevin was either neutral towards the Soviet Union or hostile. He was, for example, always against the Anglo-Russian trade union committee of the 1920s, and at the TUC in 1927 when Walter Citrine opened the debate by presenting the General Council's recommendation for the dissolution of the Committee, Bevin summed up.[68] More important in the formation of his political attitudes was his bitter hostility to the Communist Party inside Britain which he regarded, with some justification, as an extension to Russian foreign policy. There were some groups of communists within his own union, and their most dramatic confrontation came at the time of the London bus strike in May 1937.[69] The comment after 1945 that Bevin was unable to distinguish sufficiently clearly his opposition to local communists from appreciation of the international manoeuvres of the Soviet Union is not wholly without substance. The following extraordinary passage comes from a speech made by Bevin at the Labour Party Conference of 1946. It will be noted that he began with his role in 1920 against military intervention, the evidence for which is examined in

Appendix 4 to this volume. Bevin was answering the many critics of his foreign policy since Labour took office:

> The next resolution deals with the USSR. This resolution looks very innocent, but what does it imply? It implies in the first instance that I have not been sympathetic to Russia. I think that is what it is intended to imply. Is there any man in this Conference who historically did more to defend the Russian Revolution than I did? It is forgotten in this age, but when the Soviets did not have a friend I got dockers and other people to assist in forming the Council of Action and stop Lloyd George attacking them. I fought the Arcos raid and I called it silly. I fought Churchill's interventionist policy, for which we are paying now. I fought every attempt to break off relations. I helped to form in Transport House Anglo-Russian commercial relations, about which this Party do not know much. All through those years there was one thing I would not do. The thanks that I got for it was an attempt by the Communists to break up the Union that I had built. I said to Maisky on one occasion: 'You have built the Soviet Union and you have a right to defend it. I have built the Transport Union and if you seek to break it I will fight you.' That was a proper position to take up. Both were the results of long years of labour. After that there was a slightly greater respect for my view. I think that is fair.[70]

This was the Foreign Secretary of the United Kingdom speaking; well away, it may be assumed, from the official briefs of his senior advisers at the Foreign Office, who can hardly have applauded this example of their minister's bizarre vanity and parochialism. There is relatively little to record of Bevin's direct statements on Russia during the years of war except for his uncompromising support for Churchill's military intervention in Greece in December 1944. The intervention immediately became a political issue which aroused fierce passions, and of all the areas of dissent during Bevin's first two years of office, none was debated more vigorously than Greece. Opposition in the early days went far beyond the traditional Left.[71] The Labour Party met in conference on 13 December 1944, and Bevin became the main speaker on foreign affairs for the National Executive. He was a good deal more moderate than Churchill had been in the House of Commons, but he was firm and unyielding on the Greek issue, and it was plain that he believed wholly the anti-communist thesis. He did not convince the conference, but the trade union block vote carried the day for the Executive.[72]

By the spring of 1945, and before the break-up of Churchill's Coalition Government, Bevin was beginning to offer clear evidence of his general agreement with the Tories on major questions of foreign policy. He had certainly not been affected in his general appreciation of the Soviet Union by their heroism and sacrifice during the war against Germany.[73] In early April 1945 he spoke at Leeds to the Yorkshire Regional Council of the Labour Party, and while the greater part of his speech was on domestic matters – and a vigorous critique of the Tories – he concluded with a few references to foreign affairs in which he argued for a national consensus:

> I cannot help feeling that on the question of our defence, our foreign policy and our relations with other countries, there is an imperative necessity for the will of the nation to be expressed, and for a combined effort to be made

and he went on to argue that all the relevant documents should be made available to whoever was in opposition.[74] He was the main speaker on foreign affairs at the Labour Party's national conference at Blackpool just after the Coalition Government had broken up; and there was little to argue about. His famous phrase, to be widely quoted, that 'Left understands Left' was made in reference to the France of the Popular Front days, and to the lack of understanding on the part of the British Government. It did not refer to Russia as has at times been suggested. All that Bevin said on Russia was that there had always been difficulties and fears on both sides, and that the first job of a Labour government would be to remove those fears: a statement that in a few months could be characterised as ironical.

We come now to a discussion of the working capabilities and working habits of Bevin in his period as Foreign Secretary. In general, of course, his work patterns would not operate differently from those of his earlier years and especially from those in Whitehall as Minister of Labour. The problems, however, of the post-1945 years were unlike those Bevin had previously encountered, and Foreign Office procedures were similarly different. Bevin had an instinctive knowledge of labour questions that developed over many years, and this was one of the central reasons – in addition to his considerable native intelligence and organisational ability – why he was so successful as Minister of Labour. His background knowledge of foreign affairs was, by contrast, somewhat sketchy. This was not an area of politics in which he had been daily involved, and while those of his officials who have written about him have insisted that his knowledge was in fact quite remarkable, it is difficult to accept their assurances without qualification. Nicholas Henderson, for example, a member of Bevin's Private Office, thought it worthwhile to include in his memoirs Bevin's own assessment of his skills as a negotiator. Bevin's remarks came at the end of the first evening at Potsdam when he commented that Stalin seemed to him 'as a man with much on his mind and that makes him weak'; and he then proceeded to explain his views on negotiating with foreigners, saying that he had a good deal of experience before the last war, bargaining with ships' captains of all nationalities.

> These people, Stalin and Truman, are just the same as all Russians and Americans;

and dealing with them over foreign affairs is just the same as trying to come to a settlement about unloading a ship. Oh yes, I can handle them.[75]

It is surprising that Henderson should have published such a story, although he must have felt it was to Bevin's credit. It may be accepted that such simple ideas were gradually modified by more realist assumptions as Bevin began to appreciate the complexities of his new position; and Bevin was always surrounded by expert opinion. Such opinions may have been, and indeed often were, biased and prejudiced – who, for example, would now look back upon Lord Killearn as a sensible commentator on Egyptian affairs in 1945 – but at least, whatever their particular attitudes, most Foreign Office officials would be well-informed, knowledgeable and experienced in the affairs of their special interests.

Here we arrive at the most difficult problem in the evaluation of Bevin as Foreign Secretary. We must begin from the proposition that there were no fundamental differences of politics between Bevin and his senior officials. It has been suggested that there was possibly some reluctance in the early days for Bevin to accept Foreign Office advice in the matter of a coherent and consistent policy towards the Soviet Union but the argument is not convincing.[76] None of the published memoirs, autobiographies and diaries of those who worked with Bevin indicate any fundamental difference of opinion. The unpublished documents naturally show disagreements, and there were certainly a number of occasions when Bevin held back circulation of memoranda prepared by members of the Office; but the reasons were almost always related to domestic and international politics. In his early months especially, Bevin had to take careful note of public opinion in general towards the Soviet Union, a vociferous back-bench opposition within his own Parliamentary Labour Party, and public opinion in the United States. Until the Marshall Plan got under way Bevin was noticeably careful about his public statements relating to the Soviet Union. The Cabinet, it must be noted, were not privy to many of the decisions affecting foreign policy; circulation of material was not automatic within the Cabinet; no one seems to have known of the detailed discussions between Attlee and Bevin over Mediterranean policies; and only a chosen few were party to the decision to manufacture a British atom bomb.[77] The relations between Bevin and his officials are therefore of crucial importance in analysing the formulation of policy on any subject or for any area of the world.

Bevin read slowly – so almost all his commentators have said[78] – and he wrote with great difficulty. His difficulty with writing is agreed by everyone. He had a large silver fountain pen – christened 'the Caber' by Roger Makins, who in the early years was a Deputy Under-Secretary of State – and Bevin held the pen between his first and second fingers, and then, according to Henderson, just 'let his hand shake'.[79] There is abundant confirmation of Bevin's aversion to writing. M.E. Pelley noted the point in his preface to a collection of documents on the 1945 period,[80] and Henderson and Barclay both discussed Bevin's working habits at length: these did not include the writing of drafts or their subsequent correction or addition. Duff Cooper, Ambassador in Paris, had an interesting comment in his autobiography. He noted that Bevin had difficulty in writing and that 'The mere setting of words on paper was for him a long and arduous process.' Duff Cooper went on to make the point that there were disadvantages in the diplomatic world if there could be no private communication. It was sometimes helpful, he noted, for an Ambassador to be able to send a private note to his Secretary of State, and know that it would be answered in the same way. With Bevin, however, Duff Cooper never once received a letter in Bevin's own handwriting nor one which he felt had been dictated by Bevin himself. Duff Cooper added that he 'never wrote to him [Bevin] without suspecting that my letter would be laid before him with the comments of the Department, or at least with those of his Private Secretary'.[81]

The procedure for policy discussions seems to have been the usual practice of a review, with Foreign Office members and always with someone from the Private Office present, and the Foreign Secretary would indicate the general lines that he expected the relevant draft would follow. There were, however, special problems with a Bevin office deliberation. It may have been his general lack of familiarity with the issues under consideration, for a number of his contemporaries have commented on his vagueness of expression, often indeed his incoherence in speech. Christopher Mayhew, for example, who became a junior minister at the Foreign Office in October 1946, and who remained thereafter an admirer of Bevin, nevertheless wrote in his diary:

> I do wish he expressed himself better . . . he puts everything so incoherently and with so little sense of proportion or logical sequence that it is hard to follow and still harder to remember.[82]

Anthony Nutting, who often followed Bevin on foreign matters in the House of Commons, complained that 'Bevin was never exactly precise in his use of language' and that it was often difficult to develop, or continue, the thesis involved.[83] It was Valentine Lawford, a carry-over from Eden for a few months in the Private Office when Labour came to power, who provided the most detailed example of what he described as 'Bevin's complacent verbal obscurity'. The occasion was early in Bevin's tenure of office, a day or so before his first big speech on foreign affairs in the House of Commons (20 August 1945). Bevin called in a shorthand typist, with Lawford present:

> [and] slipped, as it were *con sordini*, into a rambling after-luncheon monologue, uninhibited by considerations of grammar or syntax, and punctuated less by any recognisable vocal equivalent of commas or semi-colons or full stops than by the

occasional pauses required for blowing smoke, coughing, removing tobacco leaf from his tongue or dusting ash from the lapels of his coat.

After five or six pages of shorthand, taken down by the young woman with increasing panic, Bevin finished. 'All over, Missy', he said . . . 'And Lawford here will turn that into English if he can.'[84] Lawford could, and did, and Bevin used the prepared draft to make a speech of considerable power, that reads quite smoothly in *Hansard* and was evidently appreciated by most of the House.[85] Roderick Barclay, who became Principal Private Secretary in early March 1949, offered similar examples. Of a speech made by Bevin at the United Nations Assembly in September 1950 Barclay wrote that it was very well received: 'As usual, the ideas were his, but I had to re-write it fairly extensively.'[86]

Barclay sat in at all meetings with Bevin and he was responsible for all drafts of the discussion that had taken place. From the early days of Bevin's incumbency it became the practice of the members of the Private Office to develop techniques of 'ghost-writing' for Bevin's speeches or telegrams. They tried to retain the true Bevin flavour, that is, his idiosyncratic grammar, while making clear beyond doubt what the message was intended to convey. Valentine Lawford, according to Nicholas Henderson,

> became a master Bevin craftsman. He would dash off a Bevin telegram with aplomb, and the other Private Secretaries came to model themselves on his style rather than on the true Bevin, rather as a portrait painter will sometimes prefer to work from a photograph than from real life.[87]

Bevin, Henderson went on, 'accepted these imitations; and he recognised Lawford's skill but he was not flattered, and at times showed a touching awareness of his own shortcomings': although with Bevin moods of self-criticism soon passed.

Bevin, provided with a brief, was, at the least, competent, and often masterful. It was when he spoke without an official brief, or departed from what had been offered him, that his officials became worried. They were especially concerned with his parliamentary performances. He disliked the House of Commons and was not impressive except in his set pieces. It was when he spoke 'extempor', as he termed it, that particularly troubled his officials. Parliamentary convention has always been firmly against any alteration to the transcription of words spoken on the floor of the Commons unless the rectification asked for is a straightforward matter of accuracy;[88] but in Bevin's case it would seem that the normal rules were disregarded. When he was speaking 'extempor' the written version often looked 'very odd'. Barclay described how after a period of Bevin at the Dispatch Box, he or one of his assistants would 'hurry up' to the *Hansard* reporters' room, and ask to see their draft, which on occasion would 'make no sense at all'. Members of the Private Office would therefore offer to introduce intelligibility into the text, and this would be accepted 'provided always that we did not seem to be changing the substance'. From unintelligibility to intelligibility, according to the definition of the latter by members of the Private Office, was evidently agreeable to those compiling the parliamentary record.

We may reasonably infer that most of the memoranda and instructions that went out over Bevin's name were never drafted by him, or rarely altered by him in draft. All ministers, of course, have drafts prepared for them; few even write the first draft of their major speeches, but most work over early statements and alter them, often substantially. In Bevin's case, because he rarely wrote anything except the odd sentence or two, it would seem that a greater than usual responsibility can be ascribed to the officials of the Foreign Office, especially those in his Private Office. Those memoranda and circulars held back from full or partial distribution were mainly the result of a political decision by Bevin, a matter of political judgement in terms of the impact the document might make upon opinion at home or abroad. This argument suggests a somewhat different understanding of the constant reiteration by his former officials that Bevin was his 'own man'. Certainly he was not a man to be over-ruled if his own assessment was at issue, but given the range and complexity of the problems to be considered each day, and given above all the general agreement about fundamentals between Bevin and his officials, it follows that it was the Foreign Office in its individual and collective judgement which pronounced on most questions; and it further underlines the accepted view that the most important characteristic of Bevin's conduct of foreign affairs was the continuity of approach with his predecessors.

This analysis is reinforced when Bevin's health is considered. Heart trouble seems first to have been diagnosed in the spring of 1938, and in the years preceding the war he was over-weight and he smoked and drank too much. When Dr McCall first examined him in 1943, he found no sound organ in his body except his feet; and he later described Bevin, in Bullock's words, 'as suffering from angina pectoris, cardiac failure, arterio-sclerosis, sinusitis, enlarged liver, damaged kidneys and high blood pressure'.[89] Throughout Bevin's years as Foreign Secretary his health was a major problem, and only his extraordinary determination kept him in office. He was, his doctor said, an 'unruly and undisciplined patient'. He was greedy, and found it difficult to deny himself the pleasures of over-eating and excessive drinking. Bevin had a coronary thrombosis in 1946. After speaking in the House of Commons on 25 July 1946 he collapsed, and Attlee took his place at the Paris peace negotiations which opened on 29 July. Although still ill, Bevin insisted on attending a Cabinet meeting on 7 August, and he went to Paris two days later, being convinced that no one else could do his job. He was never unwilling to recognise his own importance in the Attlee Cabinet, and it was during this period that Bevin, who had heard from Henderson about certain Cabinet decisions on Egypt, decided that he must intervene. 'You know', he said to Henderson, 'I'm not conceited, but I really think the darned Cabinet goes to pieces when I'm not there. I can't afford to be away.'[90] Bevin was ill again all through the fuel crisis of early 1947, and he was due to be in Moscow in late February 1947 with Dalton noting in his diary for 24 February that Bevin might well 'collapse completely'. There were strong rumours at this time that he would have to give up the Foreign Office on health grounds.

Attacks of angina became more serious in the last years of Bevin's life. Flying across the Atlantic was forbidden, and there were a number of occasions in these middle years when he had to leave conference rooms and lie down elsewhere. Roderick Barclay became his Principal Private Secretary in March 1949; and on their first ocean crossing together, in the *Queen Mary*, in September 1949, Bevin had a heart attack walking up the gangway. On 8 September, in Washington, he went to see the musical *South Pacific* with the Achesons, and was given a warm personal reception. He had a serious heart attack just after the performance finished, and was stretched out in the aisle, with towels soaked in ice-cold water on his face; with an intake of nitro-glycerine tablets he recovered suficiently to walk out of the theatre. Bevin was consistently foolhardy in respect of his health. On the way home, instead of going back to his own hotel, as the Achesons expected, he insisted on joining them in their apartment for a night-cap.[91]

The last two years of his life (he died in April 1951) showed a continued deterioration in his health. The general election of February 1950 had very sharply reduced the Labour majority, and it was assumed by many that Attlee would replace Bevin because of his failing health. Bevin himself was tenacious of office and in this he was encouraged by his permanent officials;[92] and he remained. Between 1 March 1950 and 31 July 1950 – a period when the Schuman Plan was under discussion and the Korean War had begun – Bevin was away from the Foreign Office for 85 out of 153 days.[93] In May 1950 when Dean Acheson came to London, he observed that Bevin was taking sedatives – Bevin at this time was recovering from a very painful operation for haemorr-hoids – and the Foreign Secretary would often doze off quite soundly during the discussion. This apparently worried Acheson a good deal more than it did Bevin's own colleagues and officials. The Foreign Office in general were more concerned with keeping Bevin as their figurehead, with his enormous authority, than with the fact, as William Strang recognised, that Bevin was operating 'at considerably less than full efficiency'.[94] (Strang was Permanent Under-Sec-retary in Bevin's last years.) It must be noted again that Bevin himself showed a remarkable tenacity in doing all he could to overcome his grave physical disabilities. He was in hospital again in February 1951 with pneumonia, and then tried to return to work. He had to be forced to leave office. When Attlee finally decided to retire him – it happened to be on Bevin's seventieth birthday – it was still an affront to Bevin's vanity. 'I've got the sack' was his greeting to his wife. He died a month later on 14 April 1951.

The suggestion that Bevin approached the Soviet Union as he would a breakaway union from the Transport Workers is not as unreasonable or capricious as is sometimes argued. Bevin's trade was that of a union negotiator, and to achieve results for his members he had to be willing to talk at length with the employers and accept that on many occasions he could not expect to win. He would, however, always have to go back to the negotiating table or certainly indicate his willingness to begin again if there had been no forward movement. A breakaway union was a very different proposition. That was treachery, a word he sometimes used in place of the more common accusation of 'being stabbed in the back', and compromise could never be on the agenda. The most obvious example in Bevin's union career is the aftermath of the London busmen's strike of May 1937, and his position towards the breakaway organisation remained implacable. Towards the Soviet Union he could not, of course, refuse to talk and negotiate, but it is necessary to be clear about the premises from which he began. He is not specifically on record as Citrine is for making no distinction between Hitler's Germany and Stalin's Russia but there can be little doubt that on this crucial question he was at one with him.[95] Within six months of the assumption of office by the British Labour Party Bevin used the comparison between Hitler and post-war Soviet foreign policy on three occasions, and there may well have been others. There can be no doubt that Bevin saw little difference between the Nazi and Soviet regimes, and since his thoughts so often blundered into public statement, when away from his prepared briefs, it was not the most felicitous assumption to be known to nurture. It was at the London Conference of Foreign Ministers that the first two examples occurred. The Conference opened in the second week of September 1945, just about a month after the surrender of Japan. On the evening of 23 September, after the deadlock on procedural matters over which the Russians proved more than usually obdurate, Bevin called on Molotov at the Russian Embassy. Clark Kerr was with him and provided the record to be found in Bevin's papers:[96]

> The Secretary of State began by saying that it seemed to him that our relationship with the Russians about the whole European problem was drifting into the same condition as that which we had found ourselves with Hitler. He was most anxious to avoid any trouble about our respective policies in Europe.

He then continued about the need for frankness and friendliness; and began the substantive part of his statement by raising the question of Tripolitania and the Dodecanese islands, and ended this first statement:

> If Mr. Molotov would tell him frankly about what was in his mind, what we were

expected to agree to, the Secretary of State would lay all his cards on the table with equal frankness.

Mr. Molotov said that he would begin by referring to what the Secretary of State had said about Hitler, perhaps rightly or perhaps wrongly.

The Secretary of State broke in to say that he did not wish the talks to start with a misunderstanding. He had not wanted to suggest that the USSR in any way resembled Hitler. All he wished to suggest was that the absence of frankness led to situations which had become irretrievable.

Mr. Molotov said that he understood. Hitler had looked on the USSR as an inferior country, as no more than a geographical conception. The Russians took a different view. They thought themselves as good as anyone else. They did not wish to be regarded as an inferior race. He would ask the Secretary of State to remember that our relations with the Soviet Union must be based upon the principle of equality. Things seemed to him to be like this: there was the war. During the war we had argued but we had managed to come to terms while the Soviet Union was suffering immense losses. At that time the Soviet Union was needed. But when the war was over His Majesty's Government has seemed to change their attitude. Was that because we no longer needed the Soviet Union? If this were so it was obvious that such a policy, far from bringing us together, would separate us and end in serious trouble.

Molotov then continued to discuss certain of Bevin's specific points about the Mediterranean and the Balkans, and towards the end of the meeting was highly critical of the recent statement of Field Marshal Wilson. He asked Clark Kerr how a Russian marshal would have been dealt with if he had made a similar statement about Great Britain.[97] A week later, two days before the end of the London conference, Bevin again made the comparison with Hitler. Pierson Dixon, Private Secretary to Bevin – a position he had occupied with Bevin's predecessor, Anthony Eden – recorded the meeting of the Foreign Ministers in his diary entry for 30 September 1945:

Supreme crisis of the Conference.
Molotov's final argument was that, as Russia withdrew her agreement to the Resolution of September 11th, the Resolution was null and void. This prompted E.B. to retort that agreements freely entered into could only be annulled by the agreement of all the parties, and that Molotov's attitude was reminiscent of Hitler. As this was being translated, Molotov went pale and blotchy and walked to the door, saying that he had been insulted. E.B. apologised and Molotov resumed his place; but after this incident it was clearer than ever that no agreement was possible.[98]

It would be difficult to find a comparable example of crass and ignorant stupidity among wartime Allies within a few weeks of final victory after six years of horrendous war; and impossible to conceive of such language from either Churchill or Eden whatever the provocation. Truman was quoted as saying of

Stalin and Molotov that 'they might be rough men, but they knew the common courtesies' whereas Bevin 'was entirely lacking in all of them, a boor'.[99]

There are two comments to be made about these Hitler references: the first is that there does not appear to be any reference to them in the memoirs of his senior Foreign Office staff or in those of other civil servants in Whitehall, some of whom must have heard of these incidents. Bevin himself, it may be noted, was fully aware of the political impropriety he had committed. We have Averell Harriman's reminiscences which reported an encounter with Bevin after he had left the meeting of 30 September:

> He appeared ashamed to have shown his ignorance of diplomatic manners. I urged him to be himself, not to deviate from his blunt-spoken ways and assured him that in the long run he would get along better with the Russians that way. But he walked on to luncheon, depressed and humiliated.[100]

Harriman was not always an accurate observer, but the point must be made that however contrite Bevin felt on this particular occasion – and humiliation is unlikely to have been the right word for Bevin's feelings – it led to no change in his political understanding. Within a few months he was using the comparison with Hitler once again to explain the direction of Soviet policy. This was at the dinner with Senator Vandenberg and Foster Dulles in January 1946, discussed above in the previous chapter.

There was one outcome of the failure of the London Conference that ought to have remained of quite minor significance. This was a broadcast on the Home Service of the BBC by the historian A.J.P. Taylor: a commentary on the results so far of the London conference already being widely discussed in the British press as ominous and alarming. Taylor's broadcast of 24 September was moderate, sensible and relevant. The main themes of the talk were that Russia was now back in the world talks, unlike the inter-war years; that history has shown that agreements after wars always take time before negotiations are resolved; that often after wars new alliances form themselves, and that it can be assumed that agreements will be reached in the end. There was a full text of Taylor's talk in the Bevin papers from which the quotations below are taken:[101]

> To judge by some newspaper comment, you'd think that there'd never been disputes at an international conference before. The historian takes a longer view. At the Conferences of Vienna in 1814, after the defeat of Napoleon, two of the victors, England and Austria, made an alliance with France, the defeated Power, against the other two Allies, Russia and Prussia. But they reached an agreement in the end. That's the important thing: the task of an international conference isn't to begin in agreement but to conclude in it. So far as an outsider can judge, the present meeting in London certainly won't reach agreement. Its main job will be to clear the way for the next meeting. But it's already possible to say that we're nearer agreement on some things than we were a fortnight ago. To reach full agreement on everything will

probably take most of the twenty years, which is the lifetime of the Anglo-Soviet Alliance.

Taylor then continued by arguing that Russia was entitled to be a Mediterranean power and he made the point that the French had a much better base at Bizerta in Tunisia than the Russians could ever have at Tripoli. He further pointed out that if the Russians had stayed in the First World War and been at the peace-making conference in 1919 they would have received much more than they were asking for now. He ended:

> The Great Powers won't trust each other until their affairs get mixed up and their affairs won't get mixed up until they trust each other. That's a deadlock insoluble in logic. It's being solved every time the Great Powers meet round a table – by argument, by disputes, by crises, even occasionally by agreement.

Taylor's broadcast was a thoroughly sensible explanation of the workings of international diplomacy; but that was not how it was received in Whitehall. Cadogan added a sarcastic comment at the end of the typed script: 'The most terse and brilliant comment I have ever seen. I should like to convey my congratulations to the BBC.' The broadcast was discussed in Cabinet, and Bevin wrote to Cripps:

> You will remember that at Tuesday's Cabinet we agreed that a recent BBC broadcast on the work of the Council of Foreign Ministers had been embarrassing in tone and I undertook to see whether some guidance when a broadcast on the same subject is given next week.
> On reflection I feel that I cannot approach the BBC with a request like this, as they are of course an independent Corporation, and are not bound in any way to accept guidance on the subject matter of their broadcasts. I wonder, therefore, if you would be good enough to help me with relation to next week's broadcast which is to be by Zilliacus. I believe you know him well, and if you could speak to him, pointing out to him the harm that the previous broadcast did, and the importance of confining himself to temperate judgements, it would, I think, be a great help.
> You could, of course, add that should he like to consult the Foreign Office as to the general line the broadcast should take, we will be very glad to help with information and background.

This letter to Cripps was dated 26 September, and there was a handwritten note on the letter to the effect that Cripps 'has spoken to Mr. Zillacus, 28. IX'.

A revealing incident. It is worth pointing out that the second reference to Hitler, this time in public session, came after the Taylor broadcast.

What must be emphasised is not the whinging reaction to criticism – that was always true of Bevin – but that the top levels of the Foreign Office were also in agreement. As far as present records reveal there was no serious opposition within the Foreign Office to the anti-Sovietism which Bevin brought into a Foreign Office whose ideas moved in an untroubled way to the Warner memorandum of the spring of 1946. It was an Office, moreover, which did all in its power to protect the man who represented them in such a dominant fashion in the Labour Cabinet. We have on record their reactions to the most serious criticism Bevin encountered from within the Parliamentary Labour Party: the foreign affairs debate in mid November 1946, at which Bevin himself was not present, being in New York, and when Attlee took his place. The large number of Labour abstentions was a serious warning to the Government, and Whitehall was not alone in recognising the danger signals. Early in the New Year 1947, an American official in London spelled out the problem to George Marshall, his Secretary of State:

> Foreign Office officials directly charged with Soviet Affairs have recently and repeatedly indicated that while there is no change in substance U.K. policy towards USSR, every move must be carefully considered and planned from point of view of protecting Bevin from Labour Party rebels . . . in light of Labour rebellion Bevin and F.O. now take greater pains to avoid impression that he is ganging up with the U.S. against Russia.[102]

The end of 1946 and the first few months of 1947 were the most testing time for Ernest Bevin and his senior officials. As discussed in the chapter which follows, it was over the Christmas–New Year period of 1946–47 that Attlee's serious criticisms of Bevin's Middle Eastern policies were largely resolved in private deliberations between the two men; and the outcome was mostly in Bevin's favour. By the time another year had passed the Labour opposition to Bevin, which had been so vigorous and vociferous in the House of Commons and elsewhere, was now diminishing fast. Henceforth, Bevin's foreign policy found increasing favour within Britain and never again was there serious parliamentary opposition.

3

A Slight Case of Heresy: Clement Attlee and the Middle East, 1945–47

Attlee was born in 1883 into a conservatively minded middle-class family. He left his public school, so his biographer wrote, 'intellectually immature and under-developed',[1] and, as with so many of his middle- and upper-class contemporaries, Attlee remained in a number of ways encapsulated within the language and traditions of his own school days. When Sir John Colville went to Chequers following the Labour victory in the general election of 1945, Attlee asked his opinion of Geoffrey de Freitas who was being considered for the position of Parliamentary Private Secretary. Colville said that he thought him charming and highly intelligent. 'Yes', replied Attlee, 'and what is more he was at Haileybury, my old school.'[2] Until he went to the East End of London to engage in social work Attlee's mind remained closed to any degree of social understanding or conscience. His university life at Oxford seems to have made little impression upon him, but what saved him from the conventional career of his class was the involvement of other members of his family in social work. His favourite brother Tom was helping in a working-men's hostel in Hoxton; an aunt was managing a club for factory girls in Wandsworth; his mother was a district visitor in a slum area, and the eldest brother was working two nights a week at a mission in Hornsey. Attlee was taken by another brother to the Haileybury Club in Stepney, and there, within a few months, he decided to stay; and this is one of the interesting differences between him and most of his contemporaries. After their 'philanthropic stint' young middle-class men and women were usually expected to return to 'normal' middle-class life. In Attlee's case he went to the Haileybury Club every week and gradually was drawn more into its activities; and it was not long before he chose to live in Stepney, where he was to remain until the beginning of the First World War. The particular character of the Haileybury Club – of which he became manager – is important to define. It was a secular not a religious mission, aiming to inculcate certain of the attitudes thought to be important at Haileybury; and it did this through military training. The Club was in fact 'D' Company of the First Cadet

Battalion of the Queen's (Royal West Surrey) Regiment, and to join the Club was to join the junior section of the Territorial Army. The adults who ran the Club took volunteer commissions, and were the Company officers. Discipline, team work, and a sense of belonging.

Attlee, who was physically small, emotionally shy and reserved, and always in his younger days lacking in confidence, began to find fulfilment in his new responsibilities; and he went much further than administrative and charitable good works. He first joined the Fabian Society, but his education and training within the labour movement only began when he became active in the Stepney branch of the Independent Labour Party. Of all the Labour prime ministers of the twentieth century Attlee had the most sustained experience of grass-roots politics. He spoke constantly at street corners, stood at dock-gates collecting money during the Irish Transport Workers' strike of 1913, led marches of protest to the local Boards of Guardians, carried banners 'from the Mile End Waste across central London to Hyde Park', and above all, since this was the biggest problem of the London ILP, tried to get closer to the trade unions and their members. Attlee, like a number of his middle-class generation, was appalled at the waste and the dirt and the misery and the exploited labour that he saw around him. He was influenced by Ruskin and the romantic ideas of William Morris; and in the condition of the early twentieth century he came to accept the untheoretical labour-socialist rhetoric of mainstream ILP politics.[3] In 1922, in what was to be his most radical period, he expressed his political creed in his address for the general election:

> Like many of you I took part in the Great War in the hope of securing lasting peace and a better life for all. We were promised that wars should end, that . . . the men who fought the war would be cared for, and that unemployment, slums and poverty would be abolished. I stand for *life against wealth*. I claim the right of every man, woman and child in the land to have the best life that can be provided. Instead of the exploitation of the mass of the people in the interests of a small rich class, I demand the organisation of the country in the interests of all as a co-operative commonwealth in which land and capital will be owned by the nation and used for the benefit of the community.[4]

These were the ideas, sentiments and feelings consonant with the majority of the new-style Labour Party after 1918; and like so many of his time, once living standards improved and the biting poverty of the early twentieth century was largely eliminated, the socialist commonwealth dreamed of in youth became easily identified with the welfare state of the third quarter of the century.

Two days after war was declared in August 1914 Attlee enlisted. His brother Tom was a conscientious objector. Attlee was in the Gallipoli campaign and later served in France. He conceived it his duty to fight, apparently with no doubts at all, and he engaged in war with the same unemotional approach that he brought to his active political life. He ended his Army service as a major, and, as was common in the inter-war years, was often referred to as Major Attlee. When the war ended he returned to Stepney, and to Labour politics. A former member of the Haileybury Club became his batman/valet/house-keeper. Attlee was elected the first Labour Mayor of Stepney (1919–20) and stood successfully for Limehouse in 1922, a constituency he continued to represent in Parliament until his resignation in 1955. In the parliament of 1922 MacDonald made him one of his two parliamentary private secretaries, the other being Jack Lawson of the Durham miners. In the 1924 Labour administration Attlee became Under-Secretary to the War Office. His minister was Stephen Walsh, a Lancashire miners' MP who, so the gossip went at the time, 'was entirely unable to conceal his reverence for generals'.[5] In the 1929–31 Government Attlee was not given a post immediately – he was heavily engaged in the drafting of the report of the Simon Commission on India[6] – but after Oswald Mosley's resignation Attlee became Chancellor of the Duchy of Lancaster and then, five months before the Labour Government broke apart, he was transferred to the office of the Postmaster-General.

In January 1922 Attlee had married. His wife was thirteen years younger with no political experience except that derived from a conservative political background. Violet Attlee was never a socialist and later became well-known for her tactless conservative comments on events of the day. It was throughout a notably happy marriage. Attlee had been a lonely young man and he lacked affection and love. Violet was good looking, lively and she adored him. The marriage provided Attlee with a peace of mind and a happiness which must have been of great importance for his political career. At the same time Violet was on occasion something of a liability. She was unhappy at Downing Street when Attlee became Prime Minister, and often resented the time he was away from her. It was understood during Attlee's tenure of office at No. 10 that work would be organised, as far as was possible, in ways that would allow the Prime Minister to spend as much time as possible with his wife. And she was at times a nuisance to the civil servants around Attlee. It may be inferred that her conservative attitudes became more pronounced as she got older. Towards the end of her life she said to her husband's future biographer: 'Most of our friends are Conservative. Clem was never really a socialist, were you darling?', to which Attlee made 'a mildly dissenting noise'; so she added: 'Well, not a rabid one'.[7]

The general election of 1931 reduced Attlee's majority to under 500 but at least he was returned. The other two Labour members of the Stepney constituency were defeated, as, of course, were all the leading Labour ministers of the 1929 Government with the exception of George Lansbury. Attlee was therefore the only other member returned who had any experience of office, and it was this 'accident' of electoral history that had profound consequences for his future career. He became deputy leader in the Commons, and, with

Lansbury and Stafford Cripps, formed the triumvirate who led the forty-six Labour MPs in opposition.

These were years of quite crucial importance for Attlee. He was exceedingly hard-working, and he gained an all-round experience in parliamentary politics that was unusual. Attlee always had a sharper understanding of social questions than Gaitskell, who many years later succeeded him as leader of the Labour Party, and he was in general more radical in his attitudes. He was the only major Labour figure to visit Spain during the Civil War, and he spoke on a hunger marchers' platform in Hyde Park in 1936 at a time when the official movement was still not recognising the communist-led NUWM. This is not to suggest that Attlee moved in any meaningful way to the Left during these years in which so many were radicalised. The statement of his position in *The Labour Party in Perspective*, first published in 1937, in no way differs from the ideas of a decade earlier and it represents succinctly and clearly the strengths and the weaknesses of the Labour socialism of his day.[8] Attlee had become Party leader in 1935 following the resignation of George Lansbury, and he was confirmed in the position after the general election of 1935; and in subsequent years. This period until the outbreak of war in September 1939 was hardly a success story in the history of the Labour Party. Attlee presided over the disavowal of the Unity Campaign and the dissolution of the Socialist League; and in the year following Munich the expulsion of Stafford Cripps, Aneurin Bevan and others of the parliamentary Left. If war had not come and a general election had been held in 1940, the psephologists have calculated that a Tory government would again have been returned.[9]

The years of war were to shape Attlee's ideas and mould his attitudes in ways that allowed him to make the transition from deputy prime minister in a Conservative-dominated coalition, to Labour prime minister in the first peacetime administration, without any political or emotional stress or strain. In the 1930s he could still envisage degrees of sabotage against a Labour administration, and throughout the decade he insisted that the lessons of 1931 showed without equivocation 'that Socialists cannot make Capitalism work'.[10] It was the experience of war-time government, and the workings of war-time controls over the economy, that convinced Attlee of the practicability of the changes he desired. Since his definition of capitalism was untheoretical, the removal of social evils, or their mitigation, was evidence that capitalist society was capable of transformation. Already at the 1943 Labour Party Conference he was asking delegates to note how much had been achieved:

I doubt if we all recognise sufficiently the progress our ideas have made. The British never know when they are beaten, and British socialists never know when they have won.

The most explicit statement of what he now believed possible in the future was made in a letter to Harold Laski in 1944. During the war years Laski had been arguing consistently for more radical action on the part of the Labour ministers who were in the government, and for a more specific commitment to social change when peace came. In a long letter dated 1 May 1944, and typed by himself, Attlee wrote a carefully argued defence of his own position and those of his colleagues: the central argument ran thus:

> Whether the post-war government is Conservative or Labour it will inevitably have to work a mixed economy. If it is a Labour government it will be a mixed economy developing towards Socialism. . . . Although you are a theorist and I am only a working politician, I think I give more and you give less attention to changes of conception than to legislative achievements. For instance, I have witnessed now the acceptance by all the leading politicians in this country and all the economists of any account of the conception of the utilisation of abundance. . . . It colours all our discussions of home economic policy. There follows from this the doctrine of full employment. . . . Take again the whole concept of State planning and the control of the financial machine by the Government and not by the Bank of England and the City. Here again I see the change since the days of 1931. In my time in our movement, now getting quite long, I have seen a lot of useful legislation, but I count our progress much more by the extent to which what we cried in the wilderness five and thirty years ago has now become part of the assumptions of the ordinary man and woman. The acceptance of these assumptions has its effects both in legislation and administration, but its gradualness tends to hide our appreciation of the facts.[11]

This identification of social welfare legislation and full employment with the road to a socialist State has become embedded within the understanding of the labour movement in Britain; and no period of its history was more powerful in its influence than the years of the Attlee administrations. When the general election of 1945 produced an overwhelming victory for the Labour Party, it was generally accepted that Labour's stated objectives could now be achieved and indeed nationalisation of the basic services and an advanced social welfare programme were put on the statute book within the first three years of office. The legislation represented a considerable instalment of economic and social reform; in particular the introduction of the National Health Service was the most advanced of any of the major industrial countries, and the nationalisation of the basic industries offered the opportunity of modernising the economic infra-structure within which private enterprise operated. At the same time full employment continued; the demobilisation of the armed forces and the transition to a peace-time economy was carried through with remarkably little friction, and between 1946 and 1950 industrial production increased by fifty per cent. There was also a minor redistribution of income, although the details are still a matter of debate.[12] As Attlee had predicted in his letter to Laski, it was a mixed economy with leanings towards a more equitable society: an advanced liberal state but with economic power, measured by the ownership of capital, still in the hands of capitalists and landlords. By the end of the 1940s, there was a choice of two roads for the Labour Government to follow: either a further extension of State ownership with the introduction of popular control and democratic measures which had so far not taken place; or a standstill on what had so far been achieved, the process of 'consolidation' as it was termed. It was the latter which was chosen and it was therefore only a matter of time, given the inherent tendency of capitalist society to generate inequality, for the momentum of change, begun after 1945, to be reversed.

The complicated reasons why the Attlee administration began seriously to falter in its final years have many times been discussed but too often in isolation one from the other. What has habitually been ignored, or where noted misunderstood, is the crucial relationship between foreign and domestic policies, and the ways in which domestic questions were integrally connected with issues of power emerging from the self-interest of the leading countries in the post-war years. It is, inevitably, a many-sided and intricate story in which, from the British side, Attlee exercised a critical role that has sometimes been missed and most often under-estimated.

The story must begin with the consensus in foreign affairs established during the Churchill coalition and carried over, unchanged, into the era of the post-war Labour governments. This agreement on foreign politics was a new departure – or largely a new departure – for the Parliamentary Labour Party as well as for the broader labour movement. The radical tradition in Britain has mostly been critical of the Conservative Party and the Establishment generally in foreign affairs. In the twentieth century the Boer War, the growth of armaments before 1914, the alliances with Tsarist Russia, the secret diplomacy of the pre-1914 years, the luke-warm attitude towards the League of Nations, the failure to oppose Japanese aggression from the early 1930s, the German–Italian intervention in Spain, and the whole policy of appeasement of the Fascist Powers – in all these matters the greater part of the labour movement found itself in sharp opposition to the Tories. Naturally there were exceptional periods and events, of which the First World War was the most obvious, and naturally also the movement always divided itself into right, centre and left groupings; but it was only during the Second World War, and the years that followed, that basic agreement with the Tories was accepted by the Labour leadership, supported by the majority votes of the right-wing trade unions at Party conferences. Whatever the equivocations of the pre-1939 decade – and they were many – there was nothing comparable with the accord on fundamentals that emerged after 1940.[13]

Attlee had gained a great deal of working experience of foreign policy issues during his long years on the Opposition front bench in the years after 1931. At the beginning of the Second World War he was certainly among the most knowledgeable of all his Labour colleagues; and in Churchill's Coalition Government – for five years from the spring of 1940 – he was a member of the three leading committees upon which the conduct of the war depended: the War Cabinet, the Defence Committee, and the Lord President's Committee, this last being responsible for the civil side of the war. Attlee was deputy-chairman of the first two, and from September 1943 chairman of the third. He was the only member of the Cabinet who sat on all three committees, and alone of Churchill's colleagues he remained throughout a member of the War Cabinet. He was formally designated Deputy-Prime Minister in February 1942, although he had always taken the chair for Churchill, when necessary, from the beginning of the new government. Apart from the eighteen months from February 1942 to September 1943, when he was Dominions Secretary, Attlee had no departmental responsibilities, and he was to be found on committees over the whole range of the war effort. He was a good committee man, and an experienced and efficient chairman. Churchill's many absences from Britain meant that Attlee was at the centre of decision-making since Churchill was punctilious in referring back all important issues to the War Cabinet. No more exacting, and rewarding, apprenticeship for his own leader-ship in the post-war period could have been devised. As he later wrote in his unimaginative and not very revealing memoirs, *As It Happened*:

> Although I became Prime Minister at a time of great difficulty for this country, and in the midst of all the international problems which arise at the end of a world war, I was, in other ways, very fortunate. With only a short intervening period, I had been in office for five years. I had been Deputy-Prime Minister and was therefore acquainted not only with all the outstanding problems, but with the course of events out of which they had developed. I had had a full experience of high and responsible office, understood the machinery of government, and knew personally the leading figures in the Civil Service and in the Fighting Services.[14]

There are some central issues to be considered within Attlee's general position on foreign affairs in the war and post-war years. On most major questions he agreed with Eden and Bevin. With the former he had developed a special relationship during the Coalition years, mainly as a counterweight to Churchill. There were, of course, differences of emphasis between all three but there were no fundamental divergences of opinion; nor, indeed, were there any unbridgeable differences between the leaderships of both major political parties in the Coalition. As Attlee wrote to Churchill during the summer of 1945, he accepted continuity in foreign policy on 'the main lines we have discussed together so often'[15] and as Bevin said in his concluding remarks in the House of Commons debate on 20 August: 'The basis of the Government's policy is in keeping with that marked out by the Coalition Government.'[16] On Germany it was what became known in Whitehall as 'Attlee's Plan' which provided the starting point for post-war policy.[17] Independence for India was, of course, a major issue on which a Churchill government would almost certainly have acted differently, and Bevin was among those in his own Cabinet who trailed behind Attlee in appreciation of the problem.[18] In his attitude towards the Soviet Union Attlee underwent an interesting if not uncommon change of front. He had paid his first visit to Russia in 1936, and while conscious of the effectiveness of the propaganda machine upon foreign visitors as well as on domestic opinion, his general impressions were favourable. Even after the Nazi–Soviet Pact, which led so many to revise sharply their opinions, Attlee took some time before he began to exhibit the anti-Sovietism prevalent in Whitehall. When Russia invaded Finland he rejected the hysteria of much contemporary opinion, and declined firmly the appeals of his French socialist colleague, Léon Blum, who was in favour of assisting the Finns at all costs, even if it meant war with Russia.[19] At this time Attlee always insisted upon the struggle against Hitler and German fascism as the central issue, and it was his recognition of Churchill as the best qualified man to guide Britain in that struggle that led Attlee, without any doubts, into the Coalition Government of May 1940.

Attlee was now at the centre of the British administration, and a stream of intelligence reports, surveys and specialist appraisals of the world situation became his staple reading. His intellectual and political attitudes, and the changes in them, are not easy to delineate precisely. Attlee was not a clubbable person, and he appears seldom in the wartime diaries and memoirs of his contemporaries. He was much overshadowed by Churchill and greatly underestimated by most of those who composed the administrative and military élites in Whitehall.[20] From his later statements, as well as from certain of his decisions during the war itself, it is probable that he developed a steadily accumulating hostility to the Soviet Union. It would have been surprising if that had not been the case, but more striking – a matter which will be described in detail – was a growing recognition of the diminishing status of Britain within the context of the power politics emerging in the last years of the war. About that there is no doubt. It was his attitude towards the Soviet Union that is more difficult to identify in any generalised fashion. He was against the Finnish 'adventure', but when Eden returned from Moscow with Stalin's demands for the recognition of the 1941 boundaries, Attlee vigorously opposed Beaverbrook who argued strongly for their acceptance. Such an agreement, he insisted, would be incompatible with the principles for which the war was being fought. No doubt the personality of Beaverbrook also entered his judgement, for Attlee hated him. In 1959 when he was asked for an appreciation of Beaverbrook after the latter's death, Attlee refused: 'He was the only evil man I ever met. I could find nothing good to say about him.'[21] In the summer of 1943 Attlee had no difficulty in accepting the Foreign Office view that it was necessary to keep Russia out of the Italian negotiations.

Anti-Sovietism was hardly a new sentiment among the decision-making élites in Whitehall, as the previous chapters in this volume have underlined;

and it became just as common among most leading Labour politicians as with their Conservative contemporaries. After the first few months of office the dogma of anti-Sovietism had fastened upon all the Labour personalities who were involved in foreign affairs in the British Cabinet, with Attlee the only partial exception. Harold Nicolson had a most revealing entry in his diary for the late summer of 1946, in which he recorded Jebb, Oliver Harvey and Hector McNeil 'distressed' by a talk Nicolson had recently given which suggested that 'There is much to be said for the Russian point of view.'[22] Nicolson had earlier quoted A.V. Alexander in a similar opposition to this approach. There was something of the Nicolson argument in Attlee's challenge to the unanimous opinion of the administrative and military groups at the top levels of Whitehall's hierarchy: a challenge to the concept of Great Britain as one of the world's Great Powers. The Great Power thesis continued throughout the years of the Labour governments to dominate strategic appraisals of the world after war, imparting a desolating influence upon the British approach to the politics of the post-war world. No one except Attlee was prepared to consider the problems in the serious terms that were required. Moreover, Attlee's own heresy in these matters has been almost ignored until the most recent years; and for at least thirty years after 1945 it came to be the received wisdom that Attlee had given Bevin a completely free hand in most areas of foreign policy.[23] When Michael Foot published the second volume of his biography of Aneurin Bevin in 1973 he emphasised the close political and personal relationship between Attlee and Bevin: 'In any dispute Attlee would invariably side with Bevin and the Defence Ministers against all comers.'[24] Foot was himself a leading figure in the opposition to Bevin's foreign policy in the immediate aftermath of war, and although Nye Bevan died in 1960 Foot had been on intimate terms with him and he also talked at length when writing the biography with Bevin's widow, Jennie Lee. The absence of any suggestion in Foot's biography that Attlee had serious criticisms of certain aspects of Labour's foreign policy was significant. It meant that no one at the time had any knowledge of the conflict of ideas, and that Whitehall in those days could contain secrets within its own corridors. When the relevant official papers began to be made available in the 1970s the story slowly emerged; but in the Harris biography of 1982 and in Bullock's third volume published a year later, the full story of Attlee's critical stance was not yet recounted.

Attlee's criticisms of British strategic thinking must have been maturing in his mind during at least the last year of the war. A ministerial committee on Armistice Terms and Civil Administration had been established in August 1943, and in the following November Attlee re-wrote its terms of reference. He was chairman, and in April 1944 it continued as the Armistice and Post-War Committee (APW), which became increasingly important as a clearing house for the many problems that inevitably proliferated as the war was obviously coming to an end. Attlee seems first to have gone on record in the early spring of 1945.[25] As noted in Chapter 1, he was chairman of the Suez Canal Committee, which, in opposition to Eden's proposal that defence of the Canal be vested in Britain 'in perpetuity' and the whole area administered 'as to facilitate the exercise of HMG's defence responsibilities', argued that it was desirable on general grounds that there should be international control, and that if this was admitted then there should be a sharing of the defence burden. The memorandum ended by referring the problems to the Cabinet for instructions[26] and was signed by Attlee as chairman. The argument was repeated by Attlee in his capacity as chairman of the Armistice and Post-War Committee on 12 April where it was noted again that the United States could be associated with Britain in the area of defence.[27]

The Chiefs of Staff had already made their protest against Attlee's proposition but the detailed argument of the Foreign Office was provided in a memorandum submitted by Eden on 13 April 1945 to the Cabinet.[28] The views expressed by Eden were to remain the guidelines for future policy after Bevin became Foreign Secretary, and their reproduction here will indicate the absence of any change in fundamental thinking on strategic issues. The Empire was assumed inviolate; the experience of two world wars had clearly reinforced the importance of the lines of communication through the Mediterranean, and while a world organisation was no doubt desirable, it was not a development that could be relied upon to safeguard Britain's special interests. Paragraphs four to six contained the core of the analysis:

> The Middle East area . . . is the meeting place of two continents, and, if Turkey is added, of three. It is thus one of the most important strategic areas in the world . . . a matter of life and death to the British Empire . . . [as two world wars have shown]. Consequently, we are bound to give the Middle East an extremely high priority . . . we cannot afford to resign our special position in the area . . . and allow our position to be dependent on arrangements of an international character.
>
> Secondly, the Middle East is the sole large source of oil outside America which is available to us. Recent studies indicate that in ten years time neither the British Empire nor even the United States will be able to exert their full war effort in case of need without the oil supplies of the Iraq–Persian Gulf area.
>
> There is a further consideration. The quality which the Middle Eastern peoples recognise above all others is strength [and an invitation to other Powers to share responsibility would be construed as 'abdication'].
>
> The position of the United States in relation to the Panama Canal is identical with our own in relation to the Suez Canal, as is the position of Russia with regard to certain areas of Eastern Europe. . . . I recommend then, to my colleagues that, pending the establishment of the world organisation and its Military Staff Committee, His Majesty's Government should secure the vital interests of the British Empire and Commonwealth in the Middle East by its own means.

The memorandum ended by noting that it would certainly help if Australia and

New Zealand offered practical assistance, and this, it needs to be remarked, was a not uncommon plea during the next few years. The response from both countries was steadily negative.

There were no further discussions of importance between the two opposed views until the Potsdam Conference of July 1945. The Coalition Government had dissolved at the end of May and Churchill had formed an interim administration. The general election was held on 5 July but because of the services' votes the result would not be declared until 26 July. Attlee flew out to Potsdam with Churchill and Eden on 15 July, and the opening session of the three-power conference, with Stalin and Truman, was held two days later.[29]

There had been various reports and notes concerning the Russian attitude towards the Montreux Convention of 1936 in the months preceding Potsdam, with Turkish diplomats round the world raising the question of the Straits in a general anti-Soviet way.[30] When Eden met Molotov on the evening of 16 July to discuss matters of the agenda and procedure at the Conference, Molotov spent some time on the various issues affecting Turkey and the Soviet Union, and Eden was sufficiently alarmed at the Russian attitude that he sent a minute to Churchill explaining his disquiet: a document important enough for him to reprint it in his memoirs.[31] Eden began the memorandum to Churchill: 'You mentioned in conversation yesterday that Russian policy was now one of aggrandizement. This is undoubtedly true.' What needs emphasising in the long quotation given below, which contains the nub of Eden's argument, are the assumptions that the Russians not only had the desire for unlimited expansion but the logistical means whereby their aims could be achieved. These are themes which run though all the Foreign Office discussions of the next few years, and it led at times to long-range predictions of Russian expansionism which on occasion bordered on the hysterical. Bevin, as will be seen, was easily influenced in these directions.

To return to Eden's communication. In paragraph 4, he wrote:

> All this brings me to the question of Russian access to the great seas. I know that you feel that her demands in this respect are just, and personally I agree with you that there is no reason why Russia should not be allowed free access to the Mediterranean. At the same time, I feel that it would be unwise to speak about this to the Russians at this meeting. We told them before that we were in favour of revising the Montreux Convention. What has been their response? To make other demands on Turkey which could result in placing Constantinople under Russian guns and would probably be the first stage in the subjection of Turkey to Russia. One must also remember that while we agree that the Russians should be free to enter the Mediterranean, they have not yet freedom to get out of it. Having achieved what they desire about Turkey, Russia's next request may be for a position at Tangier where they may give us much more trouble. And is their interest in the Lebanon a first stage to an interest in Egypt, which is quite the last place where we want them, particularly since that country with its rich Pashas and impoverished fellahin would be a ready

prey to Communism? If we were to talk generously to the Russians this time about access to the wider oceans, I fear that they would only regard it as an indication that we had not been shocked by their demands on Turkey and would proceed to make more and more demands on Persia and other countries in the Middle East.

Copies of the Eden minute were sent to Attlee and Ismay, the latter for the Chiefs of Staff. Attlee replied the next day[32] and attacked the basic assumptions upon which the Eden arguments were founded. He had two main points. The first was that no serious attention was being given to the possibilities of international control under the United Nations; and the second that the whole strategic argument about the Middle East was based upon 'an obsolete conception of imperial defence derived from the naval era' at a time when air warfare had now revolutionised defence strategy. Moreover, Eden's memorandum assumed 'a world of potentially warring great powers' (and Attlee clearly did not at this stage) and further no account seemed to have been taken of the economic and financial burdens involved. Eden did not reply until 23 July but when he did it was remarkably emollient. He noted, no doubt as a matter of course, that 'we cannot unfortunately assume that Russian policy has developed to the point where they are prepared to participate in a genuinely international security system rather than to pursue their own national interests'; and then proceeded to explain why the UK must continue to maintain its 'special position' in places like Gibraltar and the Suez area.[33]

On the same day Attlee wrote to Churchill.[34] It must be assumed that this was after receiving the minute from Eden although the editor of the British documents series places his letter before the reply by Eden to Attlee's communication of the 18th. If Attlee did write his minute to Churchill after he had read Eden's note to himself, he presumably concluded that he was not likely to get any further with Eden, and that Churchill ought to be apprised of his views. His arguments to Churchill must therefore be carefully evaluated and indeed they represent a major revision of the attitudes common to the Foreign Secretary and his permanent officials.

Attlee began by asking Churchill to look at the Middle East situation from the Russian point of view, noting that her weakness in the past had allowed other powers to gain strategic positions.

> We, in our own interests, have for long controlled the Mediterranean route which we considered vital to our interests. For this reason we hold Gibraltar and have taken part in the international control of Tangier. We, with the French as junior partner, have had in our hands the Suez Canal. Egypt, from the Russian point of view is a British satellite.

The situation now was different, and the Russians were clearly not willing to accept the results of the power politics of the past:

> It appears to me that the present demands on Turkey, the possible request for a share of the Mandate in the former Italian colonies in North Africa, the raising of the Tangier question and perhaps also the interest displayed in Syria and the Lebanon and Russian policy in Persia are all expressions of the determination of Russia to assert an equal right to have free access to the oceans and to be in a strategic position to enforce this right if necessary. This is not unnatural in the second greatest power in the world. For us to claim a voice in the settlement of the regime in the Straits is to invite a demand by Russia for a share in the Mediterranean exits and for strategic bases in those areas.

Attlee then continued to stress that we were living in a new world situation. We would not, in his opinion, get much support from the USA, and that country would never relinquish their control over the Panama Canal. But the world strategic situation had been transformed by the new dimensions of air power and the old strategic areas 'have today only a relative importance'. The only way, Attlee concluded, by which the new Russian demands could be met was within the context of the general world organisation for peace, and we should be seriously considering constructive proposals for discussion when the United Nations organisation came into being.[35]

This memorandum to Churchill must have been circulated among the top decision-makers the same day because Admiral Andrew Cunningham, the First Sea Lord, wrote in his diary entry for 23 July 1945 that Attlee 'has apparently written what appears to be a damned silly letter to the PM saying we ought not to oppose a great country like Russia having bases anywhere she wants them. What an ass!'[36] No other comment seems to have been recorded and there was no reply from Churchill. He and Attlee flew back to London on 25 July to await the results of the general election on the 26th. Attlee and Bevin then arrived back in Berlin on Saturday 28 July, and, with Attlee's views on Middle East strategy already on record, as Prime Minister he could now no longer be ignored. It was, of course, a situation that was wholly unexpected, and the next month or so was to exhibit the Foreign Office at its most effective when confronted with certain basic ideas which challenged their fundamental assumptions.

As we have seen, the Foreign Office soon discovered that Bevin could be wholly relied upon and senior officials were already making approving noises about him before they left Potsdam; but it was not sufficient to have the Foreign Secretary on your side, important though that was. They had learned during the war that Prime Ministers can over-rule the Foreign Secretary and his advisers, and there had, therefore, to be a mobilisation of all possible forces against this new heresy advocated by such a key personality at the centre of power. It was begun by Gladwyn Jebb with a memorandum dated 29 July 1945 – the day after Attlee arrived back at Potsdam – and written by Jebb while still in Berlin where he was a member of the British delegation. It was a long document whose purpose was to alert the Foreign Office and the Chiefs of Staff to the entirely new problems to which they now had to address themselves.[37] He began: 'The attached exchange of minutes between Mr Eden and Mr Attlee raises issues of the greatest importance and affects our entire foreign policy'; and he summarised Attlee's position:

> The Prime Minister suggests:
> a) that apart from other considerations, we are not in a position to resist a Russian claim physically to dominate the Straits and an attempt to place herself in a strategic position to enforce her right to have 'free access to the oceans'; and
> b) that if these objectives on the part of the Russians were obtained they would have 'only a relative importance in the light of modern war conditions now that air power transcends all frontiers and menaces all home-lands'.
> He also suggests that, in view of our economic position, we may not ourselves be able to continue to be solely responsible for the defence of the Suez Canal area and Singapore.

The first comment that needs to be made about Jebb's translation of Attlee's views is that he produced the most narrow version of the arguments that could be deduced from the original statements. Attlee was not offering a hard and fast declaration of policy; he was raising questions and asking that the situation in general and in particular should not be pre-judged in terms of the strategic conceptions of the past. Further, he was also suggesting that the newly established World Organisation might be involved in the control of sensitive strategic areas round the world; and he had ended his letter to Churchill with the plea 'that we should be ready with constructive proposals suitable to the new conditions of the world in which we have to live.'[38]

Jebb, after summarising Attlee's position in the quotations given above, then proceeded at considerable length to draw out the political conclusions from Attlee's approach. Jebb formulated a number of questionable propositions which henceforth were to become standard arguments against Russian policy: among them the consequences of Russian bases in the Straits. Jebb argued, and it was from this time taken as axiomatic, that the physical control of the Straits by Russia would mean the establishment of Bulgarian- or Yugoslav-type governments in Greece and Turkey. Jebb further noted that 'one of the weak points in our case' was that our opposition to Russian bases in the Straits had to be put alongside 'our present position in the Suez Canal'; and that if we wanted a showdown, in terms of refusing the Russians their demands while still insisting upon British rights in the Canal area, this could only be achieved with American support. Jebb covered his own position by emphasising that his paper was only setting out the problems, but the anti-Russian thrust of his analysis was quite plain; and he brought the arguments to a sharp point when he concluded by urging that the Chiefs of Staff should offer their opinions on all the fundamental questions involved in Attlee's attempted recasting of British strategy. It was a thoroughly sensible suggestion to his senior colleagues. The Foreign Office needed allies and there would be no more useful associates than the Chiefs of Staff, whose comprehension of the future was apparently entirely limited by their experiences of the past. Jebb ended his memorandum:

> The Chiefs of Staff, should be asked, as a matter of urgency:
> a) to re-examine the question of the possible establishment of Russian bases in the Straits (and the consequential establishment of pro-Russian Governments in Greece and Turkey) in the light of the Terminal [i.e. Potsdam] discussions and of the considerations advanced in paragraph 7 of this paper;
> b) to state what exactly would be likely to be the military effect of the establishment of Russian bases in the Baltic (1) with and (2) without the establishment there of corresponding British bases;
> c) to produce in rough outline the kind of 'special agreement' which we, together with our four principal Allies, might be prepared to make with Security Council;
> d) to indicate in detail the way in which, as they see it, the Military Staff Committee ought to function.

Cadogan minuted on Jebb's paper: 'This must be dealt with in the F.O. Sir O. Sargent shd first see this paper. A.C. July 30, 1945.'

There was no doubt a good deal of discussion within the Foreign Office, of which there is no written record; but the Middle East, reckoned by all to be of crucial strategic importance, must have been seriously analysed and discussed. In August 1945 the post of Minister Resident in the Middle East, occupied in the later stages of the war by Sir Edward Grigg (Lord Altrincham), was closed down. It had been a wartime appointment, had contributed much to the economic organisation of the Middle East as a whole, and was disliked by most of the diplomats and their colleagues in London.[39] This closure of the Middle East Supply Centre was just the Foreign Office re-asserting itself. Much more significant was the decision to bring representatives of all the missions and embassies in the Middle East to London for a major conference; and this must be understood as an initiative to counter the Prime Minister's criticisms of Middle East policy and strategy. By Foreign Office or Whitehall standards in general the conference was a hastily and ill-prepared affair, and there were indications of its inadequate preparation. On 24 August 1945 Pierson Dixon sent a memorandum to Orme Sargent, written as from the Secretary of State, announcing the convening of a conference of all the political representatives of the Middle Eastern countries, and setting out the heads of discussion: military, financial, medical services, economic development. Bevin was already dominated by two major themes: one was the defence of the Middle East by a confederacy of the Arab nations, and the other the economic development of the whole region with British assistance. On this latter, he wrote in the memorandum to Orme Sargent that 'we should consider also measures of social advancement which would improve trading conditions. In general, I am anxious that our Middle East policy should be such that the Russians are not given opportunities to criticise it'; and he added that he would preside over some of the meetings himself.[40]

In the spring of 1945 the British Commander-in-Chief in the Middle East had set down his ideas on the general problem of defence of the Middle East in the post-war era. He too had suggested a confederacy, although Bevin did not see his paper until after his own document had been sent from his Private Office; but after a personal discussion with Paget on the morning of 30 August 1945, and after reading Paget's memorandum, Bevin minuted: 'Ack. this. Please study this and I want this view discussed at M/East conference.' The argument Paget was making referred to the need for a shift from an emphasis upon British interests to the united interests of the Arab states in the region. If we adopt, he wrote:

> a different line of approach and instead of basing our demands on British interest we base them on the interests of all member states of the Middle East, including ourselves, there is, I suggest, a much better chance of getting what we wanted. The states of the Middle East would then feel that they have a common interest with us, as we have with them, in providing the security of the Middle East as a whole, or any member state.

He then proposed a confederacy of all the Middle Eastern States except Persia, 'which is already partially a Russian sphere of influence'. He recognised that in some cases the individual State might be too poor to be able to provide all the military requirements that were necessary; in which case Britain would, of course, make up deficiencies:

> If, as in the case of Egypt, a State cannot afford all that it requires in the way of defence, we should make up the deficiency; thus, we should guarantee adequate air defence, and in return Egypt would guarantee to provide the necessary facilities, and similarly in regard to naval forces and facilities.[41]

Two days after Dixon informed Orme Sargent of the proposed Conference, telegrams were sent to all the Middle East missions, and in the same file there is a note of meetings of top-level civil servants under the chairmanship of Sir Edward Bridges on the general organisation of affairs in the Middle East following the abolition of the post of Minister Resident. On 28 August the Cabinet were circulated with a one-page statement from the Foreign Secretary explaining the purposes of his Middle East conference:

> In particular, I would like my colleagues to consider the fundamental question whether we are to continue to assert our political predominance in the Middle East and our over-riding responsibility for its defence, or whether, alternatively, it was

thought to be essential on financial and manpower grounds that we should seek the extensive assistance of other Powers in the defence of the Middle East. The question was raised some weeks ago in connection with the problem of the defence of the Suez Canal (see Cabinet Paper W.P. (45) 197 of the 20th Cabinet in W.P. (45) 256).

His second main point related to Bevin's aspirations for a new economic policy 'which would benefit the common people'.[42]

It must be noted that Bevin and his advisers went back to the Attlee statement of early spring, and Eden's reply on 13 April, the original statements of the opposing positions. The Cabinet, of course, accepted Bevin's paper. In the meantime, the Joint Planning Staff of the Chiefs of Staff had produced a report which emphasised the importance of Cyrenaica to Britain within the defence structure of the Middle East; and four days later, on 24 August, a joint memorandum from Bevin and George Hall, the Colonial Secretary, argued the case for a British trusteeship for Cyrenaica, a matter which would automatically appear on the international agenda when the future of the Italian colonies was considered. The strategic reasons for control of Cyrenaica, which was the eastern part of what today is Libya, were that Britain had to dominate the eastern Mediterranean and thereby prevent any threat to Egypt and the Suez Canal such as had occurred in 1942. The Bevin–Hall memorandum provoked a reply from Attlee on 1 September, written in such blunt and vigorous language that it sent shock waves round Whitehall. Attlee began:

I am not satisfied with the arguments and conclusions as to the future of the Italian Colonies put forward by the Foreign and Colonial Secretaries. . . .

Quite apart from the advent of the atomic bomb which should affect all considerations of strategic area, the British Commonwealth and Empire is not a unit that can be defended by itself. It was the creation of sea-power. With the advent of air warfare the conditions which made it possible to defend a string of possessions scattered over five continents by means of a Fleet based on island fortresses have gone. . . .

Apart from strategic considerations, I can see no possible advantage to us in assuming responsibility for these areas. They involve us in immediate loss. There is no prospect of their paying for themselves. The more we do for them the quicker we shall be faced with premature claims for self-government. We have quite enough of these awkward problems already.

Cyrenaica will saddle us with an expense that we can ill afford. Why should we have to bear it? Why should it be assumed that only a few great Powers can be entrusted with backward peoples? Why should not one or other of the Scandinavian countries have a try? They are quite as fitted to bear rule as ourselves. Why not the United States. . . . [43]

The First Sea Lord noted in his diary that 'The PM misreads the lessons of the war – practically preaches unilateral disarmament and advocates not putting in our claim for trusteeship of Cyrenaica and Great Somalia.'[44]

This document of 1 September remained the basis of the critique by Attlee of the strategic ideas of the COS for the next eighteen months. He was later to enlarge his opposition to include broader political issues, especially on the nature and character of the foreign policy of the Soviet Union. He was, it must be emphasised, alone among the policy-making élites of Whitehall; and there does not seem to have been any support for his approach among the Foreign Office and certainly not among the Chiefs of Staff. Within the Cabinet there was remarkably little comment on foreign affairs. In part, but only in part, this was because on a number of controversial questions, of which Mediterranean strategy was the most important, Attlee preferred to discuss in private. The result was that Attlee's criticisms remained largely unknown to his contemporaries, and for many years after.

Attlee's 1 September memorandum on the Italian colonies was considered by the Cabinet two days later.[45] The minutes of the Cabinet discussions of 3 September summarised first the points made by Attlee, and then those against him; the combined effect is an interesting illustration of the political role played by the writers of the official minutes. This is hardly a new discovery. In the present case the comparison is striking between the 'flatness' of the summary of Attlee's arguments and the more forthright and lively style that Attlee himself had used in his memorandum of 1 September. The conclusions of this Cabinet meeting were that the whole question would be discussed at a later meeting and that the Prime Minister would consider with the Foreign Secretary the procedures to be adopted. A few days later Bevin presented a memorandum to the Cabinet for their immediate consideration. The Council of Foreign Ministers, which was meeting at this time, would be discussing the future of the Italian colonies, and Bevin asked for Cabinet direction. The most important points made were that the expected Russian claim to complete or shared control in any of the former colonies must be resisted, and that the Chiefs of Staff considered it 'essential to obtain strategic facilities in Cyrenaica'. The tone of the memorandum was moderate, with Bevin, in his introduction to the Foreign Office statement, suggesting that 'the wisest course might be to aim at keeping both Cyrenaica and the Somalilands under British military government until the World Organisation had been set up.' Only Shinwell and Aneurin Bevan are recorded as entering dissenting opinions, and the Cabinet agreed to give Bevin authority to pursue the general lines of policy he had outlined to them.[46] The discussion at the Council of Foreign Ministers on the Italian colonies took place on 14 September 1945. The Americans through Byrnes argued for United Nations trusteeship for Libya and full independence after ten years, and there were other suggestions for the East African colonies. Bevin, who spoke next, noted that Libya was two territories – Cyrenaica and Tripolitania – but he was unable to ask outright for a British trusteeship of

Cyrenaica. Such a demand would have taken Britain away from the USA and provided Molotov with a strong case for Tripolitania, for which it was known he was going to ask. So Bevin tried to play for time by asking that the whole question be referred to the Deputy Foreign Ministers, with particular reference to the ways in which the method of trusteeship might be altered if collective trusteeship under the UN did not work. It was not likely, it should be added, that either the Americans or the Russians were unaware of what was in Bevin's mind. When Molotov spoke he argued for individual trusteeship chosen by the UN and put forward a claim for the Russian administration in Tripolitania.

The discussions in the Foreign Ministers' meeting were reported to the British Cabinet the next day, 15 September. The Chiefs of Staff argued their usual position – that Cyrenaica was essential for British security in the Middle East; and when asked by Attlee they made a vigorous case for Somaliland – in their usual style of fighting the next war in terms of the one just finished:

> [Somaliland] was on the long sea route to the Middle East if the Mediterranean were out of our control, and it was also on the short sea route to India, Australia and the Far East. An unfriendly administration installed might be embarrassing to us.

Attlee, however, was able to lean with the Americans and he summed up the Cabinet's agreement to support Byrnes' scheme for collective trusteeship under UN auspices.[47] The matter was not in fact resolved at this time because procedural disputes initiated by the Soviet Union brought constructive discussion and agreement in the Foreign Ministers' Council to an end.[48]

Meanwhile the Middle East Conference had been under way. Its purpose was to re-affirm the traditional role of Britain in the Middle East and in spite of Bevin's so-called 'vision' that objective was achieved. Bevin himself reviewed his ideas in a letter to Halifax in Washington after the Conference was over:

> The benefits of partnership between Great Britain and the countries of the Middle East have never reached the ordinary people, and so our foreign policy has rested on too narrow a footing, mainly on the personalities of kings, princes or pashas. There is thus no vested interest among the peoples to remain with us because of benefits obtained. Hence it is easy for Great Britain to be blamed when difficulties arise.[49]

These were the themes that Bevin had communicated to his Cabinet colleagues at the end of the Conference, in a report of 17 September. His search was for economic and social policies that would promote the 'social betterment of the people of the region'. The United Kingdom would naturally make its contribution, in capital 'where it was needed', in equipment and in expertise.

The general approach was summed up in words that were quoted on a number of occasions: 'peasants not pashas'.[50]

It was nonsense. Britain had large-scale debts in the form of the sterling balances; there were no economic reserves to offer the Middle East; and this approach wholly and completely misunderstood the strength of Arab nationalism. Bevin, it should be noted, continued to cherish these illusions about what could be achieved in the Middle East until the end of his life, which virtually coincided with his position as Foreign Secretary; and no one within the Foreign Office, at the top level at any rate, was prepared seriously to disagree with him. The Treasury were quite a different matter. They were fully informed about the proposed Conference but from the outset made it clear that it must not raise expectations; it had to be remembered, wrote Edward Bridges in a one-page document for the Cabinet circulated before the Conference opened, 'that one of our chief objectives in the immediate future must be to reduce our war expenditure in the Middle East as rapidly as possible. We cannot afford nugatory expenditure in the Middle East.'[51] In a short memorandum to Bridges dated 13 September, one of his colleagues wrote a brief summary of the outcome of the Conference, which clearly he had not found inspiring. He obviously thought the 'visionary' ideas of the Foreign Secretary impracticable and noted that no concrete schemes were in fact suggested. He allowed himself one general comment:

namely, the haste with which the Conference was convened has to my mind made it much less useful than it might have been with better preparation. The proceedings have been rather chaotic, with quite insufficient time to prepare for the agenda of a forthcoming meeting (which often had to consider papers only laid on the table at the beginning of the meetings).[52]

In short, it was a waste of time except – and it is a large exception – that it confirmed Bevin in his belief that the Middle East was of paramount importance to the future of Britain and that within the Middle East everyone agreed that Egypt was the centre-piece of British strategy. In this he was at one with the Chiefs of Staff and his senior colleagues in Whitehall, and it meant that Attlee, if he pursued his critique of British traditional policy, would be met with the united strength of groups of important decision-makers within the administration. Only if Attlee had been prepared to encourage Dalton to use the full strength of the Treasury to oppose a continued large-scale military presence in the Middle East would the Prime Minister's ideas have prevailed; but this option, as discussed later, was not practical politics.

The Ambassador to Egypt was Miles Lampson, Lord Killearn since 1943; and his ideas as well as his general career illustrate markedly what was wrong with British policy in the Middle East and why the British were, in so many areas and quarters of life, detested. Killearn at the September 1945 Conference also demonstrated how reactionary Bevin was at this early stage of his Foreign Office career, since Killearn and Bevin found each other highly compatible. We have a description of Lampson from a diplomat who as a young man was posted to Cairo as Third Secretary and Lampson's Private Secretary. Evelyn Shuckbrugh[53] offers a devastatingly critical appraisal. He once wrote to his father that he was 'treated more or less as a hired footman' by both Lampson and his wife. Lampson, he continued in the same letter, is 'very charming when he wants to be, but entirely oblivious of the lives or interests of his subordinates and expecting everything from them. Nobody who works for him enjoys his *complicity*, if you see what I mean.' When Lampson drove through the streets of Cairo, two motor-cyclists blowing whistles preceded him; and his attitude towards the various Egyptian prime ministers during his many years of office was 'avuncular and overbearing'.

After the opening of the Middle East Conference Killearn wrote in his diary under the date 5 September 1945: 'Bevin in the chair – and very good too. He is energetic, strong, and has progressive ideas about things in general and the Middle East in particular. I *liked* him.'[54] There were similar comments running through the diary throughout the Conference. The last entry in this context was on 13 September when Killearn had an interview with Bevin: 'I like him a lot. Direct, downright and with a *most* pleasing dry humour. I hope I may have "clicked" with him – as he certainly did with *me*.' The simple, basic ideas of this clicking man were revealed when he was removed from the Embassy in Cairo and given a specially created job in South-East Asia. He was one of those diplomats whom even Bevin had to agree to move as soon as it was politically possible; and on 6 March 1946 Killearn produced what he himself described as his 'Swan-Song', which was printed and circulated to the Cabinet. It was a long despatch, beginning with an account of Killearn's tenure of office from January 1934, and including the background to the treaty of 1936 and the events of 1942 which did as much as any one episode to harden nationalist attitudes. Killearn insisted that Britain must remain in Egypt for strategic reasons, and he predicted a political explosion against the ruling monarchy unless economic conditions improved. Killearn had spent seven years in China before he came to Cairo, and as the quotation below illustrates, he had clearly learned nothing from the momentous changes in the world during the second quarter of the twentieth century:

> The Egyptians (he wrote in this memorandum) are essentially a docile and friendly people, but they are like children in many respects. They need a strong but essentially fair and helpful hand to guide them: 'firmness and justice' is the motto for Egypt, just as it used to be for the Chinese.[55]

The idea of a Middle East confederacy for defence continued to impress military circles in Whitehall. A preliminary report by the Joint Planning Staff of the Chiefs of Staff on 18 October concluded that the idea satisfied Britain's strategic requirements subject to rights of large-scale air trooping, and only if the Confederacy 'induces the Egyptians to allow us facilities which they otherwise would not concede'. Some of the minutes from within the Foreign Office were damning. The Confederacy, one said, 'is admittedly little more than a piece of camouflage designed to make the Egyptians less unwilling to play'; and another regarded the proposal as 'impracticable at present', which was Foreign Office wording for trash and twaddle.[56]

Bevin, however, remained impressed and in late October he sent Alan-brooke, the Chief of Imperial General Staff, on a tour of the Middle East to discuss the idea of a Confederacy with its rulers. It was to be part of a world visit which Alanbrooke was making of all the areas in which Britain had commitments. Of the Middle East, he wrote in his diary:

> There was no doubt that the nearer you got to Russia, the greater was the desire for some sort of co-operation in defence. Both Transjordania and Iraq were all for some such plan; it was only Egypt that was so intent on the removal of the Occupation Forces that she refused to look at the advantages to be derived from a Federation.[57]

What Alanbrooke did not appreciate was that the two countries he mentioned in favour of a Confederacy were ruled by Anglophiles regarded as stooges by all Arab nationalists, and as Elizabeth Monroe emphasised in 1961, there was no possibility of conducting an Arab policy 'so long as Britain wanted military privileges in Arab territory'. It was a lesson that Bevin was never to learn.

The Middle East was honeycombed[58] with British military bases, airfields and naval installations. The Suez area was a vast arsenal with 200,000 troops at the end of the war; and numbers were still about 40,000 by the time the Labour Government left office. The 1936 Treaty had specified 10,000. There were constant attempts in the immediate post-war years to find alternative defence centres other than Suez, but none proved viable according to the requirements of the COS. Bevin did nothing to alter the basic approach of his military advisers. His ideas remained unchanged although there was never the possibility of even a small part of their realisation. He had, wrote W.R. Louis, 'an irrepressible optimism', or it may just have been political naivety. Early in 1948, for example, he was remarking that the Russians treated all their different races on the same footing, 'and the result was that they had at their disposal one vast and homogeneous force':

> We should do the same. We must exploit the manpower resources of the Middle East by means of joint defence boards set up under treaties between HMG and each of the States concerned. . . . Thus we should have one great Middle Eastern Army. This was the more necessary now that we could no longer count on India as a manpower reserve.[59]

After the conclusion of the Middle Eastern Conference and the Foreign Ministers' Conference, the argument within Whitehall concerning British strategy in the Mediterranean area tended to die down; and for the remainder of the autumn and early winter of 1945 the leading groups in and around the Government were mainly concerned with Attlee's visit to Truman[60] and the negotiations over the American loan, which included an increasing pressure from the United States on the acquisition of bases for military purposes.[61] There were, of course, continued discussions about the Middle East and the policy élites were fully aware of the attitude that Attlee was taking towards defence problems. The First Sea Lord, Admiral Cunningham, noted in his diary after attending a Cabinet meeting on 15 September that it was 'All packed with the give away the Empire party',[62] and at a later meeting in early October, when manpower problems were under debate, he wrote, again in his diary: 'We were met with the usual arguments from the Prime Minister, who are you going to fight? and the country cannot afford it.'[63] Strategic questions did not, however, become a central matter for Cabinet decision again until early in 1946.

A meeting of the Defence Committee on 21 January 1946[64] to consider manpower problems was attended by Bevin, Morrison and Dalton, the Dominions and Service Ministers and the Chiefs of Staff or their deputies. Attlee was in the chair. Dalton noted that the financial deficit for 1946 would be nearly covered if there were reductions of munitions of £150 million and of half a million men in the forces. Attlee then proposed detailed figures for each of the three services for 30 June and the end of the year. Alexander, for the Navy, said it was more or less impossible for them to accept the reductions proposed, and Attlee replied that 'it was not necessary in present circumstances to have a large fleet ready for instant action, as there was no-one to fight.' Bevin answered the arguments for reductions in the size of the armed forces in what was his usual way. At all similar discussions he argued that any reduction in Britain's military forces would have an immediate impact upon his bargaining power round the diplomatic table. This was his constant theme, and it was used on every occasion when he was required to oppose a curtailment of Britain's military presence. He usually coupled his opposition with the statement that he was, of course, in favour of defence cuts, and that in a few months' or a year's time, when his present policies had worked themselves out, then it would be appropriate to accept reductions. In this meeting on 21 January 1946 Bevin added a comment entirely in line with the general woolliness of his thinking when he moved away from his specific briefs. Attlee had complained that almost the entire burden of defence was carried by the United Kingdom and India, and that the Dominions ought to make some contribution. Bevin answered that he thought the Dominions had begun to reconsider their position as the result of recent events; and 'he would like to see the British

Commonwealth act as a duplicate of the United Nations organisation on a smaller scale': a statement that was quite unrealistic.

A further example of Bevin's attitudes came a month later when once again, on 15 February 1946, Attlee put before his colleagues a summary of his now well-established argument that strategic assumptions concerning the Mediterranean region had to be re-examined, partly because the old assumptions no longer obtained, partly because Britain could not afford the financial burden involved in maintaining its traditional role. Bevin whined away on how the cuts

> faced him with grave difficulties in obtaining the support which he thought necessary as a backing to the Government's foreign policy . . . he asked that their strengths should not be reduced appreciably over the next three months. This would provide him with the necessary strength in the most delicate period, and providing a satisfactory solution was found to his problems he would support reductions in the second half of the year. . . . In answer to a question from the Prime Minister, Mr Bevin said that as he was in the process of the formulation of a Far Eastern policy, he considered it dangerous to weaken our naval forces further at present, as we should not then succeed in influencing decisions in this area to the extent we desired. If all went well, reductions could take place later.[65]

Attlee summed up that there would be no war for two to three years; that the United States would probably be on our side in future crises; that there was no fleet to menace the UK; that the reductions in manpower in the forces as proposed could be accepted although there were some areas where there might have to be postponements; that withdrawals of troops from Europe should be left to as late a date as possible; and that there should be enhanced inducements to skilled men either to stay on or to re-engage. Without Attlee it is unlikely matters would have been pushed along quite so fast, although this is not to suggest that the economic requirements of British society had been fully met.

Two days before this meeting, on 13 February, the Chiefs of Staff had produced a report on the question of the Italian colonies.[66] They had nothing new to say and their paper was a reiteration of all that they had been saying since at least the spring of 1945. All the existing bases in the Mediterranean were needed; 'our military object in the Middle East and Eastern Mediterranean is to maintain our predominant position in that area'; and they quoted Smuts to support their total opposition to all things Russian and their mistrust of Russian intentions.[67]

On 2 March Attlee produced yet another memorandum on 'The Future of the Italian Colonies'[68] directed specifically against the Chiefs of Staff report of 13 February, discussed above. There was little new in substance, except for one quite crucial matter, but the argument in general was perhaps more free-flowing than his previous statements. The new aspect of policy Attlee now included in the discussion related to India, and the measures which were currently being considered as firm steps towards Indian independence. The relevant passage is given below:

> Presumably, the strategic communications which it is suggested we must preserve are those with India, but the position of India is changing. It is not certain whether she will remain within the Commonwealth. She will increasingly have to depend upon her own Armies for her defence. It would appear doubtful if the time saved by the use of the Mediterranean route for the purpose presumably of reinforcing India is worth the cost. It may be suggested that we are specially interested in the oil of South Persia and Iraq, but I suggest that we are not in a position to defend this area from a determined land attack from the North. Our communications with the East Indies and Australasia could be maintained by the use of the Cape route, or, even in the latter case, through the Panama Canal if we have a close understanding with the United States.

It was in this memorandum that Attlee suggested a new way of looking at the strategic position of Britain: 'as an easterly extension of a strategic area the centre of which is the American Continent rather than as a Power looking eastwards through the Mediterranean to India and the East':[69] a concept that was not understood by the Chiefs of Staff, his contemporaries in the Cabinet or the Foreign Office.

Attlee's paper was naturally taken seriously, and with immense misgivings, by the senior officials in the Foreign Office. Gladwyn Jebb began the critique, as he had done in the closing stages of the Potsdam Conference, in a memorandum dated 8 March and addressed to Oliver Harvey, the Deputy Under-Secretary, and Orme Sargent, the Permanent Under-Secretary. The main line of Jebb's argument was that which he had already used earlier but now with much sharper emphasis: namely, that British withdrawal from any part of the Mediterranean and the Middle East could only be followed by the entry of Russia into the power vacuum. Jebb offered a dramatic, not to say hysterical, scenario: pro-Russian governments right along the northern Mediterranean coast, including Spain, at which point France would be unable to resist Soviet pressure. The consequences would be calamitous:

> there would be every chance of our being forced into the position of being, not a client state of America, but a client state of Russia. [In either case] the idea of 'Social Democracy', which represents our own 'way of life' would be snuffed out between the rival forces of Capitalism and Socialism, and our only role would merely be that of the grain [or perhaps the chaff] between the millstones.[70]

The argument that the British way of life lay between the USA and the USSR was going to be heard more of in the next two or three years. This was an early version.

Jebb's comments were followed by those of Oliver Harvey on 11 March. Harvey agreed that if Britain left the Mediterranean area Russia would move in, and 'the Mediterranean would become a second Black Sea sealed at either end.' Moreover, Russian influence would not stop at Europe but would spread southward into Africa. There were 'far weightier reasons' than narrow strategic ones for holding on to the Mediterranean region as an area of influence for Britain. And with these ideas Orme Sargent was in complete agreement:

> Our position as a World Power and therefore as a Great Power depends surely on our maintaining our position in the Mediterranean, and this not for strategic reasons but on political grounds. In other words, the Mediterranean is of vital importance to us not so much because it is our direct link with the East but because if we abandon it in present circumstances the Russians will take our place there with incalculable results not only on the Middle East but also on Italy, France, Spain and Africa.

Orme Sargent ended his minute with the point that if we had to withdraw because of lack of economic and financial strength, then certain consequences would follow inevitably, of which the most important would be that Britain henceforth could only play 'a subordinate part in the affairs of Europe and a still smaller one in the affairs of other Continents'.

Bevin then sent a memorandum to Attlee answering the latter's statement of 2 March 1946.[71] As was usual with most of the documents produced within the Foreign Office and signed by Bevin, the arguments were reproduced either verbatim or were closely related to previous minutes or memoranda of the permanent officials. So it was in this case. Gladwyn Jebb's argument that Britain represented the middle way in world politics was repeated in rather more striking language than in the original:

> The other point which influences me in the European scene is that we are the last bastion of social democracy. It may be said that this now represents our way of life as against the red tooth and claw of American capitalism and the Communist dictatorship of Soviet Russia. Any weakening of our position in the Mediterranean area will, in my view, lead to the end of social-democracy there and submit us to a pressure which would make our position untenable.

The 'red tooth and claw' phrasing was demagogy for the benefit of some of his colleagues in the Cabinet, for Bevin certainly never acted upon this kind of appreciation of capitalist society; nor would he do so in public, because the Foreign Office was now becoming increasingly conscious of the need of dollars and American support in general, and critical comment about the United States was never made. In the remainder of his memorandum Bevin emphasised the power vacuum theory which the permanent officials made so much of, and he also commented upon the need to shift Britain's military centre in the Middle East from Egypt to East Africa: a policy option already discussed by the

COS, and strongly opposed by them. Bevin then continued with one of his 'imaginative' suggestions which helps to illustrate his failure throughout his Foreign Office years to comprehend the nature of Egyptian nationalism. In the event of Britain moving, or threatening to move, its defence centre from Egypt, Bevin wrote, and one must assume this at least was his own idea: 'Egypt may well beg us to stay. It is only because she thinks there is no alternative that she is taking her present attitude.'

The months which followed were much occupied with international conferences, the Palestine problem and a sustained attack upon Bevin's foreign policy from within the Labour Party at home. Inside the Foreign Office the attitudes towards the Soviet Union steadily hardened, with Christopher Warner's memorandum on 'The Soviet Campaign against This Country and Our Response to It' and the formation of the Russia Committee among the most obvious landmarks.[72] The high point of political opposition to Bevin's policies came with the Commons debate of 18 November 1946, to which we have referred in previous chapters. Attlee, summing up for the Government in place of the absent Bevin, made a warm defence of his Foreign Secretary's policy, but only in general terms. It was a highly skilful speech which omitted reference to specific issues; it insisted that it was a united policy of the Cabinet; and above all, that there was no 'ganging-up' against the Soviet Union.[73]

Within a fortnight of this speech Attlee was writing a private letter to Bevin which indicated very clearly that he had been wholly impervious to the arguments of the past months concerning Middle East policy, and that he continued to adhere to his already firmly stated position. The letter was dated 1 December, marked Private and Personal, and typed by Attlee himself.[74] It made some striking and remarkable points, not least concerning the motivations of the Soviet Union in its foreign policy; and it must be quoted at length:

> I think that we have got to consider our commitments very carefully lest we try to do more than we can. In particular I am rather worried about Greece. The Chiefs of Staff are suggesting that we must keep our forces there for at least another year. I cannot contemplate the financial and military burden with equanimity. The political and economic situation in Greece shows no improvement. They seem to be unable to get a satisfactory government nor can they do anything but quarrel amongst themselves. Meanwhile we have to accept a good deal of criticism. I feel we are backing a very lame horse. . . . While I recognise the desirability of supporting the democratic elements in South-East Europe and while I am conscious of the strategic importance of oil, I have as you know always considered that the strategic importance of communications through the Mediterranean in terms of modern warfare is very much overrated by our military advisers, a view which is shared by some Service authorities. I agree wholeheartedly with you that the real line of the British Commonwealth runs through Lagos and Kenya. The Middle East is only an outpost position. I am beginning to doubt whether the Greek game is worth the candle.
>
> I do not think that the countries bordering on Soviet Russia's zone, viz. Greece,

Turkey, Iraq and Persia, can be made strong enough to form an effective barrier. We do not command the resources to make them so. If it were possible to reach an agreement with Russia that we should both disinterest ourselves as far as possible in them so that they become a neutral zone, it would be much to our advantage. Of course it is difficult to tell how far Russian policy is dictated by expansionism and how far by fear of attack by the US and ourselves. Fantastic as this is, it may very well be the real grounds of Russian policy. What we consider merely defence, may seem to them to be preparation for an attack. The same kind of considerations apply to the proposals by the USA for Air bases in Canada which the Russians might regard as offensive in intention.

He ended the letter by asking Bevin to be careful that if America gave economic assistance to Greece and Turkey Britain should not be expected to continue military obligations; and he warned of the American tendency to regard Britain as an outpost which they would not have to defend. On 4 December Hector McNeil cabled Bevin that the Cabinet was going to discuss the policies towards Greece and Turkey. There was, McNeil continued, considerable reluctance to continue British commitments to these countries. Bevin replied that he was shocked, since he had been working under the assumption that support for Greece and Turkey was essential if Soviet policy towards the Straits question was to be withstood: 'Am I now to understand that we may abandon this position? I really do not know where I stand.'[75]

The Bevin papers contain some notes for a possible reply to Attlee's letter which Dixon prepared, but Bevin did not write back to Attlee at this time.[76] He arrived in England after Parliament had risen, and Bevin made his report back by way of a radio broadcast on 22 December 1946. The greater part of his talk consisted of generalities without much meaning, and some were untruths, such as the great desire on the part of the British Government to co-operate with the Soviet Union: a statement that could certainly not be applied to Bevin himself. This was the nadir of Bevin's period of office; and as his biographer notes, if he had retired or died at this time, his record for the previous eighteen months would be regarded as one of failure.[77] This was especially true of the Middle East. Egypt had turned down the Sidqi agreement with Bevin and Palestine was on the edge of civil war.

Bevin's first discussion with Attlee after his return from America was at Chequers on 27 December. It was a private affair, the report of which was communicated by Bevin to Nicholas Henderson of his Private Office and whose summary is in the Bevin papers.[78] Attlee stated that he was in favour of withdrawing troops from Greece and handing the Palestine mandate over to the UN. Bevin countered this latter by saying that he wanted to defer the Palestine decision until he had tried to do a deal with Stalin over Cyrenaica; and he further said that he had it in mind to offer to withdraw troops from

Greece in exchange for the withdrawal of Soviet troops from Bulgaria – somewhat unrealistic propositions.

A few days later Attlee brought together in a formidable paper, dated 5 January 1947, all his criticisms of the Middle East policies favoured by the Foreign Secretary and the COS. He sent it to Bevin with a typically deprecating note: 'I have set down for purposes of clearing my own mind some considerations which have occurred to me on reading the papers on our policy in the Middle East. I enclose a copy in order to inform you of what is in my mind.' Attlee might have added that he was summarising in comprehensive form the arguments he had been using since at least the spring of 1945.[79]

Attlee began with a summary of the position of the Chiefs of Staff: that the United Kingdom was the heart of the Commonwealth, vulnerable to long-range weapons for which at present there was no effective defence. The only possible enemy was Russia, and the only bases from which Russia could be attacked were in the Near East. The United Kingdom must therefore maintain its influence in the region, and there were other, more traditional reasons: the security of oil supplies and the line of communication through the Mediterranean. It followed that there must be a heavy military commitment in the area, and that there must also be political support for the states of the Middle East: Turkey, Greece, Iraq, Persia, Lebanon, Syria, Transjordan; and it would be essential to maintain Britain's position in Palestine. On the other side, since a Soviet offensive was assumed, against both Western Europe and the Middle East, it would be necessary to deny the Russians any bases in the region of the Mediterranean.

It should be noted that Attlee's summary was a fair statement of the general approach of the Chiefs of Staff. It was during 1946 that they had added the argument of the need for bases for purposes of aerial attack against Russia to their long accepted strategic assumptions concerning the life-line through the Mediterranean and the safeguarding of oil supplies from the Gulf states.[80] Attlee introduced his critique of the strategy of the Chiefs of Staff by arguing that Western Europe would grow in economic strength in the coming years and that this would lead to a strengthening of Western democracy and a lessening of international tension. 'I should expect', he continued, 'that the more international tension relaxes the less possible will it be to maintain in the USSR the war mentality and war economy that has persisted since the revolution. The best hope of enduring peace lies in a change in the character of the regime in the USSR.'

Attlee then turned to the Middle East and listed the weaknesses in the military approach. It was a powerful indictment:

5. The countries we have to support in the Middle East if we are to use that area as a potential base against the USSR are weak.

a) Militarily. Only Turkey has a fighting record over any long period. They are industrially backward and lacking in scientific manpower and resources.

b) Industrially. They are backward and will require very large capital developments to be effective units.

c) Strategically. They are ill-placed to resist a strong power, especially Turkey, Iraq and Persia which border the USSR.

d) In population. The whole group, exclusive of Egypt, has less than 50 million.

e) Very vulnerable owing to their social and political composition. Greece appears to be hopelessly divided. In the other countries there is a small class of wealthy and corrupt people at the top and a mass of poverty stricken landworkers at the bottom. Their Governments are essentially reactionary. They afford excellent soil for the sowing of communist seed.

6. Our position is, therefore, made very difficult before the world and our own people. We shall constantly appear to be supporting vested interests and reaction against reform and revolution in the interests of the poor. We have already that difficulty in Greece. The same position is likely to arise in all these other countries.

Attlee then continued to emphasise the financial support that would have to be given to bolster up these weak regimes, and he ended this part of his statement by stating bluntly that he regarded the strategy he had briefly summarised 'as a strategy of despair'. The second and last part of his analysis referred to the position of the Soviet Union, and at the centre of his argument was his plea for a serious and long-searching review, with the Russian leaders, of all the issues at present in conflict. He first drew upon the evidence of history, pointing out that at the end of the nineteenth century Britain was in dispute with France at many points of the world, yet in a short time we had the Entente Cordiale. Similarly, Britain's relations with Tsarist Russia had reached crisis point with the Dogger Bank incident during the Russo-Japanese war, and we were always alarmed at Russian designs in Central Asia. Yet we fought together in the first world war. Is it not possible, asked Attlee, that, given we accept the USSR is not prepared to undertake a major war 'for some years', it might be practicable to explore the possibilities of settlement in Persia or the Dardenelles, and convince Russia that neither the United States nor ourselves have offensive intentions against her? To what extent is the ideology of the present rulers of Russia really committed to the idea of world revolution? The arguments were simply stated, and highly pertinent, and they added up to a persuasive and impressive case for serious negotiations and a more open approach to the Soviet Union.

There was, of course, no possibility that Attlee's cool and rational exposition would be acceptable either to the permanent officials within the Foreign Office or to Bevin himself. By the end of 1946 there was a consensus inside the

Foreign Office that was unshakeable. Communism was a militant ideology and on the rampage whenever and wherever the opportunity presented itself for undermining Western democracy and/or fomenting 'trouble' in the rest of the world. The 'vacuum' theory took no account of logistics; Russia was apparently capable of moving out of Europe and into Africa and the Middle East with its supply and transport problems easily and efficiently solved. There was no basis for serious negotiation in the meaning of the terms that Attlee was using; and so the senior officials began immediately to mobilise once more against the apostate within their midst. Bevin's Principal Private Secretary, Pierson Dixon, quickly arranged a meeting of top officials to discuss the Attlee letter. This was on 8 January, three days after the letter was written. The meeting was made up of Orme Sargent, the Permanent Under-Secretary, Christopher Warner, R.G. Howe, Superintending Under-Secretary of the Egyptian Department, and William Hayter.[81] Dixon had written a paper for the meeting which listed the Prime Minister's 'contentions' and the answers thereto. The general theme of the argument taken as a whole was that withdrawal would be another Munich; that to attempt an agreement now would be 'bidding from weakness'; that it was absurd to contemplate the Middle East as a neutral zone; that even if we accepted our main defence line to be in Central Africa we needed, in the atomic age, a first line of defence; and while it may be true that the Mediterranean was no longer of much use as a communications route in war 'we need to hold it in order to keep others out.' Dixon then summarised his position in the four short paragraphs given below:

1. Effect of withdrawal from Middle East would be disastrous to our position there, in the neighbouring countries, and in Europe.

2. It would lead the U.S. to dispair [sic] of us and thus effectively divide the world into an American and a Russian bloc.

3. This would heighten the probability of world war in which we should be massacred.

4. Even if Russian world domination can be discounted bear will certainly not resist pushing paw into soft places.

In the same file there is a note by Dixon, based upon information supplied by Sir Norman Brook, of the points in the Attlee memorandum that the Chiefs of Staff were taking up. The first of five items listed was the importance of Palestine in the Middle East scheme of defence arrangements, one more example of the political fog in which the military were to be found, given that Palestine was handed over to the United Nations within just over a year. What is striking about the reactions to the Attlee statement is the prompt co-ordination of all the leading groups in Whitehall that were involved in the elaboration of foreign policy (rather than its financial implications). These discussions by the administrators were followed by a long letter from Bevin to

Attlee dated 9 January 1947. Dixon drafted it and Bevin signed.[82] What was being proposed, Bevin wrote early in his letter, 'is a reversal of the whole policy I have been pursuing in the Middle East, with the assent of the Cabinet, since the Government took office'. After his usual commentary on the basic aims of his Middle East policy, namely, 'to develop the Middle East as a producing area to help our own economy and take the place of India', Bevin then continued to expound at length the arguments that Dixon had developed already for his senior colleagues. Munich on a world scale was included in the rebuttal to Attlee. Bevin's letter contained no new ideas of any kind, but was a familiar restatement of what the Foreign Office fervently believed. As such, it is an important document.

This exchange of letters between Attlee and Bevin was followed by a private meeting between Attlee, Bevin and the Minister of Defence (A.V. Alexander). There were no officials present, and no minutes were taken. We know of the meeting from a hand-written note from Pierson Dixon written on 10 January 1947 based upon confidential information supplied by Bevin.[83] As much as possible seems to have been written down by Dixon who then summarised the conclusions of the meeting. It was clear that Bevin had won most of the points discussed, except that Attlee continued to have reservations about the overall plans for Middle East defence, and it was agreed that discussions would continue with the Chiefs of Staff present. What seems to be accepted is that Attlee acknowledged his defeat at this time. At a meeting with the Chiefs of Staff on 13 January the ministers present (Attlee, Bevin and Alexander) endorsed the military view of the Middle East and its defence requirements. Later meetings of the Defence Committee and the Cabinet both accepted only quite small percentage cuts in the size of the armed forces and their financial provision. Dalton gives his version in the last volume of his *Memoirs*[84] but says nothing very specific about Attlee. Some historians have taken the version offered by Montgomery, now Chief of Imperial General Staff, as providing the definitive conclusion for Attlee's apparent change of direction, but there is no evidence except that given by Montgomery, and without corroboration that cannot be accepted without question. What Montgomery alleged was that he persuaded his other colleagues to threaten to resign if their views on 'the necessity to hold the Middle East' were not accepted; and these decisions were communicated privately to the Prime Minister. 'We heard no more about it', wrote Montgomery.[85]

There were other ways of approaching the problem. Whatever political or military decisions might be taken, there had to be both money and manpower to implement these decisions. It was the manpower issue that Attlee was to use in order to modify, if not to nullify, the unyielding positions adopted by Bevin and his advisers. The discussion of the length of service in peace-time began during the spring of 1945. Attlee himself was not opposed to conscription, but he was fully aware of the strength of feeling among his own backbenchers against the concept of compulsory national service. On a number of occasions the PLP had debated the issue of conscription, the first at the beginning of 1946 when Attlee had spoken against a motion which called for the international abolition of conscription. Support for the motion came from pacifists and those who were opposed to the Labour Government's foreign policy. Within the Government, policy decisions slowly coalesced during 1946. By mid September 1946 the Cabinet's Manpower Committee had before them a detailed memorandum from the armed services which argued for an eighteen months' minimum tour of duty, on the basis of national conscription. The arguments against a twelve-month period, especially for the Army, were carefully rehearsed. The Manpower Committee in due course forwarded its own report to the Cabinet, with a firm advocacy for conscription but with no specific recommendation as to length of service. There were, however, detailed calculations relating to the comparative use of manpower in the civil and military sectors; and it was estimated that an eighteen-month conscription period would result in 1952 in an industrial labour deficiency of between 400,000 and just over 800,000. The Defence Committee, chaired by Attlee, was the next stage; and at a two-day meeting, 16/17 October 1946, both conscription and the eighteen-month period of service were recommended. This was accepted by the Cabinet and announced by Attlee in November 1946.[86]

It was not until March 1947 that the relevant legislation was introduced into the House of Commons; but by now many things had changed. Attlee had apparently accepted the Foreign Secretary's general policy towards the Middle East, but through 1947 both the domestic and the world situation were altering rapidly. The year began with a growing coal crisis which turned into catastrophe from 20 January when the worst winter of the century – so far – continued for the next eight weeks. The consequences for manufacturing production and for employment as well as for domestic householders were severe. Abroad, the withdrawal from Greece was announced in February and in the same month the announcement was made of the end of Empire in India later in the year. The debates on conscription[87] reinforced the opposition to compulsory national service against the background of domestic troubles and impending changes in Britain's imperial position. There developed at an early stage considerable opposition to the conscription issue among Labour MPs; and Attlee was presented with a two-fold problem. On the one hand, if he gave way to the critics whose numbers and influence were considerable, he would be accused of weakness of leadership; as indeed became the case. On the other hand, he could use the argument that it was incumbent upon him to listen sympathetically to his own members on matters that they felt deeply about, and this was not a small minority with whom he was concerned. At the same time, a reduction in the length of military service would strengthen his own opposition to the policies of the COS and the Foreign Office in the Middle East. A successful amendment reducing the length of service to twelve months was carried in the House of Commons, and in all subsequent meetings and discussions Attlee consistently opposed any attempts, by the military in particular, to compromise the twelve-month rule.[88]

Britain's position in the world was indeed changing and its decline as a major power was becoming increasingly obvious. As Attlee reported to the Dominion Governments in October 1946, the reductions in British troops abroad meant

> withdrawal from Austria, Trieste, Greece, and Japan; considerable reductions in Middle East (including Palestine), and evacuation of India and Burma, all before 31 March next; also liquidation of all special post-war commitments, except Germany during the following twelve months.[89]

Bevin's policy in the Middle East was now in tatters. Egypt had always been understood to be the key strategic centre of British defence policy in the region. The Egyptians had asked for revision of the 1936 Treaty as soon as the war ended and discussions began in 1946–47 which led to the removal of British troops from installations in the Nile Delta, and their re-establishment, at huge cost, in the Suez zone. The British still had no serious appreciation of the nationalist opposition to their presence and within the next few years mounting terrorism forced the evacuation of the Suez area in 1954. The considerable British garrison in Palestine had been withdrawn in 1948; and with the independence declaration of August 1947, the road to India, the overwhelming reason for the importance of the lines of communication through the Mediterranean, now led to nowhere. As for Bevin's grandiose and wholly implausible ideas for the Middle East to replace India as a food producer, and a reservoir of manpower for a great Middle East army, where were they now? Still, apparently, in the minds of the Chiefs of Staff. In late May 1947 the Chiefs of Staff produced a detailed statement of an overall Defence Policy: 'The Overall Strategic Plan, May 1947' was its official title. It had been a long time in the making. The later years of the war had seen a large number of discussion papers and memoranda, and at the end of the war, with the defeat of Germany and Japan, the emergence of the two super-powers and the decline of Britain as a world power, new thinking and a new appraisal were required. The military consequences of the atomic age were hardly comprehended. The basic requirements of British defence policy in this statement, which was intended to be a definitive policy for the post-war years, were centred upon three basic pre-conditions: the defence of the United Kingdom; the control of communications; and 'A firm hold in the Middle East and its development as an offensive base.' To these three fundamental requirements they added a fourth which, though not essential, 'would give a most desirable addition of strength'. This was the co-operation of India and in particular the opportunities for the development of an offensive base in North-West India against the Soviet Union.

There is little that needs to be said about this statement of May 1947[90] except that it exhibited once again the ways in which the military could only see backwards in time; but one illustration may be given to indicate the realms of illusion within which the Chiefs of Staff dwelt. In their detailed discussion of the Middle East, which they recognised as a 'vital strategic area', were listed the conditions which would be required in order that an effective defence might be provided. A preliminary proviso was the rapid assistance of the United States and Dominions. The four basic requirements were:

(a) We have the right to re-enter Egypt on threat of war and develop the base facilities we shall require there.

(b) We have strategic rights in Palestine in peace.

(c) We retain the sovereignty of Cyprus.

(d) Turkey refuses Russian demands for strategic facilities in peace and opposes Russian invasion of her territory. This will modify the time factor to our advantage.

The Chiefs of Staff added two further desiderata: Greece should remain independent, not least to encourage Turkey to 'stiffen' its attitude towards the Russians; and the British position would be given greater depth if the trusteeship of Cyrenaica were granted.

The historian of the detailed evolution of the British strategy which culminated in the May 1947 Overall Strategic Plan was satisfied, in his concluding pages, that it had been well done. 'One step had followed another in steady sequence until the job was done with a thoroughness not soon to require reversal.'[91] It is not a judgement that can be endorsed. The withdrawal from India was the crucial event in British post-war policy and for at least the next twenty years military strategy failed to comprehend that Britain, in the traditional sense, was no longer an imperial power. 'In the 1950s and 1960s', Correlli Barnett has written, 'British world strategy still followed the basic patterns of the nineteenth century: a chicken that had lost its head – India – but still ran round in circles.'[92] It is an assessment that would be accepted, no doubt in different wording, by most historians.[93]

The large question which remains is to ask why it was that Attlee was unable to impose his ideas upon his Foreign Secretary. Attlee was obviously never satisfied with Bevin's Middle East policies. It needs perhaps to be noted that while he correctly judged the changing strategic situation as well as at least appreciating the possibilities of more serious negotiations with the Russians than Bevin was capable of, he did not lay emphasis upon the potent, bursting forces of Arab nationalism. He was aware, as indeed were most of Whitehall, of the problems that Jewish immigration and a militant Zionism were causing in the Middle East; but whether he recognised, as the Americans did, for example, the bitterness of the Egyptians against the British occupation is not wholly clear. Nevertheless, the question remains, and the answer inevitably is complex.

Attlee was confronted with almost the whole weight of the Whitehall administrative machine. Indeed, as far as is known, he did not have support of any significance for his critical appraisal except from Dalton and the Treasury; and the relations between Dalton and Attlee would have to be more closely examined in this context than has so far occurred. Much more important, however, are the relations between Attlee and Bevin. Attlee was elected leader in 1935; and from that time until the summer/autumn of 1947 his position was always under at least a degree of threat. He was distinctly uncharismatic, and his considerable intellectual ability, as well as his practical experience, were very often, if not generally, under-estimated. There were intrigues, of varying degrees of intensity, against his leadership in 1935 (when he was first elected), in 1939, 1943, 1945 and 1947. One of the main contenders, especially in 1945, was Herbert Morrison. Bevin himself, who was seriously considered, would never allow his name to go forward against Attlee, and it is the Bevin factor which is crucial in this analysis. Bevin was the strong man within the Labour Cabinet and since he was not prepared to enter into any intrigue involving the replacement of Attlee, there was no possibility of any significant line-up of supporters for a new leader. Herbert Morrison was the obvious contender, and the bitterness that Bevin showed towards him during the years of the Churchill government and those of the Labour administration meant that so long as Bevin remained there would always be the massive support that Bevin could command behind Attlee as leader, above all from the trade unions.

Attlee and Bevin worked closely together and while there were differences between them Attlee was content to leave Bevin in more or less control of foreign affairs. India was the great exception, and the course of events that lead to Indian independence were directed by Attlee. Bevin, without doubt, would have handled matters differently, but in most other areas, with the Middle East being the exception that has been discussed in this chapter, Bevin was left to direct foreign policies on terms agreed by himself and his senior officials in the Foreign Office. In the last resort, as we have seen in the case of the Middle East, where Attlee's position was more rational and sensible than that of Bevin and his officials, Attlee nevertheless deferred. He did so because he could not afford the disunity that outright opposition to Bevin would have brought about. It must be emphasised that Attlee shared most attitudes on world affairs with Bevin. His mind was a good deal more subtle, and he was more intelligent than Bevin, but on fundamentals there were no serious differences between them. Moreover, the Middle East question in the second half of 1947 and through 1948 was no longer the same question that it had been two years earlier; and Germany and Europe came to occupy a much more prominent position in international politics than in the immediate aftermath of the end of the war.

The differences between Attlee and Bevin faded quickly; and they were soon forgotten. Whitehall in those days could keep its secrets and when members of Bevin's Private Office and other senior officials of the Foreign Office began to write their memoirs twenty or thirty years later there were no references to the political differences over the Middle East which at the time had caused so much concern. Gladwyn Jebb, for example, who in 1945 and 1946 was the most concerned with Attlee's aberrations, has not one word in his *Memoirs* to indicate that there was a serious debate at the heart of the Government. Nicholas Henderson has described Bevin's relations with Attlee as 'totally uncomplicated',[94] and this has been the general theme in all the writings about Attlee. Kenneth Harris' biography reinforces the general belief that Attlee and Bevin agreed on all broad issues, although Harris reprints, in an Appendix, Attlee's memorandum of 1 September 1945 on the Italian colonies question. Alan Bullock provides most of the documentary material relating to the differences over the Middle East, but not in a compact form, so that the reader tends to become submerged in what is often a chronological account which covers all issues and questions with which Bevin had to deal. As remarked already in this chapter, Attlee's own account of his political career makes no mention of any disagreement with Bevin, and it is clear from the biographies of contemporaries that the arguments were kept within a very narrow group; and certainly were not available for Cabinet discussion. Until the 1980s historians have almost always followed the accepted version. It is an intriguing story, this disappearance for about three decades of Attlee's heresy, although what we know of British public opinion in the years of the Labour Government makes it plain that any change of policy of the kind that Attlee was advocating would have been met with the fiercest opposition from the many conservative parts of British society. The opposition, it may be suggested, would have been much more intense than that generated by the withdrawal from India.

4

Some Economic Factors in
Foreign Policy

The war ended earlier than had been assumed in policy discussions during 1944 and 1945, for no one had predicted the collapse of Japan so soon after the defeat of Germany. Attempted peace negotiations by the Japanese – there had been less significant efforts earlier – began with a cable from Foreign Minister Togo to the Japanese Ambassador in Moscow on 11 July 1945, suggesting the USSR as an intermediary; Russia and Japan not yet being at war with each other. The Americans had long broken the Japanese codes, and were therefore fully aware of the debate that was going on, with Sato in Moscow, urging with all the emphasis he could command that Japan should sue for peace. The fire-bombing of Tokyo had begun on the night of 9–10 March, and it continued on all major industrial cities throughout the spring and summer. General Le May's B-29s virtually eliminated Japanese industry and with that the willingness of the Japanese people to resist; and this before the atom bombs were dropped.[1]

The telegrams between Tokyo and Moscow continued throughout July; Stalin informed Churchill, accurately, of these exchanges when they met at Potsdam, and with Stalin's agreement Churchill passed on the information to Truman. It was always clear that without an understanding to save 'face' in the matter of the Emperor's position in Japanese society, the negotiations for peace on the unconditional surrender terms would always be strongly opposed, in spite of the devastation that was rapidly overtaking Japan itself.[2] On 16 July 1945 the first atom bomb was exploded at Alamogordo in the New Mexico desert, although it was still not certain that it would work when dropped by a plane. When it did, on two occasions, the end of the war was brought dramatically home to the British by the abrupt cessation of Lend-Lease two days after the formal surrender of the Japanese Empire.

Economic stock-taking, in anticipation of the end of hostilities, had provided grim reading in the spring and summer of 1945: British exports by volume were thirty per cent of their 1938 level; the net loss of shipping tonnage was just under thirty per cent, and with that loss went a sharp reduction in freight earnings. Sales of investments during the war had been over one billion pounds sterling; and there was now a massive debt, the most important items of which were the sterling balances accumulated in India, Egypt and other countries where Britain had incurred large military and other expenditures. The net change on capital account between 1939 and the end of the war was around £4,700 million. It was the largest debt in British history.[3] Estimates of the shortfall on the United Kingdom's current account began with the deficit in 1944 which had reached £2,500 million, of which £1,800 million was provided through Lend-Lease. It was assumed in the Treasury calculations – although inevitably there were differences, sometimes large, between different calculations – that there would remain a deficit on current account for the first three to five years of peace. All estimates expected a rapid increase in exports and the continuation of restrictions upon imports, in order to keep down consumption, using wartime controls. For 1946 the deficit was estimated at £750 million, falling to lower figures in succeeding years. Contemporary estimates have been shown to be too pessimistic, but this was at least in part because of a much more rapid growth in exports than anticipated.[4]

The most urgent immediate problem confronting the new Labour Government was the large deficit which their Treasury advisers expected to last for a number of years; and the abrupt cancellation of Lend-Lease pushed the Government into an application for an American loan. Keynes led the British delegation to Washington, having made strongly optimistic comments on what terms he expected to achieve, most of which were to be quite severely deflated. In Washington the political mood was very different from the days of the Roosevelt era when Morganthau had been at the Treasury. Now the State Department was in a much stronger position in relation to the Treasury and Keynes was no longer able to count upon the sympathy and the friendship with which he had become accustomed during the war years.[5] The Americans were concerned especially with three main issues: the problems of the existing sterling debts, the elimination of controls on sterling transactions (in other words convertibility), and the development of a multilateral system of world trade. The British returned in December with 3.75 billion dollars plus $650 million to cover the final settlement of outstanding Lend-Lease obligations. Repayment of the loan was to begin after five years at a rate of interest of two per cent. As Keynes told the House of Lords, the commercial terms on which the loan were granted were very favourable. The crucial question was, in fact, convertibility, and this was to come into operation one year after Congress had approved the loan.[6]

The domestic pre-occupation of Labour ministers and politicians was, above all, in the early period of the Labour Government, with the maintenance of something approaching full employment. Capitalism in its history had never provided full employment except in periods of boom, and the experience of the

Great Depression of 1929–32 had etched itself deeply into the minds and hearts of large sections of the British people. The publication of Keynes' *General Theory* in 1936 meant that economists and political scientists sympathetic to the Labour Party now had a rational basis for their ideas of increased State intervention. Many went beyond Keynes in advocating the nationalisation of the Bank of England, which they believed was crucial for the control of investment levels, and they also endorsed the nationalisation of key utilities and some other sectors of the economy, believing that State control would be able to remedy the obvious wastefulness and inefficiencies of industries such as coal and the railways. This extension of Keynes' ideas, whose importance they did not deny, reinforced their belief in the evolutionary transition to a new social order.[7] Almost everyone was afraid of a post-war boom followed by a slump – a repeat of the aftermath of the First World War – but this did not happen, and the recovery which began with the return to peace-time industry and a world desperate for exports continued throughout the years of the two Labour governments.

The problem of the balance of payments had been long foreseen before the war ended. With the end of the war with Germany in sight, Keynes set down an analysis of the financial relations between the United States and the United Kingdom and what the future might look like in the immediate post-war years. This was his 'Overseas Financial Policy in Stage III' which had been drafted in March 1945 and was circulated to the Cabinet in a revised form on 15 May.[8] Then, within three months, he was to become involved in the negotiations for the American loan, and this was followed, when the negotiations were completed, with a probing discussion of what would happen if Congress refused to ratify the loan agreement. Keynes had only a few months to live; he died in late April 1946, but in these first months of that year the discussion papers and minutes exchanged between Keynes, Richard Clarke and others sharply illuminate the financial problems of the British economy. On 20 February 1946, at the end of a paper entitled 'Relevant Facts on Rejection', Clarke summarised his views on long-term measures to remedy Britain's position without an American loan:

> *para. 15.* We should have to seek to balance the sterling area's accounts with USA and by end-1948. This would involve some developments like the following:
> (a) Pressure to increase UK agricultural production, especially sugar and dairy produce.
> (b) Long-term supply arrangements with Dominions and Argentina for meat and dairy produce.
> (c) Pressure to expand UK steel production.
> (d) Continued pressure to switch from US cotton (and development of US types in Africa).
> (e) Strong attempt to get timber from Russia (at present hopeless).

(f) Develop Middle East oil (but not easy in relation to paragraph 12).[9]

(g) Increase Rhodesian tobacco production.

(h) Rapid expansion of UK film industry.

(i) Special attempts to restore Malayan tin and rubber.

(j) Renewed attempts of gold production within the Empire.[10]

Earlier in this memorandum Clarke had commented upon the high cost of political and military expenditure (paragraphs 11 and 12); in the second of these paragraphs he had been emphatic that the extent of overseas commitments entered into would have to be very carefully examined, and he ended: 'But it is clear that they could not be even a shadow of present plans.'

Keynes wrote a minute to Sir David Waley (Third Secretary, Treasury) explaining that while he did not want to share responsibility for this paper of Clarke's, he was agreed that it should be circulated, subject to certain points which he then presented. In his first paragraph he noted that there were a number of ways, including some not mentioned by Clarke, by which the gap in the payments deficit could be met. One of these, following Clarke, was 'cutting down our military and political expenditure overseas', and in his second paragraph he elaborated the point in terms that require to be emphasised:

> I should be inclined to high-light still more than he [Clarke] has that the main reaction of the loss of the American loan must be on our military and political expenditure overseas. For I cannot believe that the gap can be bridged in practice unless we go all out in economies in that direction. As Mr. Clarke points out, that is fraught with all sorts of political consequences. It brings this out to put the orders of magnitude of the loan and of the political and military expenditure side by side. The American loan is for 937 million. In the Washington estimates the political and military expenditure was put at 600 million. The revised estimate of the latter, prior to the recent changes of policy now under consideration, was 1000 million. Thus, it comes out in the wash that the American loan is primarily required to meet the political and military expenditure overseas. If it were not for that, we could scrape through without excessive interruption of our domestic programme if necessary by drawing largely on our reserves. The interruption of our domestic programme which is politically and economically possible so long as the military and political expenditure goes on its present scale is strictly limited. The main consequence of the failure of the loan must, therefore, be a large scale withdrawal on our part from international responsibilities. (Perhaps there might be no harm, in private conversation, in letting the State Department appreciate a little more vividly than I think they do at present that this would be inevitably the most striking consequence).[11]

'Thus, it comes out in the wash that the American loan is primarily required to meet the political and military expenditure overseas.' These were not matters that in any way affected the calculations of the Chiefs of Staff in Whitehall or the senior members of the British Foreign Office. It is indeed striking that in the files of the Foreign Office in the years immediately after the end of the

Second World War there are almost no references to the economic consequence of foreign policy issues and no suggestion at all that because of
financial constraint British commitments should be carefully reviewed. The
Chiefs of Staff produced an Overall Strategic Plan in May 1947, referred to
above, of which two comments may be made: the first, that it had been a long
time in the making; and the second, that it took no account of the much
weakened economic position of the United Kingdom in the post-war world or
of the profound political changes that were taking place on a global scale. In
short, the future defence policy was a wholly unrealistic document, and only the
unsophisticated military in London could have produced it,[12] based as it was
upon the optimum situation that the military would have liked to have existed at
the beginning of the Second World War.

It was, however, the Foreign Office through Bevin that carried the political
weight inside the Cabinet and while, as we have seen in earlier chapters, the
Prime Minister was unconvinced of the Middle East strategy being pursued, he
mainly calculated his opposition in terms of manpower not financial obligations. Although there were in the first year or so of the Labour Government at
least three committees in Whitehall examining the implications of manpower
shortages, it was the Defence Committee that was the deciding factor since it
was in their deliberations that the future size of the armed forces was
determined.[13] Demobilisation went steadily forward, but too slowly, and given
the agreed view between the Foreign Office and the Chiefs of Staff there was
no serious opposition within the Cabinet. Indeed, what is notable in the
immediate post-war years is the very limited impact Cabinet discussions had
upon the general direction of foreign affairs. The senior officials continued to
argue that while there would no doubt be financial difficulties in the immediate
aftermath of war these would be overcome by Britain's imperial resources and
the skill with which financial and related problems would be administered.[14]
The most extraordinary insensibility to post-war realities is to be found,
however, in the reports of the military planners who drew up their paper plans
for future strategy without any consideration for the logistics of the real world.
This was especially true of their evaluation of the aggressive possibilities of the
Soviet Union, whose ability to reach the Channel ports, or the Persian Gulf,
was apparently unbounded.

The scale, then, of Britain's overseas government expenditure was a matter
of considerable debate at the time and has remained a matter of major criticism
of the Labour Government in the decades which followed, although the basic
postulates upon which it was founded have been less seriously questioned. It
was, let it be said again, the product of two articles of faith: the first was the
belief in the British Empire as the bedrock upon which rested Britain's claim to
have remained one of the three world powers, and the second was the Great
Power thesis. A question to be answered relates to the financial, economic and
political processes by which Britain's position in the world as a Great Power,

untenable in the long run, was apparently temporarily maintained during the first years of peace.

The statistical data upon which an assessment of Britain's economic recovery can be based can sometimes be conflicting, but the general trends are acceptable.[15] Full employment was maintained throughout, and industrial production between 1946 and 1951 increased by one-third. Feinstein estimated that Gross Domestic Product showed a slight fall between 1945 and 1948 and then increased by just over ten per cent between 1948 and 1951. Exports in 1946 more than doubled compared with the years previous. There were severe difficulties in 1947 which halted the rise in exports but from 1948 the increase each year was resumed. Between 1946 and 1952 the export of goods and services increased by some seventy-seven per cent while imports and consumption levels were quite strictly held down. Indeed, the only act of effective macro-economic planning on the part of the Labour Government, apart from a certain degree of direction of industrial location, was the continuation of wartime controls on imports and domestic consumption, and their gradual relaxation. From data which must be regarded as somewhat crude it is possible to estimate that consumer spending in real terms was about seven per cent higher in 1951 than in 1946. There were no problems on the export front in the sense that world demand remained at high level throughout the years of the Labour Government; and after, of course. The unprecedented world boom of the third quarter of the twentieth century began, on Milward's analysis, in 1945 and continued through until the early 1970s.[16] The United Kingdom had suffered physical damage during the war years, but its extent did not compare with the rest of belligerent Europe. There had been some capital investment but much of British industry was producing the rapid growth of manufactured exports on equipment which had not been renewed or replaced for many years; a matter discussed below.

There were other additional ways in which the Labour Government financed its domestic and international policies. One was the American loan, and much smaller loans from elsewhere, and another was Marshall Aid. The widely accepted view among British but not American historians, that it was Ernest Bevin's perceptive understanding that translated Marshall's general ideas into European reality, is an illusion that is still constantly repeated in current writing.[17] The Marshall speech was a conscious political statement, and the genesis of the Marshall Plan has been fully documented. In early May 1947 Acheson briefed three British journalists of the developing ideas within the American administration; and at Cleveland, speaking in place of Harry Truman, Acheson undertook a 'preliminary canter' – his words – over the ground that Marshall himself was to cover at Harvard. On 22 May 1947 John Balfour, who was Head of Chancery at the British Embassy in Washington, had lunch with Dean Acheson in the company also of Gerald Barry, editor of the

London *News Chronicle*. Balfour reported to London the main points of Acheson's conversation:

> The thoughts of responsible Administration experts seems to be turning in the direction of viewing the problems of foreign aid, beginning with aid to western Europe, in continental rather than in national terms. This trend of thought coincides with growing evidence that the mood of Congress is becoming increasing hostile to the idea of being invited to make piecemeal approaches for the emergency needs of individual countries.[18]

Balfour included with his despatch to London an article by James Reston, a well-known columnist in the *New York Times*, for 27 May. Reston's article was headed 'US Studies Shift of Help to Europe as a Unit in Crisis', and nearly a fortnight earlier Raymond Aron had referred in *Combat* to 'the more or less genuine news of a vast "Lend-Lease for Peace" plan that America is about to produce'. It must be presumed that the senior officials of the European chancelleries were not less well-informed than the world of sophisticated journalism.

Will Clayton returned from Europe during the second half of May and produced a memorandum which according to Acheson had a powerful effect upon Marshall.[19] Clayton's thesis was the rapid disintegration of Europe. It was a highly sensational document which undoubtedly exaggerated the economic problems of Europe, however much, or little, is accepted of the Milward revisionist thesis.[20] Acheson gave a short account in his memoirs of the meeting on May 28 at which Clayton expounded his views to Marshall and his colleagues. Acheson's summary read:

> Will Clayton was one of the most powerful and persuasive advocates to whom I have listened. What he said at the meeting added to his paper principally corroborative detail to illustrate the headlong disintegration of the highly complex industrial society of Europe, through the breakdown of inter-relations between the industrial cities and the food producing countrysides. Millions of people would soon die, creating a chaos of bloodshed and disorder in doing so. To organise the great effort needed to prevent this disaster would take time, but it had to begin here and now. Surely the plan should be a European plan and come – or at any rate appear to come – from Europe. *But the United States must run the show*. And they must start running it now.[21]

But the United States must run the show. The emphasis was made by Acheson in this extract from his autobiography. The same point was made later in the year by George Kennan in a lecture he gave to the National War College presented in the homely style he sometimes used: 'It doesn't work if you just send the stuff over and relax. It has to be played politically, when it gets over. It has to be dangled, sometimes withdrawn, sometimes extended. It has to be a skilful operation.'[22] As a statement of American magnanimity in the world after 1945, it will not be bettered.

Analysis of the Marshall Aid period is complicated but two matters may be briefly commented upon here. The first, which is of crucial importance, is the extent to which the acceptance of Marshall Aid offered political leverage to the United States over and within Western Europe. The answer to this question is integrally related to the second matter, namely, whether Marshall Aid really did save Western Europe from economic collapse. Milward's analysis on the economic side is that Western Europe was not collapsing but that Marshall dollars allowed some governments to continue the domestic and foreign policies which had brought about the balance of payments crisis. These are very large questions and are still under debate.[23] What can be said in general is that there is no doubt that Americans helped to maintain the high levels of investment and government expenditure, and that in very broad terms there was without question a general strengthening of capitalist power throughout Western Europe, and a weakening of the militant working-class radicalism which had come out of the defeat of fascism.[24] In the case of Britain the absence of outside funds would have involved major cuts in the import programme, and that would have meant sharp reductions in food imports from dollar sources. A Treasury paper on the economic consequences of no dollar aid estimated that the required reduction in imports of food would reduce the level of calorific intake for the population as a whole by about ten per cent compared with the immediate pre-war years.[25]

Milward has provided a breakdown by country of the expenditure of Marshall dollars on broad categories of commodities, and there are striking differences between different countries. The two countries which received the greater part of Marshall Aid were Britain (about 23 per cent) and France (between 20 and 21 per cent). These were the original allocations, based upon the existing dollar deficits, and were to be adjusted in minor ways over the years. The interesting part of the analysis for Britain is to compare the commodity expenditures of these two countries, which from the beginning were strikingly different.[26] The proportion of foodstuffs financed by Marshall dollars in the British case was the largest single category whereas for France the proportion of foodstuffs using European Recovery Program Aid was low while the imports of capital goods for the general reconstruction plan were of considerable significance. It was Pelling's argument that Britain's problems were due not so much to domestic social reform as to 'the maintenance of substantial military forces on overseas stations' as well as to a failure to control the conversion of sterling balances (by the white Dominions). Milward took strong exception to this analysis in a review of Pelling in the *Economic History Review*[27] on the grounds that the payments crisis was a general European problem, and that the Labour Government was behaving 'in the same way as the right-wing liberal foreigners of whom they were so suspicious'.

It can be agreed that economic recovery began at the end of the war; that it continued strongly through 1946 and then ran into the payments crisis of 1947; but was resumed through 1948 before American dollars under Marshall Aid began reaching Europe. Britain was not, however, in the same position as the countries of Western Europe. While France and the Netherlands had colonial wars in the Far East, and the French also had colonial possessions elsewhere, neither country had the size or importance of the Empire for the British. Tomlinson has estimated that British Government overseas and foreign investment amounted to more than eight times the aggregate current account deficit for 1946–48.[28] Marshall Aid allowed Britain a high though declining level of military expenditure to 1950 and a slow but increasing improvement in consumption: guns plus some small advance in food intake, together with a general amelioration in living standards as the product of full employment. Contemporaries who listened to the shrill cries of the Housewives' League or who read the dubious statistics of income distribution that were widely disseminated by middle-class apologists might well believe that life was becoming more intolerable as the years of peace went by, but for the majority of working people, who were the majority of the population, the favourable comparison with the decades of the years between the wars was not to be questioned.[29]

Historians have often discussed Britain's financial problems in terms of the guns or butter thesis. Bullock wrote that for many outside and inside the Labour Party 'the open choice' was 'between cutting expenditure on overseas and defence commitments and the Party's programme of social reform'.[30] Certainly, as already discussed, Marshall Aid and the earlier American Loan permitted Britain to maintain its overseas undertakings while its productive capacity, especially in the export sectors, was rapidly developed; and at the same time austerity could be slowly relaxed. There was, however, another very important source of considerable financial benefit to the United Kingdom: the sterling area, and the crucial differences of policy that London operated between the independent countries of the Commonwealth on the one hand and the dependent colonial areas on the other. The sterling area was maintained in ways which permitted foreign investment within the whole area, and after the war ended London soon found its traditional role of financial centre for investing in the Dominions. As a result a very considerable flow of capital occurred, with a leakage of dollars as one of its consequences, and a steady reduction of sterling balances as another. Almost all the investment was in the 'white Commonwealth' and notably South Africa. The colonial areas had a quite different history. Throughout the sterling area London took the decisions on the allocation of gold and dollars; but in the colonial countries within the Empire the sterling balances increased. Countries like Malaya (rubber and tin) and West Africa (cocoa) were large dollar earners and were of quite central importance in the overall payments strategy. A Colonial Office paper of 7 December 1948 reported:

> Between 1946 and 1948 the colonies have enormously increased their direct dollar earnings and these were running at an annual rate of from $600 million to $800 million during the first half of 1948. At the same time, expenditure by the colonies in the Western Hemisphere has been curtailed. It fell in spite of higher prices and the necessity to increase purchases of certain equipment for development, from $500 million in 1947 to an annual rate of $473 million in the first half of 1948.[31]

The problem for these colonial dollar earners was that Britain after the war concentrated its commodity exports upon dollar markets and was not able to supply the colonial markets with the capital goods in particular that were required. It was this which led to the steady increase in sterling balances, and since the British control of colonial currencies was operated at fixed exchange rates, the sterling area became an important support in maintaining the pound sterling as a world currency. A further, and related, matter was the physical control over colonial commerce. From the beginning of the Second World War Britain had introduced a licensing system for the control of all colonial foreign trade. It was done, in part, in order to facilitate the allocation of shipping space. There were, moreover, marketing boards for different colonial products which after 1945 bought at fixed prices, in most cases using the large trading companies as commission agents. Prices were normally fixed at below world prices and the funds thus accumulated were intended originally to build up buffer reserves in order to offset the effects of any future fall in prices for the local producers. It was a system that had been introduced during the decade before 1939 in order to alleviate the drastic fall in world prices that occurred during those years, but its function became very different in the new world situation following the end of the war, when it was shortages and rising prices for most products that dominated the world's commodity markets. For the Labour Government, the arrangements of the sterling area and the system of bulk purchase were important ways of using the resources of the colonial countries for the benefit of the metropolis. D.K. Fieldhouse, in a seminal article published in 1984, which now has become the analytical basis for most imperial and commonwealth historians, wrote that the problem was to 'account for the apparent incompatibility between Labour's virtuous principles and the government's obnoxious practices'. He continued:

> The basic fact is that between 1945 and 1951 Britain exploited those dependencies that were politically unable to defend their own interests in more ways and with more serious consequences than at any time since overseas colonies were established. Exploitation was hydraheaded, though not all were invented by Labour and few were recognised by Labour men at the time to be indefensible.[32]

The nature of the relationship was commented on very soon after the Conservatives replaced Labour as the governing party in the early 1950s. An article in *The Financial Times* (15 January 1952) by Arthur Lewis, who was at the time Professor of Political Economy at the University of Manchester and a member of the Colonial Development Corporation, analysed the sterling balances of the colonial countries since the end of the war and arrived at the same conclusions as had Fieldhouse:

> Britain talks of colonial development, but on the contrary, it is African and Malayan peasants who are putting capital into Britain. For the first time since free trade was adopted, in the middle of the nineteenth century, the British colonial system has become a major means of economic exploitation.

This single article by Lewis summarised accurately the problem of the sterling area and the ways in which its impact had changed from before 1939: in the post-war years it had become a direct means of exploitation in the interests of the United Kingdom. Lewis did not, however, make the political point that American dollars through the first Loan and then Marshall Aid, together with the economic drain from the colonial countries, allowed the Labour Government to continue with its overseas military commitments and at the same time to carry through its domestic programme of social reform. There was, inevitably, a political price to be paid to the United States, and there were also consequences for the internal development of the British economy that need further analysis.[33]

The over-riding concern with the balance of payments after 1945, and the emphasis placed upon the urgent need to increase British exports, meant that the efficiency of industry also became an issue of central importance. As Cairncross noted: 'Few governments have proclaimed more insistently the need for higher productivity.'[34] There was, with demobilisation more or less completed to the levels reluctantly agreed by the military and the Foreign Office, an almost fixed supply of labour supplemented by some immigration to produce an ever increasing volume of exports; and it was accomplished very largely on the capital equipment carried over from the war years. It was not that all Labour ministers failed to appreciate the many deficiencies in British industrial organisation, for some of them had been intimately involved in business affairs through the war years: notably Hugh Dalton and Stafford Cripps. There was evidence in abundance in the files of the Board of Trade, the Treasury and other ministries as to the weaknesses in many areas of industrial production, and much of the wartime debate was summarised in an important paper produced by the Board of Trade in October 1948.[35] A number of prominent initiatives were put in hand after 1945 and especially following the crisis year of 1947; but as Tomlinson notes, the Labour Government was committed to a consensual industrial policy, and this was not enough, for little change of the fundamental kind that was needed had been achieved by the time Labour went out of office.[36] By then, neo-classical economics wrapped in a Keynesian covering dominated economic thinking once again, and the supply side of the economy was left to market forces; with the depressing and dispiriting results that have accumulated in the past forty years.[37] The story goes back a long way.

Several decades before the First World War Britain began to suffer the consequences of being the first society to industrialise, although the consequences have become more apparent to historians than they were to most contemporary observers. It was from the 1870s that this most dynamic industrial society began to exhibit a commercial as well as a technological sluggishness that was largely masked by the continuation of Britain as a world power. The depression in prices and the reduction of profit margins after 1875 was not without its impact upon certain sections of the economy: hence the Fair Trade movement of the 1880s, and later, for somewhat different reasons, the tariff campaign of Joseph Chamberlain.[38] Britain in the nineteenth century had built its prosperity upon a group of staple trades – coal, iron and steel, heavy engineering (especially non-electrical machinery, prime movers and railway equipment), textiles and shipbuilding – and these industries made up about fifty per cent of all net industrial production, and some seventy per cent of commodity exports. What happened after the mid 1870s was that British exporters, confronted with the emergence of the United States and Germany as major industrial nations, and steadily as competitors on the world market, were able to find new markets outside Europe and the United States for their traditional type of export products. Had the economic world been limited to Europe and the Atlantic countries a major restructuring would have been forced upon the industrial economy of Britain. It was the continued expansion of the commercial world to embrace the whole geographical world that helped to produce the so-called 'over-commitment' of Britain's staple industries before 1914, and the serious problems of contraction in the years after 1918.[39] Empire was another related factor.

There were obdurate factors, institutional and social, deeply embedded within British society long before the end of the nineteenth century: a complex of economic and social structures and class-biased ideologies that inhibited flexible responses to the problems of a changing world. Early industrialisation had produced the institutions of competitive capitalism: firms with small market shares; vertical specialisation; a distributive system separate from the manufacturing sector; technical progress through practical experience; a banking system aloof from long-term industrial investment; an abhorrence of any intervention by the State; a total faith in the invisible hand of the market mechanism – in short, as Tawney expressed it, entrepreneurial initiative and managerial direction by 'rule of thumb and a nose for money'. By the end of the nineteenth century this competitive capitalism had served Britain reasonably well, if one puts to one side the cost of human suffering among large numbers of working people; and the cultural and social values among its propertied classes that success engendered had hardened into articles of faith. The world, however, continued to change and the dominant mode of industrial organisation in the twentieth century was one or other version of corporate capitalism characterised by industrial oligarchy, a managerial bureaucracy in tight control over the utilisation of the labour force, an increasing importance of scientific research and its subsequent development, and the integration of production and distribution in many sectors. Financial and industrial capital in Britain, for long sharply distinguished, now became at least partially integrated. National patterns have inevitably exhibited differences of structure and organisation, but in all the successful advanced societies of the second half of the twentieth century the 'visible' hand has been seen ever more prominently.[40]

Belief in the economic virtues of the unfettered mechanisms of the market has been tenaciously adhered to in Britain during the whole of the twentieth century by most businessmen and many academic economists. A school of neo-classical economic historians have argued that by the test of profit maximisation, within the given framework of contemporary capitalism, British entrepreneurs in the twentieth century have in general performed satisfactorily. It is, however, the 'given' conditions that must be the subject of analysis and dissection. Most businessmen, it can be agreed, will accept the economic environment in which they find themselves, and accept the restraints that are thereby imposed. Even so, when it is argued that 'we do not know why Britain grew less rapidly than her competitors' in the decades between 1860 and 1914,[41] it may be suggested that this is a negation of the historian's role. We know that the performance of the British economy, measured by rates of growth both of output and productivity, was inferior to the achievements of the United States and Germany; and we know also that the slower rates of growth before 1914 were to continue, on a comparative basis, throughout the twentieth century. Indeed, although economic growth after the Second World War was faster than at any period of the whole century, the lag behind most countries of Western Europe was 'larger, more sustained, and more conspicuous' than for any previous period.[42] It is not unreasonable to argue that there might be some relationship between the various components of the economic situation in Britain before 1914 and those in the decades which followed. Already in 1915 Thorstein Veblen, in his fascinating chapter on England in *Imperial Germany and the Industrial Revolution*, discussed some of the reasons why Britain 'was paying the penalty for having been thrown into the lead and so showing the way'. Veblen analysed obsolescence as the 'unavoidable' existence of past technological development which no longer suited the requirements of the present, but which could only be overcome by a large-scale recasting of the economy, both within individual industries and of the infrastructure in general. Here is his comment on the transportation problem:

> So, e.g., it is well known that the railways of Great Britain, like those of other countries, are built with too narrow a gauge, but while this item of 'depreciation through obsolescence' has been known for some time, it has not even in the most genial speculative sense come up for consideration as a remediable defect. In the same connection, American, and latterly German, observers have been much impressed with the silly little bobtailed carriages used in British goods traffic; which were well enough in their time, before American and German railway traffic was good for anything much, but which have at the best a playful air when brought up against the requirements of today. Yet the remedy is not a simple question of good sense. The terminal facilities, tracks, shunting facilities, and all the ways and means of handling freight on this oldest and most complete of railway systems, are all adapted to the bobtailed car. So, again, the roadbed and the metal, as well as the engines, are well and substantially constructed to take care of such traffic as required to be taken care of when they first went into operation, and it is not easy to make a piece-meal adjustment to later requirements. It is perhaps true that as seen from the stand point of the community at large its material interest, the out-of-date equipment and organisation should profitably be discarded – 'junked' as the colloquial phrase has it – and the later contrivances substituted throughout; but it is the discretion of the business men that necessarily decides these questions, and the whole proposition has a different value as seen in the light of the competitive pecuniary interests of the business men in control.[43]

There are many different kinds of obsolescence – political, social, cultural, as well as economic – and Veblen was always conscious of the distinctive cultures of individual societies. He underlined the importance in the history of modern Britain of what today we would describe as the carry-over of discrete cultural and social aspects of early or pre-industrial society. 'Church and State and Nobility', he wrote, 'are still present in effectual force', and he contrasted these 'substantial survivals' of the past with the 'broad fringe of usages, conventions, vested rights, canons of equity and propriety' that have grown out of the new industrial system itself. There has been an increasing debate in the past two decades or so concerning the ways in which the past has laid heavily upon economic development in the twentieth century, and has contributed substantially to the relative economic decline of the United Kingdom. Analysis of the 'past' is not to be confined to cultural attitudes, although these are always relevant, or to industrial attitudes derived from the ways in which industry was organised, although these too can never be ignored. The understanding of the politicians in power, or their misunderstanding; the cultural attitudes of different sections of the propertied classes towards industry; the training and scientific knowledge of the managerial class; the technical and general education of foremen and operatives; the willingness to experiment with new processes and new materials; the acceptance or resistance to new ideas – the list is almost endless – all such have their origin within the same environment which produces both retarding as well as dynamic factors.[44] When the Platt Report on the Cotton Industry (1944) remarked that the outlook of American managers was 'highly analytical and progressive', comparing them in favourable terms with their benighted counterparts in Britain,[45] it was, in part, an echo of what Matthew Arnold had noted in 1868 as a major defect in Britain's educational system and teaching. This, wrote Arnold, was the lack of 'the idea of science and systematic knowledge', an absence, he suggested, which was beginning to threaten the English business class with 'practical inconvenience'.[46]

Education is only one of a complex of factors which provide the analysis of economic decline, but in a world of increasingly sophisticated technology it has inevitably become a substantive component of change, of steadily growing importance. In Britain in the era of early industrialisation there was an indifference to general education for the ordinary people derived partly from political attitudes on the part of the propertied classes[47] and partly from the emphasis upon practicality as the essential guide to material success in industry and commerce. There was, therefore, no significant pressure group within British society for extending educational facilities to the mass of people, and the result was the slow evolution of a national system of elementary education, with the emphasis upon elementary. It is a subject much written about.[48] When *The Economist* in 1850 published a devastating critique of English education it was just as certain that the failures so heavily emphasised were of small practical significance. The comments are worth quoting. The first was in the issue of 2 March 1850:

> It is generally agreed that no civilised people are so little and so ill educated as the English. Nor can there be any doubt that our school system . . . is unworthy alike of an organising government, and of the orderly methodical spirit of the nation. It has never, within our recollection, been examined but to be condemned. It has found innumerable accusers and opponents – not one advocate. Those who have been hopelessly at variance as to the means of improving it, have cordially agreed in saying that it was an intolerable disgrace to the community.

But, *The Economist* continued, the English as a nation were not behind any other 'in either intellect or morality'; and it went on to make the point that 'mere school instruction' was a good deal less important in the training of youth than many believed. This judgement it underlined a month later, in the issue of 20 April, 1850:

> To say that our secular education is perfect would be terribly erroneous; but to say that it is unrivalled, judging from its effects by the progress and success of the

community, will not be far from the truth. That kind of education which fits men to perform their duties in life is not got in public or parish schools, but at home, in the counting house, in the lawyer's office, or the camp, or on board ship, in the shop or the factory. . . . What is most wanted in society seems to be a knowledge of our moral duties, in detail, and a general discipline of the minds of all who perform them.[49]

This emphasis upon what a foreign observer later described as 'le practical man'[50] derived in business circles both from the divergence between science and industry and the technology of early industrialisation.[51] The first stage of industrialisation was carried through without any close alliance between the scientist and the entrepreneur, although the gap may not have been as wide as some commentators have suggested.[52] Any attempt at a broad generalisation covering nearly a century's technology is a hazardous business, but it is probably true that down to the 1850s, and in some industries a later date would be appropriate, most of the technological innovations and improvements were the work of practical men working within the particular industry. The faith of the self-made businessmen in Mr Gradgrind's facts, against what they believed to be empty theorising, hardened into dogma as the decades passed, and the continued success of themselves and of Britain in general served to buttress their complacency. It was the coming of the steel age that finally ended the epoch of the practical man. With steel, the new basic material, and electricity, the new, and for many processes a greatly improved, source of power, it was increasingly difficult to improvise on an ad hoc basis; and when these two innovations came together to provide the possibilities of mass production, the scientist also moved into the centre of technological development. Or rather, this was what an increasingly complex technology demanded, and what in fact did take place in both American and German industry before 1914; but not, alas, in Britain in any comparable way. In 1913 Germany had nearly 60,000 university students compared with 9000 in Britain; and Germany produced 3000 graduate engineers a year at a time when England and Wales were graduating only 350 with first or second class honours in *all* branches of science, technology and mathematics.[53]

It was not that an appreciation of the general problem failed to develop but rather that the gap between a small minority of enlightened opinion and majority attitudes within industry proved apparently unbridgeable. This general problem was not, of course, just a question of an indifference to education or the refusal to understand the importances of technical education, but one of a wholesale reshaping of attitudes and of institutions, at all levels of society. The lack of appreciation of the importance of technical education was subtly linked with the wider problems of industrial organisation, and the need for change; and the problems of industrial organisation were themselves related to the institutional gap in Britain between manufacturing and finance, about which so much has been written.[54] There are, in sum, a complexity of causes for British industrial decline in the twentieth century; of the fact of its existence there is no serious debate after the bitter experience of the 1980s and their aftermath.

By the beginning of the Second World War the manufacturing sector in Britain was indisputably inefficient compared with those of the United States and Germany. The emphasis in the 1930s in economic thinking, however, was upon different problems. It was a decade in which, in Britain, as well as elsewhere, there was a growth in the numbers of professional economists who were, however, concerned mainly with the problems of unemployed resources: an understandable emphasis. The world economic crisis of 1929–32 had produced massive unemployment, and inevitably the question of how to put unemployed resources back to work provided most of the discussion of these years with Keynes' writings as the outstanding contribution to the debates. In Britain the structural problems of the economy were not in the forefront of economic teaching.[55] D.L. Burn did not publish his seminal *Economic History of Steelmaking* until 1940, and it was in Whitehall departments, during the war years, that British industrial performance came under highly critical review on a scale not hitherto published. There were some official reports on individual industries, and these are discussed later, but in 1948 Rostas produced his pioneering work on productivity measurements, which suggested that for the years 1935–39 output per worker, in a comparative sample of thirty-one manufacturing industries, was around 2.2 times greater in the United States than in Britain. Some later calculations put the gap even higher and in the decades following the rate of growth of both Domestic Product and productivity, while higher than at any time in the twentieth century, lagged notably behind other industrial European countries. Between 1953 and 1973 all other Western European countries had better growth figures than the United Kingdom. France, Germany, Italy and Austria each had a long run annual increase in GDP of over five per cent while the figure for the UK was three per cent.[56]

The published evidence that became available in the closing years of the war and in the immediate aftermath concerning the many inefficiencies of British industry, together with the great mass of material collected during the war years, ought to have provided the leading personalities of the Labour Government – one might also include the leaders of industry – with firm convictions about what needed to be done in order to restore Britain to a position of major importance as a manufacturing country. Why this conviction was absent, in practical terms, is considered below; but some illustration of what was known may be helpful. First there were the published reports on cotton and the coal industry which appeared before the war ended and which were much discussed at the time;[57] but the story of machine tools and above all the history of tank production, which remained for the most part in the files of the relevant departments until the official histories were published, demonstrated in striking fashion the structural and managerial weaknesses that afflicted so many sections of the British economy.

Machine tools are the bedrock of large parts of British industry and particularly of the engineering industries. The deficiencies in the range and quality of British machine tools became a commonplace of the years of rearmament before 1939 and they were a continuous problem during the war years. A report for the Historical Section of the Cabinet Office by D. Mack Smith covered the years 1940 to 1944 and it began by noting that the machine tool industry was much too small for war needs. Already before 1939 the Air Ministry had placed a large part of its orders abroad: in the USA, Sweden, Switzerland, Belgium and France. In 1940 some 30,000 machine tools had been made in Britain, and about 10,000 were imported; but there was a crucial difference between home production and those imported. The British industry made mostly standard tools while the American and German industries produced not only large numbers of standard tools but also highly specialised tools that were not available in Britain. It was not only a matter of quality; many machine tools, according to Mack Smith's report, were 'inefficiently employed', and on this question of utilisation American experts surveying British industrial organisation were reported to be very critical (para. 3). By the time the war had really got under way, from the summer of 1940, there developed a shortage of skilled labour. The industry was summed up (para. 4):

> The general purpose tools already available in industry were usually old and worn, not capable of great accuracy and high cutting speeds and the rapid machining necessary for rapid output. In any case they would require reconditioning and the addition of balancing plant. So the tendency was to lay down plant which was automatic and suitable for one line only of production, as speedier and more economical of skilled workmanship. It was typical of this that the I.C.I. came to use as many as 140 steel gauges in cartridge case production, and the six pounder gun required 300 jigs and fixtures for its breach mechanism alone.[58]

The general position within the industry improved markedly during the war years. There was a strong movement towards standardisation[59] and improved labour utilisation, with a large recruitment of female labour. Many more types of specialist machine tools were now being produced. A further report covering the period 1936 to 1945 confirmed the improvements that had taken place during the war years while still noting the serious deficiencies that remained.[60]

The many problems of the machine tool sector naturally affected the wider engineering industry, and these can be indicated by the sorry tale of tank production during the Second World War. The history of the tank offers broader considerations which go beyond the technical problems of industrial production. Society is not a collection of separate boxes in which social and industrial groups live and work independently of each other. There are a multitude of inter-relationships, influences and contacts, not all of which are overt and immediately recognisable, which bias in varying degrees social consciousness and practical activity. What, for example, were the connections during the inter-war years, and especially during the 1930s, between the lack of comprehension on the part of the Army Staff of the role of the tank in future wars, and the massive incompetence of the engineering industry to produce a reliable tank to given specifications? And why was it so difficult to develop good working relations between those who drew up the specifications and those responsible for their manufacture? There are large and subtle questions here that require an unravelling of the *zeitgeist* in twentieth-century Britain; an examination of the complex relationships between the political economy of an imperialist country in its decades of decline, and the social consciousness of those who make up its polity.

An internal memorandum on the history of the tank, by Professor D. Hay, covered the years 1936 to 1943.[61] It was in two parts, and after providing an opening summary Hay noted that 'The facts collected in the narrative, by their very multiplicity, tend to obscure what is an extremely depressing story.' A central part of the critique by Hay concentrated upon the failure of the Army Staff to perceive the role of the tank in modern warfare: as in the following bitter comments:

> The hypothetical tasks of the Army varied no more than those of the Air Force and the Navy, but in these serious logic was allowed to dictate the bases of operational equipment. The equestrian pre-occupations of the soldier was in the main a measure of the inadequacies of his mechanical equipment; service journals do not reveal sailors being nostalgic for the days of the wooden man-of-war nor airmen regretting the obsolescent [sic] of biplane or blimp.[62]

Hay ended his report with a further attack upon those responsible in the top echelons of Army Command for overall strategy in the field:

> At no point before the autumn of 1942 is the policy on tank employment thoroughly thought out; cruiser tanks are treated as anti-tank gun carriers; infantry tanks are intended for trench crossing and anti-concrete work. The German tanks may have been slower and less well-armoured but they carried armament designed to carry out a tank role. It was precisely this characteristic which made Grant and Sherman both popular and effective. The design and production of British tanks was a failure because from 1936 to 1942 the function of a tank in modern warfare was not understood and consequently not defined.[63]

Professor Hay was not quite as forthright in his published chapters in the official war history on *Design and Development of Weapons*, to which he contributed several chapters on Army weapons; but he did state bluntly that 'the General Staff requirements of 1942–43 had not been met by the end of the war as far as tanks were concerned; and the same is true of armoured cars and carriers.'[64] There is much else that could be quoted from departmental files of the war years which adds substantially to the indictment of British industrial organisation. But there is one document that deserves the attention of posterity: an uninhibited and caustic memorandum by Brigadier W.M. Blagden, dated September 1943, which on its title page carried the intriguing instruction: 'NOT TO BE QUOTED OR SHOWN TO ANYONE', a command which was underlined twice. The title of Blagden's paper was 'Confidential Note on Tank Situation 1940–3'.[65] It was a devastating document, quite stunning in its ferocity, and revealed a story of incompetence and stupidity. Blagden was scathing about the weak armament of British tanks in North Africa, and their mechanical unreliability, and he made the point which Correlli Barnett was to discuss in *The Desert Generals*, that it was the American Grants and Shermans which turned the tide at the second battle of Alamein. Blagden was equally critical of the administrative structures in Britain that were responsible for tank design, planning and production. After recounting the record of changes of personnel at the head of various sections of the Tank Board, which had been established in the summer of 1940, Blagden continued:

> One must remember that in exceptional circumstances it may be possible to design and produce a tank in two years. Within only 18 months our Tank Design Organisation had been subject to four major upheavals, of which only the first can really have been justified. It is remarkable that so much mal-administration could have been crowded into so short a period.

Quality control was never in evidence for those who had to fight in British tanks during the war, and among the most serious defects as Blagden had noted were those of the mechanical unreliability of the tank as an armoured vehicle. During the summer of 1942 Churchill was pressing General Auchinleck concerning a renewed offensive in North Africa, while Auchinleck, who had already complained several times about the poor condition of British tanks on their arrival, sent a report dated 14 July 1942 which set out in depressing detail what was wrong:

> General condition of these tanks was better than those received earlier this year, but the performance of the engines was below standard. Some higher gears could not be engaged. In a number of cases the cylinder head gaskets were blowing. All engines required tuning and adjustments to steering gear had to be carried out. In most cases clutch withdrawal levers required adjustment. All 2-pounder guns required buffer piston clearances checked. This is a Middle East modification which must be done in the United Kingdom. They were not marked, so checking had to be done. Approximately 160 items of tank fittings were deficient of which 120 were important, such as towing shackle, armament components, periscope components, power traverse control boxes. Some of these items may have been pilfered in transit.[66]

The industrial situation in Britain was not, of course, all gloom. Output in many sectors had sharply increased, and there was improvement in levels of productivity as the war progressed. There were considerable advances in the practice of standardisation – a central weakness in many industrial groups – and there was a more intelligent combination of the factors of production. The greater part of the much increased volume of output came, inevitably, from a more intensive utilisation of existing resources and capital equipment. The problem of fundamental restructuring would necessarily have to be left for the years of peace; and the crucial question for the historian is the extent to which the problem was appreciated, and then the practical steps that were taken, or not taken, in order to remedy the manifold shortcomings of the previous decades.

The main answer to the question just posed is that during the years of the Attlee governments there never emerged any critical understanding of the role and place of the manufacturing sector in an advanced society or of the long-term consequences of the relative economic decline of the previous half century. An industrial strategy involves a complex of measures which include decisions concerning the different weights of individual sectors of industry within the economy as a whole, composition of output, and the improvement of the technological base of industry. It also requires decisions about the nature and character of investment, and its source in either the private sector, or the public, or both. Furthermore, no industrial strategy in the twentieth century can succeed without a large input into research and development, and the institutional framework which will encourage scientific and technological exploration. Above all, an industrial strategy must have clear but flexible aims and objectives, and adequate powers to carry through those aims. It would certainly not mean a rigid central planning mechanism of the former East European type, but a British or European version of the Japanese Ministry of International Trade and Industry (MITI) which was established four years after Hiroshima. In Britain in the immediate post-war years such an institution would necessarily differ from the Japanese model, because of dissimilar national traditions and the historical stage at which industry already existed; but a national policy for industrial regeneration, whatever the details of its organisation, was a crucial desideratum for Britain in the years after 1945. It was not to be.

The Labour Party's manifesto for the 1945 general election, *Let Us Face the Future*, insisted that it would 'plan from the ground up'. The idea of planning had taken hold of popular imagination in the 1940s, dominated as that imagination was with the social scourge of unemployment, and the war years had shown what could be done by government action. No one, however, had any firm idea what 'planning' involved except that governments must ensure that full employment was their first priority. The planning structure that was established owed most to the civil servants in Whitehall and in particular to Edward Bridges who was secretary to the Cabinet 1938–46 and then Permanent Secretary to the Treasury and head of the Home Civil Service until his retirement in 1956. The administrative machinery established proved quite inadequate, above all because it divided planning powers from finance,[67] and it was not until 1947 that a fusion was achieved; and this, in part at least, came about by accident. Attlee offered Stafford Cripps the position of Minister of Economic Affairs in September 1947[68] and then, following Dalton's very minor indiscretion over the Budget, Cripps became Chancellor of the Exchequer.[69] The Treasury now became the most important part of the planning machinery. Edwin Plowden had been brought back to Whitehall to become Chief Planner in the newly established Central Economic Planning Staff (CEPS). Plowden was in the Treasury and very close to Robert Hall of the Cabinet Office and also to Roger Makins who was in charge of the Economic Department of the Foreign Office. The Treasury, it must be emphasised, was concerned with industrial matters only insofar as they impinged upon the balance of payments and the state of the pound. What the Treasury were primarily interested in, from the point of view of their daily responsibilities – no one anywhere in Whitehall really thought in terms of anything but short-term perspectives – was balancing the budget, ensuring the external value of the pound sterling in world markets, and managing the affairs of the sterling area, which included, of course, the sterling balances. What the Treasury was not concerned with was the general health of the economy as a whole, and in this regard, as in others, the Treasury in London was quite different from their counterparts in the civil service and in the central banks of other major industrial countries in Europe.[70]

The structural and managerial deficiencies of the British manufacturing sector in particular were sharply emphasised by the activities of the Anglo-American Council on Productivity and especially by the very large number of reports which specialist teams made of American industries. The teams visiting the United States were made up of managers, workers and specialists, and while there are criticisms to be made of the approach of many of the reports,[71] certain basic facts emerged from all the American studies, of which the most important was the extensive use of mechanisation in all parts of the manufacturing processes: to which could be added better production and control, improved layout, modern methods of costing, and standardisation. At the same time it was undoubtedly management which dominated the teams' investigations and they were by no means unwilling to draw unfavourable contrasts in respect of the attitudes of their British workers with what they generalised about the American workforce. Moreover, the management side were always ready to underline the importance of competition as a factor in high productive levels of efficiency, the implication being that British industry was subject to pervasive State control. By the time the last batch of reports were being prepared the Labour Government was running out of time, and towards the end of 1951 a Conservative administration was in power. The market was now more or less fully returned and the economic boom in the industrialised countries continued to mask the long-term problems of the British economy.

It was, as already remarked upon, the rapid demand for British exports since the war ended that contributed to the general complacency of so many influential groups of British society about its future. Full employment was now becoming an accepted part of economic life and the slow but steady relaxation of controls on consumption all contributed to the hardening of opinion against further State intervention. The increasing bitterness of conservative opinion, especially among the middle classes – the upper classes may be taken for granted – is a political factor in the closing years of the 1940s that is often overlooked or played down. It was, it needs to be emphasised, a demoralising influence upon the Labour Government even though the continued support of working people was never seriously in question. This combination of political acerbity on the part of the average conservative voter allied with the self-congratulatory stance of Labour politicians and Labour intellectuals produced a climate of opinion that was reflected in the political arguments for 'consolidation' rather than further advance in the closing years of Attlee's governments. In the preface to the third and last volume of his memoirs, published in 1962, Hugh Dalton was still ecstatic about what had been achieved:

> Here was a Labour Government, supported for the first time in British history by a great and secure majority at Westminster which, in the lifetime of a single Parliament, beat all past records of legislative output, completed the whole very wide-ranging programme on which it had been elected, and brought in changes which, in the total, so changed the social and economic life of Britain that, at the end of those five years, a new Britain was emerging, not static, not finished, but an immense improvement on pre-war Britain and containing many seeds, sowed by us innovators, of future growth. The Labour Party's High Tide came at the end of that Parliament.[72]

Dalton's euphoric commentary had been pronounced earlier by his younger intellectual friends who had published *New Fabian Essays* in 1952. Not all the essayists followed C.A.R. Crosland in his belief which he set out in the *New Fabian Essays* that we were no longer living in a capitalist society, but rather in a half-way stage to socialism; but certainly the minority of middle-class intellectuals still committed to the Labour Party were deeply impressed with what had been accomplished in the six years of Labour's rule. It is impossible to read the Labour journals of the early 1950s without being surprised by the completeness with which the Labour intellectuals and publicists had accepted the arguments that the 'savage' taxation of the personal incomes of the middle class and the rich had gone as far as was practicable, or, as some were arguing, as was morally justifiable. By practicable they meant that further taxation would stifle incentive, enterprise, risk-taking: all the stock phrases that have done such splendid service since the first tentative restraints on unbridled capitalism were suggested in the second quarter of the nineteenth century. It was Crosland who kept the income redistribution thesis in discussion among those who supported the Labour Government, not only in his 1956 *Future of Socialism* but in the revised edition of 1964 where he still wrote that 'the distribution of personal income has become significantly more equal; and the change has been almost entirely at the expense of property incomes';[73] and in stating this Crosland was only repeating what he had been writing over a decade earlier in *New Fabian Essays*. At the time that Crosland published the first edition of *The Future of Socialism* the rich in Britain were enjoying a bonanza the like of which they had not experienced at any previous time in the twentieth century. Between June 1952 – when the Tories had been in power for six months – and July 1955 the index of ordinary shares rose from 103 to 224, and there was a further sharp rise between 1955 and 1961. During the thirteen years of Tory government – 1951 to 1964 – the average market value of all securities (government bonds, fixed interest stocks and equity) slightly more than doubled. Without doing anything therefore, the average rich man more than doubled his capital; and if he had used his brains, or more likely the professional brains available, he would have done very much better.[74]

The illusion that fundamental changes were taking place in British society during the years of the Labour governments much weakened the position of the activists within the Labour Party, whether on the back benches of the House of Commons, or in the country at large. Naturally they were fully conscious of the changes in the employment situation since 1940, and they greatly appreciated the value of the new social services, and in particular the creation of the National Health Service. For those who looked about them, however, the evidence of a massive shift in income distribution was not exactly overpowering. The differences in the life-style of the middle classes and working people were as obvious as they had been before 1939. The theatre, restaurants, hotels and all other places of entertainment were prospering as never before. For many industrial workers a decent family income now depended upon the wife of the family working full or part time; and at the place of work industrial relations had not changed, whether in the private sector or in the newly nationalised industries. To the ordinary Labour voter the situation contained elements of puzzlement: to some it was demoralising. By contrast the Tory sections of Britain were steadily becoming more aggressive. In the House of Commons, after the initial demoralisation of electoral defeat, the Parliamentary Party soon received its understanding of what needed to be done. We have an account from John Freeman, who entered Parliament in 1945, and who became a junior minister. He was writing in the *New Statesman* on 14

November 1959 and explaining how the Tories dealt with the new Labour Government:

> It is interesting to recall their subsequent parliamentary strategy. The opposition front benches were not filled up with the face-less place men of the 1922 Committee. Alongside Churchill and Eden were to be seen day after day some of the ablest men in Britain . . . all personally appointed by Churchill with orders, after the briefest period of honeymoon which tactical expediency dictated, to attack all the time. I have not forgotten the tension of rising to answer questions or conduct a debate under the cold, implacable eyes of that row of well-tailored tycoons, who hated the Labour government with a passion and a fear which made them dedicated men to get it out of office and to limit the damage it could do to the world which they saw as theirs by right.

Angela Thirkell, daughter of J.W. Mackail and grand-daughter of Edward Burne-Jones, wrote a series of post-war novels which have been rather well described as 'fictionalised journalism'.[75] Their general approach might also be delineated as middle-class populism, hardly to be classed as literature but invaluable for the social historian. *Peace Breaks Out* (1946) was her first offering after the end of the war – an interesting title – and this was followed by *Private Enterprise* (1947) and *Love among the Ruins* (1947). Thirkell was, of course, a snob and she reflected remarkably well the sufferings and the miseries of middle-class England in the immediate post-war years when domestic servants were so hard to come by, foreign travel severely restricted, and the uppity lower classes had what were thought to be *their* people in power at Westminster. Foreigners, intellectuals and the working class were written about as figures of fun, and all the time the difficulties and the struggle of the middle class, their housewives in particular, were recorded with an easy, bitter, at times hysterical, flow of language. Thirkell's country was especially that of the rural gentry, now well on the Thirkell way to extinction, and since her novels sold by the thousands, in Britain and also in America, it is reasonable to assume that their message was touching the hearts of middle-class England in stirring ways. Here is just one of her more absurd passages, from *Private Enterprise*: the words of one of her female characters:

> We need a more eighteenth-century set to see us through this mess; if they were gentlemen in the proper spirit of the word, if they drank and gambled and whored . . . and put people in the pillory or cut off their ears and encouraged child-labour, I'd feel some hope for England.
>
> What I really mind is their trying to burst up the *Empire* . . . I mean like leaving Egypt and trying to give Gibraltar to the natives. If they do anything to Gibraltar, I shall put on a striped petticoat and a muslin fichu and murder them all in their baths, because TRAITORS ought to be murdered.

There are, then, many reasons why the Labour governments failed to achieve fundamental reforms of any lasting significance. What became known as the Welfare State was replicated, in different national guises, in all the advanced industrial societies of Western Europe. There was nothing specifically socialist about the elaboration of social security arrangements for they were a necessary safety net against the radicalism of many working-class groups in the two or three decades after the end of the war; and the financial structure of many welfare schemes were such that they involved a redistribution of income within the working class itself.[76] In the case of Britain a serious industrial strategy, involving a high level of investment, could only have been carried through by a stringent cut-back in military overseas expenditures. This assumes, of course, that the Labour Government would have honoured its social commitments. A sharp reduction in overseas spending could only have come about with major changes in the direction of British foreign policy, and that would have meant an unbridgeable rift with the Tory Party and their affluent supporters in Angela Thirkell country, and the end of the so-called special relationship with the United States. Above all, it would have involved serious, patient and intelligent negotiation with the Soviet Union, which may, of course, given the obduracy of Russian diplomacy, not have succeeded; but the outcome would have been different, on the central assumption that the Russians were not preparing for the first opportunity to reach the Channel ports.

These are speculative matters which it is improbable would ever have come about.[77] Bevin and the Foreign Office would never have altered their views; after the announcement of the Marshall Plan the left-wing opposition to Bevin on the back benches of Westminster faded away; American dollars in addition to the world boom that was gathering strength in the late 1940s meant that full employment and the successful export drive effectively submerged the few ideas that were about concerning the long-term weaknesses of the economy; and the colonial Empire was successfully proving its economic worth. Britain continued what were considered as the Empire's military obligations round the world; the proportion of national income expended on military commitments remained higher than any other country in Europe outside the Soviet Union; and the greater part of research and development investment was directly in the defence industries.[78] As Enoch Powell said from the platform of the Conservative Party Conference in October 1966:

He doubted if it was realised widely how much a part of our balance of payments was related to military expenditure, undertaken in foreign currency. Last year, for example, we earned a surplus of 273 million, and what converted this into a deficit of 354 million was the Government's expenditure in foreign currency, of which the largest item of 280 million was military. Thus our growing burden of external debt was not, as was often falsely alleged, to enable us at home to live beyond our means, but to finance our effort, and principally our financial effort, overseas.[79]

A concluding note on the theme of the industrial strategy that never happened. In 1971 the value of British manufactured exports was 97 per cent higher than manufactured imports; in 1975 the same comparison was 48 per cent higher; by 1980 it was down to 23 per cent; and in 1983 the British manufacturing trade went into deficit. And there it has remained.[80]

5

The British Intervention in Indo-China, 1945

At the end of the war, political conditions in Indo-China, and especially in the north, will probably be particularly unstable. The Indo-chinese independence groups, which may have been working against the Japanese, will quite possibly oppose the restoration of French control. Independence sentiment in the area is believed to be increasingly strong. The Indo-chinese Independence League, representing some ten different native political groups, is thought to carry substantial influence with between one-quarter and one-half million persons. The serious 1930 insurrection, in which over 100,000 peasants actively participated, and similar insurrections which took place in the fall of 1940 indicate that the supporters of independence are neither apathetic nor supine and are willing to fight. It is believed that the French will encounter serious difficulty in overcoming this opposition and in re-establishing French control. . . .

Pre-war French policies involved economic exploitation of the colony for France. . . .

French policy toward Indo-china will be dominated by the desire to re-establish control in order to reassert her prestige in the world as a great power. This purpose will be augmented by the potent influence of the Banque de l'Indo-chine and other economic interests. Many French appear to recognise that it may be necessary for them to make further concessions to Indo-chinese self-government and autonomy primarily to assure native support but also to avoid unfriendly United States opinion. Chief French reliance, however, will continue to be placed upon the United Kingdom, which is almost as anxious as the French to see that no pre-war colonial power suffers diminution of power or prestige.

> POLICY PAPER PREPARED BY AMERICAN STATE DEPARTMENT, 22 JUNE 1945: *Foreign Relations of the United States*, 1945, Vol. VI, pp. 567–8

France had made its first attack upon Indo-China in 1858 but it was nearly fifteen years before conquest of the whole region was officially completed. By the end of the century it had become France's most profitable colony. It was a region of different peoples, tongues and cultures. Before the war with Japan, it consisted of the colony of Cochin-China and the protectorates of Annam, Tonkin, Cambodia and Laos. There was a Governor-General who exercised supervision and control over the governments of the various territories. French rule was direct in Cochin-China and indirect through native sovereigns in Annam, Cambodia and Laos, and through a native administration in Tonkin; although it must be added that French rule was, in fact, dominant throughout the whole region.[1]

Pre-colonial Vietnam – 'Indo-China' was a Western-imposed term – had been a country of considerable educational achievements, and around eighty per cent of the people were, in some degree, literate. A nationalist spirit was fed by an indigenous educational revival in the early years of the twentieth century and between the wars various nationalist movements established themselves, some influenced by the Bolshevik Revolution of 1917. Severe repression seriously weakened the nationalist movement as a whole, especially in the 1930s, but a few groups survived, of which the communists, though quite small numerically, were potentially the most important.[2]

French colonial rule was harsh and corrupt, and when metropolitan France collapsed before the German offensive in the spring of 1940, the French colonial administration acknowledged Vichy as the legitimate authority. The Japanese were steadily putting pressure upon the French local administration, and on 27 September 1940, the Governor, Admiral Decoux, signed an agreement with the Japanese to station 6000 troops north of the Red River, and 25,000 in the south. From this time the Japanese effectively took control, and when formal hostilities with the USA and the UK began after Pearl Harbor, Japan, although continuing to operate through the French administration, began to use Indo-China as a base of increasing importance. Saigon became the headquarters of the Japanese armies in South-East Asia. In March 1945, with the end of the war in Europe a matter only of weeks, the Japanese took over completely from the French, among other reasons to forestall the possibility of Decoux moving over to the Western Allies. French resistance to the Japanese had been minuscule up to the spring of 1945, and there were only isolated incidents thereafter.[3] By contrast the Viet Minh, founded in May 1941, was growing steadily in strength. The Chinese had arrested Ho Chi Minh at the end of 1941 and kept him in prison for the next thirteen months, but it was the Chinese who first provided an umbrella under which the Viet Minh continuously enlarged its resistance activities. It was the Japanese overthrow of the French administration, however, that brought the Viet Minh into close contact with the Americans. The Viet Minh had earlier assisted in the rescue of an American pilot and his return to China, and in mid March 1945 Captain Charles Fenn, who was in charge of OSS (Office of Strategic Services) operations in Indo-China, met Ho Chi Minh in southern China, and worked out arrangements for joint co-operation. The OSS agreed to provide radio equipment and some arms and the Viet Minh offered in return intelligence information and sabotage activities. A month later OSS personnel became attached to Ho Chi Minh's headquarters which was located about fifty miles north of Hanoi. From these early contacts there developed political discussions as well as increased military action.[4]

There was another consequence of the Japanese suspension of the French administration on 9 March 1945 which is often overlooked. The Japanese took power into their own hands for two main reasons: the first, to neutralise French troops in the event of an Allied invasion, which at the time was widely anticipated; and the second, to encourage nationalist opinion within Indo-China in order to strengthen opposition against the former colonial powers. The French civilians in general were left alone, although many of the Army were killed or imprisoned, and the Japanese encouraged the individual regions to declare their independence of the French and replace French officials by their own people. Bao Dai, the emperor of Annam, abrogated the 1884 treaty which gave France 'protection' over Annam and Tonkin, and he invited Tran Trong Kim to head a government whose ministers were all Vietnamese: mainly professional people such as teachers and lawyers. An early development was to revive the older name of Vietnam, and there was a considerable growth of a mass political participation especially among the youth (whose organisations later provided the Viet Minh with large-scale support).[5]

The political and military situation in the Far East was being rapidly transformed during the spring and summer months of 1945. General Le May worked out new tactics for the huge B-29 bombers, and on the night of 9/10 March there took place the first fire-bombing raid, on Tokyo, producing a greater devastation than that of Dresden three weeks earlier. Nearly eighteen miles of Tokyo were burned out; the official death toll being later estimated at 130,000. Before the atom bombs were used more than a quarter of a million Japanese civilians had been killed in firestorm bombing raids.[6] Peace negotiations were already under way through Moscow at least six weeks before the Potsdam Conference, and the Japanese finally surrendered on 15 August 1945. Ho Chi Minh's National Liberation Committee took power in Hanoi on 19 August; the Emperor Bao Dai abdicated in the last week of August; and a Provisional Executive Committee, dominated by the Viet Minh, took over Saigon. The anti-imperialist and nationalist groups in the south were less powerful than in the north and were deeply divided among themselves, but the general support was widespread.[7] On 2 September 1945 Ho Chi Minh spoke at a rally in Ba Dinh Square in Hanoi, and he read the 'Declaration of Independence of the Democratic Republic of Vietnam' to the assembled masses. It began with the opening statement of the American Declaration of Independence of 1776, continued with the words of the French revolutionary proclamation of 1791, and followed with a bitter attack upon French colonialism:

> 'All men are created equal. They are endowed by their Creator with certain inalienable rights, among these are Life, Liberty and the pursuit of Happiness.'
>
> This immortal statement was made in the Declaration of Independence of the United States of America in 1776. In a broader sense it means: All the peoples on the earth are equal from birth, all the peoples have a right to live, to be happy and free.
>
> The Declaration of the French Revolution made in 1791 on the Rights of Man and the Citizen also states: 'All men are born free and with equal rights, and must always remain free and have equal rights.'
>
> Those are undeniable truths.
>
> Nevertheless, for more than eighty years, the French imperialists, abusing the standard of Liberty, Equality and Fraternity, have violated our Fatherland and oppressed our fellow-citizens. They have acted contrary to the ideals of humanity and justice.
>
> In the field of politics, they have deprived our people of every democratic liberty.
>
> They have enforced inhuman laws; they have set up three distinct political regimes in the North, the Centre and the South of Viet-Nam in order to wreck our national unity and prevent our people from being united.
>
> They have built more prisons than schools. They have mercilessly slain our patriots; they have drowned our uprisings in rivers of blood.

The statement continued with the recital of French crimes against the people of Vietnam; it appealed to the Allied nations who acknowledged the principles of self-determination at Tehran, Yalta and San Francisco; it underlined the struggle their people had conducted against the French, and against the fascists in the war that had just ended; and it concluded:

> For these reasons, we, members of the Provisional Government of the Democratic Republic of Viet-nam, solemnly declare to the world that Viet-nam has the right to be a free and independent country – and in fact it is so already. The entire Vietnamese people are determined to mobilise all their physical and mental strength, to sacrifice their lives and property in order to safeguard their independence and liberty.[8]

French Indo-China had not become part of the political consciousness of the ordinary people of the Western Powers during the war years. Saigon became the headquarters of the Japanese forces in South-East Asia, but there was no fighting between Japan or any of the Allies in the region, and Japan, as already noted, did not take over the full administration of the country until the spring of 1945. In the next stage of the war, Malaya and Singapore would have been the area of invasion had the Japanese Army not surrendered.[9] French Indo-China, however, was certainly not absent from the discussions among the policy-making élites in Washington and Whitehall, and the debates and arguments over Indo-China illustrated sharply and clearly the problems of nationalism, colonialism and imperialism and the political differences on these issues between the United States and Britain.

There was one constant throughout the years of war in the Far East: the unshakeable conviction on the part of the British, French and the Dutch that their 1939 colonial territories would automatically return to their Western 'owners' when the war was ended. Whatever the verbal manoeuvrings of the imperialist powers during the war years there was never a serious doubt in their minds that empires would be restored. Britain, France and the Netherlands confronted two problems: the first was the attitude of the United States, and in particular that of Roosevelt, towards the colonial question in general; and the second, which except in India was not appreciated seriously by any of the former colonial powers in the Far East, was the growth and development of nationalism and nationalist movements. In the post-war years it was of little account whether the nationalists of any one region had collaborated or not with the Japanese.[10]

Roosevelt was reflecting important sections of American opinion in his constantly reiterated opposition to the ethos of colonialism and imperialism. With some individuals and groups anti-colonialism was connected with isolationism, and during the 1930s and early 1940s both trends of opinion had been powerfully represented in Congress.[11] Isolationist attitudes were not uncommonly associated with Anglophobia, and anti-British opinions were strongly reinforced with the shattering collapse of British power in the Far East when the Japanese Army quickly over-ran Hong Kong, Malaya and Singapore, and then Burma. Criticisms of British imperialism sharply increased in the United States, and the abject surrender of Singapore was especially deplored.[12] There are many examples that can be quoted of anti-British attitudes in the United States at this time, although it was recognised in some quarters that there also existed an anti-imperialist tradition, especially associated with the Labour Party, the leaders of which were now in Churchill's Coalition Government. The public statements, however, coming from London, as well as the diplomatic communications, were clear in their insistence that the Empire was a central part of Britain's Great Power status in the world. Churchill's famous Mansion House speech in November 1942, briefly discussed above, confirmed once again the emphasis that Britain placed upon its imperial position.[13] It was not, however, Britain but France that was mainly the subject of Roosevelt's public and private statements and comments on the abomination of colonialism. Roosevelt always had an abiding distrust of General de Gaulle, and he regularly singled out French Indo-China as the example of colonialism at its worst. When Queen Wilhelmina of the Netherlands announced in December 1942 that a political union between the Netherlands and the Netherlands East Indies would be established after the war 'on the solid foundation of complete partnership' the Americans received this declaration as a response to their own anti-colonialist stance. Roosevelt was impressed and he often used the Dutch example as an example for both the British and the French. He had earlier followed the negotiations over Indian independence with close interest, although it was a subject that he learned not to confront Churchill with directly, given his own views on the iniquities of imperialist domination. The failure of the Cripps mission to India in the spring of 1942 was followed by the 'Quit India' movement launched by Gandhi. Harold Ickes wrote to the President in criticism of the British repression and Roosevelt replied on 12 August 1942: 'You are right about India but it would be playing with fire if the British Empire were to tell me to mind my own business.'[14] With the French it was different. They were not part of the Grand Alliance for which major compromises had to be made, at least in public and certainly at times round the conference table. The President's hostility to the return of the French to Indo-China continued until his death in April 1945.[15]

Sumner Welles, in a Memorial Day (30 May 1942) speech, had predicted the end of imperialism when the war was over. It was being fought, he said, to abolish discrimination between peoples on the grounds of race, creed and colour. These were themes, among many others, that were to be the concern of an important Advisory Committee on Post-War Foreign Policy which had been established within the State Department. Its existence was first reported to Whitehall by Halifax in a weekly political report dated 11 June 1942. Sumner Welles was chairman, and Halifax listed the main headings agreed:

(a) necessity for a long armistice, possibly lasting several years, before final settlement is made;

(b) the establishment of an international police force;

(c) abolition of colonial empires;

(d) equal access for all democracies to raw materials of world.[16]

The despatch went on to note that these ideas were being generally discussed in Washington at the present time.

A guest present at a private dinner given to President by Welles and attended by the Litvinoffs and Brazilian Ambassador said the President talked along lines of Welles' speech and condemned the discussion of territorial arrangements before victory as likely to arouse resentment and suspicion in America, feelings with which he personally sympathised.[17]

The membership of the State Department's Advisory Committee on Post-War Foreign Policy included Stanley Hornbeck, a senior State Department official, Isaiah Bowman, president of Johns Hopkins University, James T. Shotwell, the historian, and Mrs Anne Hare McCormick, an editorial member of the *New York Times* who was noted for her anti-imperialist views. The

Committee spent some of its time during the summer months of 1942 discussing matters of self-determination, how the principles of trusteeship could be applied, and what was the kind of international organisation envisaged for the resolution of these issues in the post-war years. Roosevelt himself strongly favoured the plan for an international trusteeship in the case of French Indo-China which would prepare the way for full independence, and until the last months before his death he pursued the idea, in contrast with his expressed views that post-war arrangements should be left open until the war was finished. Even in this case, however, Roosevelt was never clear-cut in his decisions concerning future policy, a comment that can be more strongly made in almost all areas of international diplomacy. By contrast with Roosevelt's irresolution, the British Foreign Office and the Colonial Office were firm in their support for the return of the French. The Colonial Office were even critical of what they regarded as the 'defeatism' of the Foreign Office in their attitude towards the future in the Far East. An Assistant Under-Secretary and former head of the Far Eastern Department wrote in a minute of 17 June 1942:

> There is a kind of defeatism in the Foreign Office Far Eastern outlook which is not a new phenomenon. They suffer from what to my mind is a quite fatal lack of confidence themselves in our position in the Colonies, and they seem to be fascinated by the belief that HMG must be subservient to the supposed American policy of preventing the restoration of British sovereignty in Malaya, Hong Kong, and possibly Burma, too.[18]

The Foreign Office were, however, firmer in their approach than this comment suggests. It was during 1943 that the question of Indo-China came to be increasingly discussed. The victory at the second battle of Alamein, the landings in North Africa, above all the surrender of the German 6th Army at Stalingrad, all meant that the tide of war had turned against the Germans, and the problems of the post-war world, however far away they might be, were inevitably coming into the foreground of international politics. In the case of Indo-China there were two broad considerations which affected long-term planning. The first was the question of Empire and the recognition that what happened to one colonial power could also influence the course of events in other imperial powers. The second was the future of France in Europe and the historical problems of the balance of advantages of one grouping against another. G.F. Hudson[19] set down the basic facts that Whitehall came to accept:

> It would seem unwise to base any policy on the assumption that France will be weak after the war, because she may well be able to supplement her own strength by diplomatic connections of a traditional kind. If Germany were prostrate, a revival of the Franco-Czecho-Slovak-Soviet bloc could dominate Europe, perhaps to the great detriment of British and American interests. It would appear to be a British interest that there should not be a continental European bloc in contraposition to a

group formed by the USA and the British Commonwealth, and one way to keep the French 'loose' from such a bloc would surely be to give them as far as possible a sense of common interest with ourselves as an overseas colonial Power – with the added consideration for us that outlying territories such as Madagascar or Indo-China would always be hostages to fortune in the event of France being involved in a conflict with the USA or Britain. The Americans also might appreciate this point of view if it were put to them.[20]

Churchill was reluctant to become involved with the French problems in the Far East at this time. The French had been pressing for representation on the Pacific War Council. The first meeting of the Council, with Churchill in the chair, had taken place on 10 February in London, and it was understood that meetings would either be in Washington or London. When Cadogan, who was under pressure from the French, asked Churchill for a decision on French participation in the Council – this was in late October 1943 – Churchill replied 'No need for action yet'. Cadogan argued in a further note that there were new grounds for positive action:

a refusal would confirm the French in their present suspicions that neither we nor the Americans wish to see them resume sovereignty over Indo-China. This would add to their existing sense of frustration and wounded pride. Moreover, in view of the well-known American attitude towards the restoration of colonies generally, there is much to be said for the Colonial Powers sticking together in the Far East. This included the French as well as the Dutch.[21]

The French were also demanding a military mission attached to SEAC, and again the Foreign Office were sympathetic. By the end of 1943 the basic principles of the British policy towards Indo-China were agreed within the Foreign Office; and early in 1944 the British Cabinet approved a Foreign Office memorandum on Indo-China and the French possessions in the Pacific whereby 'the French should be allowed to retain their territories after the war, subject to whatever international undertakings would result from a system of collective security.' Sir Maurice Peterson, who quoted these words, was writing to Ismay[22] explaining the Foreign Office's reasons for their position, and asking for further concessions on behalf of France. He commented on the general reasons for supporting France:

The reason which led us to this conclusion was the desirability that France should be strong and friendly to us in Europe and that a friendly French policy should be reflected in the French overseas Empire. These reasons having been considered valid, we now suggest that the same principle should be applied as far as possible to the other Far Eastern questions outstanding with the French, namely their desire (a) to have a French mission attached to Admiral Mountbatten, (b) to take a more active part in the Far Eastern war, (c) to participate in planning, and (d) to be allowed a share in political warfare in the Far East.

Sharp differences between the United States and Britain over policy matters in the Far East continued right through the closing years of the war. The Colonial Office and the Dominions Office, for example, were deeply disturbed about the ideas on trusteeship which the groups around Roosevelt were emphasising and which Roosevelt himself was so often talking about. He was clear that ultimate independence should be the objective for every colonial country in the peace that was to come, but he also recognised that certain peoples would need a period of 'tutelage' by the parent states. 'Tutelage' for Roosevelt did not mean the old-style colonialism dressed up with meaningless trappings; and he firmly believed throughout the war years until his death that the principles of self-determination set forth in the Atlantic Charter must be so organised as to create independent states from the former empires.

It has already been remarked upon that Roosevelt used Indo-China as the example of colonialism at its worst. At the Cairo Conference, in the evening of 23 November 1943, Roosevelt and Harry Hopkins met Chiang Kai-shek and his wife, and there was a wide-ranging discussion on China in the post-war world, and on colonial issues in general. Once again Roosevelt talked of trusteeship for Indo-China as 'the most the French should have', provided that it was responsible to a United Nations organisation.[23] When Roosevelt returned from Cairo and Tehran – where he also discussed colonial matters with Stalin without a British presence – he called a meeting of representatives of interested powers. There is no official American record of this meeting but Halifax reported it to London on 19 December 1943 emphasising Roosevelt's arguments why Indo-China should not be restored to France. The British Ambassador's despatch summarising the President's views caused intense irritation in London, and some overtly strong minutes of dissent were appended. Cavendish-Bentinck referred to Roosevelt's 'megalomania', G.F. Hudson expatiated upon the French economic and social achievements in Indo-China, and Cadogan followed the same line of argument:

> I have heard the President say that Indo-China should not revert to France, and he is on record as saying that the French, in that region, 'were hopeless'. I have not had the advantage of hearing him develop this theme. We'd better look out: were the French more 'hopeless' in Indo-China than we in Malaya or the Dutch in the East Indies? In what way were they hopeless? When stricken at home, they could not, of course, defend it. But was their peace-time record so bad?

Cadogan concluded with the comment that this was 'one of the President's most half-baked and most unfortunate obiter dicta'. The Foreign Secretary, Anthony Eden, noted: 'I agree.'[24]

There were also important differences over military matters. Mountbatten had a combined Anglo-American staff but until Potsdam in July 1945 there were always questions that were disputed, some with considerable bitterness.[25] Esler Dening, political adviser to Mountbatten, summarised some of the problems in an important memorandum he sent to Whitehall in February 1944. The 'Political Implications of Far Eastern Strategy' offered a clear guide to the disagreements between the American strategy for the Far Eastern war and the part which the British ought to be afforded.[26] The 'Nimitz–MacArthur' approach, Dening wrote, was that there was only a contributory role of no great significance for the British. This, he argued, was quite unsatisfactory and wholly unacceptable. In the post-war world the British Commonwealth would be 'an essential factor' in the maintenance of peace in the Far East, and to achieve that position it was essential that the British contribution to the war should be 'a principal and not a subsidiary one'. He went on further to note the importance of the struggle on the mainland of Asia, the military defeat of Japan being necessary if the cult of militarism was to be destroyed. Dening ended by emphasising the importance of the establishment of SEAC, with a combined Anglo-American staff, and noted that Anglo-American relations in the whole area covered by SEAC had already improved.

Dening sent an internal memorandum along with his official statement, in which he informed the Foreign Office that he intended to show it to General Wedemeyer, Mountbatten's American deputy. Dening further commented that he had refrained from criticising the 'tenacity' of the American opposition to the British but he then proceeded to offer a sharp appraisal of the British Chiefs of Staff for their agreement with the United States' strategy at Cairo and opined that the British representatives at the Cairo Conference (Churchill, Eden, Mountbatten and Cadogan) were not fully aware of the implications of that strategy until after the event.

Comments on the Dening memorandum inside the Foreign Office were all favourable. Cavendish-Bentinck was in complete agreement but noted that there were implications for future manpower resources, and that only 'a very small measure of demobilisation' would be possible until the war with Japan was over. Cadogan minuted:

I think Mr Dening has written a very good paper, which should be endorsed. Unless we can take an obvious part in retrieving the fortunes of the United Nations in the Far East, our prestige in that area will remain at zero. Mr Bentinck has pointed out the manpower difficulty. If that cannot be overcome, the situation will be irremediable, but there seems to me to be no doubt that we should be prepared to go to all possible lengths to overcome it.

Eden wrote that he liked it very much and would like to send it to the Prime Minister. When the memorandum was sent to Churchill Eden wrote a covering note in which he strongly supported the Dening thesis: 'We want to make it plain to the world that we have played our part in regaining our Far Eastern Empire'.[27] It was in the same month of February 1944 that the British Cabinet adopted a Foreign Office paper on Indo-China, briefly discussed above, and thus by the spring of this year the broad outlines of British policy in the Far East had been agreed. There were still occasional problems, but they were problems only of timing. Eden and the Foreign Office were constantly pressing the War Cabinet for decisions about the French and their participation in SEAC, and Churchill, who always had a reluctance to concern himself with the French in the Far East, wrote an exasperated letter to Eden, dated 21 May 1944:

> It is hard enough to get along in SEAC when we virtually only have the Americans to deal with. The more the French can get their finger into the pie, the more trouble they will make in order to show that they are not humiliated in any way by the events through which they have passed. You will have de Gaulliste intrigues there just as you now have in Syria and Lebanon.
>
> Before we could bring the French officially into the Indo-China area, we should have to settle with President Roosevelt. He has been more outspoken to me on that subject than on any other Colonial country, and I imagine, it is one of his principal war aims to liberate Indo-China from France. Whenever he has raised it, I have repeatedly reminded him of his pledges about the integrity of the French Empire[28] and have reserved our position. Do you really want to go and stir all this up at such a time as this?[29]

Roosevelt's attitude towards French Indo-China did not change in any serious way until just before his death and even then it was more likely that he was responding to the increasing pressures within his own decision-making élites for a more general support of the French claims. Stettinius, who had replaced Cordell Hull as Secretary of State, sent a long memorandum to Roosevelt on 2 November 1944 in which he set out the French and British policies in the Far East, and noted specifically how positive the British were in their actions in support of the French. He noted, for example, that the British SOE had recently received orders from the Foreign Office to have 'nothing to do' in their underground work with any Annamite or national organisation 'but to devote their efforts to the French'; and Stettinius further reported that the OWI representative in Delhi had received information to the effect that the British wanted the American OWI activities to be dampened down in Indo-China in order 'not to stir up native resistance to the Japanese and so incite the Japanese to send more troops into these areas'.[30] Roosevelt's reply, on the following day, was emphatic: 'We have made no final decisions on the future of Indo-China. This should be made clear.'[31]

On 20 January 1945 the French Provisional Government sent an uncompromising statement to the United States Government, insisting on their sovereignty over French Indo-China, quoting the Brazzaville decisions and requesting once again ships for the transport of troops to French Indo-China.[32] At Yalta, on 8 February 1945, Roosevelt had a private session with Stalin in which it was again made clear that the United States was unwilling to accept the French case; and it was only in the month or so before Roosevelt's death, on 12 April, that in a much-quoted conversation with Taussig, one of his advisers, Roosevelt offered an indication of his changing position.[33]

The pressures for a relaxation of an intransigent position on French Indo-China were coming from different parts of the policy-making establishment in Washington. The American Joint Chiefs of Staff had always been opposed to the idea of trusteeship, largely because of their insistence that there must be unrestricted American control over the islands in the Pacific taken from the Japanese; this they deemed central to post-war security. The State Department had long been divided. Cordell Hull had supported his Far Eastern Division when they accepted trusteeship with the ultimate aim of independence together with a policy of the 'Open Door'. Against this view were the State Department's European Office who cared nothing for the emerging nationalisms in the Far East, or elsewhere in the world, but who were increasingly conscious of the need for a strong France within the post-war Europe whose shape was beginning to emerge. In this they were allied to the British whose own refusal to countenance any international control over their former colonies, without their complete agreement, also worked towards limiting Roosevelt's ideas and intentions. Roosevelt himself, while scattering his opinions, forcefully expressed, whenever opportunities offered themselves, never made specific any firm proposals for the solution of colonial issues.[34] When Stettinius replaced Hull as Secretary of State the influence of the European Office became steadily more compelling. At the Yalta Conference it had been agreed that trusteeship should only be imposed if the 'mother' country agreed. In the months that followed, the increasing concern with the position and policies of the Soviet Union began to affect all other issues, and in the appreciation of global strategy it was not difficult to argue that the French should be allowed to repossess their former colonies. It was hardly necessary for de Gaulle to use the crude blackmail reported by the American Ambassador to France in March 1945, when de Gaulle said he thought the French people would be gravely perturbed if the Americans opposed their return to Indo-China, and that: 'We do not want to be Communists; we do not want to fall into the Russian orbit; but I hope that you do not push us into it.'[35]

By the date that de Gaulle made these remarks most of the crucial decisions relating to Indo-China had already been taken. The military and the top officials on both sides of the Atlantic, or most of them, knew what they wanted. Churchill could still rebuff Duff Cooper in June 1945, but this was only a matter of difference of timing within the high politics involved.[36] One of the issues still unresolved was the definition of the area covered by SEAC – known in some American quarters as 'Save England's Ancient Colonies' – and the place of Indo-China in relation to that Command. At the Cairo Conference of late 1943 Indo-China had been included within the command of Chiang Kai-shek, and therefore of the Americans; and Mountbatten, during 1944, began pushing hard for a redefinition of the geographical area of SEAC. In a personal letter to Eden in the middle of August 1944 he urged the Foreign Secretary to attempt once again to achieve a decision: 'I have felt all along that it was vital that the French should liberate French Indo-China in collaboration with us, and that they should be properly grateful for us doing it for and with them.'[37] Mountbatten continued to note that Roosevelt's attitudes made things difficult, but he suggested that the latter's approach to de Gaulle might be changing: 'I have heard rumours that the Americans are about to start making up for lost time, and are embarking on a kind of competition with us in trying to secure the good graces of the French for after the war.'

On 24 August 1944 a meeting took place between Eden with his Far East officials and Massigli, the representative of the French government in London.[38] Massigli said they had already selected de Gaulle's nominees for the Indo-China administration, with powers from the Provisional Government, and Eden underlined the point that Britain had made its position clear at the Cairo Conference: 'We were ready to give facilities where others did the same, but we have taken the line that what we have we hold.' A month later Eden once again insisted that it was essential for the recovery of British prestige in the Far East that Britain should play a 'major role' against Japan, and that its contribution should be 'not merely effective but spectacular'. One consequence that followed was that the boundaries of SEAC 'should not be treated as a purely military problem'; and Eden went on to repeat once again the argument that had become common in Whitehall:

> It cannot be legitimately argued that France has misruled Indo-China. . . . Whatever criticisms may be levelled against the French administration (as against the administrations of other colonial territories) French rule has preserved Indo-China from tyranny and other evils and has given peace and political cohesion to a territory which has no geographical or ethnographical unity.[39]

The French were in a much stronger position to press their claims after the liberation of Paris, and then of the whole of France. A decree of 21 February 1945, published in the *Journal Officiel*, established a Cabinet Committee over which de Gaulle himself presided, or, in his absence, the Minister for Colonies; the terms of reference being 'to organise French participation in all its forms in the liberation of Indo-Chinese territories and to prepare for the re-establishment of French sovereignty there'.[40] When the Japanese organised their complete take-over in mid March 1945 the result was to strengthen the French case for their involvement in Far Eastern affairs. Massigli argued strongly that the 600 officers and men of the Corps Léger d'Intervention (CLI) should be sent by air to the Far East. They were troops described as having an 'intimate knowledge' of Indo-China. French plans continued to develop. Dening informed London that they were planning to assemble a hundred administrators in Ceylon and India in preparation for the eventual take-over of Indo-China; and he asked London to note the French assumption that the invasion of Indo-China would be the responsibility of SEAC. Dening further went on record to the effect that if it was the Americans who were to be involved in the fighting, then the French would undoubtedly try to attach themselves to the forces of the United States.[41]

The Foreign Office draft for the San Francisco Conference in May 1945 emphasised the role of the French in South-East Asia as the main stabilising force in the region; and in this last summer of the war – a period when no one expected the war to end so soon – the French continued to strengthen their position with the very limited resources at their disposal.[42] At the time of the Japanese surrender, in early August 1945, there was a French mission and a civil colonial mission in Calcutta – unknown, so it appears, to the Indian Government in Delhi; and there was now a military mission at SEAC headquarters. There were still no French troops available for what was soon to be the occupation of Indo-China. It was the Potsdam Conference in July 1945 which finally settled the boundaries of the South-East Asia Command. All the areas of Indo-China south of the 16th parallel were now added to SEAC while north of that line responsibility remained with Chiang Kai-shek and his American advisers. All of Dutch Indonesia was also added to SEAC's responsibility. On 8 August Mountbatten suggested to London that negotiations ought to be finalised with the French concerning the future administration of Indo-China. There was already an agreement with the Dutch in respect of Indonesia but this had assumed a military operation against the Japanese, and therefore the subordination of the civil authorities to the military during the course of the fighting. The situation of Indo-China was thought to be quite different. At the beginning of August General Leclerc, head of the French Military Mission at SEAC, was appointed Commander-in-Chief of all French forces, and Vice-Admiral Thierry D'Argenlieu was designated future High Commissioner and Governor-General of French Indo-China whenever the situation permitted.[43] These appointments, together with Mountbatten's request for a directive concerning the future British role in Indo-China, led the Foreign Office in London to draft a memorandum in close consultation with the French, and this was sent to Mountbatten at the end of the month. This was quite different from the 1944 agreement with the Dutch, and it provoked a number of serious disagreements on Mountbatten's part; on 10 September a revised draft was sent from SEAC to London. He was then instructed to proceed on the basis of his own draft in which were incorporated quite minor changes from London. The final text was not sent to Mountbatten until 9 October, by which time the British occupation of Indo-China had been in existence for nearly a month.[44]

The central purpose of the Mountbatten draft, which after some amendment became an official document agreed to by the British and French governments, was that the British occupation forces, in respect of Indo-China south of the 16th parallel, were responsible for two main objectives: the first was the surrender and disarmament of all Japanese forces, and the second, the liberation of Allied prisoners of war and other internees of the Japanese in Indo-China. It was clearly stated that administrative responsibility throughout the region was the responsibility of the French authorities. There were certain key areas where the British would exercise necessary authority to fulfil their specific tasks, but even here the military were expected to conduct relations with the civilian population through the French administration. All matters concerning the provision of supplies for civil purposes were a matter for the French.[45]

The terms of the agreement were quite unworkable, based as they were upon a misreading of Indo-China's internal situation. Dening had been warning London for many months of the very difficult problems that would have to be faced once the war with Japan was over, and of all the commentators within the British Foreign Service he was one of the very few who had begun to understand the growth of nationalism among the peoples of the Far East. A despatch of his dated 11 December 1944 warned both against the Americans and also of the disturbed politics of the former colonies in the aftermath of war; and it was shredded by his colleagues in Whitehall. Cavendish-Bentinck in particular was wholly dismissive of Dening's analysis and advised that as the Chiefs of Staff 'have a tendency to be prejudiced against Mr Dening' it would be preferable to give this and similar recent telegrams 'the minimum circulation'.[46] The issues can be simply stated. The French had every intention of returning to Indo-China; but they had no resources, of men or matériel. Since the British military and the Foreign Office were determined to support the French repossession, only SEAC's Commander-in-Chief could arrange for a military occupation which would disarm the Japanese, release all prisoners and internees, and hand over the whole administration of the country to the French. There were two main problems which London and Paris disregarded: one was that there was no viable French administration which had not collaborated with the Japanese; and the second, of crucial importance, was the bitter hostility of the peoples of Vietnam towards the French, and their unshakeable belief that it was their inalienable right to control their own destiny. Mountbatten had glimmerings of these problems and there were occasions when he knew that what was being done was immoral and unjust. He obeyed his orders, and the evidence of his diary does not suggest a man riven with feelings of guilt. It is not the hindsight of the historian that has clarified the issues; they were appreciated at the time. The French, like the Dutch in Indonesia, were hated; they were to be put back into their former colonies by the British; and since there were not enough troops of the Allied Powers available, it was inevitable that the defeated Japanese would be brought into service: first for normal policing and then, as the nationalist movements became convinced that the British were determined to put back into power their despised colonial masters, for more active combat. General Sir William Slim was Commander-in-Chief of Allied Land Forces, South East Asia (ALFSEA). On 6 October 1945 he sent a report to London on the situation in both Indo-China and Indonesia in which the contradictions and confusions of the policies the military had to follow were enumerated very clearly.[47]

'The unfortunate situation has arisen', Slim wrote, whereby the only armed troops available for maintaining order outside the very small areas where British troops are concentrated are the Japanese; and using the Japanese, Slim went on, has 'many grave disadvantages'. For one thing we cannot disarm them; for another the Japanese do not like what they are being asked to do; and by using Japanese troops 'We earn the opprobrium of the local inhabitants and to some extent of our Allies for employing the Japanese at all.' Slim was, of course, stating the problems in mild terms. He went on to warn against the dangers of provocative actions by both the French and the Dutch – and he was certainly not just referring to the armed forces – and the result could be 'a large-scale native uprising against Europeans'; against which our present forces would be quite inadequate. He then pointed up the contradictions between what everyone had thought would be their aims and objectives, and what in fact they were now becoming involved in. A paragraph in this report encapsulates the political and moral dilemmas of what was thought to be the early months of peace:

I must confess that the directives we have been receiving from various sources seem to me to have been somewhat involved and at times contradictory. Originally I understood that the main object was to disarm the Japanese and evacuate our prisoners without getting in anyway involved against nationalistic forces or move-ment. The Secretary of State for War was particularly insistent on this point during his recent visit.[48] At the same time we were to work in the closest accord with Dutch and French authorities and to make them responsible for the general internal security. These tasks were to be achieved by using British forces to hold only key areas and Allied forces to control the areas outside. The difficulty of this is that up to the present the British forces have not been large enough to hold even the key areas and there have been practically no Allied forces to hold outside them. Japanese have therefore had to be used to supplement the British even in key areas and wholly outside. If French or Dutch are used to extend these areas I think there is little doubt that, unless the political situation improves immensely, there will be clashes. When these clashes occur, even if British troops do not have to go to the assistance of their Allies, as has already happened, the Dutch or French forces will be operating under the command of the local British Force Commander, under my higher command,

and the SAC's Supreme Command. As long as we retain this command we cannot divorce ourselves from the responsibility for their actions.[49]

The first move into Indo-China by SEAC was on 8 September 1945 when a small advanced party of engineers and medical reconnaissance detachments together with a Control Staff of the Repatriation organisation (RAPWI) flew into the Tan Son Nhut airfield near Saigon. The Japanese had been warned of their arrival, and all facilities were provided. In the following days small groups of the military arrived and on the 13th General Gracey flew in with Brigadier Maunsell, his Chief of Staff; the build-up of the 80th Brigade of the 20th Division continued throughout September, much hampered by bad weather. Towards the end of the month the whole Brigade had arrived as well as the 273 Spitfire Squadron. Gracey had commanded the 20th Division during the reconquest of Burma and was regarded as a highly efficient soldier. The Division was Indian and Gurkha, with British officers as was customary. The RAF were almost wholly British.[50]

Gracey was Commander-in-Chief of the British forces in Indo-China and in addition he was also head of the Control Commission; in that position he was under the immediate orders of Mountbatten while he reported to Slim on strictly military affairs. No political adviser became available to Gracey until some ten days after his arrival in Saigon. There is a good deal of scattered evidence concerning Gracey's own views on the internal situation in Indo-China[51] and there is confirmation of the single-mindedness with which he developed his policies from the earliest days. Gracey was convinced beyond doubt that the French had a moral and political right to re-establish themselves in their former colony, and there is equally no doubt that a commander-in-chief with a more even-handed approach would have acted differently.[52]

When Gracey and his advance guard arrived in Saigon they were received by Japanese generals, and their troops, at the airfield. The only transport available was Japanese with Japanese drivers. Gracey ignored the waiting Viet Minh delegation – his own orders were specific concerning the recognition of French authority in administrative affairs – and soon after he arrived he was in consultation with Colonel J. Cédile who had been parachuted into the country north of Saigon on 22 August and been captured by the Japanese, but had escaped on 1 September and persuaded the Japanese to continue guarding the Governor-General's palace until the British arrived. There had been a considerable riot against the French on 2 September (which Cédile later described as 'moderately serious') and by the time Gracey arrived there was a nominal Viet Minh government in Saigon and a considerable breakdown of law and order, with much pillaging, directed especially against the French. The Viet Minh Committee which was acting as the Provisional Government, took active measures after the 2 September riot to restore peace and confidence: they arrested all the Trotskyist leaders in Saigon,[53] and then members of the Coa Dai and Hoa Hao,[54] but the French population remained highly nervous. All the reports that came out of Indo-China in these early days emphasised the hatred of the French by the peoples of Vietnam; the 'veiled contempt' of the French by the Japanese, whom they knew only as a defeated nation; and the bitterness that ran through the French community. The political adviser attached to Gracey's Control Commission reported on 27 September:

> The French population here present a difficult problem. As I have said their morale is low. They combine an almost hysterical fear of the Annamites (which to my mind denotes a guilty conscience) with an intense hatred and desire for revenge. These people will constitute one of the greatest obstacles to the institution by the French of a liberal policy and its acceptance by the Annamites. If at all possible I think these people should be evacuated from Indo-China at the earliest possible moment.[55]

The Japanese Commander of all the military forces throughout South-East Asia was Field Marshal Count Terauchi. Gracey had already been in touch with him following the riots of 2 September insisting that under the Rangoon agreement[56] Terauchi had accepted responsibility for the maintenance of law and order until the arrival of the SEAC troops; but the application of the agreement was patchy, with some sections of Japanese troops standing by while French property was being ransacked. Gracey, in the weeks after his arrival, very soon tightened up control and quite quickly brought the Japanese into line with his instructions. Within a week, moreover, Gracey took a political decision which was to set the guidelines for British policy until their withdrawal. On 19 September he sent his Chief of Staff to the Viet Minh Provisional Government with a proclamation which it was intended to issue two days later. In the broad meaning of the term, he was proposing martial law. All newspapers were to be closed; all demonstrations and public meetings were prohibited; no weapons of any kind were to be carried; the Provisional Government were to cease requisitioning buildings, and they were told to provide lists of police and other armed units. The Viet Minh called a general strike but the Provisional Government formally accepted the terms of the proclamation, although asking that the ban on newspapers should be lifted, to which Gracey agreed.

Gracey insisted that his authority came from Mountbatten, but he was, without doubt, going beyond his instructions and certainly the latest orders he had received. His original directives had referred to his authority over the whole of southern Indo-China but his instructions had been narrowed just before he left Rangoon for Saigon.[57] At the time of the proclamation Mountbatten himself was in no doubt that Gracey had exceeded his delegated powers. In the famous Section E of his report to the Combined Chiefs of Staff, written in 1947 but not made public in its entirety until 1969, Mountbatten expressed his disagreement with Gracey's action:

> I felt that this proclamation – addressed, as it was, to the whole of the Southern French Indo-China and not merely to the key points – was contrary to the policy of His Majesty's Government; and since proclamations of this nature may well appear to be initiated by Government policy, I warned Major-General Gracey that he should take care to confine operations of British/Indian troops to those limited tasks which he had been set. At the same time, I approved the military measures which he proposed to take.[58]

These military measures involved instructing the Japanese not only to maintain order among the civilian population but to accept British direction whereby Japanese troops would keep the northern approaches to Saigon clear; and this would take them well beyond the designated 'key areas'. Mountbatten, on 24 September, telegraphed the Chiefs of Staff in London for further clarification of his position. He put before them the alternatives of either implementing Gracey's proclamation and assuming military responsibility throughout southern Indo-China or limiting SEAC's responsibility to the control of the Japanese Supreme Headquarters and to the original instructions to disarm the Japanese and evacuate all prisoners of war and internees.

It was not a realistic choice, and Mountbatten must have known that the second option was quite impracticable. He was, from the evidence of these days, more conscious than most of the explosive nationalisms that he was dealing with, and he must have been aware of the repercussions that would flow from Gracey's actions. Mountbatten could not have been ignorant of the general approach of the Foreign Office in Whitehall and of the fact that their attitudes were shared by the Chiefs of Staff. In the event Mountbatten found the situation in Indo-China developing beyond his control. Gracey's Proclamation was put into effect on 21 September and immediately the British Indian troops began disarming the Viet Minh police and taking back the main public buildings occupied by representatives of the Provisional Government. In the early hours of 23 September Gracey permitted the French troops under his command to release about a thousand men, mostly soldiers, who had been imprisoned since the Japanese took complete control in March. They were then armed, and by midday all the public buildings were in French hands, and the tricolour was hoisted over the town hall. The whole operation was carried through before the local officials were really aware of what was happening. It was not, however, a bloodless coup, as is sometimes suggested.[59] Harold Isaacs, an American reporter in South-East Asia whose despatches at this time provide an invaluable record, wrote later of the coup in Saigon on that day:

> With Cédile personally commanding, the French troops moved against the Hotel de

Ville, the new seat of the Viet Minh government. They attacked the Post Office and the Surété. Annamite sentries were shot down. Occupants of the buildings were either killed or taken prisoner. Records were seized and scattered. Scores of Annamites were trussed up and marched off. Foreign eyewitnesses that morning saw blood flow, saw bound men beaten. They saw French colonial culture being restored to Saigon.[60]

During that first day, with French sentries in place of the Vietnamese before the main administrative centres, the French, soldiers and civilians alike, ran amuck. The brutality of the French against the native people of Saigon continued into the day following, and as one historian has written of 24 September 1945, this was 'the day when the Vietnamese war of national liberation against France began'. On 25 September there was an appalling massacre of the French – men, women and children – in one of Saigon's suburbs, the Cité Hérodia. The Japanese stood by without any interference. The attacks on the French were almost certainly made by members of the Binh Xuygen and not by the Viet Minh, but the situation had now moved beyond the point of a negotiated agreement, given the hatreds on all sides. The issues of the Vietnamese were now clear-cut: it was independence or struggle; and the hopes expressed when the British first entered Saigon were gone for ever.

Mountbatten continued to work for a settlement. He called a meeting on 28 September when the Secretary of State for War in the Attlee Cabinet would be in Singapore. Gracey and Cédile were present, and Mountbatten emphasised the importance of negotiations with those he still called Annamites. 'At this meeting', Mountbatten wrote in the report to the Chiefs of Staff, 'the Secretary of State confirmed my impression that it was the policy of His Majesty's Government not to interfere in the internal affairs of French Indo-China.'[61]

On 1 October Mountbatten received new instructions from the Chiefs of Staff in London. These were that British Indian troops should be used throughout south Indo-China in support of the French provided that his primary responsibility for Saigon was not in any way prejudiced. These instructions he passed on to Gracey with that rider that the troops were only to be used in a preventive role and not in an offensive one. Mountbatten was, of course, fully aware of the unworkable assumptions upon which these instructions were based. He was constantly reminding London of the impossible situation in which he was operating and the grave dangers that were involved. Below is quoted a despatch dated 2 October which he sent to the Chiefs of Staff and which repeated once again the basic requirements of his command:

para 4. From our point of view every day of delay in providing sufficient French troops to enable Leclerc to take over responsibility in F.I.C. magnifies the danger that British/Indian troops may become involved in large scale fighting on French territory. Slim has pointed out that the present inadequately trained French forces are *not* capable of restoring order outside the Saigon area without the backing of the 9th C.I.D. and if they attempt to do so we may be called upon to go to their rescue. . . .

para 6. The only way in which I can avoid involving British/Indian forces is to continue using the Japanese for maintaining law and order and this means I *cannot* begin to disarm them for another three months. By that time prisoners of war and internees will all have been removed and since it will be obvious that we could physically have disarmed the Japanese long before the end of December we shall have a less and less good excuse for retaining British/Indian forces there. In fact we shall find it hard to counter the accusations that our forces are remaining in the country solely in order to hold the Viet Nam Independence movement in check.[62]

Mountbatten continued his telegram with a message to him from the Viceroy of India, who reported growing agitation inside India concerning the use of Indian troops in Indo-China and Java; and urged that Indian troops should be withdrawn as soon as possible. A truce had been negotiated on the same day that this telegram was sent but it was a fragile thing from the beginning; and breaches of the ceasefire enabled Gracey to justify extended military action. In Whitehall a meeting of the Defence Committee on 5 October agreed on the Prime Minister's direction that there was no warrant for accelerating the movement of French troops to Indo-China. The meeting, it should be noted, had before it a paper on Indo-China in which the truce was remarked upon, and this may well have influenced their decision. This report from Mountbatten was dated 2 October and its main arguments were repeated by Slim in his despatch of 5 October quoted above.

By the first days of October 1945, some three weeks after the British arrival in Saigon, the situation had become set in the ways that were to continue until the British withdrawal at the end of the year. The British Indian troops occupied Saigon and later other key points in the south, on the clear understanding that they were holding these positions until the French had sufficient troops to take over from them. Leclerc arrived in Saigon at the end of the first week in October, by which time French reinforcements were beginning to arrive, although much too slowly for those on the ground. Gracey gradually but steadily expanded the geographical area he controlled, using his own forces and bringing in increasing numbers of Japanese into military use against the Vietnamese. As important as the fighting on the ground was the use that was made on an intensive scale of the Japanese Air Force which was converted into a transport service for the Allied command. Harold Isaacs wrote in 1947:

During the first month of operations against the Annamites (October–November) the British officially revealed that Japanese planes operating with Japanese crews under British orders had flown 100,000 miles, carried 45,000 pounds of supplies, ferried 1,000 French and Indians over road-blocked areas . . . all food and supply convoys moving along the rivers were Japanese manned. All supply lines, all roads and outlying installations were guarded by Japanese soldiers.[63]

During November and December 1945 the French took over responsibilities from the British. On 23 November, when sharp fighting was still clearing roadblocks around Saigon, the French began to take over the city from the 32nd Brigade, which was due to replace the Australians in Borneo in the New Year. By 19 December French control of Saigon was completed and on 1 January 1945 a joint statement was issued by Mountbatten and Admiral D'Argenlieu that henceforth the French would assume full responsibility for the maintenance of law and order in south Indo-China except for the control and repatriation of Japanese troops. General Gracey left for India with the remainder of the 20th Division between 28 January and 7 February, and it had been agreed with the British Chiefs of Staff that SEAC would cease to have any responsibility for Indo-China once Gracey had left the country. The Combined Chiefs of Staff in Washington took some time to agree – this was the Americans, of course, who retained their mistrust of the French – and it was not until late February 1946 that a compromise arrangement was worked out whereby the French would take over control with Mountbatten remaining responsible to MacArthur for the disarmament and repatriation of the large numbers of Japanese who still remained. The last British/Indian units left Indo-China by mid April 1946.[64]

Indo-China was now back under French sovereignty: the beginning of decades of war and massive suffering for the peoples of Vietnam. We may end this section by quoting from a letter sent by a young British officer in the Indian Army who had arrived in Saigon with the first detachments of British/Indian troops. The letter was written to his former headmaster of Malvern College who passed it on to Philip Noel-Baker, at this time Minister of State at the Foreign Office. The letter was dated 18 November 1945, and it began:

I am sorry to write to you, to bring you evil tidings, but my duty is clear. I carry but the sad and dwindling hopes of men of goodwill, of all honest incorruptible peoples. I bear no malice to any, but the truth must be known, for else we will drift into our fourth world conflagration. God willing, we will be heard and truth will conquer.

The Annamites ruled Saigon in peace and good order as indeed they do to this day in Hanoi. When the British arrived to disarm the Japs the Annamites prepared to welcome the carriers of liberty, the liberators of Europe, of Africa, of the Philippines, of China – they prepared banners 'Welcome to the Allies, to Britain, to the Indian troops', they paraded the streets standing on the airfield road on either side for five miles – but they were mistaken – poor blind sheep. We came, we saw; we armed the French, who are more trigger happy than children of six, the battle began, we fought, we slaughtered, we established a bridgehead to enable the French to conquer the country, to re-impose a corrupt, inefficient, wicked government on a peaceful civilised race, who are denied the very égalité, fraternité, liberté – the essence of

France. Oh! when will the world realise the truth. We have blindly or wickedly let down those who have put their trust in us. We have preferred the easy way – but the world is a smaller place than it is and we shall rue the day we set foot in French Indo-China unless something is done to put right a wrong.[65]

The young officer continued in this impassioned way and insisted that there ought to be a United Nations investigation. Noel-Baker's reply to the head-master of Malvern is also worth reprinting, partly because it reflects how men of the type that Noel-Baker was[66] can fall so easily into the paths of discreditable opportunism when in high office, but also because of the unpleasant unctuous-ness of his last sentence:

> [After thanking the sender for the letter.] Although I am prepared to believe that French colonial administration is not perfect – whose is? – I feel that he gives a rather romantic and oversimplified picture of conditions there. As you know, my own belief is that the only way in which these conditions can be eventually improved is the work of the specialised agencies and other organs of the United Nations organisations. I am returning Williams' letter to you [Footnote: no, I am keeping it]. I find it very encouraging to see so many boys of his age feeling as deeply as this about such social questions.[67]

It is difficult to know precisely when the Japanese troops began to be employed in a combat role for the 'law and order' phrase was always or nearly always used to describe their role: and it is unlikely that we shall ever know the complete story. The most likely period is the days following the coup d'état carried out by the French and approved and supported by General Gracey. This was 24 September 1945 and it was on that day, and the day following, as we have seen, that the French, military and civilians, ran amuck in Saigon; and their brutalities and murders were succeeded by similar barbarities on the nationalist side.[68] Certainly from early October the 'law and order' role included a military role, and throughout the months of October and November, at a time when the newspapers of Britain were retailing the horrors inflicted upon Japanese prisoners of war and civilian internees, the British in Indo-China were steadily increasing the part which Japanese soldiers played in the front line.

It was following the events of 24 and 25 September that Gracey took a very firm control of what was always a very difficult situation. He delivered an ultimatum to Marshal Terauchi that his officers and troops had to be co-operative in maintaining order in Saigon, or he would be held as a war criminal; and from this time the 'co-operation' of the Japanese steadily improved. There was inevitably reluctance on both sides. The Indians and Gurkhas had been fighting the Japanese in Burma and they had bitter memories of their brutal enemy. On the Japanese side the Army in Indo-China had never been defeated in battle and their reluctance to assist the British to promote the cause of the despised French was understandable. The exact number of deserters from the Japanese Army to join the Viet Minh and the Vietnamese nationalists is not known but at the least it was several hundreds. The myth that Vietnamese nationalism was largely the product of Japanese support was widely accepted in France and in Whitehall, but certainly the British Foreign Office at this time was always dismissive of the phenomenon of nationalism, which they obviously did not understand, whether in the Middle East or the Far East. There was some arms supply from the Japanese to the Vietnamese but it was not on a large scale, and most of the Viet Minh were poorly armed in the south.[69]

Serious fighting continued throughout October and November, with October being the most difficult period for the British command. This was when the Japanese began to be used extensively. The official history of the Indian armed forces noted that 'All the dirty work, to fight and disarm the Annamites, was assigned to the Japanese troops,'[70] and the historian of the 4/10 Gurkhas, after noting that the Japanese were freely used in the difficult operations of these days, emphasised that 'a satisfactory result of their use was greatly to reduce the casualties among our troops.'[71] Casualties on the Allied side, which now included the Japanese, were given in the SACSEA War Diary at the end of October. The listing was of total casualties from the initial landing of the British until 29 October:

British and Indian:	Killed 18;	Wounded 51;	Missing 3
French:	Killed 17;	Wounded 34;	Missing 2
Japanese:	Killed 19;	Wounded 13;	

The Dutch and American figures were negligible; those for the Annamites 'estimate only and not for publication' were 391 killed by British troops and 441 arrested. A further note added that there were no reliable figures for the nationalists killed by either the French or the Japanese.[72] French killings would almost certainly have been greater than the British. Their record in this period of the French repossession of Indo-China was shameful. The official British military historian, describing operations in one area during November and quoting the British figures, added: 'Casualties among the rebels in the French sector were reported to be much higher':[73] the official language for butchery. It would, however, be inadmissible to suggest that instructions to British troops were in any way different from those of 'normal' warfare. The Operations Instruction of the 100 Indian Infantry Brigade, 27 October 1945, made the position quite clear that the usual ruthlessness of war and the principles of warfare were to be strictly observed:

> There is no front in these operations: we would be dealing with bands of guerillas and are likely to meet opposition on flanks and rear; we may find it difficult to distinguish friend from foe. Same vigilance against ambushes and doubtful friends

as one observed in North-West Frontier of India would be required all over. Also beware of 'nibbling' at opposition. Always use the maximum force available to ensure wiping out any hostiles we may meet. If one uses too much no harm is done. If one uses too small a force and it has to be extricated we will suffer casualties and encourage the enemy.[74]

Relations between the British and the French at the level of senior officers were excellent. Leclerc found Gracey most sympathetic; a good deal more so than Mountbatten. By contrast the French rank and file had to have it explained that because Indians were coloured peoples they were part of the British forces and on 'our' side, and must not be subject to the racist prejudice and abuse that the French lower ranks so often engaged in.[75] Relations, too, with the Japanese, again at the senior officer level, were also good. Harold Isaacs, one of the very few newspaper correspondents who was in Indo-China for most of this early period, summarised in a book of 1947 the accounts that he had been sending back to *Newsweek* during the months of late 1945:

> There was no secret about the use of Japanese troops against the Annamites. The British command did make it quite difficult for correspondents to get first hand information on this subject, and they forbad Japanese officers to talk to newsmen. . . . The British spokesman announced on October 18 that the head quarters had thanked General Terauchi, the Japanese commander, 'with highest praise' for his co-operation. The British were delighted with the discipline shown by the late enemy and were often warmly admiring, in the best playing-field tradition, of their fine military qualities. It was all very comradely.[76]

A question of some importance to the historian is the very limited impact of the British military intervention upon British public opinion in the United Kingdom; and indeed the question could be extended to world opinion. One important reason was that Indonesia, also subject to British intervention, this time on behalf of the Dutch, received world-wide publicity. There were many strikes by dockworkers in Australia, Ceylon and elsewhere against the loading of arms for the Indonesian intervention, and the whole episode gripped the imagination of many peoples of the world in the way that Indo-China did not. The first stage of the conflict in the latter country was over much more quickly, of course, and no doubt more important was the aftermath of the war in Europe itself. Nevertheless, it was a Labour Government that was directing the intervention and the use of Japanese troops would have been inconceivable in August 1945, only two months before they were in fact used as combat forces. What is striking about the domestic politics of Britain is that the use of Japanese troops went almost completely unnoticed. There were a few questions in the House of Commons about the British intervention but none that was a direct statement to be answered by Government spokesmen.[77] The left-wing journals and newspapers carried the occasional paragraph about Indo-China but no one seized upon the use of Japanese troops to destroy, at least temporarily, a national liberation movement. This is true of the *New Statesman, Tribune, Reynolds News* and the *Daily Worker*, each of which carried some material but nothing which compared with the reports in *Newsweek* by Harold Isaacs. It is not certain that there was a correspondent from Britain in Indo-China for the five and a half months of the British intervention, and this must help to account for the meagre reporting that was published. The Indian press, as would be expected, was more open with regular reports, and it reflected the growing anger at the use of Indian troops in both Indo-China and Indonesia. S.A. Dange, already in September, was reported in the Bombay communist paper *People's War* protesting in a session at the Paris meeting of the World Federation of Trade Unions at the employment of Japanese troops alongside the British Indian troops:[78] but even in the Indian communist press in general it was Indonesia that was mostly written about.

There was also misinformation or more likely disinformation. Tom Driberg, who visited French Indo-China in September, cabled a report to *Reynolds News*, for which he was a regular contributor, on the situation in Saigon. It was published under the heading 'Why Japs Are Used as Police' on 30 September 1945. He wrote that the central fact of the Saigon situation was that the small British force had to rely upon a much larger Japanese Army to help it 'in the job of re-imposing an intensely unpopular French regime on an ardently national-ist people, the Annamites'. The situation was not, however, to be compared with that in Greece, for two reasons: one, that the Viet Minh had never fought the Japanese; and two, the nationalist movement was financed and put into office last March by the Japanese. We know from Driberg's other reports that he interviewed Gracey and other British officials and military, and it was obviously from these that he obtained his mistaken views of the local situation. Driberg, however, used his eyes, and ears, and his understanding of the French was accurate, but he ended this report with the words: 'In my view General Gracey has done all that it was possible to do in an almost impossible situation.'[79] It must not therefore be surprising that public opinion in the United Kingdom, even the considerable left-wing movements at this time, could become somewhat confused about what was really happening. In general it may be said that the labour movement as a whole continued to accept the disingenuous statements from the Labour front bench when the matter of Indo-China was occasionally, only very occasionally, up for discussion. Bevin, on 24 October, provided a statement for the House of Commons that gathered together all the half-truths and untruths that provided the British Govern-ment's justification to the world for what they were perpetrating in South-East Asia. In Indo-China, Mr Bevin said in his opening words, it was the Japanese who had followed the policy of encouraging the growth of nationalism, and the Viet Nam Republic had been established in August with Japanese arms and backing. The British, under General Gracey, went in for the purposes which were well known, namely the disarmament of the Japanese and the evacuation of prisoners and internees. Unfortunately in fulfilling these primary duties Gracey had to contend with 'continual looting and attacks by Annamite armed bands on French civilians and property'. With Gracey's encouragement a truce was arranged between a senior French officer and Annamite representatives to run from 2 October. The truce, however, was soon broken by further Annamite attacks and Gracey was forced to take action in order to 'ensure the proper execution of his task'. As the Prime Minister had made clear on 17 October, the British Government had no wish to become 'unnecessarily involved' in the administration or political affairs of territories that were not British and their object was to withdraw at the earliest possible opportunity. The French, as the Commons would be well aware, issued a declaration of policy on 24 March 1945 which would give the peoples of Indo-China 'a wide measure of autonomy'; and Bevin then went on to praise the French for their liberal attitude which 'has been reflected in the very conciliatory manner in which the local French representatives have dealt with the Annamite leaders'.[80] Half-truths and untruths: it was a louche statement of lies.

The British Chiefs of Staff would not have been satisfied with any other outcome. In early November there was sent to the Cabinet Offices a paper on 'British Strategic Interests in the Far East'.[81] It was based on a full study issued as a Staff Paper by the Chiefs of Staff dated 21 February 1945 (COS (45) 120 (O) PHP). As with many of the strategic assessments at this period, it noted that war between the United Kingdom and the United States was unthinkable, and that any further threat from Japan could be discounted 'unless she receives assistance from Russia'. The general conclusion, which again was common to all the strategic assessments of 1945 and after, was that the only threat to Britain's interests could come from a hostile USSR 'with probably China, Japan or both to some extent under her control'. The memorandum was summed up:

Provisionally therefore, we consider that our further strategic requirements will be:

(a) to ensure that no potentially hostile power, in particular Russia, should become established in China south of the Yangtze;

(b) to maintain a chain of forward naval and air bases, held either by ourselves or the United States, stretching from Hong Kong to the Aleutians, through the Pescadores, Formosa, the Philippines, the Carolines, the Marshalls, and the Midway Islands in order to control sea and air routes to the South and East from Soviet and Japanese bases.

(c) to provide against penetration of this line of forward bases, and for the possibility of delay in the full development of the United States war effort, we must maintain, in co-operation with the French and the Dutch, an alternative system of bases along a general line from French Indo-China to Samoa through Borneo, the Celebes, the Admiralty and Solomon Islands and Fiji. The security of French Indo-China is of particular importance to the defence of South-East Asia as a whole.

This was one of so many examples of the lack of comprehension of the position of Britain in the post-war world in terms of economic weight and political authority. Military fantasies of this kind were interwoven with the demonstration that planning for future security was grounded firmly upon the experience of the war just concluded.

British military intervention in French Indo-China was over by the end of 1945 and the combat troops were already on the way to the more perverse problem of the Dutch and Indonesia. Indo-China was the first intervention of this kind initiated by the new Labour Government in Britain; and because it was over so quickly, against the background of all the many problems of converting from war to peace that the United Kingdom was involved with, it remained forgotten in the collective memory of the British people. It has also been forgotten, for the most part, by British historians (but not by Americans). Alan Bullock wrote his massive third volume of Bevin at the Foreign Office in 1983, when all the departmental records were available; and there are two specific references to the military intervention. The first, on p. 32, is a discussion of the problems of both Indo-China and Indonesia with the British 'caught in the cross-fire and denounced by both sides and their sympathizers. In Indo-China this was for only a limited time and the British handed over with relief to the French in the spring of 1946.' The second reference, on p. 152, simply notes that a nationalist government had established itself before the Allied Powers arrived and in Indo-China 'General Gracey was forced to intervene in support of the French'; but that from mid October 1945 the French were able to take over 'ever increasing responsibility for restoring their control'. And there the historical account ended, with no discussion of what 'control' meant or why the British felt themselves obliged to intervene in order to save the position for the French. A year after Bullock's volume appeared there was published a detailed survey of the Labour Government in office: *Labour in Power 1945–1951* by Kenneth Morgan; an interesting and informative book in which, however, there is no mention at all of the British intervention in Vietnam.

Vietnam has been a battlefield of the world since 1945. It lies within the area of the killing fields, although the term was not originally applied to Vietnam. During the decades of the Cold War wars were always being fought in regions of South-East Asia; human beings were always being tortured, murdered and on occasion butchered en masse. The responsibility and blame lies with many groups and certain of the countries of the advanced industrial world. What would have been the history of Vietnam if the British, through their military intervention, had not made certain that the French would take over, below the 16th parallel, before Christmas Day 1945?

Appendix 1

Extracts from C.F.A. Warner, 'The Soviet Campaign against This Country and Our Response to It'

2 April 1946*

The reports from the Embassy in Moscow on recent Soviet pronouncements, in particular the election speeches made by Stalin, Molotov and other members of the Politbureau and the publicity campaign in connexion with the elections to the Supreme Soviet, bring out the following points in the Soviet Government's declared policy:-

(a) The return to the pure doctrine of Marx-Lenin-Stalinism.
(b) The intense concentration upon building up the industrial and military strength of the Soviet Union.
(c) The revival of the bogey of external danger to the Soviet Union.

2. The return to Marx-Lenin-Stalinism includes of course the glorification of Communism as the inevitable religion of the future, the natural antagonism between Communism on the one hand and imperialism and capitalism on the other (both Russia's major allies being regarded as imperialistic and capitalistic); the natural antagonism between Communism and Social Democracy; the Soviet Union's duty to propagate Communism; and all the rest of the doctrine. In other words, the Soviet Union has announced to the world that it proposes to play an aggressive political role, while making an intensive drive to increase its own military and industrial strength. We should be very unwise not to take the Russians at their word, just as we should have been wise to take Mein Kampf at its face value. . . .

4. The Soviet Union is no doubt war-weary, and, as the Soviet leaders have proclaimed, wants a prolonged peace to build up her strength. But she is practising the most vicious power politics, in the political, economic, and propaganda spheres and seems determined to stick at nothing, short of war, to obtain her objectives. Having regard to the declarations of policy referred to above, it would be very rash to assume that her present political strategy and tactics are short-term only.

*Reprinted in full, DBPO, Ser. I, Vol. VI, HMSO, London 1991, No. 88, pp. 345–52.

5.   Soviet spokesmen and apologists, from M. Maisky during the war onwards, have been at pains to explain that Russia's acquisitive policy everywhere is due to not unnatural suspicion. But the Soviet authorities in their press and broadcasts seem now to be at pains to intensify this suspicion among their own people. Can it be, in reality, a convenient excuse for an aggressive policy; after all, at the end of the war, the only two countries that could threaten Russia were her allies, Great Britain and America, and these, as any good Soviet observers must have reported, were only too anxious to relax and demobilise? Or again, are anxiety about the internal situation in Russia and the need to apply the spur to their own people the principal motives? Whichever of these explanations be correct, the fact remains that Russian aggressiveness threatens British interests all over the world. The Soviet Government are carrying on an intensive campaign to weaken, depreciate and harry this country in every possible way. There is no guarantee that this is not going on indefinitely. The tempo and the pressure may vary for tactical reasons. But the revival of the Marx-Lenin ideology, and the fact that this country is under the present Government the leader of Social Democracy in Europe and is at the same time the less formidable of the two great 'imperialist and capitalist' powers, suggests on the contrary that the attack on this country will continue indefinitely. If this be so, concessions and appeasement will merely serve to weaken our position while the Soviet Union builds up her industrial and economic strength; therefore we must defend ourselves.

6.   Russia's policy is normally coordinated over the whole field and she will no doubt direct her attack equally against our strategic, political and economic interests, using military, economic, propaganda and political weapons and also the driving force generated by Communism. And Communism in this connexion must be viewed not merely as a political creed but as a religious dogma and faith which can inspire such fanaticism and self sacrifice as we associate with the early Christians and the rise of Islam and which in the minds of the believers transcends all lesser loyalties towards family, class or even country. We must therefore study this Russian aggressive policy as a whole in all its different manifestations, and not only make up our minds what measures we should take to defend ourselves against the Soviet Union's present manoeuvres, but also to try to foresee the future development of her campaign against us and how we can meet it. We should also consider whether, in some directions at least, we should not adopt a defensive-offensive policy.

7.   As regards Russia's use of the military weapon, the Chiefs of Staff have endorsed the opinion expressed in the J.I.C.'s recent paper (J.I.C. (46)1(0) of 1st March) that the Russians do not wish to get involved in another war for at least the next five years and the Chiefs of Staff are considering their plans on this assumption. We understand that they will be making their recommendations shortly. It is relevant however to the political problems which concern the Foreign Office to remark that in their use of military pressure, in areas affecting our vital interests or those of the Americans, the Russians will, of course, have to rely on their own appreciation to judge how far they can go without making war inevitable. As in the case of Hitler and Poland, they may miscalculate. In their anxiety to justify themselves to the British people and the world His Majesty's Government may have misled Hitler. We should always keep this in mind in dealing with the Russian problem now.

8.   In the economic sphere, the broad lines of Russian policy are clear. It is entirely

selfish. It is at the same time ideological. They are ruthlessly despoiling the countries occupied by the Red Army, in the guise of booty, restitution and reparation. Simultaneously, they are using their puppets to gear the economics of these countries to the Soviet machine. They are contributing nothing to United Nations international efforts to restore economic stability and the free flow of trade and transport. They are making exclusive commercial treaties and securing a predominant share in the control of basic industries from Germany and the Adriatic right across to Manchuria. By this means they hope to control the whole economic life of this vast area for the benefit of the Soviet Union, in order to speed up the achievement of their own long-term industrial development. In doing so they are reducing the standard of living throughout this area to the Soviet level, partly presumably in the process of coordinating the economic life of the whole area, partly because it is not good for their own internal propaganda that the many Soviet citizens who are likely to move about in that area should see that Russia's satellites have a higher standard of living than the Soviet Union.

9.   Russia's foreign economic policy thus serves political, economic and ideological ends simultaneously. It will speed up the achievement of her own vast plan of industrial and military development. It will make an enormous area economically, and therefore politically, dependent upon herself. It will serve the spread of Communism and it will give the Kremlin a tremendous economic weapon to use in the Marx-Leninist struggle against capitalism and for Russian imperialistic political ends.

10.   To the extent that it is successful it will destroy the hopes of world prosperity based upon a free economy. . . .

28.   To sum up, the Soviet Government both in their recent pronouncements and in their actions have made it clear that they have decided upon an aggressive policy, based upon militant Communism and Russian chauvinism. They have launched an offensive against Social Democracy and against this country. They must have realised already that their clumsiness is alarming the whole non-Communist world, and in particular American public opinion, and is thus consolidating opposition to them and support for His Majesty's Government. They will very probably adopt henceforth more subtle tactics and lay themselves out to allay these suspicions. But it would be in the highest degree rash to suppose that they will drop their policy of challenging this country, which they must regard as the leader of Social Democracy and the more vulnerable of the two great Western powers. The interests of this country and the true democratic principles for which we stand are directly threatened. The Soviet Government makes coordinated use of military, economic, propaganda and political weapons and also of the Communist 'religion'. It is submitted, therefore, that we must at once organise and coordinate our defences against all these and that we should not stop short of a defensive-offensive policy. If general approval is given to these propositions, further study should be given as a matter of urgency to the various suggestions outlined in this memorandum.

Appendix 2

'The Soviet Union is no doubt war-weary': A Note on the Ravages of War on the Eastern Front in the Second World War

The war on the eastern front in the Second World War had a character that was qualitatively different from that in Western Europe or North Africa. All war is brutalising but that which the Germans conducted against Britain and the United States broadly accepted the recognised rules of war. As in all wars, there were atrocities committed on both sides; often deliberate, sometimes the result of mistakes. There were, and still are, many disputed areas – the intensive bombing of civilians, for example, and above all the savagery against resistance movements and the retaliation against civilian populations. For most of those in uniform, however, warfare on the western fronts was carried through within the general rules of international military law. On the eastern front, in sharp and bitter contrast, it is not possible to make clear distinctions between the treatment of the armed forces or the civilian populations or the partisans. The war waged by the German Army and their satellites against the Soviet Union was conducted with a murderous bestiality from the first day of the Wehrmacht's invasion in late June 1941.

Recognition of the barbarous nature of the eastern war has never entered into the consciousness of ordinary people in Western Europe nor, it must be added, into the understanding of the decision-making élites. The words quoted in the title of this Appendix are from a memorandum which was circulated within the British Foreign Office in early April 1946. Its author was C.F.A. Warner, the Superintending Under-Secretary of the Northern Department, which concerned itself with Russian, Polish, Czechoslovak and Scandinavian affairs, and the memorandum is reprinted in part in Appendix 1. Documentation relating to the incorporation of the Wehrmacht, from its highest commanders to the rank of file soldiers, into the machinery of extermination, is now extensive. In 1978 Christian Streit brought together the research of a quarter of a century and established the responsibility of the Wehrmacht, alongside the organs of the security forces, notably the *Einsatzgruppen*, for the appalling and hideous atrocities inflicted upon millions of the peoples of the Soviet Union.[1] We may leave aside for the present the much debated thesis so brilliantly developed by Arno Mayer concerning the relationship between the German military failures on the eastern front and the 'Final Solution'[2] and rest upon his detailed enumeration of the horrors of the German war. The quotation which follows relates to the autumn of 1941 when the military campaign was already beginning to falter:

> The massacre of Soviet Jews was closely interrelated not only with the increasing brutality of the military campaign but also with the intensifying mistreatment of the civilian populations. If the mass murder of Jews aroused little indignation, let alone resistance, it was not because it was carefully hidden but because its unique and absolute horror was submerged in an atmosphere of rampant naked violence. The local populations became indifferent to the torment of the Jews less because of any residual Judeophobia than because they, too, were being terrorised and brutalised, even if to a lesser extent. The torture and killing of Jews, allegedly in reprisal for resistance, contributed to this general reign of terror, as did the fearsome presence of the Wehrmacht.[3]

Jürgen Förster, whose own writings on these questions are important, quoted Ernst Nolte on the war against the Soviet Union as the 'most monstrous war of conquest, enslavement and extermination' in modern times.[4] In the past two decades or so Western scholars have begun, in a more intensive way than hitherto, to put together the costs of war and their consequences in the post-war history of the Soviet Union. An example is the volume edited by Susan J. Linz, *The Impact of World War II on the Soviet Union*.[5] There were earlier studies including the research paper written by Wassily Leontieff for the American Office of Strategic Services in 1944 and the symposium of 1949 published by the American Academy of Political and Social Sciences.[6] Of immediate relevance in the latter is the paper by Abram Bergson, J.J. Blackman and A. Erlich, 'Postwar Reconstruction and Development in the USSR', in which it was noted: 'Russia's loss of property as a result of the war was huge by any standard; possibly it totalled as much as, if not more than, a quarter of the total prewar stock in the country as a whole.'[7] With statistics lacking in comprehensiveness exact calculations are not possible. Susan Linz, in the volume already quoted, estimated that if war-related population losses were taken into account when carryover costs were estimated, then the post-war burden imposed upon the Russian people was between eighteen to twenty-five years' earnings, or work effort, of the 1945 labour force.[8] It was the enormous destruction in the main pre-war industrial areas of the Soviet Union that made the issue of foreign aid, and, more salient, the matter of reparations, of such major importance in Soviet diplomacy.

We must return to the question touched upon in the second paragraph above. How did it come about that neither the barbarism of the war nor the scale of destruction made any significant impact upon public opinion, however defined, in the countries of the Atlantic Alliance? In Germany the conduct of the Wehrmacht has always been distinguished from that of the security forces, and on the eastern front it was the outrages committed by the Red Army during the advance into Germany as well as the sufferings of German prisoners of war that overshadowed the much greater inhumanity of the war on the eastern fronts. When a TV documentary was shown in 1979 in Germany which chronicled the crimes of the Wehrmacht in the war against the Soviet Union, the reaction of the public was extremely hostile and generally disbelieving. In other countries of Western Europe and certainly in Britain, it has been the mass murders of the Holocaust which have submerged all other memories except, to a more limited extent, the conduct of the Japanese in the Far East.

These considerations do not conclude the matter. Harrison Salisbury, towards the end of his agonising story of Leningrad's 900 days' siege, examined the various estimates of the death toll and explained the various figures that have been given at different times:

> The death toll was minimised for political security reasons. The Soviet government for years deliberately understated the military and civilian death toll of World War II. The real totals were of such magnitude that Stalin, obviously, felt they would produce political repercussions inside the country. To the outside world a realistic statement of Soviet losses (total population losses are now estimated at well above 25 million lives) would have revealed the true weakness of Russia at the end of the war.[9]

Contributors to the Susan Linz volume have accepted a figure of around twenty million dead, about half being attributed to military casualties and half civilian, with the male population suffering much the heavier losses within the military totals in particular.[10] Official Soviet statistics in 1946 produced the figure of seven million dead, and such calculations were only seriously revised after Stalin's death. More accurate data on Soviet material and population losses were available in the West, but any deductions that might have been made concerning the military weaknesses of the Soviet State and society were ignored; George Kennan, Frank Roberts and C.F.A. Warner all assumed in their important analyses of the spring of 1946 that the Russians were concentrating all their efforts upon reconstruction and building up their industrial strength (true) and that their military strengths remained at levels which would allow of rapid movement beyond their own boundaries and those of the countries of Eastern Europe which they controlled. This was untrue. Western intelligence may have been fully aware of the high rate of demobilisation of the Russian armed forces, but this was a perception that wholly escaped the minds of the élites in Whitehall. In 1947 Harry Schwartz published *Russia's Postwar Economy*[11] in which he estimated that around ten million of the armed forces had been returned to civilian life by the end of 1947. This figure was higher than that stated by Nikita Khruschev in 1960, but it was roughly of the same order. Khruschev claimed that the size of the Soviet armed forces was 11,365,000 in 1945 and 2,874,000 in 1948: and most Russian specialists now seem to agree that his figures were generally accurate.

This question has been explored in detail by M.A. Evangelista, who has refuted the belief common in the immediate post-war years as well as in later decades that the Soviet Union offered an overwhelming threat to Western Europe in the late 1940s.[12] Evangelista not only accepted the high rate of Soviet demobilisation but insisted that the very large number of Soviet divisions so often quoted falsified the real situation in that the Soviet division was much smaller than Western divisions and lacked the 'extensive logistical and support services of Western Divisions'. The central mistake, Evangelista argued, was to count the number of divisions and not the total of manpower. Moreover:

> Although, based on their capabilities or functions, the Western forces in early postwar Europe were not particularly suited to wage another war, the Soviet forces were even less so. Soviet troops were not capable of executing the type of invasion that many Western observers expected during the early postwar period. Soviet forces were severely lacking in many important components of military capability, including transportation, equipment and troop morale.

They were not the 'highly mobile and armoured spearhead' of much Western popular and military writing.[13]

The peoples of the Soviet Union were indeed 'war-weary'. The trauma of the war years remained with those who had suffered the destruction and the pillage and the millions of deaths to the end of their lives.

Appendix 3

Christopher Hill at the Foreign Office, 1944–45

The question of Russian studies in the United Kingdom became a matter for serious discussion within the Foreign Office during 1944. It was becoming increasingly obvious that there was a marked shortage of Russian specialists, and comparison with the situation in the United States was always unfavourable to Britain. Accordingly, the Foreign Office established a Committee on Russian Studies whose terms of reference were agreed in June 1944:

> to consider means of ensuring that adequate facilities existed in this country for the study of the Russian language, arts, science, history etc. and generally for the study of Soviet institutions and forms of political, economic and social organisation.[1]

A circular letter of 16 May 1944 had been sent to universities and other interested bodies explaining that a committee had been established under the chairmanship of Sir Orme Sargent, and there was also notification in the national press. The first meeting of the Committee was in June 1944 when the subjects to be considered were divided into three main groups: (a) library and research facilities; (b) facilities for teaching Russian studies; (c) exchange of students; three sub-committees were formed according to this division. Each sub-committee had a chairman and a secretary. Principal Sir J.F. Rees (University College, Cardiff) was chairman of (a); Professor le Gros Clark (University of Oxford) of (b); and Professor Ifor Evans (University College, Swansea, and British Council) of (c). Christopher Hill, on secondment to the Foreign Office, was secretary of sub-committee (b).

The secretary to the main committee, reporting to Orme Sargent, was Geoffrey Wilson (Manchester Grammar School and Oriel College, Oxford). Wilson was on the staff of the Foreign Office from 1940, first in the Moscow Embassy and then in Whitehall and he was to have a distinguished public career.[2] Hill in 1944 and 1945 was to be his main assistant.

The Committee on Russian Studies was not a major initiative of the Foreign Office, which had many matters of much greater importance to attend to in the last year of the war, and the work of the Committee proceeded quite thoroughly but at a fairly leisurely pace. Most of the work of the sub-committees at this stage was assembling information from academic institutions throughout Britain and it was not until 18 January 1945 that Geoffrey Wilson informed Orme Sargent of the completion of all three reports of the sub-committees. The full Committee was then circularised, and a third meeting was held in late April 1945. Orme Sargent was not present and Wilson was voted into the chair. Also present were Professors W.J. Rose (School of Slavonic Studies), Ifor Evans, le Gros Clark, and P.M. Blackett (University of Manchester); Mr G.A. Birkett (University of Glasgow); Mr Ramsden (Federation of British Industries); Messrs Seymour and Ledward (British Council); and Miss Hedley, Hill and Smollett of the Foreign Office. After this meeting Orme Sargent wrote to R.A. Butler on 2 May 1945, who replied two days later:

> Many thanks for your letter of May 2nd. I shall look forward to seeing your report on Russian studies in this country. It is clearly a matter of importance and you may be sure that I will take a personal interest in it.[3]

In mid June 1945 Clark Kerr, Ambassador in Moscow, telegrammed that he had read all the reports of the sub-committees and that he hoped progress would now be made. The Foreign Office would have liked to get the matter of student exchange raised at the Potsdam Conference in July, but Lord Cherwell blocked the idea, and this produced irritated minutes from senior members of the Northern Department, notably C.F.A. Warner and Brimelow.[4]

Christopher Hill, the subject of this Appendix, continued to be involved in the affairs of the Committee although there was little action during the summer months, and he left the Foreign Office in August 1945 to return to his Fellowship at Balliol College, Oxford.

There were two matters of potential controversy connected with the proposals being considered for the work of the Committee. The first came out of the discussions of sub-committee (b). The problem was the shortage of teachers of the Russian language, its history and institutions. The report of sub-committee (b) set out the matter:

(ii) *Difficulties of the inter-war period*

(a) The principal handicap to the development of Russian studies, which began to expand rapidly during and after the war of 1914–18, was the political tension and suspicion existing between Great Britain and the USSR which prevented normal intercourse between the two countries. (It is assumed that the 20 years Treaty of Alliance with the USSR will remove this fundamental obstacle). . . .

(b) The shortage of teachers can partially be met by pooling, either between universities or colleges . . . or between departments within a university. . . . But there will remain a serious gap between demand and supply of teachers, which will be increased by the following recommendation: Whilst recognising the valuable services rendered in the past by teachers of Russian origin (but not Soviet citizens) the Sub-Committee feels that their employment in future (except possibly in junior language and literature posts) would not be in the best interests of Anglo-Soviet co-operation or indeed the development of Russian studies in this country. The Sub-Committee strongly recommends that the above point be brought to the notice of all university authorities.[5]

The report then went on to consider the ways in which the numbers of teachers might be increased, and these included the use of personnel trained for the armed services during the war, Soviet citizens, and American teachers of 'non-Russian origin'. The point was stressed in the sub-committee's summary recommendations that any employment of Soviet citizens should only be arranged 'through diplomatic channels'.

Minute 15 of the third meeting of the full Committee – discussed briefly above – read as follows:

> Mr. Birkett drew attention to the undesirability from the political point of view in the post-war period of employing as teachers of Russian, Poles who were unable or unwilling to return to Poland. It was agreed that an addition to this effect should be made to the report of sub-committee (b) and this point (in addition to the undesirability of employing White Russian émigrés for the same purpose) should be made known to Local Education authorities by the Ministry of Education in a confidential circular, the text of which should be agreed by the Ministry of Education and the Foreign Office.[6]

As far as can be discovered from the files up to August 1945 no action one way or another was taken upon this recommendation. The second matter of potential controversy was of quite minor importance. After the public announcement of the establishment of the Committee on Russian Studies, D.N. Pritt, on behalf of the Society for Cultural Relations with Soviet Russia (SCR), regretted the fact that the Society was only being 'consulted' and was not a member of the Committee. Wilson, in a minute of 21 September 1944, wrote: 'I have seen Mr Pritt and set his apprehensions at rest for the time being. . . . I think they want to be helpful and so long as they are not in on what is happening we shall always run the risk of being sniped at from the Left.' Hill added a further minute: 'The SCR has in fact been very helpful to Sub-Committee (b). I agree with Mr Wilson'; and Orme Sargent initialled. The SCR was later suggested by Hill among a list of organisations that might be invited to join the full Committee which included the Royal Society, Chatham House and the British Academy. There were at least three minutes which could be read as offering strong objections to the inclusion of the SCR, but again, up till August 1945, no firm decision seems to have been taken.[7]

The Cold War soon submerged most of the ideas and proposals of the Committee on Russian Studies, and it remained a very small footnote in the history of Anglo-Russian relations, until 1987. In that year Jonathan Cape published a book entitled *The Secrets of the Service: British Intelligence and Communist Subversion, 1939–1951*. The author was Anthony Glees, and the contents of the volume are indicated by the title. This Appendix is concerned only with nine pages of the text (pp. 279–88) which deal with part of Christopher Hill's temporary attachment to the Foreign Office in 1944–45. The heading of these nine pages is 'A Marxist in the Foreign Office' and the commentary by Glees is limited to the connection of Christopher Hill with the Committee on Russian Studies.

Christopher Hill was born in 1912; read history at Balliol College, Oxford; was a Fellow of All Souls in 1934; spent 1935–36 in academic research in Moscow; was an assistant lecturer at University College, Cardiff, from 1936–38; and then returned to a Fellowship at Balliol College where he remained, except for the years of war, until his retirement. He became Master of Balliol in 1965 and retired in 1978. He joined the Communist Party in the early 1930s and resigned in 1957. In the decades since 1945 he published steadily in his chosen field of seventeenth-century Britain, and his reputation as a scholar of outstanding ability was increasingly recognised by the academic community round the world.[8]

In June 1940 Hill volunteered for the Field Security Police and within two days was offered an officer's training course. He was commissioned and rose to the rank of Major. In late 1942 he was seconded to the Research Department of the Foreign Office and later transferred to the Northern Department which dealt with Russian questions. In August 1945 he went back to Oxford. Throughout his period in the Foreign Office Hill remained a junior member at the administrative level. Most of his work was concerned with routine relations with the Moscow Embassy and reports for his superiors in the Foreign Office on events in Russia. His involvement in the work of the Committee on Russian Studies was only a small part of his daily routine; he became secretary of one of the sub-committees, as already noted, and general factotum to Geoffrey Wilson, the secretary to the full Committee.

Anthony Glees, in his nine pages of text, suggests that it was surprising that a communist should be admitted to the administrative level of the Foreign Office; that it remains uncertain whether Hill was 'vetted' before his secondment;[9] and in one area in which Hill is supposed by Glees to have paid a significant part, namely the Committee on Russian Studies, there is more than a suggestion that Hill was motivated by his communist beliefs rather than the objectivity which Glees assumes to be the standard of the Foreign Office. Glees hedges most of his statements on these matters with qualifications of one kind or another, no doubt to avoid an action for libel, but many readers of his pages might certainly gain the impression that there was a good deal that was dubious about Hill's work for the Committee.

By way of introduction let it be noted that Glees failed to consult the greater part of the documentation in the Public Record Office that relates to Hill's work with the Committee; that in his nine pages of text there are at least eight factual mistakes and a major error; and that the analysis presented is a distortion or a misreading, or both, of the evidence, all of which is in the public domain. It is unusual, it needs to be emphasised, in this kind of writing about intelligence matters, for *all* the evidence to be available for consultation; but in the case of Christopher Hill, the allegations made against him can be checked by reference to the Foreign Office files in the Public Record Office. There is no indication that any files have been withheld; and this would be unlikely, since the subject matter was not sensitive.

There are five pieces in the PRO at Kew that are concerned with the work of the Committee until August 1945. For readers not familiar with government documents at Kew, a 'piece' is a folder which contains one or more files. Some include many files. Each piece, and each file, has a classified number of identification. There were two pieces in 1944 that contained material on the Committee on Russian Studies, and three in 1945. Glees only used the first piece of 1945: FO 371/47884. This is a bulky folder containing twenty-nine files, but Glees quoted only the piece number (three times) and never the relevant file within the piece, or the date of the statement referred to. This would be normal scholarly practice, for obvious reasons, since without the file or date reference, readers would have to search through the twenty-nine files if they wanted to follow a particular matter through the original sources.

The central and crucial error Glees commits is to believe that Hill was the dominant personality in the work of the Committee. On p. 279 Glees writes that 'it was decided to set up a Committee on Russian Studies under the leadership of Christopher Hill', and he repeats this two pages later when he suggests that it was Geoffrey Wilson who asked Hill to 'lead' the Committee. It is difficult to imagine or to reconstruct how Glees arrived at this conclusion. It is clear from his very muddled account of the work of the Committee over a year and a half that he could not have read many of the relevant files, but whichever files he did read, or skim through, it should have become apparent that this was a Foreign Office committee, and Foreign Office committees do not have 'leaders'. They have a chairman and a secretary and so many members. Apart from Geoffrey Wilson, whose name is mentioned once but whose position as secretary to the Committee is not revealed, no other person is referred to as being involved. Readers were not told who was chairman of the Committee, and the fact that three sub-committees were established to carry through the work of the main Committee was also not mentioned. For Glees, then, the Committee on Russian Studies was Hill, and Hill was the Committee on Russian Studies. So it was Hill 'who proposed'; Hill who 'recommended'; Hill who 'suggested'; Hill who 'insisted'; Hill who 'tried to get Churchill to raise this matter at Terminal' (that is, the question of student exchanges at the Potsdam Conference).

While Glees failed to read the necessary documents of the Committee on Russian Studies, commonsense might have reminded him that Foreign Office committees are established and organised in ways that are common to Whitehall in general. The Committee on Russian Studies had a rather larger number of members who were not civil servants than in most Foreign Office committees, but its procedures followed traditional lines. It remained a Foreign Office committee, and senior members of the Office would see all or some of the papers as they desired. The head of the Northern Department, for example, who was not a member of the Committee on Russian Studies, initialled a number of files and wrote an occasional brief comment; and while Orme Sargent left most of the work of the Committee to Geoffrey Wilson, final decisions would remain with the senior officials. The work that Wilson did in the organisation of the Committee's enquiries was recognised at the third meeting in late April 1945 when the Committee expressed 'its warm thanks' to him.[10]

Glees offers his own gloss on the various recommendations of the Committee, never making clear whether such recommendations were in the reports of the sub-committees or in the minutes of the main Committee, but there is no indication in his text that he actually knew how the Committee's work was arranged. Since Hill, according to Glees, was the dominant figure in the decision-making, all that Glees required was an interpretation of the recommendations arrived at in order to show that they all tended towards a close accommodation to the requirements of increased Soviet influence. Thus, the various suggestions concerning the extension of teaching facilities were summed up by Glees in a remarkable conclusion:

> A cynic might think Foreign Office funds were going to be used to set up what amounted to a school for Soviet sympathisers and Fellow-Travellers. The fact that they were to be given the Stalinist line in their instructions emerges clearly from another minute (reinforcing the earlier unpleasant notion that Russian was only to be taught by those who were politically reliable. (p. 284)

Glees presumably based most of this argument upon the recommendation first put forward in the report of sub-committee (b) and later endorsed by the full Committee concerning the restricted use of Russian and Polish émigrés in the teaching of Russian studies. There are several points that need to be made. The first is that the very limited field of Russian studies in Britain before 1939 had certainly included among their teachers a high proportion of Russian émigrés, and that this fact had not been unnoticed. In the particular political situation of the closing years of the war, there was a widespread sentiment that the aftermath of war should see the continuation of wartime collaboration; and it was sensible to suggest that the teaching of Russian studies should not be in a position to be criticised for obvious bias by a large proportion of its teachers. Glees provides an untrue version of the recommendations. He actually suggests that Hill was insisting – Glee's emphasis – that 'the teaching of things Russians should be conducted by Soviet citizens which, in effect, meant Stalinists selected by the KGB' (p. 282). This is the second point that must be made. No one in sub-committee (b) or in the main Committee ever suggested that existing teachers, in any institution, whatever their views, should be discharged. What was done was to draw attention to the problem of the acute shortage of Russian teachers if there was to be expansion and the need in the medium and long run to remedy the shortfall in numbers. In the shorter term the report of sub-committee (b) recommended that the gap might be filled, as noted above, with individuals trained as war-time interpreters, and with Soviet citizens and American teachers. The third point to be made is that until Hill left the Foreign Office in August 1945 all these matters remained recommendations, and no decisions seem to have been taken, or implemented. The matter of finance, for example, had not been seriously discussed.[11]

In order to make his case against Hill appear as compromising as possible, Glees spent just over two pages of his nine considering a small book which Hill wrote in 1945 under a pseudonym: K.E. Holme, *The Soviets and Ourselves: Two Commonwealths*. It was, as would be expected both of its author and of the climate of opinion at this time, sympathetic in its appraisal of the Soviet Union. There was nothing in the book which in any way drew upon Hill's work within the Foreign Office – except his familiarity with current Russian sources – but Glees used it to explain to his readers that a favourable opinion of the Soviet Union in 1945 was likely to get in the way of that 'detached and objective view' that was expected of Foreign Office officials.

When the evidence of the many files on the working of the Committee on Russian Studies up to the end of the war is set against the account produced by Glees in his 1987 volume, we are confronted with a most extraordinary misrepresentation. Christopher Hill took no decisions of any kind. He was in no position to take any decisions. He could insist upon no matter. He was a junior administrative officer, on a secondment that would end when the war ended. In his internal correspondence within the Foreign Office, where young men are encouraged to express their own views clearly and precisely, he was scrupulous in stating plainly whether it was his own views that were being stated, whether Geoffrey Wilson agreed with them, or whether they summarised the views of a Committee. The question remains of the motivation of the author of *The Secrets of the Service*. Glees was writing a book on communist subversion. He found a communist in a junior administrative position in the Foreign Office: ergo, there must be subversion. Glees lights upon the Committee on Russian Studies, flicks through a small part of the documentation, misunderstands and certainly distorts what he reads, and then produces an account that is false testimony. It needs to be stated firmly and clearly that there is no truth in the insinuations and innuendos that are made against Christopher Hill. The Public Record Office, it must be said again, offers all the material on which such a judgement is made. The evidence is open to everyone.

Appendix 4

Ernest Bevin and the Defence of the Russian Revolution

The Annual Conference of the Labour Party met in Bournemouth in June 1946. There had been continuous criticism of Labour's foreign policy since the Government had taken office in July 1945, and the foreign affairs debate on the morning of Wednesday, 12 June, was wide-ranging and vigorously expressed. The debate was opened by P.J. Noel-Baker, a member of the National Executive and Bevin's Minister of State.[1] Bevin provided the closing speech, in which he discussed seriatim the critical resolutions before the Conference (all of which, unless withdrawn, being lost by the use of the block votes of the big unions). Then Bevin came to the resolution dealing with Russia, which called for 'friendship and co-operation . . . with the progressive forces throughout the world, and in particular with the USSR, and that such a policy should override British imperial interests'.[2]

The resolution, said Bevin at the beginning of his comments on this section, 'implies in the first instance that I have not been sympathetic to Russia':

> Is there any man in the Conference who historically did more to defend the Russian Revolution than I did? It is forgotten in this age, but when the Soviets did not have a friend I got dockers and other people to assist in forming the Council of Action to stop Lloyd George attacking them. I fought the Arcos raid and I called it silly. I fought Churchill's interventionist policy, for which we are paying now. I fought every attempt to break off relations. I helped to form in Transport House Anglo-Russian commercial relations, about which this Party do not know much. All through those years there was one thing I would not do. The thanks I got for it was an attempt by the Communists to break up the Union that I had built.[3]

The statement that Bevin was largely responsible for the movement in Britain against military intervention in Russia after the end of the First World War has been widely accepted. In the first volume of his biography, Alan Bullock provided a version of the events of 1920 and in the third volume he summarised Bevin's role in 1920 taking 'the lead in stopping the shipment of arms and setting up a Council of Action, with the threat of widespread strikes, if Lloyd George intervened on the side of Poland against Russia'.[4]

Military intervention against the newly established Soviet Republic had steadily increased throughout 1918, many months before the war with Germany was finally over.[5] It became known in Moscow in early March 1918 that the Allied Powers had suggested to Japan that armed forces be landed in Vladivostock. On 14 March the matter was raised by Lees Smith[6] in the House of Commons. From this time the press came under an increasing degree of censorship with the reporting of news from Russia, the most affected almost certainly being Morgan Philips Price, the *Manchester Guardian* correspondent in Russia, whose despatches for about half a year were not allowed to be used.[7] The main source of military information came from within the House of Commons, where radical liberals such as Joseph King, and others among the Labour group, constantly asked questions of the relevant ministers.

By the last few months of 1918 the labour movement in Britain, in both the political and industrial groups, was becoming increasingly aware of the intervention against Russia. In September the Second International had warned its affiliated organisations about the dangers of the policies the Allied Powers were pursuing in Russia; and at the beginning of 1919 (18 January 1919) a meeting in London in the Memorial Hall, Faringdon Road, established a 'Hands off Russia' Committee. Some three hundred and fifty delegates were present from most of the left-wing groups and organisations. The purpose of the Conference was to prepare for a general strike unless allied intervention in Russia was brought to an unconditional end, and a committee of fifteen was appointed to take the movement further. Among this committee were Jack Tanner, Albert Inkpin, Sylvia Pankhurst and Harry Pollitt.[8] In the same month Pollitt was appointed London District Secretary of the Boilermakers. From this time the agitation increased but not to the point, even in this tumultuous year of 1919 – the most potentially explosive year of the whole inter-war period – of achieving political strikes against Government policy.[9] Local Hands off Russia committees were formed in many parts of the country, and by the spring the Executive Committee of the Labour Party had issued a press statement which expressed 'an emphatic opinion that an arrangement should be made which will lead to the immediate cessation of hostilities and the safe withdrawal of British troops from Russian soil'. When the Labour Party Conference met at Southport on 25 June 1919 the chairman, in his opening address, declared bluntly: 'We must resist military operations in Russia and the perpetuation of conscription at home'; and a composite resolution was put forward in unequivocal terms:

> This Conference protests against the continued intervention by the Allies in Russia, whether by force of arms, by supply of munitions, by financial subsidies, or by commercial blockade; it calls for the immediate cessation of such intervention; it demands the removal of the censorship, so that an unbiased public opinion may be formed upon the issues involved; it denounces the assistance given by the Allies to those reactionary bodies in Russia as being a continuation of the war in the interests of financial capitalism, which aims at the destruction of the Russian Socialist Republic, and as being a denial of the rights of peoples to self determination; and it instructs the National Executive to consult the Parliamentary Committee of the Trades Union Congress, with the view to effective action being taken to enforce these demands by the unreserved use of their political and industrial power.

There was no dissent in the body of the Conference concerning the opposition to the Government's policy towards Russia, but there was considerable debate about the use of industrial action for political ends. On the vote being taken, the resolution was carried by 1,893,000 to 935,000. Between the end of June and the September meeting of the Trades Union Congress there were public meetings of the Hands Off Russia movement in many parts of the country, and the issue was a major one at the Congress. With much enthusiasm, the resolution quoted below was carried with only one dissentient. Just as important were the proposer and seconder. J.H. Thomas was not known for his radical views and he it was who moved the resolution, which was seconded by Tom Shaw, MP, another well-known moderate. The resolution read:

> That this Congress, in view of the general desire of the country, and the repeated declarations of the Government prior to, during, and since the recent general election, as reiterated to the deputation from the Parliamentary Committee which interviewed the leader of the House of Commons [Mr Bonar Law] on May 22 last, instructs the Parliamentary Committee to demand of the Government the repeal of the Conscription Acts, and the immediate withdrawal of British troops from Russia, and failing this, demands that a Special Trade Union Congress be called immediately to decide what action shall be taken.

During October and November the *Daily Herald*, which, under the editorship of George Lansbury, played a central role in the political agitation of these times and not least in the campaign against the Conscription Acts and the intervention in Russia, reported an increased number of meetings throughout Britain; and resolutions continued to pour in to Westminster and 10 Downing St. A deputation from the Parliamentary Committee of the TUC had presented the Prime Minister with the resolution passed at the Glasgow Congress, and a special Congress was convened to hear the report back. Before this a conference of the Hands Off Russia Committee had established itself on a national basis, with W.P. (Pat) Coates from the British Socialist Party as national secretary and Harry Pollitt as national organiser. The reconvened Trades Union Congress, having heard the report from their Parliamentary Committee, demanded the right to send a delegation to Russia to make 'an independent and impartial enquiry into the industrial, economic and political conditions of Russia'. The composition of the delegation became a joint TUC–Labour Party affair, and it was to leave England on 27 April 1920.[10] Many things happened before they left. The military offensive of the White armies in Russia, which had appeared so promising in early October 1919, quite suddenly was brought to a halt and by mid November it had become a rout, with the forces of Koltchak, Denikin and Yudenitch all in retreat. Early in November Lloyd George hinted at the readiness of the British Government to abandon its anti-Russian policies, although even the most right-wing Labour leaders, gullible in most matters, were cautious about accepting the Prime Minister at his word. In January 1920, after further soothing phrases from Lloyd George, a group of self-styled moderate leaders from both the trade union side and the Labour Party issued a statement (*Manchester Guardian*, 29 January 1920) which indicated continued disquiet at government policy towards Russia, and warned about the danger of war if Poland continued to refuse to discuss peace terms with Russia and if conflict escalated into violent military action. As Graubard noted, the manifesto concluded with some remarkably prescient comments:

> The Polish Army is already in occupation of Russian Territory. If its invasion of Russia is repelled by the Soviet forces, we shall undoubtedly be told that this is an attack upon Poland, and that it is our duty to stand by the State we have created. We should then be committed to support this war, not owing to any policy sanctioned by the country, but to acts of the Polish army instigated by obscure diplomatic intrigues. The whole results of the war which we have just fought and the victory we have gained – the end of militarism, the reduction of armaments, the firmer establishment of democracy, openness in diplomacy, a more unified Europe, a more secure peace – all are menaced by these intrigues. We shall do our best to oppose Britain's entrance into any war that this may give rise to.[11]

We may ignore the illusions spelt out in the penultimate sentence about what had been achieved by the 'war to end war', and note that by the spring of 1920 the military situation had changed once again. The Polish forces were now advancing into Russia, and they took Kiev on 12 June. By the end of the month they were once again in retreat and by mid July the Russians were threatening Warsaw. In July the British government had despatched a note to Russia requesting an immediate armistice, and on 3 August Lord Curzon, the Foreign Secretary, sent a further note promising war if the Russian advance was not halted.

While the military situation thus fluctuated the militant sections of the labour movement in Britain were intensifying their efforts to end the support of the British Government for the Poles. The latter's advance into Soviet Russia in the spring of 1920 was accepted as an act of aggression that could only have taken place with active material support from Britain and France; and there were renewed efforts to prevent supplies of arms from Britain reaching Poland. Harry Pollitt, in his autobiography, described the developing agitation in the East End of London. He was at this time working with Sylvia Pankhurst's Workers' Socialist Federation, which concentrated especially at the dock gates in Poplar. The dramatic episode of the *Jolly George* on 10 May 1920, when dockers refused to continue loading the ship when it was discovered that munitions were among the cargo, received wide publicity. It was, Pollitt wrote, 'the result of two years' tremendously hard and unremitting work on the part of a devoted band of comrades in East London';[12] and it was followed within a week by the triennial conference of the Dockers' Union at which Ernest Bevin moved the resolution condemning the export of arms and congratulating their London members on their action.

On 22 May 1920 there was published a manifesto asking for a national conference to consider a twenty-four-hour strike in support of peace with Russia. Among the signatories were Robert Smillie (president, Miners' Federation of Great Britain), Tom Mann (general secretary, Amalgamated Society of Engineers), John Bromley (general secretary, Associated Society of Locomotive Engineers and Firemen), Alex Gossip (general secretary, Furnishing Trades Association) and G. Cameron (general secretary, Amalgamated Society of Carpenters and Joiners). The appeal attracted considerable attention, and the Hands Off Russia Committee distributed several hundred thousand leaflets which reprinted the text.[13]

The Labour delegation to Russia returned at the end of June 1920, and they issued an interim report which appeared in the press on 12 July.[14] There was a vigorous attack on the policy of intervention and the economic blockade and they singled out for especial criticism the recent renewal of hostilities on the Polish front. It is always difficult to assess 'weight' in matters of this kind, but it is probable that the report of the British delegation had the most important impact of any single publication on political attitudes in general towards the Russian question. Hostilities were, however, continuing and the situation looked menacing, with *The Times* of 5 August suggesting in a leader that 'we stand upon the edge of a crisis fraught with possibilities only less tragic' than those of August 1914. On the same day[15] Arthur Henderson, in his capacity as national secretary of the Labour Party, sent a telegram to every local Labour Party in the country:

Extremely menacing possibility extension Polish–Russian war. Strongly urge local parties immediately organise citizen demonstrations against intervention and supply men and munitions to Poland. Demand peace negotiations, immediate raising blockade, resumption trade relations. Send resolutions Premier and Press. Deputise local M.P.

The following Sunday the *Daily Herald* produced a special edition with the headline:

'Not a Man, Not a Gun, Not a Sou'. On 9 August a joint conference of the Parliamentary Committee of the TUC, the Executive of the Labour Party and of the Parliamentary Labour Party was convened and it was agreed to ask immediately for an interview with the Prime Minister. This took place on the day following, 10 August, and Bevin was appointed their main speaker. It was an unusual choice for Bevin was not a member of any of the labour movement's senior committees and it was clearly a result of the reputation that he had so quickly obtained following his outstanding performance at the Shaw inquiry a few months earlier.[16] An early biographer of Bevin explained the new position that Bevin had now achieved because of the nation-wide publicity that his advocacy of the dockers' case had brought him:

> Bevin had cause to congratulate himself in that August 1920. In a period of no more than six months his position in the Labour movement had changed entirely. At the beginning of the year he had been a forceful but still comparatively obscure official of the Dockers' Union. Now he was among the best known, most controversial and most powerful leaders of the whole Labour movement.[17]

The delegation which saw Lloyd George on 10 August reported back to a specially convened national conference; and it was this conference, on 13 August 1920, which accepted the recommendation to establish a national Council of Action, and to encourage every locality to form their own Councils. The resolution introducing the Councils of Action was moved by J.R. Clynes and J.H. Thomas, and a second resolution empowered the leadership to take industrial action in the event of a declaration of war against Soviet Russia. It was a quite unprecedented occasion.[18]

The military situation on the Polish front, however, once again changed dramatically. The Russians were defeated before Warsaw on 15 August, and the Red Army began a general retreat. During the autumn of 1920 the Poles and the Russians concluded an armistice, and in Britain the threat of war quickly subsided; as did the aims and purposes of the Councils of Action, which, by November 1920, had largely ceased to function.

Appendix 5

Cards on the Table: A Note on the International Department of the Labour Party

Denis Healey took over the position of secretary to the International Department of the Labour Party early in January 1946. The Department had been without a secretary since William Gillies, 'a cantankerous Scot . . . was compelled to retire' a year earlier.[1] Healey, educated at Bradford Grammar School and Balliol College, Oxford, had been a Movement Control Officer during the war years, and had seen active service in Sicily and Italy. He was already on the list of Labour Party candidates when the war in Europe ended, and he attended the Labour Party Conference in May 1945 while still in the Army. He made a brilliant left-wing speech at the Conference which attracted the notice of certain of the leading personalities of the Party, including Hugh Dalton and Harold Laski, representing the right and the left wings of the Party respectively. Healey was encouraged to apply for the position of international secretary, to which in due course he was appointed. His own story of these days will be found in his autobiography, *The Time of My Life*, published in 1989.

When he joined the International Department Healey found himself with two main duties. The first was the rebuilding of contacts with the other socialist parties of the world, and especially those of Europe; and the second was the explanation and interpretation of Labour's foreign and colonial policies to the labour movement in Britain. In the first two years of Ernest Bevin's period of office as Foreign Secretary, as noted in the main text, there was widespread discontent with many aspects of the Government's foreign policy. The first two annual conferences after the war, those of 1946 and 1947, exhibited the sharpness of the criticisms. Healey must have very quickly adjusted his views to those of Bevin and the Foreign Office, for he gives no evidence or indication in his autobiography that he experienced any difficulty in interpreting the Government's views on international affairs from his early days in the office. He became very close to Bevin, and to the middle rank of officials in the Foreign Office. As he wrote in his memoirs: 'Bevin gave me a pretty free run of the Foreign Office, and I made many friends among its officials, notably Gladwyn Jebb . . . and Evelyn Shuckbrugh.'[2]

The relationship between the International Department and the Foreign Office was always close during Healey's period of office as secretary. It was, however, a connection that would have been seriously mistrusted had the extent of the contact been publicly known. At the 1946 Labour Party Conference there was a great deal of criticism from the floor about the personnel of the Foreign Office, and of the fact that Bevin had made no changes of significance to its internal working and organisation.[3] As will be illustrated below, the need for secrecy on this matter of the close relations between Transport House and Whitehall was well understood by both sides, and while the better informed critics were conscious of the relationship with the Foreign Office, the wider public remained unaware that the International Department was for purposes of practical politics an arm of the Foreign Office propaganda machine.

Much of the contact between Healey and the Foreign Office must have been on a personal level, but there is enough documentation in the files of both the Foreign Office and the International Department to sustain the argument that is being made here. It would seem that from the early days of Healey's tenure of the office the material published by the International Department was always agreed either by a civil servant or by a junior minister, or both. Towards the end of 1946, for example, the proofs of a pamphlet, *Approach to Foreign Policy*, were sent by Healey to Mr Kinna, Room 52, 11 Downing Street. Healey's covering letter dated 22 November 1946 began:

> Dear Mr Kinna
> As suggested by you on the telephone this afternoon, I am enclosing the galley proofs of the article on the Foreign Office by Mr Wells. I should be grateful if you would pass these on to the person suggested since it will need some bringing up to date, and some re-writing.

Kinna then sent the proofs on to E.J. Passant with a covering note: 'Could you please make any changes in the attached. Wells is in New York . . . ' On 25 November there was an internal minute to Kinna. The authorship is uncertain, but the handwriting looks like that of Pierson Dixon, of Bevin's Private Office; and since all the correspondence quoted here is taken from the Bevin papers at the PRO, Dixon is not unlikely to have provided the comment, which began:

> 1. Under USA. I have marked the second sentence beginning 'There has been close collaboration . . . ' Do we want – or do the Labour Party want – to suggest 'ganging-up', which the Secretary of State strongly repudiates?

The minute continued with strong criticism of most of the rest of the pamphlet mainly on the grounds that the information provided on individual countries was too scanty to be useful. Kinna then sent a minute to the Southern Department asking them 'to add or rewrite sections on Yugoslavia, Albania and Bulgaria'. When Kinna returned the page proofs to Healey, he drew particular attention to the phrasing of the 'close collaboration with the USA . . . and you will no doubt wish to alter or omit this sentence'. In the final published version the phrase was in fact still retained although many of the other corrections were accepted.[4]

There was an episode in 1947 which made explicit the care that was expected to be taken to dissociate the International Department from the Foreign Office. In the early spring of 1947 Gladwyn Jebb produced a long policy statement which he called 'Stocktaking II'. He noted at the beginning that Orme Sargent had circulated a memorandum entitled 'Stocktaking after VE-Day' on 11 July;[5] and Jebb's memorandum was an exercise in summarising the main developments in the two years since Orme Sargent's paper was written. It had a one-page foreword by Orme Sargent dated 20 March 1947 and it was thought important enough to be printed. During the next two months there was a good deal of discussion within the Foreign Office, and between the senior officials and Bevin, who was for some of the time in Moscow. There was a telegram from Moscow on 2 April 1947 to the effect that the Foreign Secretary had read Jebb's memorandum and commented 'that it was well done' but he was not willing for it to be circulated until at least the end of the Moscow Conference. A month later, on 3 May, Jebb sent a minute to Orme Sargent in which he said that Pierson Dixon, of Bevin's Private Office, had reported that Bevin did not want the Jebb memorandum circulated to his colleagues but that he might perhaps be willing to agree to circulate it to Heads of Missions. Dixon had further commented that more useful would perhaps be a short paper which refuted the arguments in R.H.S. Crossman's recent pamphlet *Keep Left*; and Jebb added that naturally he was prepared to do this but further suggested that it might be helpful for Orme Sargent to have a discussion with Bevin first. Orme Sargent followed this with a short note to Bevin hoping that the Jebb memorandum could be circulated to Heads of Missions. The reasons why Bevin was unhappy with Jebb's draft were never clearly stated, but it may be inferred from the various minutes that were being circulated that Bevin was unwilling to allow a wide circulation at this time to such a vigorous and firm anti-Soviet document. There was a brief memorandum from Dixon to Bevin, for example, on 9 May 1947 reminding the Foreign Secretary that he was going to look at the Jebb paper again: and Dixon asked whether it should be 'circulated for information only, very secretly, to the Heads of Missions abroad'.[6] Jebb took up the suggestion of a reply to Crossman's *Keep Left* pamphlet and there was a discussion within the Office as to whether it might form the basis for a pamphlet; and then Dixon, on 14 May, wrote a short minute that 'Rather unfortunately, Labour Party bringing out a pamphlet on foreign affairs . . . without consultation with us.'[7]

While these discussions had been going on within the Foreign Office, a quite independent initiative had been developing from the International Department. The details that follow are from the papers of the International Department in the Labour Party archives. On 21 April 1947 Healey wrote to Dalton, Chairman of the International Sub-Committee, asking if there was any objection to a pamphlet on foreign affairs being published in time for the Annual Conference 'providing there is no serious objection from the Foreign Office'; and Healey attached a draft. On the same day he sent another draft to Hector McNeil, Bevin's Minister of State, and McNeil replied on the 24 April, endorsing the draft in general but also making a number of suggestions and amendments. McNeil wrote that he had 'enjoyed reading it. I think it distinguished, not only by its honesty, but by its appearance of honesty – honesty like justice always needs a little good dressing.' In McNeil's handwriting on this letter to Healey was scribbled: 'Dalton agreed. Friday 25 April.' This, then, was how the pamphlet *Cards on the Table* came to be published.[8]

To return to the Jebb memorandum. On 9 May 1947 Jebb wrote to Orme Sargent, the Permanent Under-Secretary. His minute is given below in full:

> The Secretary of State saw me this morning and discussed 'Stocktaking II' and my memorandum on Mr Crossman's pamphlet [*Keep Left*]. He is taking Stocktaking II away with him for the weekend to re-read, and will then let us know whether he thinks it is suitable for circulation to Heads of Missions – which, of course, on your instructions I strongly urged.
>
> As regards my comments on Mr Crossman's pamphlet, it seems that the Secretary of State himself had used many of the arguments which it contained in a discussion which he had with the Labour Party Foreign Policy group last Monday, and he does not, therefore, propose to

circulate it, as such, before the Margate conference, especially as there are doubts whether Mr Crossman would make much progress there.

Most Confidential
On the other hand, the Secretary of State thought that many of my arguments might quite suitably be embodied in some Labour Party Headquarters pamphlet, which might be published after the Margate conference is over, and he thought I might then get in touch with Mr Denis Healey and discuss ways and means with him, provided, of course, that such co-operation was kept very dark. He also thought that Mr Gee (who will by then, I hope, be our Labour Adviser) might be associated with such talks.[9]

Dixon's suggestion of 14 May, quoted above, that the Labour Party were bringing out their own pamphlet without prior consultation with the Foreign Office was not true since, as we have noted, Hector McNeil had been involved at an early stage, and it must be presumed that before the Margate Conference of the Labour Party opened on 26 May 1947 the Foreign Office and their ministers had all told each other how *Cards on the Table* came to be published. It may be correct for Bullock to suggest[10] that Bevin was surprised to learn that the pamphlet was being written by Transport House, but it was disingenuous to write that 'What pleased Bevin most was that someone else in the Labour Party had made the case for him.'[11] Jebb's minute to Orme Sargent of 9 May, quoted above, had repeated Bevin's suggestion that the Foreign Office and the International Department should collaborate in a publication to be put out under the imprint of the Labour Party; a partnership that should be kept 'very dark'.

On the first day of the Margate Conference Konni Zilliacus drew attention to *Cards on the Table*, quoted the comment that 'America provides the money while we provide the men', and condemned the arguments in general as contrary to the principles of foreign policy upon which the Labour Party had been elected in 1945. He was followed by Crossman who pointed out that foreign policy was to be debated later in the week and that therefore at this stage he would raise procedural matters concerning the provenance of the pamphlet. Who had written it? Had it been approved by the Foreign Secretary? Had it the authority of the National Executive? Was it an official statement or merely a discussion statement? Dalton replied with an unsatisfactory and equivocal statement and promised a considered reply from the Executive later. Later in the week, on Wednesday afternoon, Dalton made a further statement in which he remarked that 'the silly story that it was prepared in consultation with officials in the Foreign Office is quite untrue'; and that *Cards on the Table*, while not committing the National Executive in every detail, was published as a contribution to the discussion and interpretation of foreign policy.

Dalton's version of the incident in his diary is somewhat different. After noting that he had agreed to the publication of the pamphlet, on the understanding that McNeil would check its political reliability, Dalton continued:

When, therefore, I was suddenly asked at Margate whether the National E.C. was in agreement with it, I had to hedge. To have said 'Yes' would have been a plain untruth, since they had not seen it; to have said 'No' would have quite discredited the pamphlet and its author. Therefore I adopted a challenging tone and said that, as this question had been put, I would most gladly let them have a definite answer before the Conference closed. Then we had a long jaw in the National E.C., several members taking great objection to the pamphlet. I had to keep rather quiet as to my own individual role in the matter which was not, I think, known to all my colleagues.[12]

Over twenty years later Healey offered a further gloss on Dalton's story. In a book published in 1971 Healey is reported as saying that

> The Executive held meeting after meeting, and it wasn't until almost the last one that Dalton, under repeated prodding from Shinwell, admitted that he had cleared it for publication. Up to that point he let it appear that I had done this entirely off my own bat without consulting anyone.[13]

Almost a further twenty years on Healey wrote in his autobiography that he had consulted with McNeil and Chris Mayhew, the latter's name being mentioned for the first time in the documentation so far consulted.[14]

There are several points that emerge from this story. The first is that the National Executive were highly conscious of the discontent that had prevailed within the labour movement during the first two years of its office concerning Bevin's handling of foreign affairs. It was, as discussed above in the main text, a discontent that was soon to die away with a quite remarkable change in the climate of political opinion. The second is that it confirms the close contact between the Foreign Office and the International Department. What we do not know about the *Cards on the Table* episode is whether McNeil consulted any of his civil servants when he received Healey's draft; and presumably we shall never know. In his letter of 24 April which commented on Healey's draft he noted that he had asked the Department to verify some figures about displaced persons, but there is no indication about a political consultation. The addition of Mayhew's name is interesting, and the combination of McNeil and Mayhew certainly meant that the mainstream opinion within the Foreign Office was adequately represented, for both were wholly at one with Bevin and his senior officials in their anti-Sovietism. The third point is the obvious one that *Cards on the Table* makes it abundantly clear that Denis Healey was in total agreement with the Foreign Office view, central to their policies, that the Soviet Union was a potentially aggressive power, waiting only for an opportunity to move its armies into Western Europe or the Middle East. Over forty years later, Healey recanted:

> Like most Western observers at this time, I believed that Stalin's behaviour showed that he was bent on the military conquest of Western Europe. I now think we were all mistaken. We took too seriously some of the Leninist rhetoric pouring out from Moscow, as the Russians took too seriously some of the anti-Communist rhetoric favoured by American politicians.[15]

In the meantime, although Healey does not make the point, there were forty years of Cold War.

There is a footnote that may be added. Anthony Eden lunched early in June 1947 with Bruce Lockhart and the latter recorded the occasion in his diary. Eden had talked of *Cards on the Table*, which he said had been published before the Labour Party Conference presumably to strengthen Bevin's hand and, it must be assumed, with Bevin's approval:

> The pamphlet, Anthony said, was patronising to the USA and offensive to Russia. He was going to attack it at the weekend when he was to receive the freedom of Warwick. He was going to call it 'diplomacy by insult' (At Warwick he did!).[16]

Notes

Introduction

1. The Polish question; Trieste; the Baruch Plan; the Iranian crisis of 1946; the division of Germany – all have been suggested as turning points of some kind in the relations between Russia and the Western Powers. Naturally their importance varies widely and, naturally also, all points of friction contributed to the longer-term hostilities of the Cold War; but by themselves, even with the central issue of Germany, any one episode, crisis or major confrontation must be evaluated in context and within a global historical framework.

2. There were, of course, other exceptions in addition to those mentioned in the text. Philip Darby's *British Defence Policy East of Suez, 1947–1968*, Oxford, 1973, was a remarkable reconstruction based largely upon interviews and discussions with leading military and political contemporaries; and J. Frankel, *British Foreign Policy, 1945–1973*, London, 1975, a very helpful political sociology, especially in its discussion of the conservatism of the decision-makers.

3. E.H. Carr, *What is History?*, London, 1964, p. 24.

4. Quoted in Z.S. Steiner, *The Foreign Office and Foreign Policy, 1898–1914*, Cambridge, 1969, p. 113.

5. H.G. Nicholas, ed., *Washington Despatches, 1941–1945: Weekly Political Reports from the British Embassy*, London, 1981, 25 August 1945, pp. 608–9.

6. J.L. Gaddis, 'The Emerging Post-Revisionist Synthesis on the Origins of the Cold War', *Diplomatic History*, Vol. 7, Summer 1983, pp. 171–90; with a useful bibliography.

7. The first detailed published account seems to be R. Smith and J. Zametica, 'The Cold Warrior: Clement Attlee Reconsidered, 1945–7', *International Affairs*, Vol. 61, No. 2, Spring 1985, pp. 237–52.

8. R. Smith, 'A Climate of Opinion: British Officials and the Development of British Soviet Policy, 1945–7', *International Affairs*, Vol. 64, No. 4, Autumn 1988, p. 646; idem, 'Ernest Bevin, British Officials and British Soviet Policy, 1945–7', in A. Deighton, ed., *Britain and the First Cold War*, London, 1990, pp. 32–52.

9. O. Harvey, *The War Diaries of Oliver Harvey*, ed. J. Harvey, London, 1978, pp. 62–3.

10. I. Deutscher, *Stalin: A Political Biography*, Oxford, 1961, p. 538.

11. See below, Appendix 2.

12. D. Healey, *The Time of My Life*, London, 1989, p. 101.

13. There is a large amount of disparate material to be found in the departmental records for 1946. See also the reports of interviews with the new ambassadors of both the USA and Britain; the accounts of experienced visitors (M. Philips Price in the *Manchester Guardian* and the *Glasgow Herald* in December 1945) and the reports of the Labour Party delegation of July/August 1946. Throughout most of the same year the Moscow despatches to London carried accounts, sometimes verbatim, of the weekly lectures on foreign policy delivered by, mostly, Russian academics; and these provide interesting insights into the more sophisticated opinion in the Russian capital. They will be found in FO 371/56762 and /56834.

14. The most recent detailed account in English is A. Deighton, *The Impossible Peace: Britain, the Division of Germany, and the Origins of the Cold War*, Oxford, 1990. The book was discussed in a

review article by D. Reynolds, 'Britain and the Cold War', *Hist. Journal*, Vol. 35, No. 2, 1992, pp. 501–3.

15. H.M. Hyndman, *The Record of an Adventurous Life*, London, 1911, p. 245.

1. The Mind of the Foreign Office

1. *The Memoirs of Lord Gladwyn*, London, 1972, p. 106. Gladwyn Jebb, as he was known before his peerage, wrote his memoirs just before the thirty-year rule for Public Records was introduced; and reliance upon his own papers and his memory produced a number of somewhat blurred and sometimes inaccurate accounts of events in which he himself played a prominent part.

2. Sir John Tilley and S. Gaselee, *The Foreign Office*, London, 1933, p. 88. The first eleven chapters – the quotation in the text is from Ch. 4 – were written by Tilley, who had been Chief Clerk to the FO.

3. Most of the details in this paragraph are taken from the work of Z.S. Steiner, *The Foreign Office and Foreign Policy, 1898–1914*, esp. Ch. 1. On the 'homogeneity' thesis see Peter G. Boyle, 'The British Foreign Office View of Soviet–American Relations, 1945–6', *Diplomatic History*, Vol. 3, 1979, pp. 307–20. Referring to the top officials in Whitehall and Washington, he wrote: 'The world view of these men in 1945–6 comes across very clearly – it was the view of the British upper class at the end of the Second World War' (p. 308).

4. Christina Larner, 'The Amalgamation of the Diplomatic Service with the Foreign Office', *J. Cont. Hist*, Vol. 7, No. 1, 1972, pp.107–26.

5. Tilley and Gaselee, *The Foreign Office*, p. 85. The generalisation is still true of contemporary Britain. A TV production in December 1986 filmed an interview of two candidates before the final selection board of the Foreign Office. One, a young woman, Charterhouse and Cambridge, had recently spent five weeks in Israel and was asked a question about the Palestinian homeland, and whether she thought the claim justified. After thought she decided it was, because of the Holocaust, and she was then gently reminded that the Palestinians were Arabs. The whole interview was at a very dispiriting level. The second candidate, a young man, comprehensive school and Oxford, was foolish enough to try to argue the case for abolition of nuclear weapons. The young woman was accepted, among other reasons, for her charming manners, or so the Board said; the man failed. There is an account in *The Observer*, 14 December 1986, by Alan Rusbridger. The programme was shown as part of the 'Forty Minutes' series on BBC 2.

6. Steiner, *Foreign Office and Foreign Policy*, p. 213.

7. Political radicalisation had extended to sections of the working class during the later years of the 1930s – metal workers in particular – and to some groups of the middle classes, with the Left Book Club playing an important part; and to the Jewish population of all social classes. However, in spite of the tumultuous events of the years before 1939, psephologists have always maintained that had there been no war, the Conservative Party would have probably won the general election in 1940. It was the war which extended the anti-Tory sentiment of large numbers of the British people. For the general background, see P. Addison, *The Road to 1945: British Politics and the Second World War*, London, 1975; J. Saville, *The Labour Movement in Britain: A Commentary*, London, 1988, Chs 4 and 5.

8. For a somewhat neglected text, Joseph Frankel, *British Foreign Policy 1945–1973*, London, 1975, provided a stimulating analysis of the various factors involved in the determination of foreign policy decisions; and for a specific analysis of the conservative social and political background against which decision-making was formulated, see the section 'Traditions and Other Obstacles to Rationality', pp. 101 ff.

9. *The Diaries of Sir Alexander Cadogan, 1938–1945*, ed. David Dilks, London, 1971: 'It was a methodical, orderly household, hierarchical to a degree not easy to realise at this distance of nearly a century. Not only did Earl Cadogan strictly discourage any disagreement among themselves. Explaining to a friend why, when nearing eighty, he still felt diffident about uttering to his brother what would look like a criticism, Sir Alec Cadogan recalled how often as a child he had heard the remark: "Don't contradict your brother, he is older than you." And so we never offered criticisms to each other, at least never from a younger to an older.' Introduction, p. 1.

10. Gladwyn, *Memoirs*, p. 70: of Cadogan he wrote: 'Careful, cautious, reserved, conventional,

THE POLITICS OF CONTINUITY

clearly shy, clearly repressed emotionally, he was nevertheless a man of quiet charm and native intelligence.' Gladwyn wrote these words before Cadogan's *Diaries* were published, the content of which greatly surprised him.

11. One must not, of course, be too prim about adolescent behaviour. No doubt it happens, or it happened, to all of us. There is the story of Jean-Paul Sartre in his very early twenties, on the roof of the Sorbonne with a friend, throwing water onto the pedestrians below, with the cry: 'Thus pissed Zarathustra.'

12. Writing of the period when Neville Chamberlain became Prime Minister in May 1937, A.J.P. Taylor has a characteristic comment: 'the staff of the Foreign Office had little confidence in the government. Sir Robert Vansittart, the Permanent Under-Secretary, was set on resisting Germany. He paraded his resolution in an ornate literary style and also in more irregular ways, such as passing information to Churchill and stirring up opposition to the government in the press. Yet the attitude of Vansittart and the other professionals was singularly unpractical. They could only re-iterate that Hitler should be resisted, and had no idea how to do it.' *English History, 1914–1945*, Oxford, 1965, p. 405.

13. So Orme Sargent told Bruce Lockhart: *The Diaries of Sir Robert Bruce Lockhart, Vol. 2: 1939–1965*, ed. K. Young, London, 1980, 6 January 1946, p. 516.

14. Sir Llewellyn Woodward, *British Foreign Policy in the Second World War*, London, 1962, p. xxvi.

15. *DNB 1960–1969*. The author was P.H. Gore-Booth.

16. The political review is in the Cadogan *Diaries*, pp.116–20; and the March 1938 quotation is on p. 63.

17. Gladwyn, *Memoirs*, p. ix.

18. Cadogan, *Diaries*, pp. 686–7. The omissions are in the printed text. When officials in the Foreign Office wanted to quote left-wing opinion, the *New Statesman* was their most common source. Barrington Ward was editor of *The Times*, 1941–48. This was a period when *The Times* offered a critical appraisal of certain aspects of British foreign policy, and when it could certainly not be described as an organ of official opinion; for which see Iverach McDonald, *The History of The Times. Vol. 5: Struggles in War and Peace, 1939–1966*, London, 1984. The 1944 intervention in Greece was sharply criticized (pp. 117–26). For a general survey, see A.J. Foster, 'The Politicians, Public Opinion and the Press: The Storm over British Military Intervention in Greece in December 1944', *J. Cont. Hist.*, Vol. 19, No. 3, 1984, pp. 453–94; idem, 'The British Press and the Coming of the Cold War', in A. Deighton, ed., *Britain and the First Cold War*, London, 1990, pp.11–31.

19. *Diaries*, pp. 696–7. Churchill's speech is in *Hansard*, 5 Ser., Vol. 407, Cols 396–428, 18 January 1945. It began with a ferocious attack on ELAS/EAM. Churchill did not mention *The Times* by name; the newspaper was identified in the same debate by a Labour member. E.H. (Ted) Carr was assistant editor of *The Times* 1941–46. What Iverach McDonald makes clear is that many of the offending leading articles were the work of several hands, especially of Donald Tyerman as well as Carr, and that they were always edited carefully by Barrington Ward unless he was away from the office. Carr's general approach to international politics at this time was provided by his *Conditions of Peace*, London, 1942, a substantial volume of 275 pages.

20. *Diaries*, p. 604.

21. John Colville, *The Fringes of Power: Downing Street Diaries. Vol. 1: 1939–October 1941*, paperback edn. London, 1986, 6 March 1941, p. 430. Colville has similar comments elsewhere in his diaries, one of which is quoted below. His account of life on the troop deck for five weeks from England to South Africa is worth reading: *Vol. 2: 1941–April 1955*, paperback edn, London, 1986, pp. 21–42. Colville's diaries are superior to those of Cadogan. Among other defects Cadogan spatters his comment with prep school expressions such as 'silly bladders', 'beastly', 'silly', 'ass'. It seems a not uncommon characteristic that some members of the British upper classes never quite recover from their school or university days.

22. Colville, *Fringes of Power*, Vol. 2, p. 139.

23. Lockhart, *Diaries*, Vol. 2, p. 236.

24. Piers Dixon, *Double Diplomacy: The Life of Sir Pierson Dixon. Don and Diplomat*, London, 1968, p. 166. Dixon was Private Secretary first to Eden and then to Bevin, November 1943–December 1947.

25. Lockhart, *Diaries*, 7 February 1943, p. 226.

26. *The Times*, 1 and 4 January 1943.

27. Ibid., 1 January 1943.

28. K.B. Smellie, *A Hundred Years of English Government*, London, 1937, Ch. 10, 'The Machinery of Administration since 1918', includes a useful summary and discussion of the Haldane Report; and it further provides a summary of all subsequent Reports relevant to administration up to the date of publication.

29. Cadogan, *Diaries*, pp. 501–2.

30. Bruce Lockhart's wartime *Diaries* are full of Whitehall's criticisms and complaints about the Foreign Office and the lack of co-ordination within Whitehall; summarised by Kenneth Young in his Introduction, Vol. 2, p. 19 ff.

31. Cmd. 6420, reprinted in Appendix III to Lord W. Strang, *The Foreign Office*, London, 1955, pp. 214–22.

32. FO 800/463, 11 February 1946.

33. *Labour Party. 1946 Conference Report*, p. 152.

34. There were many examples in the papers circulating in Whitehall; after the thirty-year rule was introduced, American historians began, rather slowly, to comment on the complacency, as well as the illusions, displayed by London: 'At times', one has written, 'the Foreign Office exhibited an incredible, almost irresponsible optimism about its ability to manipulate American opinion and actions'; R.M. Hathaway, *Ambiguous Partnership: Britain and America, 1944–47*, New York, 1981, p. 52. There is a more extended discussion below in this chapter, in the Washington section.

35. CAB 65/52, WM (45) 39, 3 April 1945.

36. FO 371/50912, 11 July 1945, reprinted in G. Ross, *The Foreign Office and the Kremlin . . . 1941–45*, Cambridge, 1984, Document 39, pp. 210–14. Evelyn Shuckbrugh, *Descent to Suez: Diaries 1951–56*, London, 1986, emphasised that Anthony Eden's views were similar to those quoted in the text: 'He did believe that we had responsibilities, experiences and qualities of thought of a world-wide nature which we ought not to jeopardise', (p. 18). Shuckbrugh was Private Secretary to Eden 1951–54, but these comments would certainly apply to Eden throughout his official career.

37. 'Even in the heyday of Empire, imperial ideas were not a coherent nation-wide orthodoxy but were criticised and opposed by many Englishmen. Nevertheless, the national involvement in the Empire was an important reality at all social levels and was by no means limited to the upper and upper-middle classes. Not only was the Empire the source of Britain's military and economic power and of national pride, but it also provided many individual Britons with a good income, with outlets for their energy, and with opportunities for their careers': Frankel, *British Foreign Policy*, pp. 221–2. Frankel then continued with a discussion of the increasing burden of Empire in the post-war world, a matter which is considered below in Chapter 4. On the question of terminology, there came about a consideration of the most appropriate usage: was it to be Commonwealth, British Commonwealth, or the established British Empire? Attlee, after a Dominion Premiers' Conference, raised the matter in the House of Commons on 2 May 1949 and concluded that he thought it better 'to allow people to use the expression they like best'. W.I. Jennings, a constitutional academic lawyer, in a letter to *The Times*, 6 June 1949, suggested that 'Empire' was associated with 'imperialism' which was 'the deadliest of the political sins. "Commonwealth" made political conditions slightly less difficult.'

38. For an introduction to the literature, see B. Porter, *The Lion's Share: A Short History of British Imperialism, 1850–1983*, 2nd edn, London, 1984, esp. Ch. VIII for the inter-war years.

39. J.M. Mackenzie, *Propaganda and Empire: The Manipulation of British Public Opinion, 1880–1960*, Manchester, 1984, p. 256.

40. P.S. Gupta, *Imperialism and the British Labour Movement, 1914–1964*, London, 1975, is an excellent introduction; and see the bibliography in J. Saville, 'Britain: Internationalism and the Labour Movement between the Wars', in F. van Holthoon and M. van der Linden, eds., *Internationalism in the Labour Movement, 1830–1940*, Leiden, 1988, pp. 565–82.

41. All political and diplomatic histories of the late 1930s and the early war years must consider the issue of isolationism: see the excellent volumes by W.L. Langer and S.E. Gleason, *The Challenge to Isolation, 1937–1940*, New York, 1952, and *The Undeclared War*, New York, 1953; and the detailed account in D. Reynolds, *The Creation of the Anglo-American Alliance 1937–1941: A Study in Competitive Co-operation*, London, 1981. On the issue of anti-imperialism and anti-colonialism the literature is again considerable. All studies and biographies of F.D. Roosevelt have

to consider his views of the question. The most wide-ranging analysis, with a comprehensive bibliography, is W. Roger Louis, *Imperialism at Bay, 1941–1945: The United States and the Decolonisation of the British Empire*, Oxford, 1977. For a British historian's approach, see D. Cameron Watt, *Succeeding John Bull: America in Britain's Place 1900–1975*, Cambridge, 1984.

42. Churchill's statement was on 9 September 1941: *Hansard*, 5 Ser., Vol. 374, Col. 69. Reynolds, *Creation of the Anglo-American Alliance*, provides a perceptive analysis of contemporary thinking among the political leaders on both sides of the Atlantic in Ch. 10 'A New Deal for the World?'.

43. Wendell Willkie (1892–1945) went on a special mission for Roosevelt in September–October 1942 to the Middle East, China and Russia. In a statement made at the conclusion of his visit, he said: 'We believe that it is the world's job to find some system for helping colonial peoples who join the United Nations cause to become free, independent nations': *Keesings Contemporary Archives*, 1942, p. 5401; and for Willkie, *Dictionary of American Biography, Supplement Three*, 1973.

44. CAB 65/28, 18 November 1942, quoted in M. Gilbert, *Road to Victory: Winston S. Churchill, 1941–1945*, paperback edn, London, 1989, p. 254.

45. Lord Lugard developed the theory of 'indirect rule' which became the orthodoxy of British colonial policy in the first half of the twentieth century. Margery Perham wrote the standard biography of Lugard in two volumes, 1956 and 1960. She herself was a prolific commentator on colonial issues in the post-war years.

46. W.K. Hancock (1898–1988), Professor of History at Adelaide University, 1924–33; Birmingham University, 1934–44; Chichele Professor of Economic History, Oxford, 1944–49; Director of Institute of Commonwealth Affairs, 1949–56; he then returned to Australia.

47. After the failure of the Cripps Mission in the spring of 1942, against the background of the Japanese military successes in South-East Asia, there were serious riots and disorders in India, beginning August 1942; the Congress leaders were put in jail where they remained for most of the rest of the war: V.P. Menon, *The Transfer of Power in India*, London, 1975. An American historian summed up: 'The survival of the Congress Party indicated that the British would not – indeed could no longer – take repression to its logical conclusion and that the assertion of imperial authority in August 1942 was the last act in a long running drama': R.A. Callahan, *Churchill: Retreat from Empire*, Wilmington, Del., 1984, p. 208.

48. *Hansard*, 5 Ser., Vol. 385, Col. 912, 26 November 1942.

49. The speech was made on 25 November 1943, before a private meeting of the UK branch of the Empire Parliamentary Association (EPA), and published by the Association under the title *Thoughts on the New World*; reprinted in full in *Selections from the Smuts Papers. Vol. VI: December 1934–August 1945*, ed. J. van der Poel, Cambridge, 1973, pp.456–68. In this speech Smuts moved into romantic nonsense at considerable length about the British Empire, a theme in which he fervently believed (for which see the quotation in the same para. of the text). A year earlier on 28 December 1941 *Life* magazine of New York had featured an article by Smuts in which the same exaggerated sentiments were expressed: that the British Commonwealth was 'the widest system of organised human freedom which has ever existed in human history'. Smuts was highly influential in political circles in Britain. Louis, *Imperialism at Bay*, p. 209, characterised the Smuts interview in *Life* 'as one of the most skilful propaganda pieces of the entire war': a generalisation that may be doubted.

50. *Smuts Papers*, Vol. VI, p. 462.

51. *Hansard*, 5 Ser., Vol. 305, Col. 939, 26 November 1942.

52. Louis, *Imperialism at Bay*, Ch. XI.

53. K. Harris, *Attlee*, London, 1982, pp. 201–7.

54. CAB 66/65, WP (45) 256, paras 4 and 5, 13 April 1945. Eden's memorandum 'Defence of the Middle East' was produced in reply to questions raised by the Suez Canal Committee whose chairman was Attlee (CAB 66/63, WP (45), 197, 20 March 1945). Attlee's unorthodox political position on the future of Britain in the Middle East is considered in detail in Chapter 3 below.

55. Below, Chapter 3.

56. Nicholas, ed., *Washington Despatches*, 25 August 1945, pp. 608–9.

57. Quoted in Callahan, *Churchill: Retreat from Empire*, p. 177.

58. Cadogan, *Diaries*, Dilks' Introduction, p. 20.

59. T. Burridge, *Clement Attlee: A Political Biography*, London, 1985, pp. 171–2, 175–6. The

extension of the terms of reference in November 1943 are set down in CAB 65/38, WM (43), 155, 16 November 1943.

60. Victor Frederick William Cavendish-Bentinck (1897–1990) succeeded to the title of the 9th Duke of Portland in 1979. After his wartime career in Whitehall he became Ambassador to Poland, from which Embassy his appointment was 'terminated', the term used in the FO List (to be compared with the usual 'resigned' or 'retired'). There was controversy about Cavendish-Bentinck's departure from the Foreign Office: the subject was debated in the columns of the *Guardian* between Patrick Howarth, who wrote the obituary notice (3 August 1990), and the present author (7 August) with a further reply from Howarth on 15 August 1990.

61. J. Lewis, *Changing Direction: British Military Planning for Post-War Strategic Defence, 1942–1947*, London, 1988, pp. 52–4 and Ch. 3.

62. Gladwyn, *Memoirs*, pp. 131–7. Gladwyn Jebb described his exit from the Post-Hostilities Planning Staff as 'towards the end of 1944, I seem to remember that I rather faded out of this strictly strategic picture' (p. 137). The fuller story is told, although not as clearly as could be wished, in Lewis, *Changing Direction*, Ch. 4, esp. p. 122 ff.

63. The note is reprinted in full in Lewis, *Changing Direction*, App. 3 (ii), pp. 350–53.

64. Among those who took the side of the military, at least in part, were Cavendish-Bentinck, Frank Roberts and R.M. Hankey (for the last two named, see the essays in J. Zametica, ed., *British Officials and British Foreign Policy 1945–50*, Leicester, 1990). Against the military were Cadogan, Orme Sargent and Christopher Warner, head of the Northern Department. For a sample of the views expressed see the files in FO 371/40740 and various minutes of 7–9 June 1944. There is a good brief summary of the controversy between the FO and the COS in Ross, *Foreign Office and the Kremlin*, Introduction, pp. 50–51.

65. A. Bryant, *Triumph in the West, 1943–1946: Based on the Diaries and Autobiographical Notes of Field Marshal the Viscount Alanbrooke*, London, 1959, p. 242.

66. CAB 79/82. COS (44) 346 (O) (13), Confidential Annex, 24 October 1944. The three procedures agreed for dealing with politically sensitive papers relating to the Soviet Union are reprinted in Lewis, *Changing Direction*, p. 134.

67. V. Rothwell, *Britain and the Cold War, 1941–1947*, London, 1982, is one example. He characterises Warner's memorandum 'The Soviet Campaign against This Country and Our Response to It' (FO 371/56832/ N 6344, 2 April 1946) as 'in a sense an apologia for his relatively favourable stance towards Soviet Russia of the later war years'. Such a statement, as my text suggests, reflects a failure to understand the diplomatic problems the FO confronted during the war years.

68. Maclean defected to the Soviet Union, with Guy Burgess, on 25 May 1951. There is a useful bibliography, and some general, sensible guesswork, in Sheila Kerr, 'The Secret Hotline to Moscow: Donald Maclean and the Berlin Crisis of 1948', in A. Deighton, ed., *Britain and the First Cold War*, London, 1990, pp. 71–87.

69. As Ross notes in *The Foreign Office and the Kremlin*, p. 51; and illustrated by Document 28, pp. 166–72, which brings together extracts from the Planning Staff papers, June 1944–June 1945.

70. Quoted in J. Edwards, *The British Government and the Spanish Civil War, 1936–1939*, London, 1979, p. 33.

71. FO 371/47881, 2 April 1945: reprinted in Ross, ed., *Foreign Office and the Kremlin*, Document 35, pp. 119–200.

72. Ibid., pp. 202–3.

73. Ibid., Document 39, pp. 210–14 together with Annexe by Bruce Lockhart, pp. 214–17.

74. Ibid., p. 214.

75. 'Future Defence Policy in the Suez Canal Area'. Report of the Suez Canal Committee CAB 66/63, WP (45) 197, 20 March 1945. See note 54 above.

76. As above, in note 54: CAB 66/65, WP (45) 256, 13 April 1945.

77. Anne Deighton, 'The "Frozen Front": The Labour Government, Division of Germany, and the Origins of the Cold War, 1945–7', *International Affairs*, Vol. 63, No. 3, Summer 1987, pp. 449–65.

78. The literature is voluminous. The items listed in this note offer a brief selection of differing views – often strong views – on what has been rightly called the Greek Tragedy. P. Auty and R. Clogg, eds, *British Policy Towards Wartime Resistance in Yugoslavia and Greece*, London, 1975, provides an important series of articles from political contemporaries, military activists and

academic historians. G. Kolko, *The Politics of War: Allied Diplomacy and the World Crisis of 1943–1945*, London, 1969, Ch. 8, offers an independent left-wing summary, and other left-wing accounts include H. Richter, *British Intervention in Greece*, London, 1986, and M. Sarafis, ed., *Greece: From Resistance to Civil War*, Nottingham, 1980. Most of the writings of C.M. Woodhouse, at one time in command of the military mission in occupied Greece and later a Conservative MP, are concerned with the events in Greece during the war years and after, and their point of view is that of a moderate conservative and firm anti-communist. The political issues involved in the British military intervention and the situation that developed thereafter continue to be passionately debated. A British TV series on the Greek Civil War in 1986 evoked vehement debate. A feature article by Richard Gott in the *Guardian*, 5 July 1986, was followed in succeeding weeks by a mass of letters, only a selection of which could be printed. See especially the issues of 10, 12, 23 and 25 July; and both *The Times* and *The Daily Telegraph* carried considerable material. There is a recent doctoral thesis: John Sakkas, 'British Public Opinion and Intervention in Greece, 1944–1949' (PhD, University of Hull, 1992).

79. *Hansard*, 5 Ser., Vol. 407, Col. 400. 18 January 1945. There was a particularly effective speech in this debate from Seymour Cocks, Cols 467–79.

80. A. Bullock, *The Life and Times of Ernest Bevin. Vol. 2: Minister of Labour 1940–1945*, London, 1967, pp. 340–47; M. Foot, *Aneurin Bevan: A Biography. Vol. 1: 1897–1945*, London, 1962, pp. 477 ff. The description of the Central Hall meeting is in ibid., pp. 486–7.

81. Among the more critical speeches in the debate on 20 August, *Hansard*, 5 Ser., Vol. 413, were those from Lyall Wilkes, Cols 305–11 (Greece); Michael Foot, Cols 336–41 (Greece); Peart, Cols 357–60 (Socialist policy); Woodrow Wyatt, Cols 366–9 (India).

82. *Franco's 'Neutrality' and British Policy*, Union of Democratic Control, 1944, 16pp; Raymond Carr, *Spain, 1808–1975*, 2nd edn, Oxford, 1982, wrote that the 'Blue Division, of 18,694 men, largely Falangist volunteers', left for the Russian front in July 1941, and was withdrawn in November 1943, having lost 4000 dead (pp. 712–13). Some sources give much higher figures for the number of Spaniards fighting in Russia. The Russians were especially hostile to these Spanish fascists for their destruction of Catherine the Great's palace at Tsarskoye Selo. (George Kennan to Washington, 3 February 1946, *FRUS*, 1946, Vol. V, p. 1034.)

83. The most polemical work during the war years which, because it was published in Britain by Left Book Club, achieved a wider circulation than it could normally expect, was Thomas J. Hamilton's *Appeasement's Child: The Franco Regime in Spain*, London, 1943. Hamilton was the *New York Times* correspondent in Spain for two years from August 1939. Selections from the correspondence between Hitler, Mussolini and Franco were published by the Department of State in a booklet, *The Spanish Government and the Axis*, European Series No. 8, Washington, 1946; and there is additional information in *Documents on German Foreign Policy 1918–1945*, Series D, Vol. XI, Washington, 1960. The declaration at Potsdam relating to Spain was unequivocal: 'The three Governments feel bound however to make it clear that they for their part would not favour any application for membership put forward by the present Spanish government, which, having been founded with the support of the Axis Powers, does not, in view of its origins, its nature, its record and its close association with the aggressor States, possess the qualifications necessary to justify such membership [of the United Nations].'

84. D. Little, 'Red Scare, 1936: Anti-Bolshevism and the Origins of British Non-Intervention in the Spanish Civil War', *J. Cont. Hist.*, Vol. 23, No. 2, April 1988, pp. 291–311, p. 295. This excellent article summarises part of the author's *Malevolent Neutrality: The United States, Great Britain and the Origins of the Spanish Civil War*, Ithaca, NY, 1985.

85. Thomas Jones, *A Diary with Letters, 1931–1950*, Oxford, 1954, pp. 210–11.

86. Carr, *Spain, 1808–1975*, p. 679.

87. (Sir) Lawrence Collier's lone position inside the FO is well documented by Jill Edwards, *The British Government and the Spanish Civil War, 1936–1939*, London, 1979, pp. 137, 160–61, 172–3, 212.

88. CAB 286, fols 91–7, 'Committee of Imperial Defence, Chiefs of Staff Sub-Committee Report: Balance of Strategical Value in War as between Spain as an Enemy and Russia as an Ally', reprinted in Edwards, *The British Government and the Spanish Civil War*, App. G, pp. 228–32; and see ibid., pp. 210–215, for a general summing up. The reference to Basil Liddell Hart in the text is especially to his book, widely discussed at the time, *The Defence of Britain*, London, 1939.

89. Churchill's comments on Spain are in *Hansard*, 5 Ser., Vol. 400, Cols 768–72, 24 May

1944; the extract in the text to Roosevelt is from Sir Llewellyn Woodward, *British Foreign Policy in the Second World War*, Vol. IV, London, 1975, p. 29. Gilbert, *Road To Victory*, paperback edn, London, 1989, p. 777, makes a brief reference to Churchill's speech in the Commons but fails to notice the many adverse comments it produced.

90. 18 December 1944: Nicholas, ed., *Washington Despatches*, pp. 480–81.

91. *FRUS*, 1945, Vol. V, p. 667. The new Ambassador was Norman H. Armour.

92. *Hansard*, 5 Ser., Vol. 413, Col. 296, 20 August 1945. There was widespread dismay, first registered by the critical speeches on Bevin's attitude towards Spain in this foreign affairs debate.

93. *Labour Party. 1946 Conference Report*, pp. 166–7.

94. Woodward, *British Foreign Policy*, Vol. IV, Ch. XLVII.

95. FO 371/49589/ Z 7338/233, 12 June 1945.

96. F. Hoyer Millar, FO 371/49589/ Z 9328, 14 August 1945.

97. T.J. Low, 'Bases in Spain', in H. Stein, ed., *American Civil-Military Decisions*, Alabama, 1963, pp. 667–702, with editorial comments, pp. 703–5. This is a useful study of the ways in which pressure groups, working within the defence forces and Congress, gradually altered policies towards Spain. In particular, the US Air Force needed bases in addition to those in the UK, and the Navy required ports in the Mediterranean.

98. The Left opposition within the British Labour Party, centred upon the Keep Left group, began rapidly to disintegrate during 1948; and Spain, among other causes, was a victim. Among the many aspects of the Spanish question that remain to be researched are the letters and memoranda which Republicans in exile sent to the Labour Party, or to leading individuals in the Labour Party. See for example the long document dated 29 July 1946 sent to the executive of the Labour Party by socialist exiles in Mexico: Labour Party, International Department, Box 5, Spain, 1946.

99. H. Macmillan, *The Blast of War, 1939–1945*, London, 1967, always used the term 'bandit' to describe the resistance inside Greece.

100. For a good summary for the immediate post-war years from the French point of view, see Anne Dulphy, 'La politique de la France à l'égard de l'Espagne franquiste 1945–9', *Revue d'histoire moderne et contemporaine*, tome XXXV, Jan–Mars 1988, pp. 123–40; and for a detailed survey of the Labour Government and Spain: Qasim bin Ahmad, 'The British Government and the Franco Dictatorship, 1945–1950', Ph.D., London, 1987.

101. Arno J. Mayer, *Politics and Diplomacy of Peacemaking: Containment and Counter-Revolution at Versailles, 1918–1919*, New York, 1967, pp. 875–6.

102. Lloyd George, *The Truth about the Peace Treaties*, Vol. 1, London, 1938, pp. 325–6, referred to Churchill as 'the most outspoken and persistent advocate of military intervention.' All histories of this period make the same point.

103. Quoted in L. Fischer, *The Soviets in World Affairs: A History of Relations between the Soviet Union and the Rest of the World*, Vol. 1, London, 1930, p. 274.

104. D. Marquand, *Ramsay MacDonald*, London, 1977, p. 384. For the general background, see R. W. Lyman, *The First Labour Government*, London, 1957, esp. Chs 14 and 15; and for the Zinoviev Letter, with a review of the literature, *DLB*, Vol. IX, 1992, Special Note, pp. 111–24.

105. D.F. Calhoun, *The United Front: The TUC and the Russians, 1923–1928*, Cambridge, 1976, passim; W.P. and Z. Coates, *A History of Anglo-Soviet Relations*, London, 1944, esp. Chs IX–XII.

106. Working-class criticism was mainly to be found among the politically right-wing of labour movements, and on the extreme Left, among the anarchist or semi-anarchist organisations such as the Spanish POUM, or Trotskyist groupings; and there were marked differences between different countries. The absence of any significant Trotskyist movement in Britain was in contrast with countries like France or the United States; for an introduction to this important question, see John Saville, 'May Day 1937', *Essays in Labour History 1918–1939*, in A. Briggs and J. Saville, eds, London, 1977, esp. pp. 259–70.

107. M. Gilbert, *Winston Churchill: The Wilderness Years*, Book Club edn, London, 1981, p. 161.

108. H. Nicolson, *Diaries and Letters, 1930–1939*, ed. N. Nicolson, London, 1966, p. 342.

109. The French were especially interested in shifting the war onto an anti-Bolshevik crusade although they had some powerful allies among the British politicians and senior military officers. As A.J.P. Taylor observed, *English History 1914–1950*, p. 469, note 1: 'The motives for the projected expedition to Finland defy rational analysis', except on the anti-Bolshevik thesis. M. Gilbert's *Second World War*, London, 1989, has a short paragraph on p. 42, stating the decision to intervene militarily, but with no comment.

110. Colonel Moore-Brabazon became Minister of Aircraft Production in May 1941, and, at a semi-official meeting at which trade unionists were present, suggested that it would be in British interests if Germany and Russia fought each other to a standstill. Jack Tanner, general secretary of the Engineer's union, told the story at the September 1941 TUC Conference.

111. Above, pp. 27–8.

112. *FRUS*, 1945, Vol. V, 23 April 1945, p. 253.

113. D. Yergin. *Shattered Peace: The Origins of the Cold War and the National Security State*, Boston, 1977, pp.164–5; J.V. Forrestal, *The Forrestal Diaries*, ed. W. Millis, New York, 1951.

114. L.P. Elwell-Sutton, *Persian Oil: A Study in Power Politics*, London, 1955. Elwell-Sutton was an eminent Persian scholar at the University of Edinburgh. A more recent account is D. Yergin, *The Prize: The Epic Quest for Oil, Money and Power*, London, 1991, which records that 'Between 1945–1950, Anglo-Iranian [Oil Company] registered a £250 million profit, compared to Iran's £90 million in royalties. The British government received more in taxes from Anglo-Iranian than did Iran in royalties. To aggravate matters still further, a substantial part of the Company's dividends went to its majority owner, the British government, and it was rumoured that Anglo-Iranian sold oil to the British Navy at a substantial discount' (pp. 451–2).

115. *FRUS*, 1946, Vol. VII, pp. 362–3; and for the background of the Iranian crisis: J. Frankel, 'The Anglo-Iranian Dispute', *The Year Book of World Affairs*, in G.W. Keeton and G. Schwarzenberger, eds, 1952, pp. 56–74; Gary H. Hess, 'The Iranian Crisis of 1945–46 and the Cold War', *Political Science Quarterly*, Vol. 89, No. 1, March 1974, pp.117–46; L. L'Estrange Fawcett, 'Invitation to the Cold War: British Policy in Iran, 1941–47', in Anne Deighton, ed., *Britain and the First Cold War*, London, 1990, pp. 184–200.

116. Hugh Dalton, Diary, 27 March 1946, quoted in Alan Bullock, *Ernest Bevin. Foreign Secretary, 1945–1951*, London, 1983, p. 236.

117. Truman used the argument of the possibility of war over Iran to persuade Averell Harriman to take the Embassy in London: Bullock, *Ernest Bevin*, Vol. 3, p. 236, quoting H. Feis, *From Trust to Terror*, 1970, pp. 82–3.

118. E.M. Mark, 'Allied Relations in Iran, 1941–1947: The Origins of a Cold War Crisis', *Wisconsin Magazine of History*, Vol. 59, Autumn 1975, pp. 51–63; p. 62 for the statement in the text.

119. There is a considerable literature on the immediate post-war history of Iran, but what is generally played down or not mentioned at all was the hatred of the Iranian people towards the British in particular: for which see Yergin, *The Prize*, Ch. 23.

120. *FRUS*, 1946, Vol. VI, pp. 694–6 for Kennan's report to Washington. A note on p. 695 quotes from a memorandum written by H. Freeman Matthews, Director of the Office of European Affairs, which read in part: 'Stalin's speech of February 9 constitutes the most important and authoritative guide to post-war Soviet policy.... It should be given great weight in any plans which may be under consideration for extending credits or other forms of economic assistance to the Soviet Union.'

121. *New York Times*, 4 April 1946. Budenz was born into a Catholic family and he rejoined the Catholic Church five days before his public withdrawal from the *Daily Worker* and the Communist Party. Within forty-eight hours he had been appointed a professor at the Catholic University of Notre Dame, but soon moved to Fordham, where he taught for ten years. Budenz, David Caute wrote, was 'The most famous and successful ex-Communist informer of the post-war period': *The Great Fear: The Anti-Communist Purge under Truman and Eisenhower*, New York, 1978, p. 123. There is another well-documented account of anti-communist hysteria in M. Isserman, *Which Side Were You On: The American Communist Party during the Second World War*, Westleyan UP, Conn., 1982.

122. *FRUS*, 1946, Vol. VI, p. 696, n. 43.

123. Ibid., pp. 706–7.

124. Ibid., p. 709.

125. 'The Sources of Soviet Conduct' by 'X', *Foreign Affairs*, July 1947, pp. 566–82.

126. Yergin, *Shattered Peace*, pp. 170 ff; J. and G. Kolko, *The Limits of Power: The World and United States Foreign Policy, 1945–1954*, New York, 1972, Ch. 2; Forrestal, *Diaries*, New York, 1951, pp.135–40.

127. J. Stalin, *War Speeches, Orders of the Day*, London, 1945, quoted in I. Deutscher, *Stalin. A Political Biography*, Oxford, 1949, p. 538.

128. Yergin, *Shattered Peace*, p. 170. There is now a not inconsiderable commentary on

Kennan's ideas and attitudes, in addition to his later exegesis of his own writings of the immediate post-war years: G. Urban, 'From Containment to . . . Self-Containment: A Conversation with George F. Kennan', *Encounter*, September 1976, pp.10–43; L. Labedz, 'The Two Minds of George Kennan: How to Un-Learn from Experience' (1979), *Survey*, Vol. 30, No. 1/2, March 1988, pp. 223–9; D. Mayers, 'Young Kennan's Criticisms and Recommendations', *Biography*, Vol. 8, No. 3, 1985, pp. 227–47; idem; 'Soviet War Aims and the Grand Alliance: George Kennan's Views, 1944–1946', *J.Cont. Hist.*, Vol. 21, No. 1, 1986, pp. 57–79.

129. Harold to Frida Laski, 30 July 1946: Archives, Brynmor Jones Library, University of Hull.

130. S. Greenwood, 'Frank Roberts and the "Other" Long Telegram: The View from the British Embassy in Moscow, March 1946', *J. Cont. Hist.*, Vol. 25, No. 1, 1990, pp. 103–22, with a brief introduction by Sir Frank Roberts, pp. 103–4.

131. See below, pp. 52, 136–7.

132. Roberts' summary of Kennan's Long Telegram is in FO 371/56840/ N 3369, dated 2 March 1946. Roberts added a note suggesting that the Kennan despatch would help to encourage the USA to 'eschew wishful thinking, and to take a more realistic line in regard to the Soviet Union'.

133. All three despatches are in FO 371/56763; the first, 14 March, in file N 4146; the second, 17 March, in file N 4065; and the third, 18 March, in file N 4157.

134. The Peace Conference, mid August to mid October 1946, was attended by representatives of twenty-one nations. It had been preceded by a Council of Foreign Ministers, 25 April to 16 May. The British records of the Peace Conference are in FO 371/57334–94; the American in *FRUS*, 1946, Vols III and IV. Bullock, *Ernest Bevin*, Vol. 3, Ch. 7, 'Paris Summer 1946', pp. 259–306, and the opening pages of Ch. 8 provide most of the detailed background of the discussions.

135. FO 371/56835/ N 11644 contains Roberts' despatch to Bevin, dated 4 September 1946, and the minutes in London. It was widely circulated, and Brimelow's minute was typed. Thomas Brimelow (1915–), educated New Mills Grammer and Oriel College, Oxford, served in Moscow as head of the Consular Service June 1942–June 1945; thereafter in the Northern Department. He received a knowledge allowance for Russian language in October 1951; became head of the Northern Department in August 1956; and PUS 1973–75.

136. The Northern Department covered Czechoslovakia, Denmark, Estonia, Finland, Iceland, Latvia, Lithuania, Norway, Poland, the Soviet Union and Sweden. The Southern Department was responsible for Turkey, Greece, Yugoslavia, Bulgaria, Hungary, Romania, Albania and Danubian General. Warner was proficient in Turkish and Persian.

137. Some parts of British public opinion had understood. The *New Statesman*, 6 October 1945, had a full-page article following the breakdown of the first Conference of Foreign Ministers; and a middle paragraph commented: 'On one point we should be absolutely clear. There is cant talk of "appeasement" of Russia, and a parallel drawn between the Soviet encroachments and those of Nazi Germany before the war. The parallel is stupid, misleading and extremely dangerous. For the first object of Soviet policy is to preserve the peace. To believe otherwise is to display ignorance or prejudice. There are few homes in Russia which have not lost a bread-winner; the devastation and horror through which Russia has passed is the uppermost thought in the mind of every Soviet citizen. We have no doubt that Stalin spoke with precise honesty when in his interview with Senator Pepper (published in *The Daily Telegraph* of October 2) he pointed out that the Russians "have made the greatest sacrifices of any of the Allies. They have gone without adequate food, clothing and housing during this long war. It would be suicidal for us to do anything but devote all our efforts and resources to giving the people the things they have so long done without." ' See Appendix 2 below.

138. Bevin to Attlee, 10 April 1946: FO 800/501; and note the beginning of the use of the term 'social-democratic'.

139. This is not to suggest that there were no covert operations before the Information Research Department (IRD) was established. As P. Weiler shows in the most detailed study so far made of the disruptive activities supported by both the American State Department and the British Foreign Office, measures to ensure the break-up of the World Federation of Labour were put in hand as soon as the organisation was founded in the autumn of 1945. In the case of Sir Walter Citrine, opposition began when the Nazis brought Russia into the war: *British Labour and the Cold War*, Stanford, 1988, Chs 2 and 3. The beginnings of the Russia Committee are in FO 371/56885 and for later in 1946, 371/56883 and /56886. The article by R. Merrick, 'The Russia Committee

of the British Foreign Office and the Cold War, 1946–7', *J. Cont. Hist.*, Vol. 20, No. 3, 1985, pp. 453–68 is helpful for its documentation but lacks historical perspective. There are two especially useful articles on British propaganda and the IRD in particular: Lynn Smith, 'Covert British Propaganda: The Information Research Department, 1944–7', *Millennium: Journal of International Studies*, Vol. 9, No. 1, 1980, pp. 67–83; R.J. Fletcher, 'British Propaganda since World War II – A Case Study', *Media, Culture and Society*, Vol. 4, No. 2, 1982, pp. 97–109.

140. Born 1869, Secretary for the Dominions 1945–October 1947, then Lord Privy Seal, and Leader of the House of Lords: K.O. Morgan, *Labour in Power, 1945–1951*, Oxford, 1984, p. 54.

141. FO 371/56885, 14 May 1946. Bevin was opposed to Lord Addison's suggestion of co-operation with the Vatican.

142. FO 371/56784/ N 6733, 17 May 1946. Hall-Patch was a financial expert who was transferred from the Treasury to the Foreign Office in June 1944 with the rank of Assistant Under-Secretary of State.

143. Ibid. The Warner memorandum was circulated to the Prime Minister, Bevin, Morrison, Lord Addison, A.V. Alexander, George Hall (Colonies), Pethwick-Lawrence (India), J.J. Lawson (War), Lord Stansgate (Air), J.J. Westwood (Scotland). The memorandum is in FO 371/56832/N 6344 and dated 2 April 1946. It is reprinted in part in Appendix 1 and in full in *DBPO*, Ser. I, Vol. VI, No. 88, HMSO, London, 1991, pp. 345–52.

144. FO 371/56866/ N 5769, 5 October 1946. *Tass* issued the text of the Stalin–Werth interview on 24 September 1946: *Keesings Contemporary Archives*, 5–8 October 1946, p. 8153.

145. FO 371/56887/ N 14752, 7 November 1946.

146. For examples of his general thinking, see the correspondence between Warner and Maurice Peterson, Ambassador in Moscow: FO 371/56887/ N 15843, 29 October and 15 November 1946. An important statement by Sir Nigel Ronald, dated 7 November, is in the same piece: file N 14732.

147. A report from the Chiefs of Staff on 'The Strategic Position of the British Commonwealth' (CAB 131/2, DO (46) 47, 2 April 1946) says nothing that had not been stated before or that was subsequently to appear, except at greater length, in their supposedly definitive defence strategy in 1947, reprinted in Lewis *Changing Direction*, App. VII.

148. FO 800/501, 19 January 1946.

149. FO 371/56832/ N 5502, 9 April 1946.

150. Peterson's interview with Stalin was on 27 May 1946; and Peterson's summary of the conversation is in FO 371/56784/ N 6984. The instructions to Peterson before he met Stalin are in this same piece, following the meeting with Bevin, and it is worth noting that the Middle East was the first item. On Greece, the instructions read: 'If Greece is raised, Stalin should be told frankly that if the Soviet Government start again to make trouble for us in Greece, there will bound to be differences between us.' Peterson's summary included the comment that 'The omission of all references to Greece, Persia and Eastern Thrace is interesting.' In this piece, 371/56784, there are occasional references in various files to the ways in which Anglo-Soviet relations might be improved; but the suggestions remained on the level of cultural exchanges. One note stressed the good relations between the Soviet and UK lawyers at Nuremberg.

151. FO 371/56768 / N 10977, 23 August 1946. The Labour Delegation's report to their National Executive Committee is also in the FO files: 371/56769/ N 12327, 26 September 1946, from which the quotations in the text are taken. The Ambassador, Peterson, also wrote a short and not very helpful report to London: FO 371/56767/ N 10621.

152. There is, of course, a copy of the delegation's report in the files of the National Executive Committee, Labour Party Archives, August 1946, National Museum of Labour, Manchester. Laski's letters to his wife are in the Brynmor Jones Library, University of Hull.

153. See below, Appendix 2.

154. This has now become a commonplace among most historians, and it was not unknown among many contemporaries in the aftermath of the war: 'Russia's foreign policy, whether you approve or not, has one distinguishing characteristic, it knows exactly where it is going; besides this, where to stop, when to reduce its speed, and even when to retreat. And the limit Moscow sets is the line beyond which lies the imminent threat of war', J. Alvarez del Vayo, *The Last Optimist*, London, 1950, p. 354. As my text goes on to suggest, the execution of Russian foreign policy was often far from sensible or skilful, although del Vayo's last words can be accepted.

155. A review by D. Cameron Watt of B.R. Kuniholm's *The Origins of the Cold War in the Near*

East: Great Power Conflict and Diplomacy in Iran, Turkey and Greece (1980) in *Middle Eastern Studies*, Vol. 18, No. 2, April 1982, is critical of the concept of the Northern Tier, which, he writes, 'is a geopolitical concept with neither political not cultural unity', and he rightly points out it makes no sense to describe events in Greece as 'being part of the same sub-set as those in Iran or Afghanistan' (pp. 217–19).

156. The Dean of Canterbury, Hewlett Johnson, had an interview with Stalin on 7 July 1945 and at the request of Clark Kerr raised the question of the Russian wives. There were about fifteen or sixteen wives involved. The memorandum from Clark Kerr to London quoted Stalin as saying that 'there was clearly something wrong and that he would be able to put it right. He then corrected himself, saying that he would 'probably' be able to put it right.' *DBPO*, Vol. 1, No. 89, Potsdam, p. 164.

157. FO 371/44538/ AN 3159.

158. FO 371/44539/ AN 3224, 23 December 1945.

159. Quoted in John L. Gaddis, 'The Insecurities of Victory: The United States and the Perception of the Soviet Threat after World War II', in M.J. Lacey, ed., *The Truman Presidency*, Cambridge, 1989, p. 255, note 68.

160. *The Memoirs of the Rt. Hon. Anthony Eden: Full Circle*, London, 1960, p. 6.

161. There are two articles which among others suggest that Bevin's position in relation to the Soviet Union was not always in line with certain of his officials: Merrick, 'The Russia Committee'; the second, somewhat more definite in its generalisations, R. Smith, 'Ernest Bevin, British Officials and British Soviet Policy, 1945–47', in Anne Deighton, ed., *Britain and the First Cold War*, London, 1990, pp. 32–52. Both have missed relevant material in the Foreign Office files and the Bevin papers regarding Bevin's private views of the Soviet Union from the time he took office, and both have failed to appreciate that Bevin had also a public, political role to play. Above, pp. 5 ff.

162. Bullock, *Ernest Bevin*, Vol. 3, pp. 313–14, discusses first the *New Statesman* articles and then on p. 314 the Stalin–Werth interview without noting any Foreign Office response. The *New Statesman* had a leading article on 24 August, and then the first of a series called 'Re-orientations' on 31 August, continued 7, 21 and 28 September 1946.

163. The main public reaction to the Stalin interview, for which see n. 144 above, came from Anthony Eden, who on 25 September 1946 declared that it offered to Allied diplomacy 'an important opportunity which all would welcome'. His speech was at Stratford-upon-Avon.

164. John Platts-Mills was expelled in 1948; Konni Zilliacus, Leslie Solley and Lester Hutchinson in 1949: J. Schneer, *Labour's Conscience: The Labour Left, 1945–51*, London, 1987, Ch. 5.

165. The disintegration of the Keep Left group, and the acquiescence in Bevin's foreign policy by many former critics, was connected with the changing attitude towards the United States and the Marshall Aid agreements. It was also, of course, a direct response to the hardening line of Soviet policy in Eastern Europe.

166. FO 800/493, 5 May 1947. Bullock, *Ernest Bevin*, Vol. 3, p. 396, adds a further sentence from Jebb: 'With the advent of the Labour Government (as C. admits) a fresh and determined effort was made to secure this vital co-operation'; a statement that is not true.

167. Merrick, 'The Russia Committee', defined 'defensive-offensive policy' as the 'development of a propaganda campaign against international communism wherever it rears its head, exposing it as totalitarianism, and also uncovering the various Soviet "myths" which they propagated in justification of their policy.' 'In addition', wrote Warner, 'we could, in every country, where social democrats, "liberals", progressive agrarian parties etc. are fighting a battle against communism, give our friends all such moral and material support as is possible, without going so far as actually to endanger their lives or organisation' (p. 457).

168. Healey's *Cards on the Table* is analysed in some detail in Appendix 5.

169. The summary of the conversation, from which the extract in the text was taken, is in FO 800/513. The dinner party with these two leading Republicans had been agreed with Byrnes, the American Secretary of State.

170. Bullock, *Ernest Bevin*, Vol. 3, wrote that Bevin was 'furious' when he learned that Byrnes had arranged the Moscow meeting without his agreement being sought (p. 199). In the Bevin papers, FO 800/501, there is a good deal of material on the Moscow Conference and much about the disagreements between the US and the UK delegations. Bohlen, Kennan and Harriman were

privately critical of Byrnes. A postscript by Roberts read: 'In Mr Kennan's words "they hope Mr Bevin will fight his battle personally with Mr Byrnes." '

171. Bevin had used the 'bear' image at an off-the-record meeting with the diplomatic correspondents of the British press on 1 January 1946, after his return from the Moscow conference. Bullock, *Ernest Bevin*, Vol. 3, pp. 214–16, reports this meeting at length but no source is quoted.

172. Callahan, *Churchill: Retreat from Empire*, makes the point that Churchill not only set out to woo the Americans from the outset of their first meeting at Placentia Bay, August 1941, but his version of the Roosevelt–Churchill relationship in his memoirs 'tends to obscure the intricate mixture of friendship and wariness, co-operation and competition that characterised the partnership' (p. 168).

173. Cf. R. Hathaway, *Ambiguous Partnership: Britain and America 1944–47*, New York, 1981: 'Anglo-American partnership was not a natural or inevitable part of the structure of world politics. It was fragile, in constant need of nurture. . . . As the war entered its final phase in the autumn of 1944, it was still unclear in which direction future Anglo-American relations would move' (p. 15). The literature on the tensions and conflicts between the two English-speaking powers is extensive. Christopher Thorne, *Allies of a Kind: The United States, Britain and the War against Japan 1941–1945*, London, 1978, is a comprehensive study of Anglo-American relations in the Far East. Churchill's post-war writings omit some important material relevant to the controversies over military strategy in particular. Forrest C. Pogue's biography, *George C. Marshall, Organiser of Victory, 1943–1945*, New York, 1973, is essential reading for the Mediterranean versus Overlord debate; and see also Mark Stoler, *The Politics of the Second Front: American Military Planning and Diplomacy in Coalition Warfare, 1941–1943*, Westport, Conn., 1977. The English official history is in J. Ehrman, *Grand Strategy. Vol. V: August 1943–September 1944*, London, 1956.

174. Nicholas, ed., *Washington Despatches 1941–1945*, p. 567. According to Isaiah Berlin's introduction to this volume, the reports were delivered on Thursday afternoon and corrections and additions added. Berlin is regarded as having written most of the despatches. His absences from Washington are recorded in a footnote, p. xiii.

175. R.M. Hathaway, *Ambiguous Partnership*, Ch. 2 'The Economics of Partnership'.

176. Lord Charles Moran, *Winston Churchill: The Struggle for Survival, 1940–1965*, London, 1966: an appraisal to be recorded several times by Moran.

177. Quoted in Christopher Thorne, 'Indo-China and Anglo-American Relations 1942–1945', *Pacific Hist. Rev.*, Vol. 45, February 1976, pp. 73–96, 74 n. 2: Hornbeck to Cordell Hull, 3 January 1944, Hornbeck Papers, Hoover Institution, Stanford University.

178. F.L. Block, *The Origins of International Economic Disorder: A Study of United States International Monetary Policy from World War II to the Present*, Berkeley, 1977, esp. Ch. 3.

179. R.N. Gardner, *Sterling–Dollar Diplomacy: Anglo-American Collaboration in the Reconstruction of Multilateral Trade*, revised edn, New York, 1969, Chs 1–4; J. and G. Kolko, *The Limits of Power*, Chs 1–6.

180. L.S. Amery, *The Washington Loan Agreement: A Critical Study of American Economic Foreign Policy*, London, 1946, p. xi.

181. Richard Law (1901–80), later Lord Coleraine, was a personal friend of Eden; became Minister of State at the Foreign Office in the autumn of 1943.

182. FO 371/38523/ AN 1538/16 45. Alan Dudley, its author, had been appointed Acting Principal in 1943.

183. *DBPO*, Ser. I, Vol. IV, 1987, 11 January 1946, p. 40.

184. *Foreign Office List*, 1949: Obituary.

185. Hathaway, *Ambiguous Partnership*, has several examples. On p. 222, for example, there is a comment about Foreign Officials' criticism of the record of the United States with regard to the admittance of Jewish refugees; and the reference for note 75 refers only to Donnelly. Anyone reading the Foreign Office American files at this time would always be tempted to quote Donnelly: he offered such strikingly biting comments.

186. FO 371/44538/ AN 2767.

187. FO 371/44539/ AN 3788, 19 December 1945. On this particular occasion Laski was taking part in a three-day atomic bomb conference organised by the *Nation*. There had been a considerable correspondence over this Laski visit. The most important items are in the Bevin Papers. Halifax wrote to Bevin on 12 November 1945 suggesting that the Laski visit was 'a mistake'

at a time when the Loan agreement was being considered and he expressed his opinion that he hoped the visit could be 'postponed' by some means or other. He made a further reference two days later: 'I hope that you will be able to arrange for Laski not (repeat not) to accept it [an invitation to speak in the Mid-West during his visit]': FO 800/512. After Bevin had explained he could not interfere Halifax wrote back saying that he understood the difficulties but that the powerful Catholic interest, which was strongly anti-British, were considering public protests against Laski 'in view of his recent strictures against their Church' (this was probably a reference to Laski's vigorous polemics against Franco Spain). Halifax in this same letter of 20 November, while accepting that Laski could probably not be prevented from coming to the United States, although clearly this is what Halifax would have preferred, went on to ask 'whether an appeal could be made to him to keep off controversial topics while he is here at a time when Anglo-American relations are exceptionally delicate'. In the event the British Embassy were able to prevent 'large-scale demonstrations against Laski. There was a small and orderly picket line': FO 371/44539/ AN 3788, 10 December 1945.

188. FO 371/44539/ AN 3872, minute dated 27 December, 1945.

189. Robert M. Hutchins was one of America's most famous educationalists: see W. McNeill, *Hutchins' University: A Memoir of the University of Chicago 1929–1950*, Chicago, 1991, and M.A. Dzuback, *Robert M. Hutchins: Portrait of an Educator*, Chicago, 1991. Both books were reviewed by Sheldon Rothblatt, *London Review of Books*, 13 February 1992.

190. FO 371/51606/ AN 587, 5 March 1946.

191. Elliott V. Converse III, 'U.S. Plans for a Post-War Overseas Military Base System, 1942–1948', Ph.D dissertation, Princeton, 1984, Ch. 1.

192. M.S. Sherry, *Preparing for the Next War: American Plans for Post-War Defense*, New Haven, Conn., 1977, esp. Ch. 6. There is a detailed bibliography in Melvyn P. Leffler, 'The American Conception of National Security and the Beginnings of the Cold War, 1945–48', *Amer. Hist. Rev.*, Vol. 89, No. 2, April 1984, pp. 346–81. For the Joint Strategic Survey Committee, see R. Schaffer, 'General Stanley D. Embick: Military Dissenter', *Military Affairs*, Vol. 37, October 1973, pp. 89–105; M.A. Stoler, 'From Continentalism to Globalism: General Stanley D. Embick, the Joint Strategic Survey Committee, and the Military View of American National Policy during the Second World War', *Diplomatic History*, Vol. 6, No. 3, Summer 1982, pp. 303–21.

193. The 'fifth' freedom was originally a US proposal to allow aircraft to pick up passengers, mail and freight at locations not in the country of origin or the ultimate destination. The UK and other European countries vigorously opposed this proposition on the grounds that it would mean a complete domination by the US in the immediate post-war years. For general accounts: Alan P. Dobson, 'The Other Air Battle: The American Pursuit of Post-War Civil Aviation Rights', *Hist. Journal*, Vol. 28, No. 2, 1985, pp. 429–34; D.R. Devereux, 'British Planning for Post-War Civil Aviation, 1942–1945: A Study in Anglo-American Rivalry', *Twentieth Century British History*, Vol. 2, No. 1, 1991, pp. 22–46.

194. RG 165, ABC 092 USSR (11–1–44), Modern Military Branch, National Archives, Washington quoted in Sherry, *Preparing for the Next War*, p. 182, note 53.

195. Lisle A. Rose, *Dubious Victory: The United States and the End of World War II*, Kent State, 1973, p. 33 ff.

196. The common view of the Warsaw rising is set out in two official British histories: Ehrman, *Grand Strategy. Vol. V: August 1943–September 1944*, pp. 369–76; and Sir Llewellyn Woodward, *British Foreign Policy in the Second World War*, Vol. III, London, 1973, pp. 202–17. It is now generally agreed that the Soviet forces, although they reached the outskirts of Warsaw, were in no fit condition to take the city, and German counter-attacks drove them back in some sectors as much as nearly a hundred kilometres. The controversial question is the refusal of the Russians to allow Allied planes to use their airfields, and this is also a debatable issue. There is a succinct account in P. Calvocoressi and G. Wint, *Total War: Causes and Courses of the Second World War*, London, 1972, pp. 481–4. What is not disputable is the very marked adverse reaction to the Russian refusal among the countries of the Western Powers.

197. See Chapter 2 below.

198. Most details are taken from Robert L. Messer, 'Paths Not Taken: The United States Department of State and Alternatives to Containment, 1945–6', *Diplomatic History*, Vol. 1, No. 4, Fall 1977, pp.297–319. There was an interesting follow-up to the Messer article: E. Mark,

'Charles E. Bohlen, and the Acceptable Limits of Soviet Hegemony in Eastern Europe: A Memorandum of 18 October 1945', *Diplomatic History*, Vol. 3, No. 2, Spring 1979, pp. 201–13.

199. *Politics and Diplomacy of Peacemaking.* The Prologue, pp. 3–30, offers a summary of this massively documented history.

200. Quoted in Messer, 'Paths Not Taken', pp. 301–2; with Czechoslovakia the exception.

201. Charles (Chip) Bohlen had entered the Foreign Service in 1929 and studied Russian in Paris. For an illuminating account of the pre-1939 training of young American diplomats in Russian studies, see F.L. Popas, 'Creating a Hard Line Towards Russia: The Training of State Department Soviet Experts, 1929–1937', *Diplomatic History*, Vol. 8, No. 3, Summer 1984, pp. 209–26. There is disagreement among historians as to the political and intellectual consequences of what Yergin calls the 'Riga' axioms: Yergin, *Shattered Peace*, emphasises the apparently fixed views of the pre-war Russian experts, especially Kennan, while H. de Santis, *The Diplomacy of Silence: The American Foreign Service, the Soviet Union and the Cold War*, Chicago, 1980, suggests a greater responsiveness, especially during the later years of the second world war. Popas himself argues that 'the Eastern European Division officers were trained to perceive the Soviets in rigidly ideological terms which left little room for accommodation' (p. 218, note 24). George Kennan, on the evidence of the Long Telegram, certainly fits these last observations, at least for this period.

202. Its full text has been reprinted in *Diplomatic History*, Vol. 1, No. 4, Fall 1977, pp. 389–99, and its contents have been analysed in detail in Messer, 'Paths Not Taken'.

203. C.E. Bohlen, *Witness to History, 1929–1969*, New York, 1973, p. 240; and see p. 318 n. 50 in Messer's 'Paths Not Taken'.

204. Trygie Lie, *In the Cause of Peace: Seven Years in the United Nations*, New York, 1954, pp. 29–30.

205. 'For Kennan the telegram was a great professional triumph. Cables and letters of commendation poured in, and Byrnes himself characterised Kennan's analysis as splendid. Along with the unexpected success of his telegram, Kennan's fortunes abruptly changed from being an obscure diplomat about to leave the Foreign Service to a generally acknowledged expert on Soviet affairs.' 'My official loneliness came . . . to an end. My reputation was made': Mayers, 'Soviet War Aims and the Grand Alliance', p. 75. The Kennan quote is from his *Memoirs: 1925–1950*, London, 1968, p. 295.

206. For a detailed account, see Deighton, *The Impossible Peace.*

207. The most important in 1946 were the Council of Foreign Ministers in Paris from late April; the Peace Conference, attended by twenty-one nations, from mid August to mid October; and the meetings of the UN General Assembly and Security Council in New York in November and December. Bevin was away from London for 157 days: Bullock, *Ernest Bevin*, Vol. 3, p. 259.

208. Bullock, *Ernest Bevin*, Vol. 3, has considerable discussion of the Palestine problem, the pagination of which is set out in detail in the Index; and see also, from a substantial literature, E. Monroe, 'Mr Bevin's Arab Policy', St Antony's Papers, No. II, 2, 1961; two articles by R. Ovendale, 'The Palestine Policy of the British Labour Government, 1945–46', *International Affairs*, Vol. 54, No. 3, July 1979, pp. 409–31, and 'The Palestine Policy of the British Labour Government, 1947: The Decision to Withdraw', ibid., Vol. 56, No. 1, January 1980, pp. 73–93; A. Nachmani, '"It is a Matter of Getting the Mixture Right": Britain's Post-War Relations with America in the Middle East', *J. Cont. Hist.*, Vol. 18, No. 1, 1983, pp. 117–40.

209. To the effect that Britain's stock rose and fell according to the strength or otherwise of anti-Soviet sentiment in the United States. This was a common assumption throughout the first two years of the Attlee administration, and was illustrated, directly or implicitly, many times in the Foreign Office files.

210. The writings of Margaret Gowing are the essential introduction to British atomic history. The January 1948 agreement was summed up by her as comparable with the same kind of negotiations characteristic of Anglo-American relations in the atomic field for the previous five years: 'promises forgotten, former discussions misrepresented, facts stood on their heads, sheer administrative muddle, with departments pulling in different directions': *Independence and Deterrence: Britain and Atomic Energy. Vol. 1: Policy Making*, London, 1974, p. 261.

211. FO 371/62420/ UE/ 176.

212. The publication referred to was almost certainly the League of Nations, *Industrialisation and World Trade*, Geneva, 1946, a monograph which had a considerable influence upon contemporary economists and economic historians.

213. FO 371/62279/ UE 1164.

214. FO 371/62420/ UE 678/176/53.

215. The details of American bases in Britain are in Duncan Campbell, *The Unsinkable Aircraft Carrier: American Military Power in Britain*, London, 1984. There is a more extended treatment of the present text in John Saville, 'The Price of Alliance: American Bases in Britain', *Socialist Register*, London, 1987, pp. 32–60.

2. Ernest Bevin as Foreign Secretary

1. S. Bryher, *An Account of the Labour and Socialist Movement in Bristol*, Bristol, 1929; A. Bullock, *The Life and Times of Ernest Bevin. Vol. 1: Trade Union Leader, 1881–1940*, London, 1960: Chs 1 and 2 for the most detailed account of Bevin's early life.

2. 'Commonsense' was used by Antonio Gramsci to describe the ways in which ordinary people perceive the world they live in: often uncritically, incoherently and not seldom in contradictory fashion. The task of the political Left was to develop, in more coherent patterns, the positive aspects of social thought: Gramsci called it 'good sense'. Gramsci's own discussion is in *Selections from the Prison Notebooks*, ed. Q. Hoare and G.N. Smith, London, 1971, esp. pp. 323–43, 419–25. There is a brief introduction to Gramsci's ideas in R. Simon, *Gramsci's Political Thought*, London, 1982; 'Gramsci, Antonio', *Dictionary of Marxist Thought*, ed. T. Bottomore, Oxford, 1983.

3. John Saville, 'The Ideology of Labourism', in R. Benewick, R.N. Berki and B. Parekh, eds, *Knowledge and Belief in Politics*, London, 1973; idem, *The Labour Movement in Britain*, for a brief discussion of labour-socialism, pp. 27–31.

4. Bevin's role in the General Strike is discussed in Bullock, *Ernest Bevin*, Vol. 1, Ch. 12. The final meeting with Baldwin was a pathetic affair with only Bevin trying to press for a statement on conditions for the return to work. See also the account in R. Page Arnot, *The Miners: Years of Struggle*, London, 1953, pp. 446–50.

5. The acceptance of office by Ramsay MacDonald in January 1924 to form the first minority Labour government meant that a number of right-wing members of the General Council of the TUC, who accepted government office, had to retire from the General Council and their places were taken mainly by trade union leaders more to the political Left. These included A.A. Purcell and George Hicks: Calhoun, *The United Front*, pp. 46–7. After the collapse of the General Strike there was a general shift to the Right among most of the trade union leaders.

6. H. Pelling, *A Short History of the Labour Party*, London, 1961, Ch. V.

7. J. Fyrth, *The Signal Was Spain*, London, 1986, p. 265.

8. The discussion in Bullock, *Ernest Bevin*, Vol. 1, pp. 600–601 offers a different account. It was written before the relevant Government papers were open for inspection. K. Middlemass, *Politics in Industrial Society: The Experience of the British System since 1911*, London, 1979, pp. 225–6, quoting PREM 1/218, February 1937, wrote: 'In February 1937 Bevin and Citrine actually offered Baldwin, the then Prime Minister, a bargain: union help with the difficulties of the rearmament programme in return for committee of investigation into the question of holidays with pay; and in due course Bevin served on the Amulree Committee.' For the discussion on rearmament in the 1930s, see R. Miliband, *Parliamentary Socialism*, London, 1961, pp. 220 ff and Ch. 8; and for a different view, J. Saville, 'May Day 1937', esp. pp. 248–59.

9. TGWU *Quarterly Report* (December 1936).

10. *TUC Report, 1937*, p. 70.

11. I am greatly obliged to John Horner for allowing me to quote from his unpublished memoir. The story has now appeared in the history of the Fire Brigades Union, V. Bailey, ed., *Forged in Fire*, London, 1992, pp. 321–2.

12. Bullock, *Ernest Bevin*, Vol. 1, pp. 651–4 reports the reactions of some of Bevin's closest colleagues to the offer of the Ministry of Labour. Arthur Deakin was one of those who urged Bevin to accept only the Ministry of Supply or the Ministry of Economic Warfare; or, suggested Deakin, something like the Ministry of Munitions in the First World War.

13. There is a splendid story in Douglas Jay, *Change and Fortune: A Political Record*, London, 1980, which illustrates why Bevin was successful at the Ministry of Labour. Jay was at the Ministry of Supply and they were having trouble with the Wool Controller who objected to all measures

designed to slim down the industry and release labour for more specifically war purposes. Bevin was appealed to, and a meeting was organised. All senior officials attended from many departments: 'Bevin opened the proceedings with the words: "What's all this, Sir 'Arry" [Sir Harry Shackleton, the Wool Controller]; and Sir Harry replied with a none too brief catalogue of his grievances. In the dignified and deferential silence which followed, Bevin turned his huge head full face to Sir Harry, and observed: "If many people have behaved like you, Sir 'Arry, we should have lost this war by now." Not being accustomed to being addressed thus before such a distinguished company, the Wool Controller was speechless. "What you've got to do", added Bevin, "is as follows. . . . That concludes the meeting. Thank you". It had lasted less than half an hour, and Bevin had spoken in all for about two minutes. We had no further trouble from the wool industry' (pp. 98–9).

14. Bullock, *Ernest Bevin*, Vol. 3, p.109.
15. Ibid.
16. Dalton, *The Fateful Years: Memoirs 1931–1945*, London, 1957, pp. 467–75 which provide a very reasonable account of the switch in offices between Bevin and himself.
17. J. Wheeler-Bennett, *King George VI: His Life and Reign*, London, 1958, p. 638; *The Observer*, 23 August 1959.
18. Jay, *Change and Fortune*, pp. 129–30.
19. Bruce Lockhart's account of this lunch is in the *Diaries*, Vol. 2, pp. 528–9.
20. The conversation at Potsdam is in Sir N. Henderson, *The Private Office: A Personal View of Five Foreign Secretaries and of Government from the Inside*, London, 1984, pp. 22–3. The information about Maiden Lane was from George Matthews, former assistant general-secretary of the British C.P. (letter 20 January 1989) to whom I am much obliged.
21. *Diaries*, p. 778.
22. Lockhart, *Diaries*, p. 500, 30 August 1945.
23. Gladwyn, *Memoirs*, p. 176.
24. The literature is considerable. Gladwyn Jebb in his *Memoirs* has some interesting chapters on the pre-war Foreign Office (Chs 4–6); R. Rhodes James has a good account in his biography of *Anthony Eden* (London, 1986) of Eden at the Foreign Office (Ch. 5) and the immediate pre-war situation (Ch. 6). There is a bibliography in the Historical Association booklet, K. Robbins, *Appeasement* (1988), and a large-scale study by D. Cameron Watt, *How War Came: The Immediate Origins of the Second World War, 1938–1939*, London, 1989.
25. Rhodes James, *Anthony Eden* has a number of references to the hostility towards de Gaulle by both Churchill and Roosevelt. When Eden was considering taking the position of Viceroy of India early in 1943, his biographer commented: 'Had Eden gone to India, the first result would almost certainly have been the removal of de Gaulle as leader of the Free French. Churchill, in Washington again, found American feeling running strongly against the Algiers-based French Committee of National Liberation and de Gaulle as its chairman, and, given his own antipathy to this prickly and often uncongenial genius, was very sympathetic to this attitude' (p. 273). For a detailed account, see F. Kersaudy, *Churchill and de Gaulle*, London, 1981.
26. W.F. Kimball, 'Churchill and Roosevelt: The Personal Equation', *Prologue*, Vol. 6, pp.169–82; F.L. Loewenheim, H.D. Langley and Manfred Jonas, eds, *Roosevelt and Churchill: Their Secret Wartime Correspondence*, New York 1975.
27. All studies of Roosevelt during the war years comment on the relationship with Cordell Hull, the Secretary of State. An example: 'Hull had practically nothing to do with wartime foreign policy. He did not go to Casablanca, and when he asked to see the minutes he was told they were not available. He was kept in the dark about the President's policy towards the French, which Ickes thought was "one of the most astonishing things I have heard for a long time" ': Ted Morgan, *FDR: A Biography*, London, 1986, p. 68. Roosevelt used Sumner Welles, a personal friend, for much of his dealings with the State Department, although Welles resigned early in August 1943 because of potential scandal about his homosexuality. The first top conference Cordell Hull attended was the Quebec meeting in August 1943.
28. Sir Roderick Barclay, *Ernest Bevin and the Foreign Office* (privately printed, London, 1975) is frank in his summing up of Bevin's wife, (pp. 60–61). When on visits abroad, she apparently complained regularly about being neglected, and when one of the women secretaries accompanied her shopping 'this was liable to be a painful experience'. Mrs Bevin had the habit of turning the shop upside down and then walking out without making a purchase. 'She was', Barclay writes

'always delighted to receive presents, and not above indicating this to her foreign hosts'. Frank Giles, *Sundry Times* (London, 1986), was in the Private Office when Bevin first became Foreign Secretary, and wrote of Mrs Bevin as 'a tiresome old body if ever there was one, endlessly bothering Ernie, at his busiest moments, with minutiae of domestic social life, or complaining to us about where she had been placed at an official lunch or dinner' (p. 39).

29. Gladwyn, *Memoirs*, pp. 176–7.

30. The 'scheming little bastard' is from an interview with Sir Trevor Evans: B. Donoughue and G.W. Jones, *Herbert Morrison: Portrait of a Politician*, London, 1973, pp. 345–6; the 'sneers and jibes' in *The Second World War Diary of Hugh Dalton, 1940–1945*, ed. B. Pimlott, London, 1986, 23 October 1944; and the 'little bugger' quote from Francis Williams, *Nothing So Strange*, London, 1970, p. 218.

31. Foreword to Francis Williams, *Ernest Bevin: Portrait of a Great Englishman*, London, 1952, p. 8.

32. Bevin's speech was at Bristol on 29 April 1944; and K. Zilliacus, *I Choose Peace*, Penguin Special, London, 1949, pp. 108–9 provides a longer extract of Laski's article.

33. N. Henderson, *The Private Office*, p. 38.

34. J. Colville, *The Fringes of Power: Downing Street Diaries Vol 2: October 1941–April 1955*, paperback edn, London, 1986, p. 272. The hardback edition of 1985 was a single volume; the paperback edition is in two volumes with additional material in Volume 2. For another comment on Bevin's propensity to gather unto himself any success that might be around: C. Mayhew, *Time to Explain: An Autobiography*, London, 1987, p. 93.

35. Bevin's comment to Mayhew is recorded in *Time to Explain*, diary entry for 3 June 1947, p. 103. Harris, *Attlee*, London, 1982, Ch. 21, provides a straightforward summary of the negotiations leading to independence.

36. P. Ziegler, *Mountbatten: The Official Biography*, London, 1985, pp. 349–482. Cf. Edwina Mountbatten, 11 February 1946: 'Bevin is behaving like the worst conservative diehard': Broadlands Archive, C 249, quoted in Ziegler, p. 315. (The Mountbatten Archives are now at Southampton University.)

37. E.H. Carr had been writing occasional leaders from 1937. He began working full-time as assistant-editor from January 1941.

38. McDonald, *The History of The Times*, Vol. 5, pp. 133 ff. Carr's *Conditions of Peace* offers a good introduction to his ideas at this period.

39. Gladwyn, *Memoirs*, p. 175.

40. Barclay, *Ernest Bevin and the Foreign Office*, p. 84.

41. F. Williams, *A Prime Minister Remembers*, London, 1961, p. 149.

42. V. Rothwell, *Britain and the Cold War, 1941–1947*, London, 1982, p. 230. Dr Rothwell's appreciation of Bevin is almost completely at variance with that being presented in this volume. In particular Dr Rothwell argues that Bevin was determined to do everything in his power to develop improved relations with the Soviet Union until sometime in late 1947. A.J.P. Taylor supported this last point while offering serious criticism of other sections of the book: review in *London Review of Books*, 18 February 1982, p. 5.

43. *The Memoirs of General the Lord Ismay*, London, 1960, p. 403. Ismay's exact words were: 'almost the first words that he said when I greeted him at the airport . . .'

44. C.L. Sulzberger, *A Long Row of Candles: Memoirs and Diaries, 1934–1954*, London, 1969, p. 423.

45. F.O. Roberts, 'Ernest Bevin as Foreign Secretary', in R. Ovendale, ed., *The Foreign Policy of the British Labour Governments, 1945–1951*, Leicester, 1984, p. 23.

46. Eden, *Full Circle*, p. 5.

47. *Hansard*, Vol. 413, Cols 312–13, 20 August 1945.

48. 'H.N. Brailsford', *Dictionary of Labour Biography*, ed. J.M. Bellamy and J. Saville, Vol. 2, 1974, pp. 46–53, with bibliography of writings and sources.

49. Saville, 'Britain: Internationalism and the Labour Movement between the Wars'.

50. *Labour Party. 1937 Conference Report*, p. 207.

51. *The Record*, January 1938, p. 154: quoted in Bullock, *Ernest Bevin*, Vol. 1, p. 622.

52. Walter Citrine had put a resolution to Congress for the complete support for the League of Nations over the Abyssinian question (*TUC Report 1935*, p. 349) and Bevin followed with the resolution noted in the text.

53. '[The] high-minded imperialism of the *Round Table*' was Bullock's phrase, *Ernest Bevin*,

Vol. 1, p. 627. High-minded imperialists differ from the more earthy kinds, who are concerned only with money, by concentrating upon high-minded words which justify the practices of earthy imperialism. For a sympathetic account of Lionel Curtis, see the obit. in *The Times*, 25 November 1955, and the entry in the *DNB*, 1951–60.

54. Bevin spoke on 22 November 1938, and his speech was published in *International Affairs*, Vol. XVIII, No. 1, 1939, pp. 56–76.

55. Williams, *Ernest Bevin*, p. 209.

56. *Labour Party. 1939 Conference Report*, pp. 243–5.

57. Bullock, *Ernest Bevin*, Vol. 1, p. 634. G.D.H. Cole, *A History of the Labour Party from 1914*, London, 1948, devotes six pages (pp. 359–65) to the 1939 Conference, and does not mention Bevin. For the political background to the Conference, which expelled Stafford Cripps, Nye Bevan, G.R. Strauss and others for their advocacy, among other matters, of a Popular Front, see M. Foot, *Aneurin Bevan*, Vol. 1, pp. 270 ff; Saville, 'May Day 1937', esp. pp. 270–76.

58. The best documented account is P. Weiler, *British Labour and the Cold War*, Ch. 1: a book of meticulous scholarship. See also S. Basdeo, 'The Role of the British Labour Movement in the Development of Labour Organisation in Trinidad, 1929–1938', *Social and Economic Studies*, Vol. 31, March 1982, pp. 40–73.

59. Internal discussion, CO 850/135/15/20657/38, 28 July 1938.

60. Lord Citrine, *Men and Work: An Autobiography*, London, 1964, Ch. 21.

61. CO 888/2, 2 August 1942.

62. Weiler, *British Labour and the Cold War*, Ch. 3; A. Carew, 'The Schism within the World Federation of Trade Unions: Government and Trade Union Diplomacy', *Internat. Rev. Social History*, Vol. 29, Part 3, 1984, pp. 297–335.

63. FO 800/461/F 7205/186/10. This conversation, it should be noted, took place just over a month after the end of the war with Japan, and a few days before British troops landed in Indo-China; for which see Ch. 5 below.

64. This phrase 'right across the throat of the British Commonwealth' was in a major debate on foreign policy in the House of Commons opened by Churchill: *Hansard*, Vol. 415, 7 November 1945, Col. 1342.

65. It needs to be underlined that if the decisions on India had been left to Bevin and the Foreign Office, India would not have achieved independence in 1947. The critical evidence is Bevin's memorandum to Attlee dated 1 January 1947 in which he argued for delay, basing himself on the unrealistic analysis that he was constantly applying to the Middle East; and had he won the argument, the same disasters would have followed. The matter is considered further in the closing section of this chapter. The memorandum mentioned is in FO 800/470.

66. There was one quite central difference between Bevin's perceptions of the Middle East when he entered office and those from late 1946 on. He never altered his insistence upon the importance of the Middle East to Britain, as the quotation in the text makes clear; but from late 1946 the British Government had to take increasing account of American attitudes and approaches. There is a not wholly satisfactory discussion in A. Nachmani, ' "It is a matter of Getting the Mixture Right" ', and a much more extensive treatment in W. Roger Louis, *The British Empire in the Middle East, 1945–51*, Oxford, 1984.

67. Arcos was the Russian State Trading Agency. It was a joint stock company registered under British law and engaged in normal commercial activities, although it shared the same building as the Russian Trade Delegation whose activities were regulated by the 1921 Trade Agreement (and whose offices enjoyed diplomatic immunity). The Arcos offices were raided on 12 May 1927 and the search warrant also included the headquarters of the Trade Delegation. It was an episode of the anti-Soviet years that followed the Zinoviev Letter of 1924: Fischer, *The Soviets in World Affairs*, Vol. 2, pp. 680–98; W.P. and Z. Coates, *History of Anglo-Soviet Relations*, London, 1944, pp. 267 ff; Calhoun, *The United Front*, p. 347 ff.

68. Calhoun, *The United Front*, Ch. 6, esp. pp. 379–87.

69. There is a detailed account of the history of trade unionism among London busmen in H.A. Clegg, *Labour Relations in London Transport*, Oxford, 1950, and see also T. Corfield, *TGWU Record*, March 1962, pp. 42–5.

70. *Labour Party. 1946 Conference Report*, p. 167.

71. *The Economist*, 9 December 1944, accused Churchill of reviving 'the Bolshevik bogey'; and for a succinct introduction to the Greek tragedy, see G. Kolko, *The Politics of War*, Ch. 8, 'The

Greek Passion'. General British reaction is analysed in Foster, 'The Politicians, Public Opinion and the Press'.

72. 'Bevan got the applause, but, thanks to the trade union block vote, Bevin got the decision (2,455,000 to 137,000) to the relief of Churchill who never forgot the debt he owed to Bevin for his intervention at a moment when an adverse vote by the Labour conference could have seriously shaken his authority': Bullock, *Ernest Bevin*, Vol. 2, p. 346.

73. So Bullock avers: *Ernest Bevin*, Vol. 3, p. 106.

74. Bullock, *Ernest Bevin*, Vol. 2, pp. 349–50.

75. Henderson, *The Private Office*, p. 22.

76. This question was considered above, in the Moscow section of Chapter 1, pp. 59 ff. Another example of the argument is R. Smith, 'A Climate of Opinion: British officials and the development of British/Soviet policy, 1945–7, *International Affairs*, Vol. 64, No. 4, Autumn 1988, pp. 631–47. Dr Smith's argument in this article is confused and inadequately documented, and fails to make clear the sharp differences between Attlee and Bevin on certain issues in the first two years of the Labour Government. See note 161 above, in the Moscow section of Chapter 1.

77. The writings of Margaret Gowing are the essential starting point for any understanding of the history of atomic weapons in the United Kingdom. There is a summary of certain of her conclusions in 'Nuclear Weapons and the "Special Relationship"', in W. Roger Louis and H. Bull, eds, *The Special Relationship: Anglo-American Relations since 1945*, Oxford, 1986, Ch. 7. See also J.L. Gormly, 'The Washington Declaration and the "Poor Relation": Anglo-American Atomic Diplomacy, 1945–46', *Diplomatic History*, Vol. 8, No. 2, Spring 1984, pp. 125–44; N. Wheeler, 'The Attlee Government's Nuclear Strategy, 1945–51', in A. Deighton, *Britain and the First Cold War*, London, 1990, pp. 130–45.

78. Barclay, *Ernest Bevin and the Foreign Office*, p. 36, is an exception: 'Mr Bevin had left school at the age of eleven, and though quite a quick reader, writing was still a rather laborious business.' This is not the most commonly expressed view, which would have agreed with Henderson, who wrote that 'Bevin took things in much less easily by reading than by word of mouth': *The Private Office*, p. 37.

79. *The Private Office*, p. 36.

80. *DBPO*, Ser. I, Vol. II, 1985, p. xxi.

81. *Old Men Forget*, London, 1955, pp. 360–61.

82. Mayhew, *Time to Explain*, p. 113.

83. A. Nutting, *Europe Will Not Wait*, London, 1960, p. 20.

84. V. Lawford, 'Three Ministers', *Cornhill Magazine*, No. 1010, Winter 1956–57, pp. 94–5. For an interesting, in part critical, account of Bevin as Foreign Secretary, see the chapter in K.O. Morgan, *Labour People. Leaders and Lieutenants: Hardie to Kinnock*, Oxford, 1987.

85. *Hansard*, Vol. 413, Cols 283 ff, 20 August 1945.

86. Barclay, *Ernest Bevin and the Foreign Office*, p. 74.

87. Henderson, *The Private Office*, p. 36

88. 'Verbal corrections are allowed to be made in the report of speeches in the daily part for reproduction in the bound volume, but only if, in the opinion of the Editor, they do not alter in any way the general sense of the speech made': Sir Thomas Erskine May, *A Treatise on the Law, Privileges, Proceedings and Usage of Parliament*, ed. Sir Gilbert Campion, 14th edn, London, 1946, p. 253. The 21st edn, London, 1989, p. 211, has almost identical wording.

89. Bullock, *Ernest Bevin*, Vol. 3, p. 288.

90. Henderson, *The Private Office*, p. 35.

91. Dean Acheson, *Sketches from Life, of Men I Have Known*, London, 1961, pp. 27–8: quoted in Bullock, *Ernest Bevin*, Vol. 3, p. 727.

92. The general effects of Bevin's deteriorating health were commented on by a number of his contemporaries who were in close contact. Bullock, *Ernest Bevin*, Vol. 3, p. 759, quotes from the diary of Kenneth Younger who had succeeded Hector McNeil as Minister of State; and Lord Franks recalled how meetings had to be adjourned on several occasions in the last eighteen months of Bevin's life because of attacks of angina: Bullock, *Ernest Bevin*, Vol. 3, pp. 727–8. What Bullock does not emphasise sufficiently is the independence Bevin's ill-health and absence from the Office allowed his senior officials; and it was, as my text suggests, the recognition that his name and authority counted for so much that the Foreign Office in general encouraged him to continue in position.

93. Bullock, *Ernest Bevin*, Vol. 3, p. 757.

94. Bullock in Vol. 3 refers on a number of occasions to Bevin's ill-health and his rapidly declining capacity in the last years of his life. See the Index pagination under Bevin, Ernest . . . 'health declines'.

95. Two weeks after the invasion of Russia in June 1941, Duff Cooper at the Ministry of Information asked Citrine for a statement supporting Churchill's speech on Anglo-Russian co-operation. Citrine refused: 'I honestly believe that Russia is not fighting for any principle which we cherish.' His attitude changed, at least in public, in line with the rapidly growing wave of pro-Russian sentiment throughout Britain among the working people, and Citrine and other leaders of the TUC decided to form an Anglo-Soviet Trade Union Committee. After a visit to Eden to get his approval, Eden wrote to Churchill: 'You know Citrine's feeling about Communism, which he expressed again with undiminished emphasis, even going so far as to say that, were he given a choice between life under Nazi or Soviet rule, he would be in doubt as to which to choose. Nevertheless he feels that some contact between the trade union movement and the Soviets is inevitable, and that being so, he wished to control it and to put his men in charge of it': quoted in Weiler, *British Labour and the Cold War*, p. 56, from Eden to Churchill, 22 August 1941, PREM 4/21/3. Citrine's own memories of this period, somewhat different from the sentiments expressed in 1941, are in the second volume of his autobiography, *Two Careers*, London, 1967.

96. FO 800/501: present were Molotov, Gusev (Ambassador), Pavlov (Interpreter) and Clark Kerr who signed the record 'A.C.K'. Bullock's summary is on pp. 132–3, Vol. 3, and it conveys a different impression from my present text; in particular, it does not underline the impact the Hitler reference must have had upon Molotov.

97. Field Marshal Sir Henry Maitland Wilson made a blunt anti-Soviet statement in Washington (he was head of the British Joint Staff) which among other matters emphasised his disquiet at Russian potential aggression in the Balkans. An account was published in the *Baltimore Sun*, 21 September 1945, and on the following day in the London *Times*.

98. Dixon, ed., *Double Diploma*, p. 19.

99. Byrnes' comment is in *Speaking Frankly*, New York, 1947, p. 79; Truman in Eben Ayer's Diary, 7 August 1945: quoted in Yergin, *Shattered Peace*, p. 434, note 27.

100. W. Averell Harriman and E. Abel, *Special Envoy to Churchill and Stalin, 1941–1946*, London, 1976, p. 507.

101. FO 800/478, which contains a complete copy of the broadcast, and all the subsequent correspondence quoted in my text. A.J.P. Taylor made no reference to this broadcast in his *Personal History*, London, 1983.

102. W. Gallman to George Marshall, Records of the Department of State, National Archives, Washington, 841. oo/2-2-47: quoted C. Anstey, 'The Projection of British Socialism: Foreign Office Publicity and American Opinion, 1945–50', *J. Cont. Hist.*, Vol. 19, No. 3, 1984, pp. 417–51, 435.

3. Clement Attlee and the Middle East, 1945–47

1. Harris, *Attlee*, p. 9.

2. Colville, *The Fringes of Power*, Vol. 2, p. 262.

3. Saville, *The Labour Movement in Britain*, pp. 12–22, 27 ff.

4. Quoted in Harris, *Attlee*, p. 55.

5. *Dictionary of Labour Biography*, ed. J.M. Bellamy and J. Saville, Vol. 4, 1977, p. 189.

6. Harris, *Attlee*, pp. 75 ff.; Gupta, *Imperialism and the British Labour Movement, 1914–1964*, pp. 113–18 and passim. Members of the Simon Commission were selected to ensure a cautious and sober report.

7. Harris, *Attlee*, p. 56.

8. It was published as a Left Book Club volume; for the political background, see Saville, 'May Day 1937'.

9. D.E. Butler, *The Electoral System in Britain*, London, 1963, p. 184.

10. C.R. Attlee, *The Labour Party in Perspective*, London, 1937, p. 130.

11. K. Martin, *Harold Laski (1893–1950): A Biographical Memoir*, London, 1953, pp. 159–62, for the complete text of the letter.

12. J. Saville, 'Labour and Income Redistribution', in R. Miliband and J. Saville, eds, *Socialist Register*, London, 1965, pp. 147–62; and for a more extended treatment of the whole subject, A.B. Atkinson, *The Economics of Inequality*, 2nd edn, London, 1983.

13. The literature is considerable. J.F. Naylor's interesting survey, *Labour's International Policy: The Labour Party in the 1930s*, London, 1969, provides a brief summary of the 1920s in his opening chapter. There is an excellent liberal account in C.L. Mowat, *Britain Between the Wars*, London, 1955.

14. Attlee, *As it Happened*, London, 1954, p. 151.

15. Attlee to Churchill, Most Secret, 8 June 1945, Attlee Papers, 2/2 (Churchill College, Cambridge), quoted in R. Ovendale, Introduction to Ovendale, ed., *The Foreign Policy of the British Labour Governments, 1945–1951*, Leicester, 1984, p. 5.

16. *Hansard*, Vol. 413, Col. 287, 20 August 1945. The comment quoted referred to the policy towards UNRRA, but the words sum up the general approach of Bevin's speech. In the columns which followed he defended with vigour both the Churchill Intervention in Greece and the non-intervention policies towards Franco Spain.

17. T.D. Burridge, *Clement Attlee: A Political Biography*, London 1985, pp. 175 ff.

18. For a further summary of the differences between Bevin and Attlee over Indian independence, see Bullock, *Ernest Bevin*, Vol. 3, pp. 359–61.

19. T.D. Burridge, *British Labour and Hitler's War*, London, 1976, Ch. 3; and for Blum, Dalton, *The Fateful Years*, pp. 290–93.

20. There were some exceptions but positive judgements on Attlee do not seem to have been common in contemporary diaries. For later assessments that were favourable, *The Memoirs of General the Lord Ismay*; Colville, *Fringes of Power*, Vol. 2, p. 262.

21. Quoted in Harris, *Attlee*, p. 194.

22. H. Nicolson, *Diaries and Letters, 1945–1962*, London, 1968, pp. 71–2.

23. Williams, *A Prime Minister Remembers*, p. 149.

24. Foot, *Aneurin Bevan*, Vol. 2, p. 89.

25. There is still research to be done on Attlee's political attitudes in respect of foreign affairs during the Second World War.

26. 'Future Defence Policy in the Suez and Canal Area': Report by the Suez Committee. CAB 66/63, WP (45) 197, 20 March 1945.

27. 'Compulsory Military Service': Report of the Armistice and Post-War Committee. CAB 66/64, WP (45) 242, 12 April 1945.

28. 'Defence of the Middle East': CAB 66/65, WP (45) 256, 13 April 1945.

29. For the controversy around Attlee accompanying Churchill to the Potsdam Conference, see Harris, *Attlee*, pp. 258–62.

30. In 1936 the Turks had asked for an international conference to reconsider the clauses in the Treaty of Lausanne (1923) which demilitarised the Bosporus and the Dardenelles. The Montreux Convention of 1936 allowed the Turks to refortify the Straits, and also permitted the Russians to send through naval ships of any size except aircraft carriers and submarines, while limiting non-Black Sea countries to light warships. The Montreux agreement was signed by Britain, France, Greece, Yugoslavia and the Black Sea powers.

31. See the second volume of Eden's memoirs, *The Reckoning, 1938–1945*, London, 1965, pp. 546–7. There are slight verbal differences between this version and that printed in *DBPO*, Ser. 1, Vol. I, No. 176, dated 17 July 1945, pp. 352–4.

32. *DBPO*, Ser. I, Vol. I, No. 179, 18 July 1945, pp. 363–4.

33. Ibid., No. 238, pp. 575–6.

34. Ibid., No. 236, 23 July 1945, pp. 573–4.

35. The earliest discussion, of any length, of the documents quoted and referred to in the text was in Smith and Zametica, 'The Cold Warrior'. It is an article with which the present writer is in general agreement except for the conclusion on p. 251, which relates to the reasons why Attlee stopped pressing his heretical views upon Ernest Bevin. The matter is discussed below.

36. Cunningham Diary, British Library Add. MSS. 52578. Cunningham seems always to have spelt Attlee's name as Atlee.

37. *DBPO*, Ser. I, Vol. I, No. 459, 29 July 1945, pp. 990–94.

38. Quoted above: *DBPO*, Ser. I, Vol. I, No. 236, p. 574.

39. Altrincham wrote a personal letter to Bevin dated 25 August 1945 (FO 800/475) which begged him not to allow the complete break-up of the Middle East Supply Centre because of the expertise it commanded. 'There is no place where mishandling of inseparable political and economic problems can do more immediate and lasting harm [than Egypt].' The diplomats, Altrincham wrote, were 'unfamiliar' with economic problems, and unless there was 'strong civil and local control' he predicted an 'explosion in Egypt'. Bevin sent a soothing reply which suggested that he might call upon Altrincham again 'when I have made my mind up how to proceed'. The diplomats won, of course, although this is not to suggest that Altrincham knew many of the answers to the problems of the Middle East. He was arguing in the later stages of the war for seven divisions to be permanently stationed in the Middle East.

40. FO 800/475, 24 August 1945. While this memorandum obviously came from the Secretary of State it was in fact signed by P.J. Dixon, Bevin's Private Secretary.

41. FO 371/45252/E 6528. Paget's memorandum was originally dated 20 April 1945. It was after a meeting with Bevin on 30 August 1945 that Paget sent him a copy of his paper, noting that 'It gives only the bare bones of the idea, and there are obvious snags such as the reactions of USA and the Russians; but I do not think they should be insurmountable. Moreover, I believe that, if the Middle Eastern States could be brought to realise that they have a common security interest with us as we have with them, we should stand a better chance of obtaining our defence requirements.' It would be difficult to find a more striking illustration of the political innocence of some members of the British military élite.

42. FO 800/475, 28 August 1945, and also in CAB 129/1, CP (45) 130, 28 August 1945. For the general background of the early months of the Labour Government's approach to the Middle East, and for Bevin's attitudes in particular, see Louis, *The British Empire and the Middle East, 1945–1951*, Introduction, pp. 1–50 and passim.

43. CAB 129/1 CP (45) 144, 1 September 1945.

44. Cunningham Diary, BL Add. MSS. 52578, 3 September 1945.

45. CAB 128/1, CM (45) 27, 3 September 1945. Alanbrooke, the CIGS, wrote in his diary for 3 September: 'We were shaken by Attlee's new Cabinet Paper in which apparently the security of the Middle East must rest on the power of the United Nations; we have enough experience in the League of Nations to be quite clear that, whilst backing this essential and idealistic organisation, something more political is also required': Bryant, *Triumph in the West*. Later in the month Alanbrooke had a meeting with Bevin at which the latter requested him to undertake a mission to the Middle East to look into the Paget suggestion of a military Confederation; for which see ibid., pp. 491 ff.

46. CAB 128/1, CM 30 (45), 11 September 1945. Smith and Zametica, 'The Cold Warrior', suggest on p. 244 that 'Bevin was forced to accept vague proposals for promoting British control over Cyrenaica and Somaliland until the machinery of the UN Trusteeship Council had been set up.' This is a misreading of the Cabinet minutes, for Bevin got endorsement of all his proposals in the final Cabinet authorisation and his suggestion that 'the wisest course' would be for military control until the World Organisation had been set up was a typical Foreign Office formulation, since once military control had been established it would not have been difficult to delay any takeover from the UN. As my text suggests, Bevin did not have the support of the Americans, and he had therefore to block any immediate decision when the issue was considered at the Council of Foreign Ministers. The document which Smith and Zametica omit from their discussion is the memorandum from Bevin dated 10 September (CAB 129/2, CP (45) 162) in which he set out at some length the arguments for trusteeship by the British and in particular the importance of resisting the Russian's claim to any of the Mediterranean territories. It was this document which the Cabinet had before them at their meeting of 11 September, discussed above in this note.

47. CAB 128/3, CM (45) 32, Confidential Annex, 15 September 1945.

48. There is a summary of the London Conference of Foreign Ministers in Bullock, *Ernest Bevin*, Vol. 3, pp. 129–37; and for a fuller publication of the key documents, see *DBPO*, Ser. I, Vol. II.

49. Quoted in Bullock, *Ernest Bevin*, Vol. 3, p. 155: FO 800/484, 12 October 1945.

50. Bevin's report to the Cabinet: CAB 129/2, CP (45) 174, 17 September 1945.

51. T/236/205. Bridges' one-page memorandum was dated 30 August 1945, and signed EEB. It is contained in a piece of about twenty quite thin files which offer illuminating material on

the general approach of the Treasury to the Middle East questions. Bridges, in the quotation given in the text, goes on to make the simple point that any further expenditures would continue to swell the sterling balances. The Treasury insisted on being represented. Bridges has an internal note in which he wrote: 'We marched on Sir Alexander Cadogan and told him that we thought Overton and Croft should also attend the meeting. Sir Alexander Cadogan agreed.'

52. This was in a short note to Bridges, dated 13 September. Not signed.

53. Shuckbrugh, *Descent to Suez*. pp. 4–7. The quotations which follow come from these pages.

54. *The Killearn Diaries, 1934–1946*, ed. and introduced by T.E. Evans, London, 1972, pp. 347–50. Trevor Evans, formerly a diplomat and later professor at Aberystwyth, offers a very different account of Killearn than that which can be read in Shuckbrugh's volume.

55. FO 371/53288, 6 March 1946. There is a thorough discussion in Louis, *The British Empire in the Middle East*, Ch. 6: 'Egypt: British "Evacuation" and the "Unity of the Nile Valley"'. For a sharp critique of British policy, see the memorandum by Brigadier C.O. Quillian dated 15 October 1951, prepared for *The Times*. Quillian was a regular soldier who was head of the Political Intelligence Department at GHQ, Middle East from 1942. He was engaged by *The Times* in August 1945: 'A reference to my past letters will show that I am not being wise after the event when I say that the Foreign Office has contributed substantially to the present mess by its lack of understanding of Egypt and its people, and its apparent disregard of Egyptian history. It started early in 1945, when a sympathetic Saadist government asked if the Egyptian contribution to the war effort had not earned treaty revision. It was not until 1946 that we even agreed to listen to their request, and then, when negotiations did start, the Egyptian delegation – not to mention lots of British observers – got the impression that the F.O. thought it was dealing with a defeated enemy who had to be made to put its name on the dotted line': McDonald, *History of the Times*, Vol. 5, p. 184. There are a number of references to Quillian in Louis' volume, and they add up to a profile of an interesting, and exceedingly well-informed, personality.

56. FO 371/45254/ E 8025, 18 October 1945.

57. Bryant, *Triumph in the West*, p. 500.

58. The description is from Louis, *The British Empire in the Middle East*, p. 10.

59. FO 371/69192, 10 January 1948. Louis, *British Empire in the Middle East*, after quoting a slightly longer extract from the same file, has two comments on following pages: 'The daring breadth and imaginative scope of this grand design was worthy of Lord Curzon and Imperial architects of an earlier era' (p. 106); and 'So barren was the fruit of Bevin's general Middle East policy that critics then and later believed that it would have been decidedly better to have vigorously cultivated the tradition of Little England' (p. 107).

60. Attlee flew to Washington on 9 November 1945, with Sir John Anderson in tow, after telling a Mansion House audience that he was going to discuss world affairs with Truman, and Mackenzie King of Canada, 'in the light, the terrible light, of the discovery of atomic energy'. He was concerned especially with matters relating to the earlier agreements on atomic energy and the availability and distribution of raw materials for atomic energy. The story is told in detail in the definitive study by Margaret Gowing, *Independence and Deterrence: Britain and Atomic Energy*, Vol. 1.

61. Many of the papers relating to overseas bases have been reprinted: *DBPO*, Ser. 1, Vol. IV.

62. Cunningham Papers, BL Add. MSS. 52578, 15 September 1945.

63. Ibid., 5 October 1945.

64. Defence Committee minutes: DO (46) 3rd Mtg., 21 January 1946 in CAB 131/1.

65. CAB 131/1, DO (46) 5th Mtg., 15 February 1946. It needs perhaps to be noted that the argument Bevin was using in these months had no basis at all in the facts of the international situation, or the diplomacy which derived from those facts. There was taking place throughout 1946 a sharp reduction in the size of the armed forces of the Soviet Union as well as in those of the United States. For some brief facts on the Soviet Union, see below, Appendix 2.

66. CAB 131/2, COS (46) 43 (O), 13 February, 1946.

67. Field Marshal Smuts could always be relied upon to support the most intransigent position in respect of the Soviet Union: a subject for further research.

68. CAB 132/2, DO (46) 27, 2 March 1946.

69. Ibid., para. 8. The words quoted in the text were followed by a closing sentence to the paragraph: 'I have not taken into consideration here any results that may flow from the development

of Atomic warfare'; and his final sentence asked that the Chiefs of Staff should consider the strategic arguments involved in the memorandum.

70. Jebb's minute was typed. The words in the quotation in the text that are included in square brackets were handwritten additions.

71. CAB 131/2, DO (46) 40, 13 March 1946.

72. Above, pp. 50 ff.

73. *Hansard*, 5th Ser., Vol. 430, Cols 578–90, 18 November 1946.

74. Attlee to Bevin, FO 800/475, 1 December 1946.

75. Hector McNeil was now Minister of State at the Foreign Office in place of Noel Baker. His letter to Bevin, and the latter's reply of 5 December, are in FO 800/468. There is a discussion of these events in Bullock, *Ernest Bevin*, Vol. 3, pp. 339–40, including a long extract from Attlee's memorandum of 1 December which omits, towards the end of the letter following the sentence 'Fantastic as this is, it may very well be the real grounds of Russian policy', the next two sentences which read: 'What we consider merely defence, may seem to them to be preparation for attack. The same kind of considerations apply to the proposals by the USA for Air bases in Canada which the Russians might regard as offensive in intention.'

76. These notes by P.J. Dixon, Bevin's Principal Private Secretary, are important for their clear exposition of the thinking of a senior member of the Foreign Office at this time which was shared by all his colleagues: FO 800/475, 9 December 1946 and marked Top Secret. Dixon began by listing the 'points of friction' which he defined as Turkey, Persia, Greece and, to a lesser degree, Iraq and Afghanistan, and these for him were 'the nub of Anglo-Soviet relations'. The obvious solution on paper, he wrote, would be to agree with the Soviet Union that the area of 'points of friction' should be regarded as a 'neutral zone'; and he continued: 'But it is doubtful whether such an idea is practical politics. (1) Nature abhors a vacuum, or, to change the simile, the protective pad would not be a dry pad: and it would soak up. In other words, Russia would certainly infiltrate into a "neutral zone". (2) A neutral zone in the 'points of friction' countries would mean the loss of the British position in Egypt and Arabia, as well. It would, in fact, bring Russia to the Congo and the Victoria Falls. (3) The Mediterranean is no longer of use to us as communication route in war. Our interest in retaining our position is to keep others out. With the Russians in the Mediterranean we should lose our influence in Italy, France and North Africa. (4) It may well be true that Russia thinks in exaggerated terms of her own security and is thus led to interpret defensive measures on our part as potential offensive measures. But her exaggerated sense of security, which is almost indistinguishable from an imperialist instinct, would lead her to fill a vacuum, if it was there to fill. (5) In an atomic age, we cannot afford to dispense with a first line of defence. Even if a neutral zone was feasible, which is questionable, can we risk having no front line or defence between Central Africa and Russia? (6) In any case, our central African main defence exists only on paper. What happens if we get into trouble in the next ten or fifteen years, having lost our position in the Middle East and Eastern Mediterranean?'

Bringing 'Russia to the Congo and the Victoria Falls': an interesting exposition of the 'domino' theory in British diplomatic papers of this period.

77. Bullock, *Ernest Bevin*, Vol. 3, p. 345.

78. FO 800/475, 28 December 1946.

79. FO 800/476, 5 January 1947. Bullock, *Ernest Bevin*, Vol. 3, pp. 349–50, described Attlee's memorandum as 'the most radical criticism Bevin had to face from inside the Government during his five and a half years as Foreign Secretary'. Bullock also says that 'it went much further than Attlee's arguments of the previous summer in favour of withdrawal from the Middle East.' But this is not true, for all the arguments used had been presented by Attlee in previous notes and memoranda. The importance of this present document of 5 January 1947 was that it brought together all the themes and arguments of the previous two years to produce a single, coherent statement of an alternative policy.

80. Summarised in Smith and Zametica, 'The Cold Warrior', p. 246.

81. FO 800/476, 8 January 1947.

82. Bullock, *Ernest Bevin*, Vol. 3, p. 350: 'After discussion with his officials, Bevin sent Attlee a long reply of eight foolscap pages which Dixon appears to have drafted.' The Bevin letter is in FO 800/476, 9 January 1947.

83. FO 800/476, 10 January 1947. Marked Top Secret and Confidential, it was quite a short handwritten document with the internal classification of M/E 47/5. No indication of those

circularised. On the same day there was a meeting of Gen 75 now reconvened as Gen 163 which took the decision to manufacture a British atom bomb; for which see Gowing, *Independence and Deterrence*, Vol. 1, Chs 6 and 7; and also idem, 'Britain, America and the Bomb', in D. Dilks, ed., *Retreat from Power: Vol. 2: After 1939*, London, 1981, pp. 120–37.

84. H. Dalton, *High Tide and After: Memoirs, 1945–1960*, London, 1962, Ch. 23.

85. Viscount Montgomery, *Memoirs*, London, 1958, p. 436.

86. The history of the discussions within the Labour administration over conscription is set out clearly in F. Myers, 'Conscription and the Politics of Military Strategy in the Attlee Government', *J. Strategic Studies*, Vol. 7, No. 1, March 1984, pp. 55–73. The Defence Committee meeting is in CAB 131/1, DO (46) 28th Mtg., 17 October 1946; and the Cabinet agreement in CAB 21/2070, CM (46) 90 Mtg., Confidential Annex, 24 October 1946. Attlee reported the decision to the House of Commons: *Hansard*, 5th Ser., Vol. 43, Cols 37–44, 12 November 1946.

87. For a detailed account of the vigorous actions of Labour backbenchers opposed to the principle of conscription, or to any lengthy period of service, see H.B. Berrington, *Backbench Opinion in the House of Commons, 1945–1955*, Oxford, 1973, pp. 47 ff.

88. *Hansard*, 5 Ser., Vol. 430, Cols 37–44, 12 November 1946.

89. Quoted in Myers, 'Conscription and Politics of Military Strategy', p. 80: CAB 21/1861, 20 October 1947.

90. COS (47) 102 (O), reprinted in Appendix to Lewis, *Changing Direction*.

91. Ibid.

92. Correlli Barnett, *Britain and Her Army 1509–1970*, London, 1970, p. 481.

93. As an example, see the analysis in Darby, *British Defence Policy East of Suez, 1947–1968*: written before the Public Records were open.

94. Henderson, *The Private Office*, p. 37.

4. Some Economic Factors in Foreign Policy

1. E. Larrabee, *Commander-in-Chief: Franklin Delano Roosevelt, His Lieutenants and Their War*, London, 1987, Ch. 10.

2. American Intelligence was reading Japan's radio codes; and they had all the intercepts from Tokyo. Japan began serious attempts at a negotiated peace early in July 1945 when the Japanese Foreign Minister instructed the Japanese Ambassador in Moscow to enquire whether the Russians would act as intermediary for a settlement; the USSR not yet being at war with Japan. It was made clear that Japan wanted an end to the war but that unconditional surrender could not be insisted upon, since that would impugn the honour of the Emperor. For an account of these developments, see Lisle A. Rose, *Dubious Victory: The United States and the End of World War II*, Kent State, 1973, pp. 322 ff; *FRUS 1945: Conference of Berlin*, I, pp. 874 ff.

3. There is a convenient summary in A. Cairncross, *Years of Recovery: British Economic Policy, 1945–51*, London, 1985, Chs 1–3. Much of the evidence presented by writers on these matters are taken from the official data set out in *Statistical Material during the Washington Negotiations*, Cmd. 6707, December 1945. There are useful summary tables in the excellent article by J. Tomlinson, 'The Attlee Government and the Balance of Payments, 1945–1951', *Twentieth Century British History*, Vol. 2, No. 1, 1991, pp. 47–66.

4. Cairncross, *Years of Recovery*, Ch. 1; and for the approach of the Labour Government in its early days of office, see the speech of Attlee, *Hansard*, Vol. 413, Cols 955 ff, 24 August 1945.

5. A point made by all the writers on this period: Block, *The Origins of International Economic Disorder*, Ch. 3. The most succinct summary of the negotiations is in Cairncross, *Years of Recovery*, Ch.5; and a fuller account, L.S. Pressnell, *External Economic Policy Since the War. Vol. 1: The Post-War Financial Settlement*, HMSO, London, 1987, Ch. 10.

6. R. Eatwell, *The 1945–1951 Labour Governments*, London, 1979, Ch. 4; and see the references in n. 15, below.

7. The approach of the Labour Party, worked out during the war, was set out in a pamphlet written by Hugh Dalton, assisted by Gaitskell, Jay and Durbin, with whom he had been closely associated during the 1930s. This was *Full Employment and Financial Policy* (1944): a statement basically of Keynesian principles on the side of demand management, coupled with the kind of

physical controls that were proving useful during the war years. For the pre-war discussions, see Elizabeth Durbin, *New Jerusalems: The Labour Party and the Economics of Democratic Socialism*, London, 1985, esp. Part 2.

8. Cairncross, *Years of Recovery*, pp. 90 ff.

9. Paragraph 12 related to military and political expenditure abroad, and here Clarke was probably referring to the extent of Middle East expenditure.

10. Sir Richard Clarke (ed. Sir Alec Cairncross), *Anglo-American Economic Collaboration in War and Peace*, Oxford, 1982, p. 151, para. 15.

11. Ibid., p. 152. Keynes' note was dated 22 February 1946.

12. The text of the 'Overall Strategic Plan' is reprinted in Lewis, *Changing Direction*, App. 7; and see above, Chapter 3, pp. 145–6.

13. The Secretary to the Cabinet, Norman Brook, drew attention to the three different ministerial committees which were discussing manpower problems and the size of the armed forces: PREM 8/319, quoted in Cairncross, *Years of Recovery*, pp. 386–7. Hugh Dalton, writing of the period when he was Chancellor of the Exchequer, reprints a long letter he sent to Attlee on 20 January 1946 protesting vigorously against the Cabinet's refusal to accelerate demobilisation: *High Tide and After*, Ch. 23.

14. This was the basic theme of a memorandum distributed by the Foreign Office to overseas missions: 'Effect of Britain's Financial Position on Foreign Policy'. FO 371/45694, 9 February 1945.

15. The standard work of reference is still C.H. Feinstein, *National Income, Expenditure and Output of the United Kingdom, 1855–1965*, Cambridge, 1972. There are a number of general surveys, apart from Cairncross, *Years of Recovery*. An early analysis was in G.D.N. Worswick and P.H. Ady, *The British Economy, 1945–1950*, Oxford, 1952, and a survey of longer span, J.C.R. Dow, *The Management of the British Economy, 1945–1960*, Cambridge, 1964. W. Loth, *The Division of the World, 1941–1955*, London, 1988, offers a global interpretation, in a somewhat indifferent translation. Loth missed Milward's important book of 1984.

16. A.S. Milward, *The Reconstruction of Western Europe, 1945–51* rev. paperback edn, London 1987, esp. Ch. 1.

17. Bullock, *Ernest Bevin*, Vol. 3, p. 404 and K. Morgan, *Labour in Power, 1945–1951*, Oxford, 1984, p. 270, both exaggerate the importance of Bevin's initiative; and see also R. Mayne, *The Recovery of Europe*, London, 1970, pp. 104–5. Milward is among those who deny what he calls 'an agreeable myth': *The Reconstruction of Western Europe*, p. 61, note 6.

18. T 236/1887, 29 May 1947.

19. Dean Acheson, *Present at the Creation: My Years in the State Department*, London, 1970, p. 230. The Clayton memorandum is in *FRUS*, 1947, Vol. III, 'The European Crisis', 27 May 1947, pp. 230–32.

20. Milward, *The Reconstruction of Western Europe*, offers a convenient summary of the argument of his book in Ch. 14, 'Conclusions'.

21. Acheson, *Present at the Creation*, pp. 231–2.

22. Quoted in Gaddis, *Strategies of Containment*, New York, 1982, p. 38, note.

23. One of the most extended treatments of the Marshall plan and its evolution is M. Hogan, *The Marshall Plan: America, Britain and the Reconstruction of Western Europe, 1947–1952*, Cambridge, 1987, with some important differences from Milward. Hogan accepts the argument in my text that Marshall Aid was an important factor in helping Western Europe to develop into the beginnings of a version of the integrated market of American capitalism. C.P. Kindleberger, *Marshall Plan Days*, Boston, 1987, is a sparkling collection of essays with a specific critique of Milward in Ch. 14, 'Did Dollars Save the World?', pp. 245–65.

24. For the vigour of the working-class movements in Western Europe, see Weiler, *British Labour and the Cold War*, passim.

25. 'Economic Consequences of Receiving No European Aid', CAB 129/128, CP (48) 161, 23 June 1948: quoted in Milward, *Reconstruction of Western Europe*, p. 100. The Cabinet signed the Marshall Aid agreement two days after the discussion of this paper. The text of the agreement is given in H. Pelling, *Britain and the Marshall Plan*, London, 1988, App. B, pp. 153–65.

26. Milward, *Reconstruction of Western Europe*, pp. 101 ff. West Germany was a special case: Milward, ibid., p. 99; Hogan, *Marshall Plan*, passim and esp. Ch. 3.

27. Pelling, *Britain and the Marshall Plan*, p. 10; reviewed by Milward, *Economic History Review*,

Vol. XLIII, No. 3, August 1990, p. 509. It is odd that such a perceptive historian as Milward should not appreciate the difference in scale in terms of overseas commitments between Britain and the other countries of Western Europe, even including the colonial expenditures of both the Dutch and the French.

28. Tomlinson, 'The Attlee Government and the Balance of Payments', p. 65.

29. It was *The Economist* from about 1947 which was providing its readers with conclusions from the current statistical date to show that 'At least ten per cent of the national consuming power has been forcefully transferred from the middle classes and the rich to the wage-earners'(3 January 1948). This broad generalisation was confirmed by the Board of Inland Revenue's 92nd Report for 1948–49; and in 1950 *The Economist* published a pamphlet on personal incomes which referred to a 'Vast redistribution of incomes'. It was not until Richard Titmuss published a Fabian Tract, No. 323, *The Irresponsible Society* in 1959, and later his book, *Income Distribution and Social Change*, London, 1962, that the statistical evidence was subject to serious critique. For a general examination of the ideas of this period, see Saville, 'Labour and Income Re-distribution'.

30. Bullock, *Ernest Bevin*, Vol. 3, p. 363.

31. CO 537/3089/19128/89/23: quoted in A.E. Hinds, 'Sterling and Imperial Policy, 1945–1951', *J. Imperial and Commonwealth History*, Vol. 15, No. 2, January 1987, pp. 162–3. The discussion in the text has leaned heavily upon Tomlinson's article cited above in note 28.

32. D.K. Fieldhouse, 'The Labour Governments and Empire–Commonwealth, 1945–51' in R. Ovendale, ed., *The Foreign Policy of the British Labour Governments, 1945–1951*, Leicester, 1984, p. 95.

33. There was, inevitably, a considerable discussion at the time of the sterling balances, the dollar gap and the UK's external financial problems. In 1946, for example, the Fabian Society published A.C. Gilpin, *India's Sterling Balances*, with a trenchant foreword by G.D.H. Cole. The author made the point that 'the sterling balances are in real terms a forced loan by the people of India to the people of Britain.' There is a great deal of material in the Treasury papers, including a copy of a lecture delivered by Sir Frederick Leith Ross, on the sterling balances, in Cairo, 16 January 1947: T 236/761; and in the same file there is a detailed report made to the Egyptian government on Egypt's sterling balances by M. Paul van Zeeland. A contemporary journal, *The World Today*, had a number of useful articles including 'Sterling in 1947', Vol. III, No. 1, January 1947, pp. 63–72. In 1949 *The Times* reprinted in pamphlet form six special articles with the correspondence they stimulated in *The Dollar Gap*. In 1952 G.D.N. Worswick and P. Ady edited an important collection of essays on *The British Economy 1945–1950*; and in the following year R. Palme Dutt in *The Crisis of Britain and the British Empire* provided a Marxist analysis which contained much relevant material but which, while based upon considerable research, was not as tightly organised or structured as the subject demanded. There has been relatively little discussion until the last fifteen years/or so when a new generation of scholars have begun examining once again. There are a number of exceptions to this last statement, of which Gardner, *Sterling–Dollar Diplomacy*, is among the most important.

34. Cairncross, *Years of Recovery*, p. 499. Cairncross added on the following page that while the Labour Government failed to raise productivity levels to those of the most efficient European producers, it was doubtful whether any government effort could have done more: an argument that requires serious debate.

35. Board of Trade, 'General Support of Trade', EC (43) 4, 15 October 1948: CAB 87/63.

36. J. Tomlinson, 'Mr Attlee's Supply-Side Socialism: Survey and Speculations', *Discussion Papers in Economics*, Brunel University, No. 9101, 1992, pp. 22–3. As will be appreciated from the text which follows, my analysis goes back further in time than Dr Tomlinson – with whose general argument I am in agreement, and not least his critique of the volume by S. Blank, *Government and Industry in Britain: The FBI in British Politics, 1945–1965*, London, 1973, to the effect that top managerial levels of British industry were a good deal less co-operative after 1945 than Blank suggests. They were also, in many sectors, uncomprehending.

37. K. Smith, *The British Economic Crisis*, Harmondsworth, 1984; S. Pollard, *The Wasting of the British Economy: British Economic Policy 1945 to the Present*, 2nd edn, London, 1984.

38. For the Fair Trade movement, see B.H. Brown, *The Tariff Reform Movement in Britain, 1881–1895*, New York, 1943; and for the latter, J. Amery, *Joseph Chamberlain and the Tariff Reform Campaign*, London, 1969, as the introduction to a considerable literature.

39. 'The Great Depression [of the 1870s and 1880s] was not great enough to frighten British

industry into really fundamental change': E.J. Hobsbawm, *Industry and Empire*, London, 1968, p. 160, and Ch. 9 for an excellent introduction to the problem of economic conservatism. An early statement of the 'over-commitment' thesis was in D.H. Aldcroft and H.W. Richardson, *The British Economy 1870–1939*, London, 1969, esp. Ch. 5.

40. A.D. Chandler, *Visible Hand: The Managerial Revolution in American Business*, Cambridge, Mass., 1977; idem, 'The Growth of the Transnational Industrial Firm in the United States and the United Kingdom: A Comparative Analysis', *Econ. Hist. Rev.*, Vol. 33, No. 3, August 1980, pp. 396–410. B. Elbaum and W. Lazonick, eds, *The Decline of the British Economy*, Oxford, 1986, provides detailed surveys of the most important sectors of the British economy, with a useful introduction by the editors in Ch. 1.

41. R.C. Floud, 'Britain 1860–1914: A Survey', in R. Floud and D. McCloskey, eds, *The Economic History of Britain since 1700. Vol. 2: 1860 to the 1970s*, Cambridge, 1981, p. 25.

42. Ibid.; Sir Alec Cairncross, 'The Post-War years 1945–1977', p. 375.

43. T. Veblen, *Imperial Germany and the Industrial Revolution*, 1915; 1939 reprint with introduction by Joseph Dorfman, New York, 1939, pp. 130–31.

44. The literature grows apace. Apart from the works already cited there may be noted M.J. Wiener, *English Culture and the Decline of the Industrial Spirit, 1850–1980*, Cambridge, 1981; and a useful symposium, D. Coates and J. Hilliard, eds, *The Economic Decline of Modern Britain: The Debate between Left and Right*, Brighton, 1986.

45. *Report of the Cotton Textile Mission to the United States, March–April 1944*, HMSO, London, 1944. For a commentary on the Platt Report and also that of the *Board of Trade Working Party: Cotton* (1946) see Caroline Miles, *Lancashire Textiles: A Case Study of Industrial Change*, Cambridge, 1968, Ch. 3. L. Rostas contributed a long review article on the Platt Report: 'Productivity of Labour in the Cotton Industry', *Economic Journal*, Vol. 55, June–September 1945, pp. 192–205.

46. Matthew Arnold, *Higher Schools and Universities in Germany*, 2nd edn, London, 1882, pp. 191–2.

47. Some of the older texts of educational history documented the opposition to the schooling of the children of working people with an emphasis that has at times been forgotten in more recent histories. See as an example, Frank Smith, *A History of English Elementary Education, 1760–1902*, London, 1931. Historians from outside Britain have sometimes understood the social dynamics of educational history in more penetrating ways than native writers: an example is the sophisticated work of François Bédarida, *A Social History of England, 1851–1990*, 2nd edn, London, 1991.

48. The many works by Brian Simon provide an introduction; and among recent writing, G.W. Roderick and M.D. Stephens, *Where Did We Go Wrong?: Industrial Performance, Education and the Economy in Victorian Britain*, Brighton, 1981.

49. Over 140 years later *The Economist* carried an article on 'The Machinery of Growth' with the sub-title: 'Innovation is central to economic growth. How does it happen? Why are some companies and countries better at it than others?' The article, published in the issue of 11 January 1992, concluded with two sentences: 'Only that intangible, vital quality, the environment of active brains and productive skills in which companies operate, is non-transferable. To change it, governments need to start at the school gates.'

50. D.L. Burns, *Economic History of Steelmaking*, Cambridge, 1940, p. 6, quoting S. Jordan, *Revue de l'industrie du Fer en 1867*, p.79: 'les maitres de forge ont horreur de la théorie et des théoriciens, et rien ne vaut pour eux que le *practical man*'; the district referred to was South Staffordshire.

51. Margaret 'Espinasse, 'The Rise and Fall of Restoration Science', *Past and Present*, No. 14, November 1958, pp. 71–89, for a discussion of early-eighteenth-century England.

52. A.E. Musson and E. Robinson, 'Science and Industry in the Late 18th Century', *Econ. Hist. Rev.*, Vol. 13, No. 2, December 1960, pp. 222–44.

53. The figures in the text are from Hobsbawm, *Industry and Empire*, pp. 152–3. His Ch. 9 is an excellent summary of the general problems of relative decline before 1914. For an analytical account of the abject failure of the English educational system to provide the necessary training for increasing numbers of scientists and technologists in an ever-changing economy, see Julia Wrigley, 'Technical Education and Industry in the Nineteenth Century', in L. Elbaum and W. Lazonick, eds, *The Decline of the British Economy*, Oxford, 1986, pp. 162–88, together with a comprehensive bibliography.

54. For an introduction, with a useful bibliography, M.H. Best and J. Humphries, 'The City

and Industrial Decline, in Elbaum and Lazonick, eds, *The Decline of the British Economy*, pp. 223–39.

55. There were two main centres of economic teaching at university level in Britain during the 1930s: Cambridge and LSE, and at the latter Lionel Robbins and F. von Hayek were offering versions of neo-classical economics with the market as central. They were bitterly opposed to Keynesian ideas.

56. L. Rostas, *Comparative Productivity in British and American Industry*, Cambridge, 1948, pp. 89–90, for the comparisons between the USA and the UK; and for the figures quoted in the text at the European level, Keith Smith, *The British Economic Crisis*, Ch. 4.

57. For cotton, see note 45, above; and for coal, the Reid Committee Report: *Coal Mining: Report of the Technical Advisory Committee, March 1945*, Cmd. 6610. A. Beacham reviewed this Report at length in *Economic Journal*, Vol. LV, June–September 1945, pp. 206–16.

58. CAB 192/510, 'Machine Tools, 1940–1944' (D. Mack Smith). The report covered nine typed pages.

59. 'During 1942 thirty-two types were rationalised and sixty four stopped altogether': ibid., para. 4.

60. CAB 102/508: W.C. Hornby and Miss J. Embery, 'Machine Tools and Production Programmes, 1936–1945'. W. Hornby later published *Factories and Plant*, HMSO and Longmans, 1958, which further discussed the machine tool industry; and for a detailed survey of the serious problems of British manufacturing industry during the war years, see Correlli Barnett, *The Audit of War: The Illusion and Reality of Britain as a Great Nation*, London, 1986, 'Part 2: Reality – The Industrial Machine', pp. 55–183.

61. CAB 102/85: 'Design and Production of British Tanks' Pts I and II, 1936–June 1940; July 1940–June 1943, by Professor D. Hay. His opening summary, after noting that Britain had originally evolved the idea of a tank, included these comments: 'Yet tactically, technically and quantitatively the British army's armoured forces in 1939 compared unfavourably with those of Germany, although the re-equipment of the Wehrmacht had started, almost from scratch, in 1933' (para. 2).

62. For devastating criticisms along these lines, see the writings of Correlli Barnett, esp. *The Desert Generals*, London, 1960, and *Britain and Her Army, 1509–1970*.

63. CAB 102/85, Hay, para. 17. *The Economist*, 14 December 1946, pp. 942–3, had an informative and highly critical article on the superior achievement of the German tank manufacturers over their British counterparts. It ended: 'The high production [of German tanks] was achieved by the whole industry, and the honours for this must be credited to their organisation, which was able to introduce a progressive system of rationalisation into the factories and to co-ordinate an adequate supply of components, thus providing German troops with first class vehicles in large numbers. Fortunately, it is not by tanks alone that even twentieth century wars are won.'

64. M.M. Postan, D. Hay and J.D. Scott, *Design and Development of Weapons: Studies in Government and Industrial Organisation*, HMSO, London, 1964, p. 366.

65. CAB 102/854/152630. The memorandum was fifteen typed foolscap pages.

66. Quoted in M. Gilbert, *Road to Victory: Winston S. Churchill 1941–1945*, paperback edn, London, 1989, p. 145, note 6.

67. There is a useful, brief account in R.S. Barker, 'Civil Service Attitudes and the Economic Planning of the Attlee Government', *J. Cont. Hist.*, Vol. 21, No. 3, 1986, pp. 473–86. See also Cairncross, *Years of Recovery*, Ch. XI, and the interesting volume of memoirs by Edwin Plowden, *An Industrialist in the Treasury: The Postwar Years*, London, 1989.

68. It was an important move by Cripps that came about in rather peculiar circumstances, following a meeting where Cripps was explaining to Attlee why Ernest Bevin should succeed him as Prime Minister. Harris, *Attlee*, pp. 347–50, tells the accepted story.

69. For which see B. Pimlott, *Hugh Dalton*, paperback edn, London, 1985, Ch. 29.

70. Pollard, *The Wasting of the Economy*, Ch. 4.

71. A. Carew, *Labour Under the Marshall Plan*, Manchester, 1987, Ch. 9, where the author discusses the bias against the labour side in the choice of representative and the consequent bias in the balance of the industrial reports. There is no mention of the Anglo-American Reports in Plowden's memoirs.

72. H. Dalton, *High Tide and After*, p. xii.

73. C.A.R. Crosland, *The Future of Socialism*, rev. edn, London, 1964, p. 31.

74. For a fuller exposition of the Fabian illusions concerning the achievements of the Labour administrations, see Saville, 'Labour and Income Redistribution'; and for a City of London's Radical view of the 1950s, N. Davenport, *The Split Society*, London, 1964. Davenport wrote a financial column for the *New Statesman* in the 1930s.

75. D. Pryce-Jones, 'Towards the Cocktail Party', in M. Sissons and P. French, eds, *The Age of Austerity*, London, 1963, p. 216. The quotations which follow in the text are taken from this essay. There is still research to be done which would examine and analyse the social consciousness of the upper and middle classes in the years of the Labour governments. Peter Fleming, for example, published in 1951 *The Sixth Column*: a story of attempted Soviet subversion of Britain whose central theme, however, was the decline in the spirit of the British people under the post-war Labour administrations: D. Hart-Davis, *Peter Fleming: A Biography*, London, 1974, pp. 327–9.

76. *The Economist*, 1 April 1950, quoting from the ECA Report, *Facts on the British Economy*, 1950.

77. I use the word 'improbable' in the sense defined by G.K. Chesterton: that the 'impossible' can always happen, but the 'improbable' rarely.

78. Smith, *The British Economic Crisis*, is particularly good on the contribution of research and development to economic growth.

79. *Guardian*, 15 October 1966.

80. Recent analyses of the performances of the British economy include William Keegan, *Mrs Thatcher's Economic Experiment*, London, 1985, and the less radical C. Johnson, *The Economy under Mrs Thatcher, 1979–1990*, London, 1991.

5. The British Intervention in Indo-China, 1945

1. There is a large literature on the background to the wars post-1945: J.C. Sterndale Bennett, 'Indo-China', from a set of briefing papers prepared by the Far Eastern Department of the FO: 371/46309/F 8165, 4 October 1945; P. Devillers, *Histoire du Viet-Nam de 1940 à 1952*, Paris, 1952; J. Chesneaux, *Contribution a l'histoire de la nation vietnamienne*, Paris, 1955; J. Buttinger, *Vietnam: A Dragon Embattled*, 2 Vols, London, 1967; L. Allen, *The End of the War in Asia*, London, 1976; A.W. Cameron, ed., *Vietnam Crisis: A documentary History. Vol. 1: 1940–1956*, Ithaca, NY, 1971.

2. For the pre-war political situation in addition to the works cited in note 1, Ellen S. Hammer, *The Struggle for Indo-China*, Stanford, 1954, esp. Chs. 3, 4 and 6; Buttinger, *Vietnam. Vol. 1: From Colonialism to the Vietminh*.

3. The war years are covered in Buttinger, *Vietnam*, Vol. 1; Y. Toru, 'Who Set the Stage for the Cold War in Southeast Asia?', in Y. Nagai and A. Iriye, eds, *The Origins of the Cold War in Asia*, New York, 1977, pp. 321–37; Ralph B. Smith, 'The Japanese Period in Indo-China and the Coup of 9 March 1945', *J. South-East Asian Studies*, Vol. 9, No. 2, September 1978, pp. 268–95. There was some resistance to the Japanese take-over of 9 March, 1945. At Dong San, near Lang Son, a French border post commander refused to surrender, and it took the Japanese three days to capture the fort. All its military and civilian personnel were killed. The question of outside aid, requested by the French of the Combined Chiefs of Staff in Washington, remained a highly controversial issue in the months following. Some help was forthcoming, but it has been debatable whether the quality of the French troops in Indo-China at this time justified extensive assistance, even had it been available. Churchill sent a special message to General Marshall, 19 March 1945, urging any support that was practicable: quoted Gilbert, *Road to Victory*, paperback edn, p. 1254, note 1; and see also C. Cruickshank, *SOE in the Far East*, Oxford, 1983, Part 2, Ch. 4, for a bitter, controversial account of the mistakes he considers were made by the politicians of the Western Allies.

4. Allen, *End of the War in Asia*, Ch. 4; C. Fenn, *Ho Chi Minh: A biographical Introduction*, New York, 1973; J. Lacouture, *Ho Chi Minh*, London, 1969; J. Pluvier, *South-East Asia from Colonialism to Independence*, Oxford, 1974, pp. 288–98, 339–42.

5. K.K. Nitz, 'Japanese Military Policy towards French Indo-China during the Second World War: The Road to the *Meigo Sakusen*, 9 March 1945', *J. South-East Asian Studies*, Vol. 14, No. 2, September 1983, pp. 328–53; idem, 'Independence without Nationalists?: The Japanese

and Vietnamese Nationalism during the Japanese Period, 1940–1945', *J. South-East Asian Studies*, Vol. 15, No. 1, March 1984, pp. 108–33.

6. Larrabee, *Commander-in-Chief*, Ch. 10, 'Le May'. The figure of 130,000 dead is given by Gilbert, *Second World War*, p. 649.

7. The attempted peace negotiations before the Japanese surrender, mentioned in the text, are briefly discussed in the opening paragraphs of Chapter 4 above. For the events of August 1945, see Buttinger, *Vietnam*, Vol. 1, Ch. VI.

8. The full text is in Cameron, ed., *Vietnam Crisis*, pp. 52–5. For discussion of the problems of the textual accuracy of the many English versions, see ibid., p. 52, note.

9. Major-General S. Woodburn Kirby, *The War Against Japan. Vol. V: The Surrender of Japan*, HMSO, London, 1969. The index provides a detailed pagination to the various stages of the planning of Operation Zipper, a large-scale landing on the coast of Malaya. It was never carried through because of the Japanese surrender, and it would, almost certainly, have been a catastrophe had it been launched. Kirby notes that: 'Despite the chaos on the beaches [he refers to a pilot operation after the war had ended] there is little doubt that, had it been necessary to take Malaya by force of arms, Operation Zipper would eventually have achieved its object' (p. 279). From the present writer's personal experience, the operative word in Kirby's sentence is 'eventually'.

10. In French Indo-China Ho Chi Minh joined forces with the American OSS; in Indonesia nationalist leaders collaborated with the Japanese; in Burma, Aung San led the Burmese National Army and changed to the side of the British in March 1945. For Aung San and the political complexities of the various national groups in Burma during the war years, see L. Allen, *Burma: The Longest War*, London, 1984, passim and esp. p. 579 ff for Aung San's change of sides.

11. There are two useful volumes by W.L. Langer and S.E. Gleason: *The Challenge of Isolationism, 1937–40*, New York, 1952, and *The Undeclared War, 1940–1*, New York, 1953. Thomas E. Hachey, ed., *Confidential Despatches: Analyses of America by the British Ambassador 1939–1945*, Evanston, 1974, pp. xvii ff, has a brief account, and see also Nicholas, ed., *Washington Despatches, 1941–1945*, passim.

12. The most substantial analysis of Anglo-American relations in the Far East during the war years is Thorne, *Allies of a Kind*; and see also idem, *The Issue of War: States, Societies, and the Far Eastern Conflict of 1941–1945*, London, 1985. The periodical literature is considerable; some items are cited in the notes which follow.

13. Above, Chapter 1, p. 22.

14. Quoted in Morgan, *FDR. A Biography*, p. 641.

15. *FRUS*, 1944, Vol. V, pp. 1205–6, for a letter from the Director of the Office of European Affairs (John Clement Dunn) to Washington which provides a succinct summary of Roosevelt's views on French Indo-China. *FRUS*, 1945, Vol. VI, pp. 293 ff, includes a number of documents which illustrate the change of attitude after Roosevelt's death. On paper the United States was still offering an equivocal policy: cf. Acheson's extract from a State Department circular of 30 August 1945 which he sent to New Delhi on 5 October 1945: 'US has no thought of opposing the re-establishment of French control in Indo-China and no official statement by US Government has questioned even by implication French sovereignty over Indo-China. However, it is not the policy of this Government to assist the French to re-establish their control over Indo-China by force and the willingness of the US to see French control re-established assumes that French claim to have the support of the population of Indo-China is borne out by future events' (ibid., p. 313). At the time this was sent to the Indian Embassy negotiations were already under way, if not completed, for the use of American ships to carry men and supplies from Europe to Indo-China in support of the French. Among the most interesting secondary literature: Gary R. Hess, 'Franklin Roosevelt and Indochina', *J. American History*, Vol. 59, No. 2, September 1972, pp. 353–68; W. LaFeber, 'Roosevelt, Churchill and Indochina, 1942–45', *American Hist. Rev.*, Vol. 80, 1975, pp. 1277–95; C. Thorne, 'Indochina and Anglo-American Relations, 1942–1945, *Pacific Hist. Rev.*, Vol. 45, February 1976, pp. 73–96; D. Cameron Watt, 'Britain, America and Indo-China, 1942–1945', in *Succeeding John Bull*, Cambridge, 1984, pp. 194–219.

16. Nicholas, ed., *Washington Despatches*, pp. 43–4.

17. Ibid. p. 44. The Sumner Welles Memorial Day speech on 30 May 1942 is discussed in Louis, *Imperialism at Bay*, pp. 154 ff. Welles emphasised the universality of the Atlantic Charter – no doubt in answer to the British gloss upon its limited scope; and he used vivid language to dramatise his theme: 'If this war is in fact a war for the liberation of peoples it must assume the

sovereign equality of peoples throughout the world, as well as the world of Americas. Our victory must bring in its train the liberation of all peoples. Discrimination between peoples because of race and colour must be abolished. The age of imperialism is ended.'

18. CO 835/35/5514, 17 June 1942.

19. G.F. Hudson (1903–1974): archaeologist; prolific writer on Middle East and Far East affairs. Associated with Chatham House and for a time during the war seconded to the Foreign Office. His best known book was probably *The Far East in World Politics: A Study in Recent History*, Oxford, 1937; 2nd edn, 1939.

20. FO 371/35921/F 4646, 28 August, 1943.

21. FO 371/41719/1294, 3 November 1943.

22. Ibid. There are several drafts of the letter in the file. The words quoted in the text are from a carbon copy.

23. When Roosevelt travelled on to Tehran from Cairo, he had a private conversation with Stalin, and he repeated his views including the suggestion that trusteeship should prepare Indo-China for independence within twenty to thirty years: *FRUS. 1943. The Conference at Cairo and Teheran*.

24. Halifax, report to Eden: FO 371/35921, 19 December 1943; the minutes quoted are in FO 371/41723, 2 February 1944.

25. Thorne, *Allies of a Kind*, passim, is always excellent on these matters; and see his article of 1976, cited above, note 15. See also G.C. Herring, 'The Truman Administration and the Restoration of French Sovereignty in Indochina', *Diplomatic History*, Vol. 1. No. 2, Spring 1977, pp. 97–117, for the coverage of American sources.

26. FO 371/41795/F 1040, 27 February 1944.

27. Ibid. In his covering note to Churchill attaching Dening's memorandum, Eden added: 'Mr Dening has had a life-time experience in Far Eastern politics.'

28. The detailed discussions between the United States, Vichy France and the Free French will be found in *FRUS*, 1942, Vol. II, pp. 123–716. There is an account of Roosevelt's general views on French Indo-China at this time in Gary R. Hess, *The United States' Emergence as a Southeast Asian Power, 1940–1950*, New York, 1987, pp. 69–82.

29. Churchill to Eden, 21 May 1944: FO 371/41719/2502. This is a much quoted letter. Churchill went on to comment that one important reason for leaving the whole question in abeyance was that 'we certainly have no plans in prospect for liberating Indo-China.'

30. *FRUS*, 1944, Vol. III, pp. 778–9: reprinted Cameron, ed., *Vietnam Crisis*, pp. 15–17.

31. *FRUS*, 1944, Vol. III, p. 780, 2 November 1944. On 1 January 1945, in a brief minute to the Secretary of State, Roosevelt reaffirmed his position: 'I still do not want to get mixed up in any Indochina decision. It is a matter for post-war. By the same token, I do not want to get mixed up in any military effort toward the liberation of Indo-China from the Japanese. You can tell Halifax that I made this very clear to Mr. Churchill. From both the military and civil point of view, action at this time is premature': *FRUS*, 1945, Vol. VI, p. 293.

32. *FRUS*, 1945, Vol. VI, pp. 295–6. The statement referred to was from the French Embassy in Chungking to the American Embassy. It began: 'The political position taken by the Provisional Government of the French Republic regarding Indo-China is plain. A few sentences will be sufficient to make it clear. First, France cannot admit any discussion about the principle of her establishment in Indochina.' The Brazzaville decisions 30 January–8 February 1944 were agreed under the chairmanship of René Pleven, Commissioner for the Colonies. The conference worked out the principles which were to be followed with regard to the former French colonies: Indo-China was to get 'a satisfactory autonomy within the frame of the French Empire'. For detail on the background to the whole of the war years, see Louis, *Imperialism at Bay*, passim.

33. *FRUS*, 1945, Vol. I, p. 124.

34. A general point made by many historians. There is a helpful summary in Hess, *The United States' Emergence as a Southeast Asian Power*, Chs 2–5.

35. *FRUS*, 1945, Vol. VI, p. 300, 13 March 1945. De Gaulle's remarks to the American Ambassador (Caffery) were quite extraordinary. The context was the aftermath of the take-over on 9 March of the whole of Indo-China by the Japanese; and de Gaulle appears in this conversation to be verging on the hysterical, or putting on a deliberate act to that effect.

36. Thorne, 'Indo-China and Anglo-American Relations', p. 87.

37. FO 371/41719/F 3948, 16 August 1944.

38. FO 371/41719/F 4028, 24 August 1944.

39. FO 371/41720/4348, para. 14. This was a printed memorandum, signed A.E., not dated; the FO date on the file was 19 September 1944.

40. Duff Cooper to Eden, FO 371/46305/F 1533, 13 March 1945.

41. FO 371/46306/F 2439, 11 April 1945.

42. A policy document from the US Department of State provided a detailed estimate of post-war conditions in the Far East: *FRUS*, 1945, Vol. VI, 22 June 1945, pp. 556–81. The French Indo-China section, pp. 567–8, quoted as the epigraph to this chapter, emphasised that the 'Chief French reliance, however, will continue to be placed upon the United Kingdom, which is almost as anxious as the French to see that no pre-war colonial power suffers diminution of power or prestige.'

43. F.S.V. Donnison, *British Military Administration in the Far East, 1943–46*, HMSO, London, 1956, Ch. XXI, pp. 405 ff.

44. Ibid. pp. 405–6.

45. Mountbatten's directives from London, and the complex situation to which they were to be applied, are discussed in all historical accounts of this period. The most helpful are Thorne, *Allies of a Kind*, Chs 31 and 32; Hess, *The United States' Emergence as a Southeast Asian Power*, Ch. 6; P. Dennis, *Troubled Days of Peace: Mountbatten and South East Asia Command, 1945–46*, Manchester, 1987, Chs 1–3.

46. FO 371/41746/F 5802, 11 December 1944, Nine months later Dening wrote to Sterndale Bennett (FO 371/46353/F 9305, 5 October 1945): 'The independence movements in Asia must be treated with sympathy and understanding. Otherwise they will become really serious. As I have indicated, they are half-baked and treated in the proper way then they should not be very terrifying. But treated the wrong way they may well, in the end, spell the end of Europe in Asia. I think we should be leaders in handling the situation in the right way. After all, it is our forces who are liberating these areas and it is the British taxpayer who is paying. Let us therefore stand no nonsense from the Dutch or the French. In the end they may well have cause to be grateful to us – though gratitude is not a very marked feature of international relations.' Dening was obviously a complex character from the evidence of his reports to London, and he found it difficult, especially after the war ended, to accept the policies of many of the military. His relations with Mountbatten steadily worsened, for which see a remarkably vitriolic letter about Mountbatten and SEAC headquarters: FO 800/461, 29 January 1946. Dennis, *Troubled Days of Peace*, pp. 180–88, discusses some of the problems of the growing tension between Mountbatten and Dening.

47. FO 371/46309/F 8661, 20 October 1945.

48. J.J. Lawson, Secretary for War in the new Attlee Government, visited the Far East during September and October 1945, and was in conference in Singapore with Mountbatten, Slim, Gracey and other senior officials and military at the end of September.

49. FO 371/46309/F 8661, 20 October 1945. In the same file as the letter from Slim, there was a report, dated 14 October, by the Joint Planning Staff which simply reaffirmed the original, and quite unworkable, directives that British responsibility should be limited to holding a few key areas until both Dutch and French forces arrive in sufficient number.

50. Kirby, *The War Against Japan*, Vol. V, pp. 297 ff.

51. The senior French military in Indo-China thought highly of Gracey: not an approval which over time has become commendable. The relationship between Leclerc and Gracey was especially cordial: A. Dansette in his biography of Leclerc described it as 'La bonne entente', (*Leclerc*, Paris, 1952, p. 190). In 1953 the Royal Central Asian Society heard a lecture on the contemporary situation in Vietnam, and Gracey made an interesting intervention. He began: 'I hope that this excellent address today has told those who were doubtful about it what a magnificent job of work the French are doing in this almost impossible situation. . . . I went out there after the war and saw the French after they had been through a most uncomfortable time with the Japanese . . . their resistance movement was excellent. . . . I was welcomed on arrival by the Viet Minh, who said "Welcome" and all that sort of thing. It was a very unpleasant situation, and I promptly kicked them out. They are obviously Communists.' *J. Royal Central Asian Society*, Vol. 40, July–October 1953, pp. 213–14. For a favourable appraisal, D.J. Duncanson, 'General Gracey and the Viet Minh', ibid. Vol. 55, 1968, pp. 288–97; and the same author's *Government and Revolution in Vietnam*, Oxford for Chatham House, 1968.

52. Hammer, *The Struggle for Indo-China*, argues this case strongly, pp. 115–16; and see also Dennis, *Troubled Days of Peace*, Chs 2, 3 and 8.

53. For the Trotskyist movement see Milton Sachs, 'Marxism in Vietnam', in F.N. Trager, ed., *Marxism in South-East Asia: A Study in Four Countries*, Stanford, 1959, pp. 102–70. Ta Thu Than, the most prominent leader of the Vietnamese Trotskyists, was killed by the Viet Minh in the autumn of 1945.

54. For a brief summary of Cao Dai and Hoa Hao see J.S. Olson, ed., *Dictionary of the Vietnam War*, New York, 1988. Both had private armies. At the end of the war Hoa Hao was the only movement in the south to rival the Viet Minh.

55. FO 371/46309/F 8120, 16 October, para 15. H.N. Brain's memorandum was written on 27 September 1945.

56. Kirby, *The War Against Japan*, Vol. V, pp. 298 ff; Dennis, *Troubled Days of Peace*, pp. 37 ff.

57. Donnison, *British Military Administration*, pp. 407–8.

58. Mountbatten, *Post-Surrender Tasks: Section E of the Report to the Combined Chiefs of Staff by the Supreme Allied Commander, South East Asia, 1943–1945*, HMSO, London, 1969, para. 26: reprinted Cameron, ed., *Vietnam Crisis*, pp. 58–9.

59. For example by Dennis, *Troubled Days of Peace*, p. 47.

60. Harold Isaacs, *No Peace for Asia*, New York, 1947; reprinted with new introduction, 1967, p. 153.

61. Mountbatten, *Post-Surrender Tasks: Section E of the Report*, para. 31.

62. CAB 122/512/SEACOS 500, 2 October 1945; also in FO 371/46309/F 7789.

63. Isaacs, *No Peace for Asia*, p. 159.

64. Kirby, *War Against Japan*, Vol. V, pp. 304–6, for the details of the withdrawal order of British troops.

65. FO 371/46310/F 11815, 17 December 1945. The father of this young man also sent extracts from a letter received from his son to the Foreign Office: FO 371/46310/F 11326, 8 December 1945. Both letters from Saigon were written on the same date, 18 November, 1945.

66. Philip John Noel-Baker, (1889–1982), born into a Quaker family. Educated Bootham School and Kings College, Cambridge. Served in Friends' Ambulance Unit during First World War. Fervently anti-war during the 1930s, and wrote a much-publicised book, *The Private Manufacture of Armaments. Vol. 1: 1936*. Minister of State, Foreign Office 1945–46. Awarded Nobel Peace Prize, 1959. Created Life Peer, 1977.

67. FO 371/46310/F 11815.

68. The story has been told in all the histories already cited. George Rosie, *The British in Vietnam*, London, 1970, is an excellent but neglected text of competent investigative journalism; written before the public records were available. One of the most useful pieces of research Mr Rosie undertook was a close reading of the official histories of many of the individual regiments which took part in the Vietnam intervention, and they proved most revealing.

69. The argument that the Japanese were largely responsible for the nationalist movement is to be found in many of the Foreign Office papers of this period, both during the closing months of the war and in the period which followed. It was not a unanimous view. See, for example, an interesting memorandum 'Report on Political and Economic Conditions in Saigon Region' which offered a very down to earth analysis; highly critical of the French and sensible about the Annamite leadership, as they were still referred to. The authorship of this report is not clear but it reads like Brain, Gracey's political adviser, and it was written around the second week in October 1945: FO 371/46309/F 8953. An important analysis of Vietnamese nationalism during the months between the 9 March 1945 take-over by the Japanese and their surrender in August is in Vu Ngu Chieu 'The Other Side of the 1945 Vietnamese Revolution: The Empire of Vietnam, March–August 1945', *J. Asian Studies*, Vol. 45, No. 2, February 1986, pp. 293–328; and see references cited in note 5 above.

70. Bisheshwar Prasad (General Editor), *Official History of the Indian Armed Forces in the Second World War. Post-War Occupation Forces. Japan and South-East Asia*, Combined Inter-Services Historical Section, India and Pakistan, New Delhi, 1958, pp. 204–5. As my text makes clear, the use of Japanese troops was unknown, or virtually unknown, in Britain at the time they were being used; yet in Saigon the daily newspaper for the armed services was publishing the facts. The *Times of Saigon* was a daily two-sided foolscap sheet, duplicated, and edited and published by the Psychological Warfare section, SACSEA Commission, Saigon. The file in FO 959/4 begins with

No. 25, 10 October 1945. No. 38, 23 October 1945, carried a report of an official communiqué which included the news that 'Japanese troops supported by armoured cars manned by troops of the 16th Cavalry extended the perimeter west of Cholon against slight opposition...', and there were regular references in most of the official statements to the activities of the Japanese. It was noted in the issue of 7 November that twenty Japanese aircraft were taken over by the RAF in Saigon and put into use: 'All Jap flyers "vetted" by RAF before they became operational'; and it was from this communiqué that Harold Isaacs obtained the information on the mileage etc. flown by the Japanese quoted above in my text, (pp. 196–7).

71. B.R. Mullaly, *Bugle and Kukri: The Story of the 10th Princess Mary's own Gurkha Rifles*, 1957, quoted in G. Rosie, *The British in Vietnam*, London, 1970, p. 93.

72. W.O. 172/1789/SACSEA War Diary, 25–31 October 1945. Operational Summary (up to 22.00 hours 29 October 1945). The interesting inclusion, of course, is the figures for the Japanese. The Table was headed: 'Total casualties . . . by British forces . . . '.

73. Kirby, *The War Against Japan*, Vol. V, p. 304.

74. Prasad, ed., *Official History of the Indian Armed Forces*, p. 199.

75. Gracey to Leclerc, 12 December 1945: Gracey Papers, 40, King's College, London, quoted in Dennis, *Troubled Days of Peace*, p. 177. Gracey's protest was sharp, and in the accepted tradition of Indian Army officers. It spoke of 'The camaraderie which exists between Officers of the Indian Army and their Gurkha and Indian soldiers. . . . Our men, of whatever colour, are our friends, and must not be considered "black" men'.

76. Isaacs, *No Peace for Asia*, p. 158. *Newsweek* published short notes on Indo-China and the military intervention from 3 September 1945. The first article which by-lined Isaacs seems to have been in the issue of 26 November. In March 1946 *Harper's Magazine* published Isaacs with the heading: 'Peace comes to Saigon', and in which Isaacs summed up his experiences: 'With the war's end came the rising of the Annamites which in the south the French could counter only by the grace of Britain and by the extensive use of Japanese troops against the insurgents.'

77. On 11 October Sir T. Moore asked the Prime Minister what principles were being followed by Allied Commanders in respect of Japanese assistance, and Attlee gave the blandest of replies; to which Moore replied: 'How can the Rt. Hon Gentleman reconcile that reply with the Press reports one constantly sees to the effect the Allied commanders are using Japanese troops to administer liberated territory, which apparently they do with arrogance?' *Hansard*, Vol. 414, 11 October 1945, Cols 397–8.

78. Dange's report appeared in the Bombay *People's War*, the communist weekly, on 7 October 1945. In the same issue Mohan Kumaramangalam, former president of the Cambridge Union, and now one of the youngest members of the Central Committee of the CPI, quoted the *Times of India* of 23 September 1945 whose correspondent in Vietnam had reported armed Japanese patrols patrolling the streets of Saigon alongside Indian soldiers. For Kumaramangalam, see *Dictionary of Labour Biography*, Vol. V, 1979, pp. 132–4.

79. It must be emphasised that Tom Driberg remained much more aware of what was happening in Vietnam than most of the backbenchers in the House of Commons. He was acutely conscious of the corrupt nature of the regime in Saigon, and his writings in *Reynold's News* were forthright in their condemnation of the British support for the restoration of French imperialism. In the same paper on 18 November 1945 Harold Laski condemned the British intervention in Indo-China and Indonesia in the most vigorous terms. It is still fair to comment, as my text does, that Indo-China made almost no impression on the organised labour movement in Britain. Driberg throughout was the most consistent. On 28 January 1946 he asked Noel-Baker about the British withdrawal (*Hansard*, Vol. 418, Cols 526–7). The latter, in part of his reply, gave the small totals of British and Indians killed, and added that while there were no accurate figures for the 'Annamites and Tonkinites' the estimate was about 2,700. Noel-Baker also repeated the usual official statement that 'British troops . . . have been engaged on a purely military task, and their presence has had nothing to do with the political or constitutional problems of the country.'

80. This statement by Bevin was in the form of a written answer to a question: *Hansard*, Vol. 414, 24 October 1945, Cols 2149–50: reprinted in Cameron, ed., *Vietnam Crisis*, pp. 65–6. The statement by Attlee, referred to by Bevin, was in the same *Hansard* volume, 17 October, Col. 115.

81. FO 371/46415/F 9628. Cabinet 2nd Revise. Far Eastern Civil Planning Unit. British Strategic Interests in the Far East, 1 November 1945.

Appendix 2

1. C. Streit, *Keine Kamaraden: Die Wehrmacht und die sowjetischen Kriegsgefangenen*, Stuttgart, 1978.
2. A. Mayer, *Why Did the Heavens Not Darken?*, London, 1990.
3. Ibid., pp. 272–3.
4. E. Nolte, *Der Faschismus in seiner Epoche*, Munich, 1965.
5. Totowa, NJ, 1985.
6. *Annals: The Soviet Union since World War II*, ed. P. Moseley.
7. Ibid., p. 53.
8. 'World War II and Soviet Economic Growth, 1945–1953', in Linz, ed., *The Impact of World War II on the Soviet Union*, pp. 24–5.
9. H. Salisbury, *The 900 Days: The Siege of Leningrad*, new edn, London, 1986, p. 517.
10. S. Fitzpatrick, 'Post-War Soviet Society', in Linz, ed., *The Impact of World War II on the Soviet Union*, pp. 130–32.
11. Syracuse, 1947.
12. 'Stalin's Postwar Army Reappraised', *International Security*, Vol. 7, No. 3, 1982–83, pp. 110–38.
13. Ibid., p. 120.

Appendix 3

1. FO 371/47885/ N 4847, 3 May 1945. The first discussion of the Committee was in mid 1944: FO 371/43375 and 43376.
2. Geoffrey Masterman Wilson: born 1910; educated Manchester Grammar School and Oriel College, Oxford. Called to the Bar, 1934. After leaving the Foreign Office in 1945 Wilson held a number of important positions in Whitehall and in the international community. He ended his career as a civil servant as chairman of the Race Relations Board, 1971–77. Created KCB 1969.
3. FO 371/47885/ N 4847, 4 May 1945.
4. FO 371/47886/ N 9100, 3 August 1945. Brimelow wrote: 'It is annoying that Lord Cherwell succeeded in wrecking our plans for having this subject mentioned at Terminal.'
5. The reports of the three sub-committees are in several files, but are all brought together in FO 371/47884/ N 4470, 23 April 1945.
6. FO 371/47884/ N 4554.
7. The Wilson minute, 21 September 1944, reporting his interview with D.N. Pritt, is in FO 371/43376/ N 5664; and Hill's suggested list of organisations, including the SCR, was in a memorandum he sent to Orme Sargent: FO 371/47884/ N 3052, dated 6 March 1945.
8. For insight into the kind of person Christopher Hill was, and is, see the reminiscences which provide the foreword to the festschrift in his honour: D. Pennington and K. Thomas, eds, *Puritans and Revolutionaries: Essays in Seventeenth-Century History presented to Christopher Hill*, Oxford, 1978.
9. It is improbable that Hill was not vetted before he received his commission. His political views were easily ascertained. He had been to Russia for a year in the mid 1930s, and in 1940 he edited a book of three essays on the English Revolution of 1640 (with that title) including one of his own essays which immediately became well-known. The publishers were the communist publishing house, Lawrence & Wishart.
10. FO 371/47884/ N 4654, Minute 19.
11. This was an important matter which does not seem to have been resolved, certainly not before Hill resigned from the Foreign Office. C.F.A. Warner, the head of the Northern Department, warned very early against any assumption that unlimited government funds would be available: FO 371/43375, 5 June 1944. Hill was a firm advocate of financial arrangements independent of the Government: FO 371/47885/ letter of 13 June 1945 to Edward Carter, librarian of the RIBA, who had just become chairman of a newly established committee. The last

references to Hill before he returned to Oxford University are in FO 371/47886/ N 8304 to N 10220.

Appendix 4

1. P.J. Noel-Baker became Minister of State at the Foreign Office in Attlee's first round of appointments. He was a League of Nations man, and occupied a centrist position within the Labour Party leadership. Bevin did not like him and Noel-Baker had almost no influence within the Foreign Office. He was replaced by the more acceptable Hector McNeil in October 1946.

2. *Labour Party. 1946 Conference Report*, p.157.

3. Ibid. p. 167. There is a longer version of this quotation in the text, Chapter 2, p. 100.

4. Bullock, *Ernest Bevin*, Vol. 1, pp. 133–42; idem, Vol. 3, p. 105. The story continues to run. Cf. Denis Healey in 1989: 'Yet it was not anti-Communism that made him [Bevin] oppose Soviet policy: indeed, as a young man he had led a dockers' strike against the loading of supplies for the British forces of intervention against the Bolsheviks': *The Independent Magazine*, 7 October 1989.

5. M. Philips Price, *Manchester Guardian* correspondent in Russia 1917–18, published a sixteen-page pamphlet in August 1918: *The Truth About Allied Intervention in Russia*, reprinted Great Malvern, Worcester, 1985. The literature on intervention is wide-ranging; it includes Vol. 1 of Louis Fischer, *The Soviets in World Affairs, 1917–1924*, London, 1930; S.R. Graubard, *British Labour and the Russian Revolution*, Cambridge, Mass., 1956; R. Ullman, *Anglo-Soviet Relations 1917–1921*, esp. Vol. 1, Princeton, 1961; S. White, *Britain and the Bolshevik Revolution*, London, 1979.

6. H.B. Lees-Smith (1878–1941), *Dictionary of Labour Biography*, Vol. 9, pp. 175–81.

7. Tania Rose, 'Philips Price and the Russian Revolution', Ph.D., University of Hull, 1988.

8. Among the sources for the original formation of the Hands Off Russia committee in January 1918: H. Pollitt, *Serving My Time*, London, 1941, Ch. VI, 'London and the Russian Revolution'; W.P. and Z. Coates, *A History of Anglo-Soviet Relations*, pp. 135 ff; Graubard, *British Labour and the Russian Revolution*, Chs IV and V. This last volume is especially useful for the year 1919 and not least for its detailed coverage of the *Daily Herald*.

9. Running through this agitation in 1919 and 1920, until the armistice of the autumn of 1920 between the Russians and the Poles, was the much debated question of industrial action. As the text of this Appendix makes clear, even the extreme right wing of the labour movement agreed to the wording of the resolutions of this period, but there was never the intention on the part of J.H. Thomas and his like-minded colleagues of accepting the practice of strike activity to achieve the political ends they were formally supporting. Such an acceptance would have been wholly contrary to their understanding of British constitutional principles. For a helpful discussion of the contemporary situation, and the attitudes of various leading personalities, see L.J. Macfarlane, 'Hands Off Russia: British Labour and the Russo-Polish War, 1920', *Past and Present*, No. 38, December 1967, pp. 126–52.

10. For the 1920 delegation to Russia, see *Dictionary of Labour Biography*, Vol. 8, pp. 257–61.

11. Graubard, *British Labour and the Russian Revolution*, pp. 88–9

12. Pollitt, *Serving My Time*, p. 118.

13. The complete list of the members of the Hands Off Russia national committee was published on the front page of the *Labour Leader*, 20 May 1920; and reprinted in *DLB*, Vol. 9, p. 106.

14. There were two interim reports from the Labour delegation to Russia, both published in early July. The first, issued very soon after the delegation arrived back in Britain, called for the immediate ending of military intervention; and the second was an appeal for an immediate peace and a freeing of trade in order to alleviate the enormous privations of the Russian people. The full *Report*, edited by L. Haden Guest, was issued late in July 1920.

15. The exact date seems uncertain. It was either 4 or 5 August. G.D.H. Cole, *A History of the Labour Party from 1914*, p. 105, gives 4 August 1920.

16. Bullock, *Ernest Bevin*, Vol. 1, Ch. 6.

17. Williams, *Ernest Bevin*, p. 88.

18. *Daily Herald* and *The Times*, 14 August 1920. The background to these decisions of August

1920 has been explained in Coates' and Graubard's works, and Macfarlane's article – already noted above; a further account is Stephen White, 'Labour's Council of Action, 1920', *J. Cont. Hist.*, Vol. 9, No. 4, October 1974, pp. 99–122, with the argument summarised in *Britain and the Bolshevik Revolution*, London, 1979, pp. 30–51. White's summary of events is mostly accurate, but his main contention is to play down the extent of *political* opposition to the war of intervention, and to emphasise the general anti-war sentiment of war-weariness. This down-beat approach is a corrective to certain of the more triumphalist accounts which exaggerate the extent of revolutionary consciousness, but it also reduces the significance of what was happening. It is always necessary to distinguish as precisely as possible the political consciousness of the militants as compared with the ordinary working people, but especially for the year 1919 it is important not to underestimate the potential for change among the masses. In particular White gives much too little attention to the role of the *Daily Herald*, and while he recognises the importance of the Delegation to Russia in 1920, he does not relate it to the political movement against intervention which culminated in the August 1920 decisions. This approach has been followed by James Hinton, *Protests and Visions: Peace Politics and Twentieth-Century Britain*, London, 1989, pp. 82–5.

Appendix 5

1. D. Healey, *The Time of My Life*, London, 1989, p.74. Gillies deserves more attention than he has so far received. There is material for the war years in A. Glees, *Exile Politics during the Second World War*, Oxford, 1982.

2. Healey, *The Time of My Life*, p. 107.

3. *Labour Party. 1946 Conference Report.* The foreign affairs debate, opened by Noel-Baker and summed up by Bevin, is between pp. 148–69. Bevin had begun to move some of the worst appointments, such as Lord Killearn from Cairo, in the early months of 1946.

4. Bevin papers, FO 800/463.

5. FO 371/50912, reprinted as Document 39 in Ross, *The Foreign Office and the Kremlin*, pp. 210–17.

6. FO 371/67587 C/ UN 2622.

7. FO 800/493.

8. International Department, Labour Party Archives, Box 11. C. Anstey, 'The Projection of British Socialism: Foreign Office Publicity and American Opinion, 1945–50', *J. Cont. Hist.*, Vol. 19, No. 3, 1984, pp. 417–51, has misunderstood the sequence of events and Jebb did not contribute to *Cards on the Table*. This misunderstanding does not detract from her excellent article.

9. FO 371/67587 C/ UN 2622, 9 May 1947.

10. Bullock, *Ernest Bevin*, Vol. 3, p. 397.

11. Ibid., p. 398.

12. *The Political Diary of Hugh Dalton, 1918–1940, 1945–1960*, ed. B. Pimlott, 1986, p. 393.

13. B. Reed and G. Williams, *Denis Healey and the Politics of Power*, London, 1971, pp. 60 ff. The minutes of the National Executive Committee for 27 May 1947 report that the meeting of the NEC was convened only for the purpose of considering the procedure for the statement to be made to the Conference about *Cards on the Table*.

The meeting lasted two hours, and the resolution naming Dalton to make the agreed statement was passed by twelve votes to five. No names were recorded nor were the arguments summarised. Among those present were Harold Laski, Nye Bevan, Shinwell and Mrs Braddock. There was a further development. On 28 May a meeting of the newly elected NEC considered a news item published in the London *Evening News* of 27 May which purported to give the names of four members who were opposed to the views expressed in *Cards on the Table*. The secretary was asked to make enquiries and report to the next meeting of the NEC. This was held on 25 June and Morgan Phillips said that he had interviewed a number of persons – no names were given – and he gave the possible source of the newspaper report. It was agreed that no further action should be taken. NEC minutes, Labour Party Archives, Manchester.

14. Healey, *The Time of My Life*, p. 106.

15. Ibid. p. 101.

16. Lockhart, *Diaries*, Vol. 2, entry for 5 June 1947, p. 611.

Bibliography

1. A Note on Manuscript Sources

The most important repository of source materials for the study of British government, and its foreign policy, is the Public Record Office, Kew, London. The PRO have produced useful leaflets which list for the Cabinet and the main departments of State the ways in which the collections have been catalogued; and these guides are the starting point for research. There are still quite a large number of files that remain closed, in spite of the thirty-year rule, but the remaining documentation is enormous. For the post-war years the Cabinet minutes are in CAB 128, and Cabinet papers in CAB 129. The Prime Minister's Office is in PREM 8 (correspondence and papers, 1945–51); general political correspondence of the Foreign Office is in FO 371, under country and subject heading; and the important Bevin papers are in FO 800/435–513. The publication of government documents, mostly relating to foreign affairs, has proceeded slowly; a list to 1992 is given below in section 2.

Beyond the PRO are collections of the private papers of politicians and other public personalities, and these, together with the papers of relevant organisations, are to be found scattered round the United Kingdom. There is additional Attlee material, for example, in the Bodleian Library, Oxford, and there are also further Attlee and Bevin papers in Churchill College, Cambridge. Most published biographies provide lists of relevant private papers and their location; and among the most useful, which together cover the subject matter of the present volume, are A. Bullock's *Ernest Bevin*, Vol. 3, London, 1983, pp. 858–9; B. Pimlott's *Hugh Dalton*, paperback, London, 1985, pp. 717–19; and K.O. Morgan's *Labour in Power 1945–1951*, London, 1984, pp. 515 ff.

The location of the official papers of organisations will normally also be given, with the TUC archives at the Modern Record Centre, University of Warwick, and the Labour Party archives at the National Museum of Labour History, Manchester, among the most important.

2. Printed and Official Documents

Coal Mining. Report of the Technical Advisory Committee, March 1945, Cmd. 6610
Report of the Cotton Textile Mission to the United States, March–April 1944, HMSO, London, 1944

Board of Trade Working Party: Cotton, 1946

E C A Report. Facts on the British Economy, 1950

Documents on British Policy Overseas, Series 1, 1945–1950, HMSO, London
   Vol. I: *The Conference at Potsdam, July–August 1945*
   Vol. II: *Conferences and Conversations 1945: London, Washington and Moscow*
   Vol. III: *Britain and America: Negotiations of the United States Loan, August–December 1945*
   Vol. IV: *Britain and America: Atomic Energy, Bases and Food, December 1945–July 1946*
   Vol. V: *Germany and Western Europe, August–December 1945*
   Vol. VI: *Eastern Europe, 1945–1946*

Foreign Relations of the United States (annual in many volumes)

Mountbatten, Earl, *Report to the Combined Chiefs of Staff by the Supreme Allied Commander, South East Asia 1943–1945*, HMSO, London 1951

Mountbatten, Earl, *Post-Surrender Tasks: Section E of the Report to the Combined Chiefs of Staff by the Supreme Allied Commander, South East Asia 1943–1945*, HMSO, London, 1969

Ross, G., ed., *The Foreign Office and the Kremlin: British Documents on Anglo-Soviet Relations, 1941–1945* (with Introduction), Cambridge, 1984

Statistical Material Presented during the Washington Negotiations. Cmd. 6707, December 1945

3. Works of Reference

Annual Bibliography of British and Irish History, Royal Historical Society
Annual Register
Dictionary of American Biography, with *Supplements*
Dictionary of Labour Biography
Dictionary of Marxist Thought, ed. T. Bottomore, Blackwell, Oxford 1983
Dictionary of National Biography
Dictionary of Twentieth-Century History, 1914–1990, ed. P. Teed, Oxford, 1992
The Foreign Office List and Diplomatic and Consular Year Book (annual)
Hansard's Parliamentary Debates
Keesings Contemporary Archives
Labour Party. Annual Conference Reports
The Times House of Commons Guide 1945
Trades Union Congress. Annual Conference Reports
United States in the World Economy, Washington 1943; reprinted HMSO, London, 1944

4. Secondary Sources

(i) Books

Acheson, D., *Sketches from Life, of Men I Have Known*, London, 1961
Acheson, D., *Present at the Creation: My Years in the State Department*, London, 1970
Addison, P., *The Road to 1945: British Politics and the Second World War*, London, 1975

Alexander, G.M., *The Prelude to the Truman Doctrine: British Policy in Greece 1944–1947*, Oxford, 1982

Allen, L., *The End of the War in Asia*, London, 1976

Alperovitz, G., *Atomic Diplomacy: Hiroshima and Potsdam. The Use of the Atomic Bomb and the American Confrontation with Soviet Power*, London, 1966

Anderson, T.H., *The United States, Great Britain and the Cold War, 1944–1947*, London 1981

Andrew, C. and Dilks, D., eds, *The Missing Dimension: Governments and Intelligence Communities in the Twentieth Century*, London, 1984

Attlee, C.R., *The Labour Party in Perspective*, London, 1937

Bailey, V., ed., *Forged in Fire: The History of the Fire Brigades Union*, London, 1992

Balfour, M., *Propaganda in War, 1939–1945*, London, 1979

Barclay, Sir R., *Ernest Bevin and the Foreign Office, 1932–1969*, privately printed, London, 1975

Barker, E., *The British between the Superpowers, 1945–1950*, Toronto, 1983

Barnett, C., *Britain and Her Army, 1509–1970*, London, 1970

Barnett, C., *The Collapse of British Power*, London, 1972; reprinted Gloucester, 1984

Barnett, C., *The Audit of War. The Illusion and Reality of Britain as a Great Nation*, London, 1986

Bartov, O., *The Eastern Front, 1941–5: German Troops and the Barbarisation of Warfare*, London, 1986

Baylis, J., *Anglo-American Defence Relations, 1939–1980: The Special Relationship*, London, 1981

Berle, B.B. and Jacobs, T.B., eds. *Migrating the Rapids 1918–71: From the Papers of Adolf A. Berle*, New York, 1973

Block, F.L., *The Origins of International Economic Disorder: A Study of United States International Monetary Policy from World War II to the Present*, Berkeley, 1977

Blum, J., ed., *The Price of Vision: The Diary of Henry A. Wallace, 1942–1946*, Boston, 1973

Bohlen, C.E., *Witness to History, 1929–1969*, New York, 1973

Bond, B., *British Military Policy between the Two World Wars*, Oxford, 1980

Briggs, A. and Saville, J., eds, *Essays in Labour History, 1918–1939*, London, 1977

Bryant, A., *Triumph in the West, 1943–1946: Based on the Diaries and Autobiographical Notes of Field Marshal the Viscount Alanbrooke*, London, 1959

Bullock, A., *The Life and Times of Ernest Bevin. Vol. 1: Trade Union Leader, 1881–1940*, London, 1960

Bullock, A., *The Life and Times of Ernest Bevin. Vol. 2: Minister of Labour, 1940–1945*, London, 1967

Bullock, A., *Ernest Bevin. Foreign Secretary, 1945–1951*, London, 1983

Burnham, P., *The Political Economy of Post-War Reconstruction*, London, 1990

Burridge, T., *British Labour and Hitler's War*, London, 1976

Burridge, T., *Clement Attlee: A Political Biography*, London, 1985

Buttinger, J., *Vietnam: A Dragon Embattled*, 2 vols, London, 1967

Byrnes, J.F., *Speaking Frankly*, New York, 1947

Byrnes, J.F., *All in One Lifetime*, New York, 1958

Cadogan, Sir A., *The Diaries of Sir Alexander Cadogan, 1938–1945*, ed. D. Dilks, London, 1971

Cairncross, A., *Years of Recovery: British Economic Policy, 1945–51*, London, 1985

Calhoun, D.F., *The United Front: The TUC and the Russians, 1923–1928*, Cambridge, 1976

Callahan, R.A., *Churchill: Retreat from Empire*, Wilmington, Del., 1984

Calleo, D.P. and Rowland, B.M., *America and the World Political Economy: Atlantic Dreams and National Realities*, Bloomington, 1973

Calvocoressi, P. and Wint, G., *Total War: Causes and Courses of the Second World War*, London, 1972

Cameron, A.W., ed., *Vietnam Crisis: A Documentary History. Vol. 1: 1940–1956*, Ithaca, NY, 1971

Campbell, T.M., and Herring, G.C., eds., *The Diaries of Edward R. Stettinius Jnr. 1943–1946*, New York, 1975

Carr, E.H., *Conditions of Peace*, London, 1942

Carr, E.H., *What is History?*, London, 1964

Carr, R., *Spain, 1808–1975*, 2nd edn, Oxford, 1982

Caute, D., *The Great Fear: The Anti-Communist Purge under Truman and Eisenhower*, New York, 1978

Caves, R.E. and Krause, L.B., eds, *Britain's Economic Peformance*, Brookings Institute, Washington, 1980

Cerny, P.G., *The Politics of Grandeur: Ideological Aspects of de Gaulle's Foreign Policy*, Cambridge, 1980

Chandler, A.D., *Visible Hand: The Managerial Revolution in American Business*, Cambridge, Mass., 1977

Charlton, M., *The Price of Victory*, London, 1983

Chesneaux, J., *Contribution à l'histoire de la nation vietnamienne*, Paris, 1955

Citrine, Walter (Lord), *Men and Work: An Autobiography*, London, 1964

Citrine, Walter (Lord), *Two Careers*, London, 1967

Clarke, Sir Richard, *Anglo-American Economic Collaboration in War and Peace, 1942–1949*, ed. A. Cairncross, Oxford, 1982

Coates, D. and Hilliard, J., eds, *The Economic Decline of Modern Britain: The Debate between Left and Right*, Brighton, 1986

Coates, W.P. and Z., *A History of Anglo-Soviet Relations*, London, 1944

Cole, G.D.H., *A History of the Labour Party from 1914*, London, 1948

Colville, J., *The Fringes of Power: Downing Street Diaries. Vol. 1: 1939–October 1941*, paperback edn, London, 1986

Colville, J., *The Fringes of Power: Downing Street Diaries. Vol 2: 1941–April 1955*, paperback edn, London, 1986

Cooper, Diana, *Trumpets from the Steep*, one vol. edn, London, 1979

Cooper, Duff, *Old Men Forget*, London, 1953

Cooper, R.W., *The Nuremberg Trial*, London, 1947

Crockatt, R. and Smith, S., eds, *The Cold War, Past and Present*, London, 1987

Cruickshank, C., *SOE in the Far East*, Oxford, 1983

Dallek, R., *Franklin Roosevelt and American Foreign Policy*, Oxford, 1979

Dalton, H., *The Fateful Years: Memoirs 1931–1945*, London, 1957

Dalton, H., *High Tide and After: Memoirs 1945–1960*, London, 1962

Dalton, H., *The Second World War Diary of Hugh Dalton, 1940–1945*, ed. B. Pimlott, London, 1986

Dalton, H., *The Political Diary of Hugh Dalton, 1918–1940, 1945–1960*, ed. B. Pimlott, London, 1986

Dansette, A., *Leclerc*, Paris, 1952

Darby, P., *British Defence Policy East of Suez, 1947–1968*, Oxford, 1973

Darwin, J., *Britain and Decolonisation: The Retreat from Empire in the Post-War World*, London, 1988

Deighton, A., *The Impossible Peace: Britain, the Division of Germany, and the Origins of the Cold War*, Oxford, 1990

Deighton, A., ed., *Britain and the First Cold War*, London, 1990

Deist, W., ed., *The German Military in the Age of Total War*, London, 1985

Dennis, P., *Troubled Days of Peace: Mountbatten and South-East Asia Command, 1945–46*, Manchester, 1987

Devillers, P., *Histoire du Viet-Nam de 1940 à 1952*, Paris, 1952

Dilks, D., ed., *Retreat from Power: Studies in Britain's Foreign Policy of the Twentieth Century. Vol. 2: After 1939*, London, 1981

Dixon, P., *Double Diploma: The Life of Sir Pierson Dixon. Don and Diplomat*, London, 1968

Dobson, A.P., *American Wartime Aid to Britain, 1940–1946*, London, 1985

Donnison, F.S.V., *British Military Administration in the Far East, 1943–46*, HMSO, London, 1956

Donoughue, B. and Jones, G.W., *Herbert Morrison: Portrait of a Politician*, London, 1973

Dow, J.C.R., *The Management of the British Economy, 1945–1960*, Cambridge, 1964

Duncanson, D.J., *Government and Revolution in Vietnam*, Oxford, for Chatham House, 1968

Durbin, E., *New Jerusalems: The Labour Party and the Economics of Democratic Socialism*, London, 1985

Eatwell, R., *The 1945–1951 Labour Governments*, London, 1979

Eden, A., *The Memoirs of the Rt. Hon. Sir Anthony Eden: Full Circle*, London, 1960

Eden, A., *The Reckoning, 1938–1945*, London, 1965

Edwards, J., *The British Government and the Spanish Civil War, 1936–1939*, London, 1979

Ehrman, J., *Grand Strategy. Vol. V: August 1943–September 1944*, London, 1956

Elbaum, B. and Lazonick, W., eds, *The Decline of the British Economy*, Oxford, 1986

Elwell-Sutton, L.P., *Persian Oil: A Study in Power Politics*, London, 1955

Erickson, J., *The Road to Stalingrad: Stalin's War with Germany*, London, 1975

Erickson, J., *The Road to Berlin: Continuing the History of Stalin's War with Germany*, London, 1983

Fall, B., *The Two Viet-Nams: A Political and Military Analysis*, 2nd edn, New York, 1967

Feinstein, C., *National Income, Expenditure and Output of the United Kingdom, 1855–1965*, Cambridge, 1972

Fenn, C., *Ho Chi Minh: A Biographical Introduction*, New York, 1973

Fischer, L., *The Soviets in World Affairs: A History of Relations between the Soviet Union and the Rest of the World*, 2 vols, London, 1930

Floud, R. and McCloskey, D., eds, *The Economic History of Britain since 1700. Vol. 2: 1860 to the 1970s*, Cambridge, 1981

Foot, M., *Aneurin Bevan: A Biography. Vol. 1: 1897–1945*, London, 1962

Foot, M., *Aneurin Bevan: A Biography. Vol. 2: 1945–1960*, London, 1973

Forrestal, J.V., *The Forrestal Diaries*, ed. W. Millis, New York, 1951

Frankel, J., *British Foreign Policy, 1945–1973*, London, 1975

Freeland, R.M., *The Truman Dotrine and the Origins of McCarthyism*, New York, 1975

Gaddis, J.L., *The United States and the Origins of the Cold War*, New York, 1972

Gaddis, J.L., *Strategies of Containment*, New York, 1982

Gaddis, J.L., *The Long Peace*, New York, 1988

Gardner, R.N., *Sterling–Dollar Diplomacy: Anglo-American Collaboration in the Reconstruction of Multilateral Trade*, Oxford, 1956; rev. edn, New York, 1969

Gaulle, Charles de, *War Memoirs*, 3 Vols, London, 1955–60

George, David L., *The Truth about the Peace Treaties*, Vol. 1, London, 1938

Gilbert, M., ed., *A Century of Conflict, 1850–1950: Essays for A.J.P. Taylor*, London, 1966

Gilbert, M., *Winston Churchill. The Wilderness Years*, (various editions, London, 1981)

Gilbert, M., *Winston Churchill, Vol. VII: Road to Victory, 1941–1945*, London, 1986

Gilbert, M., *Second World War*, London, 1989

Giles, F., *Sundry Times*, London, 1986

Gilpin, A.C., *India's Sterling Balances*, Fabian Society, London, 1946

Gimbel, J., *The Origins of the Marshall Plan*, Stanford UP, 1976

Gladwyn, Lord, *The Memoirs of Lord Gladwyn*, London, 1972

Glees, A., *The Secrets of the Service: British Intelligence and Communist Subversion, 1939–1951*, London, 1987

Goldsworthy, D., *Colonial Issues in British Politics, 1945–1961*, Oxford, 1971

Gowing, M., *Independence and Deterrence: Britain and Atomic Energy. Vol 1: Policy Making*, London, 1974

Graubard, S.R., *British Labour and the Russian Revolution, 1917–1924*, Cambridge, Mass., 1956

Grigg, J., *1943, The Victory that Never Was*, London, 1980

Gupta, P.S., *Imperialism and the British Labour Movement, 1914–1964*, London, 1975

Hamilton, T.J., *Appeasement's Child: The Franco Regime in Spain*, London, 1943

Hammer, E.J., *The Struggle for Indo-China*, Stanford, 1954

Hancock, W.K., *Argument of Empire*, Penguin Special, London, 1943

Hancock, W.K. and Gowing, M., *British War Economy*, HMSO, London, 1949

Harbutt, F.J., *The Iron Curtain: Churchill, America and the Origins of the Cold War*, Oxford, 1986

Harriman, W.A. and Abel, E., *Special Envoy to Churchill and Stalin, 1941–1946*, London, 1976

Harris, K., *Attlee*, London, 1982

Hart, B.H. Liddell, *Memoirs*, London, 1965

Harvey, O., *The War Diaries of Oliver Harvey*, ed. J. Harvey, London, 1978

Hathaway, R., *Ambiguous Partnership: Britain and America, 1944–47*, New York, 1981

Henderson, Sir N., *The Private Office: A Personal View of Five Foreign Secretaries and of Government from the Inside*, London, 1984

Herring, G.C., *Aid to Russia, 1941–1946: Strategy, Diplomacy, the Origins of the Cold War*, New York, 1973

Hess, G.H., *The United States' Emergence as a South-East Asian Power, 1940–1950*, New York, 1987

Hobsbawm, E.J., *Industry and Empire*, London, 1968

Hogan, M.J., *The Marshall Plan: America, Britain and the Reconstruction of Western Europe, 1947–1952*, Cambridge, 1987

Hutton, G., *We Too Can Prosper: The Promise of Productivity*, London, 1953

Isaacs, H.R., *Scratches on Our Mind*, New York, 1958

Isaacs, H.R., *The Cold War in Asia*, New York, 1974

Ismay, Lord, *The Memoir of General the Lord Ismay*, London, 1960

Isoart, P., ed., *L'Indochine Française, 1940–1945*, Paris, 1982

James, R. Rhodes, *Anthony Eden*, London, 1986

Jay, D., *Change and Fortune: A Political Record*, London, 1980

Jenkins, R., *Nine Men of Power*, London, 1974

Jones, B., *The Russia Complex: The British Labour Party and the Soviet Union*, Manchester, 1977

Jones, T., *A Diary with Letters, 1931–1950*, Oxford, 1954

Judt, T., *Resistance and Revolution in Mediterranean Europe, 1938–1948*, London, 1989

Kennan, G., *Memoirs, 1925–1950*, London, 1968

Kennan, G., *Memoirs, 1950–1963*, Boston, 1972

Kersaudy, F., *Churchill and de Gaulle*, London, 1981

Killearn, Lord, *The Killearn Diaries, 1934–1946: The Diplomatic and Personal Record of Lord Killearn (Sir Miles Lampson) High Commissioner and Ambassador Egypt*, ed. and introduced by T.E. Evans, London, 1972

Kindleberger, C.P., *Marshall Plan Days*, London, 1988

Kirby, Major-General S.W., *The War Against Japan. Vol. V: The Surrender of Japan*, HMSO, London, 1969

Kirk, G., *The Middle East, 1945–1950*, London, 1954

Kitchen, M., *British Policy towards the Soviet Union during the Second World War*, London, 1986

Kolko, G., *The Politics of War: Allied Diplomacy and the World Crisis of 1943–1945*, London, 1969

Kolko, J. and G., *The Limits of Power: The World and United States Foreign Policy, 1945–1954*, New York, 1972

Kuniholm, B.R., *The Origins of the Cold War in the East: Great Power Conflict and Diplomacy in Iran, Turkey and Greece*, Princeton, 1980

Lacey, M.J., ed., *The Truman Presidency*, Cambridge, 1989

LaFeber, W., *America, Russia and the Cold War*, 3rd edn, New York, 1976

Langhorne, R., *Diplomacy and Intelligence during the Second World War: Essays in Honour of F.H. Hinsley*, Cambridge, 1985

Larrabee, E., *Commander in Chief: Franklin Delano Roosevelt. His Lieutenants, and their War*, London, 1987

Lewis, J., *Changing Direction: British Military Planning for Post-War Strategic Defence, 1942–1947*, London, 1988

Linz, S., ed., *The Impact of World War II on the Soviet Union*, New Jersey, 1985

Lockhart, Sir R.B., *The Diaries of Sir Robert Bruce Lockhart. Vol. 2: 1939–1965*, ed. K. Younger, London, 1980

Loewenheim, F.L., Langley, H.D. and Jonas, M., eds, *Roosevelt and Churchill: Their Secret Wartime Correspondence*, New York, 1975

Loth, W., *The Division of the World, 1941–1955*, London, 1988

Louis, W.L., *The British Empire in the Middle East, 1941–51*, Oxford, 1984

Louis, W.L., *Imperialism at Bay, 1941–1945. The United States and the Decolonisation of the British Empire*, Oxford, 1977

Louis, W.R. and Bull, H., eds, *The 'Special' Relationship: Anglo-American Relations since 1945*, Oxford, 1986

Lynch, A., *The Soviet Study of International Relations*, Cambridge, 1987

McDonald, I., *The History of The Times. Vol. 5: Struggles in War and Peace, 1939–1966*, London, 1984

Mackenzie, J.M., *Propaganda and Empire: The Manipulation of British Public Opinion, 1880–1960*, Manchester, 1984

McLellan, D.S., *Dean Acheson: The State Department Years*, New York, 1976

Macmillan, H., *The Blast of War, 1939–1945*, London, 1967

Macmillan, H., *Tides of Fortune, 1945–1955*, London, 1969

Maddox, R.J., *The New Left and the Origins of the Cold War*, Princeton, 1973

Mallaby, Sir G., *From My Level: Unwritten Minutes*, London, 1965

Martin, K., *Harold Laski (1893–1950): A Biographical Memoir*, London, 1953

Mayer, A.J., *Politics and Diplomacy of Peacemaking: Containment and Counter-Revolution at Versailles, 1918–1919*, New York, 1967

Mayer, A.J., *Why Did The Heavens Not Darken?*, London, 1990

Mayhew, C., *Time to Explain: An Autobiography*, London, 1987

Mee, C.L., *Meeting at Potsdam*, London, 1975

Meehan, E.J., *The British Left Wing and Foreign Policy: A Study of the Influence of Ideology*, New Brunswick, 1960

Menon, V.P., *The Transfer of Power in India*, London, 1957

Middlemas, K., *Politics in Industrial Society: The Experience of the British System since 1911*, London, 1979

Miliband, R., *Parliamentary Socialism*, London, 1961

Milward, A.S., *The Reconstruction of Western Europe, 1945–1951*, rev. paperback edn, London, 1987

Monroe, E., *Britain's Moment in the Middle East, 1914–1956*, London, 1963

Moore, R.J., *Escape from Empire: The Attlee Government and the Indian Problem*, Oxford, 1983

Moran, Lord Charles, *Winston Churchill: The Struggle for Survival, 1940–1965: Taken from the Diaries of Lord Moran*, London, 1966

Morgan, K.O., *Labour in Power, 1945–1951*, Oxford, 1984

Morgan, K.O., *Labour People. Leaders and Lieutenants: Hardie to Kinnock*, Oxford, 1987

Morgan, T., *FDR: A Biography*, London, 1986

Nagai, Y. and Iriye, A., eds, *The Origins of the Cold War in Asia*, New York, 1977

Nicholas, H.G., ed., *Washington Despatches, 1941–1945: Weekly Political Reports from the British Embassy*, London, 1981

Nicolson, H., *Diaries and Letters, 1930–1939*, ed. N. Nicolson, London, 1966

Nove, A., *An Economic History of the USSR*, London, 1972

Ovendale, R., ed., *The Foreign Policy of the British Labour Governments, 1945–1951*, Leicester, 1984

Ovendale, R., *The English-Speaking Alliance: Britain, the United States, the Dominions and the Cold War, 1945–1951*, London, 1985

Pelling, H., *Britain and the Second World War*, London, 1970

Pelling, H., *Britain and the Marshall Plan*, London, 1988

Pimlott, B., *Hugh Dalton*, paperback, London, 1985

Pitt, B., *Churchill and the Generals*, London, 1981

Plowden, E., *An Industrialist in the Treasury: The Post-War Years*, London, 1989

Pluvier, J., *South-East Asia from Colonialism to Independence*, Oxford, 1974

Pogue, F.C., *George C. Marshall: Organiser of Victory, 1943–1945*, New York, 1973

Polk, J., *Sterling*, New York, 1956

Pollard, S., *The Wasting of the British Economy: British Economic Policy 1945 to the Present*, 2nd edn, London, 1984

Porter, B., *The Lion's Share: A Short History of British Imperialism, 1850–1983*, 2nd edn, London, 1984

Postan, M.M., *British War Production*, HMSO, London, 1952

Postan, M.M., Hay, D. and Scott, J.D., *Design and Development of Weapons. Studies in Government and Industrial Organisation*, HMSO, London, 1964

Prasad, B., ed., *Official History of the Indian Armed Forces in the Second World War. Post-War Occupation Forces. Japan and South-East Asia*, Combined Inter-Services Historical Section, India and Pakistan, New Delhi, 1958

Pressnell, L.S., *External Economic Policy since the War. Vol. 1: The Post-War Financial Settlement*, HMSO, London, 1987

Reynolds, D., *The Creation of the Anglo-American Alliance, 1937–1941: A Study in Competitive Co-operation*, London, 1981

Rose, Lisle A., *Dubious Victory: The United States and the End of World War II*, Kent State, 1973

Rosie, G., *The British in Vietnam*, London, 1970

Roskill, S., *Churchill and the Admirals*, London, 1977

Rostas, L., *Comparative Productivity in British and American Industry*, Cambridge, 1948

Rothwell, V., *Britain and the Cold War, 1941–1947*, London, 1982

Salisbury, H.E., *The 900 Days: The Siege of Leningrad*, new edn, London, 1986

Sarafis, M., ed., *Greece: From Resistance to Civil War*, Nottingham, 1980

Saville, J., *The Labour Movement in Britain: A Commentary*, London, 1988

Sayers, R.A., *Financial Policy, 1939–1945* (History of the Second World War. UK Civil Series), HMSO, London, 1956

Schneer, J., *Labour's Conscience. The Labour Left, 1945–1951*, London, 1987

Sherry, M.S., *Preparing for the Next War: American Plans for Post-War Defense*, New Haven, Conn., 1977

Sherwin, M.J., *A World Destroyed: The Atomic Bomb and the Grand Alliance*, New York, 1975

Shuckbrugh, E., *Descent to Suez: Diaries 1951–56*, London, 1986

Smellie, K.B., *A Hundred Years of English Government*, London, 1937

Smith, K., *The British Economic Crisis*, Harmondsworth, 1984

Smuts, J.C., *Selections from the Smuts Papers. Vol. VI: December 1934–August 1945*, ed. J. van der Poel, Cambridge, 1973

Stein, H., ed., *American Civil–Military Decisions: A Book of Case Studies*, Alabama, 1963

Steiner, Z.S., *The Foreign Office and Foreign Policy, 1898–1914*, Cambridge, 1969

Stocking, G.W., *Middle East Oil: A Study in Political and Economic Controversy*, London, 1971

Stoler, M.A., *The Politics of the Second Front: American Military Planning and Diplomacy in Coalition Warfare, 1941–1943*, Westport, Conn., 1977

Strang, Lord W., *The Foreign Office*, London, 1955

Streat, Sir Raymond, *Lancashire and Whitehall: The Diary of Sir Raymond Streat, 1931–1957*, 2 vols, Manchester, 1987

Streit, C., *Keine Kameraden: Die Wehrmacht und die sowjetischen Kriegsgefangenen, 1941–1945*, Stuttgart, 1978

Sulzberger, C.L., *A Long Row of Candles: Memoirs and Diaries, 1934–1954*, London, 1969

Taubman, W., *Stalin's American Policy*, New York, 1982

Taylor, A.J.P., *English History, 1914–1945*, Oxford, 1965

Thorne, C., *Allies of a Kind: The United States, Britain and the War against Japan, 1941–1945*, London, 1978

Thorne, C., *The Issue of War: States, Societies, and the Far Eastern Conflict of 1941–1945*, London, 1985

Tilley, Sir J. and Gaselee, S., *The Foreign Office*, London, 1933

Titmuss, R., *The Irresponsible Society*, Fabian Tract No. 323, London, 1959

Titmuss, R., *Income Redistribution and Social Change*, London, 1962

Tomlinson, B.R., *The Political Economy of the Raj 1914–1947: The Economics of Decolonisation in India*, London, 1979

Trager, F.N., ed., *Marxism in South-East Asia: A Study in Four Countries*, Stanford, 1959

Veblen, T., *Imperial Germany and the Industrial Revolution*, with introduction by J. Dorfman, London, 1915; reprinted New York, 1939

Watt, D. Cameron, *Personalities and Policies: Studies in the Formulation of British Foreign Policy in the Twentieth Century*, London, 1965

Watt, D. Cameron, *Too Serious a Business: European Armed Forces and the Approach to the Second World War*, London, 1975

Watt, D. Cameron, *Succeeding John Bull: America in Britain's Place, 1900–1975*, Cambridge, 1984

Watt, D. Cameron, *How War Came: The Immediate Origins of the Second World War, 1938–1939*, London, 1989

Weiler, P., *British Labour and the Cold War*, Stanford, 1988

Wiener, M.J., *English Culture and the Decline of the Industrial Spirit, 1850–1980*, Cambridge, 1981

Wheeler-Bennett, J.W., *King George VI: His Life and Reign*, London, 1958

Williams, F., *Ernest Bevin: Portrait of a Great Englishman*, London, 1952

Williams, F., *A Prime Minister Remembers*, London, 1961

Williams, F., *Nothing So Strange*, London, 1970

Williams, G. and Reed, B., *Denis Healey and the Politics of Power*, London, 1971

Wittner, L.S., *American Intervention in Greece, 1943–1949*, New York, 1982

BIBLIOGRAPHY

Woodhouse, C.M., *The Struggle for Greece, 1941–1949*, London, 1976

Woodward, Sir Llewellyn, *British Foreign Policy in the Second World War*, London, 1962

Woodward, Sir Llewellyn, *British Foreign Policy in the Second World War*, 5 vols, London, 1971–76

Worswick, G.D.N. and Ady, P.H., eds, *The British Economy, 1945–1950*, Oxford, 1952

Yergin, D., *Shattered Peace: The Origins of the Cold War and the National Security State*, Boston, 1979

Yergin, D., *The Prize: The Epic Quest for Oil, Money and Power*, London, 1991

Zametica, J., ed., *British Officials and British Foreign Policy, 1945–1950*, Leicester, 1990

Ziegler, P., *Mountbatten: The Official Biography*, London, 1985

Ziegler, P., *Personal Diary of Admiral The Lord Louis Mountbatten: Supreme Allied Commander, South-East Asia, 1943–1946*, London, 1988

Zilliacus, K., *I Choose Peace*, Penguin Special, London, 1949

(ii) Articles

Acheson, D., 'Hard Words from the Veteran American Statesman: Dean Acheson in Conversation with William Hardcastle', *The Listener*, 18 June 1970

Acheson, D., 'Dean Acheson Talks to Kenneth Harris', *The Listener*, 8 April 1971

Adamthwaite, A., 'Britain and the World, 1945–9: The View from the Foreign Office', *International Affairs*, Vol. 61, No. 2, Spring 1985, pp. 223–35

Allen, L., 'Studies in the Japanese Occupation of South-East Asia', *Durham Univ. Journal*, Vol. 33, 1971–72, pp. 120–32

Anstey, C., 'The Projection of British Socialism: Foreign Office Publicity and American Opinion, 1945–50', *J. Cont. Hist.*, Vol. 19, No. 3, 1984, pp. 417–51

Barker, R.S., 'Civil Service Attitudes and the Economic Planning of the Attlee Government', *J. Cont. Hist.*, Vol. 21, No. 3, 1986, pp. 473–86

Bartov, O., 'Soldiers, Nazis, and the War in the Third Reich', *J. Modern History*, Vol. 63, No. 1, March 1991, pp. 44–60

Bell, P.M.H., 'Censorship, Propaganda and Public Opinion: The Case of the Katyn Graves', *Trans. Roy. Hist, Soc.*, 5th Ser., Vol. 39, 1989, pp. 63–83

Bergson, A., Blackman, J.H. and Erlich, A., 'Post-War Reconstruction and Development in the USSR', *Annals of the American Academy of Political and Social Science*, May 1959, pp. 52–71

Blank, S., 'The Impact of Foreign Economic Policy', in D. Coates and J. Hillard, eds, *The Economic Decline of Modern Britain*, Brighton, 1986, pp. 205–19

Boyle, P.G., 'The British Foreign Office View of Soviet–American Relations, 1945–6', *Diplomatic History*, Vol. 3, No. 4, Fall 1979, pp. 307–20

Boyle, P.G., 'The British Foreign Office and American Foreign Policy, 1947–8', *J. American Studies*, Vol. 16, No. 3, December 1982, pp. 373–89

Boyle, P.G., 'Britain, America and the Transition from Economic to Military Assistance, 1948–51', *J. Cont. Hist.*, Vol. 22, No. 3, July 1987, pp. 521–37

Brett, T., Gilliat, S. and Pople, A., 'Planned Trade, Labour Party Policy and United States Intervention: The Successes and Failures of Post-War Reconstruction', *History Workshop*, No. 13, Spring 1983, pp. 130–42

Brooke, S., 'Revisionists and Fundamentalists: The Labour Party and Economic Policy during the Second World War', *Hist. Journal*, Vol. 32, No. 1, 1989, pp. 157–75

Bullock, A., 'Ernest Bevin, Foreign Secretary', *The Listener*, 14 October 1982

Burridge, T., 'Great Britain and the Dismemberment of Germany at the End of the Second World War', *Internat. Hist. Rev.*, Vol. 3, No. 4, October 1981, pp. 565–79

Carew, A., 'The Schism within the World Federation of Trade Unions: Government and Trade Union Diplomacy', *Internat. Rev. Social History*, Vol. 39, Part 3, 1984, pp. 297–335

Chandler, A.D., 'The Growth of the Transnational Industrial Firm in the United States and the United Kingdom: A Comparative Analysis', *Econ. Hist. Rev.*, Second Ser., Vol. 33, No. 3, August 1980, pp. 396–410

Chieu, Vu Ngu, 'The Other Side of the 1945 Vietnamese Revolution: The Empire of Vietnam, March–August 1945', *J. Asian Studies*, Vol. 45, No. 2, February 1986, pp. 293–328

Cockett, R.B., ' "In wartime every objective reporter should be shot": The Experience of British Press Correspondents in Moscow, 1941–5', *J. Cont. Hist.*, Vol. 23, No. 4, October 1988, pp. 515–30

Cottam, R., 'The United States, Iran and the Cold War', *Iranian Studies*, No. 3, Winter 1970, pp. 2–22

Cox, M., 'Western Capitalism and the Cold War System', in M. Shaw, ed., *War, State and Society*, London, 1984, pp. 136–94

Crofts, S.W., 'The Attlee Government's Economic Information Propaganda', *J. Cont. Hist.*, Vol. 21, No. 3, 1986, pp. 453–71

Deighton, A., 'The "Frozen" Front: The Labour Government, the Division of Germany, and the Origins of the Cold War, 1945–7', *International Affairs*, Vol. 63, No. 3, Summer 1987, pp. 459–65

Deutscher, I., '22 June 1941', *New Left Review*, No. 124, November–December 1980, pp. 86–92

Devereux, D.R., 'British Planning for Post-War Civil Aviation, 1942–1945: A Study in Anglo-American Rivalry', *Twentieth-Century British History*, Vol. 2, No. 1, 1991, pp. 22–46

Divine, R.A., 'The Cold War and the Election of 1948', *J. American History*, Vol. 59, No. 1, June 1972, pp. 90–110

Dobson, A.P., 'The Other Air Battle: The American Pursuit of Post-War Civil Aviation Rights', *Hist. Journal*, Vol. 28, No. 2, 1985, pp. 429–34

Dulphy, A., 'La politique de la France à l'égard de l'Espagne franquiste, 1945–9', *Revue d'histoire moderne et contemporaine*, tome XXXV, jan–mars 1988, pp. 123–40

Duncanson, D.J., 'General Gracey and the Vietminh', *J. Royal Central Asian Soc.*, Vol. 55, 1968, pp. 288–97

Economist, 'British and German Tanks', Vol. 151, 14 December 1946, pp. 942–3

Elwell-Sutton, L.P., 'Political Parties in Iran, 1941–1948', *Middle East J.*, Vol. 3, Winter 1949, pp. 45–62

Evangelista, M.A., 'Stalin's Post-War Army Re-appraised', *International Security*, Vol. 7, No. 3, 1982–83, pp. 110–38

Fieldhouse, D.K., 'The Labour Governments and the Empire-Commonwealth,

1945–1951', in R. Ovendale, ed., *The Foreign Policy of the British Labour Governments, 1945–1951*, 1984, pp. 83–120

Förster, J., 'The Wehrmacht and the War of Extermination against the Soviet Union', *Yad Vashem*, Vol. 14, 1981, pp. 7–34

Foster, A.J., 'The British Press and the Coming of the Cold War', in A. Deighton, ed., *Britain and the First Cold War*, London, 1990, pp. 11–31

Foster, A.J., 'The Politicians, Public Opinion and the Press: The Storm Over Military Intervention in Greece in December 1944', *J. Cont. Hist.*, Vol. 19, No. 3, December 1984, pp. 453–94

Frazer, R., 'Did Britain Start the Cold War? Bevin and the Truman Doctrine', *Hist. Journal*, Vol. 27, No. 3, 1984, pp. 715–27

Gaddis, J.L., 'The Emerging Post-Revisionist Synthesis on the Origins of the Cold War', *Diplomatic History*, Vol. 7, No. 3, Summer 1983, pp. 171–90

Gaddis, J.L., 'The Insecurities of Victory: The United States and the Perception of the Soviet Threat after World War II', in M.J. Lacey, ed., *The Truman Presidency*, Cambridge, 1989, pp. 235–72

Gerber, L.G., 'The Baruch Plan and the Origins of the Cold War', *Diplomatic History*, Vol. 6, No. 1, Winter 1982, pp. 69–95

Gorodetsy, G., 'The Origins of the Cold War: Stalin, Churchill and the Formation of the Grand Alliance', *Russian Review*, Vol. 47, No. 2, April 1988, pp. 145–70

Gowing, M., 'Britain, America and the Bomb', in D. Dilks, ed., *Retreat from Power: Studies in Britain's Foreign Policy of the Twentieth Century, Vol. 2: After 1939*, London, 1981, pp. 120–37

Gowing, M., 'Nuclear Weapons and the "Special Relationship" ', in W.R. Louis and H. Bull, eds, *The Special Relationship: Anglo-American Relations since 1945*, Oxford, 1986, pp. 117–28

Greenwood, S., 'Bevin, the Ruhr and the Division of Germany: August 1945– December 1946', *Hist. Journal*, Vol. 29, No. 1, 1986, pp. 202–12

Greenwood, S., 'Frank Roberts and the "Other" Long Telegram: The View from the British Embassy in Moscow, March 1946', *J. Cont. Hist.*, Vol. 25, No. 1, 1990, pp. 103–22

Harbutt, F., 'Churchill, Hopkins, and the "Other" America: An Alternative Perspective on Anglo-American Relations, 1941–1945', *Internat. Hist. Rev.*, Vol. 8, No. 2, pp. 236–62

Harrison, M., 'Stalinist Industrialisation and the Test of War', *History Workshop*, No. 29, Spring 1990, pp. 65–84

Herring, G.C., 'Lend-Lease to Russia and the Origins of the Cold War, 1944–1945', *J. American History*, Vol. 56, No. 1, June 1969, pp. 93–114

Herring, G.C., 'The Truman Administration and the Restoration of French Sovereignty in Indo-China', *Diplomatic History*, Vol. 1, No. 2, Spring 1977, pp. 97–117

Hess, G.H, 'Franklin Roosevelt and Indo-China', *J. American History*, Vol. 59, No. 2, September 1972, pp. 353–68

Hinds, A.E., 'Sterling and Imperial Policy, 1945–1951', *J. Imperial and Commonwealth History*, Vol. 15, No. 2, January 1987, pp. 148–69

Holland, R.F., 'The Imperial Factor in British Strategies from Attlee to Macmillan, 1945–1963', *J. Imperial and Commonwealth History*, Vol. 12, 1984, pp. 165–86

Hudson, D.J., 'Vandenberg Reconsidered: Senate Resolution 239 and American Foreign Policy', *Diplomatic History*, Vol. 1, No. 1, Winter 1977, pp. 46–63

Jackson, S., 'Prologue to the Marshall Plan: The Origins of the American Commitment for a European Recovery Program', *J. American History*, Vol. 65, March 1979, pp. 1043–68

Kent, J., 'Anglo-French Colonial Co-operation 1939–1949', *J. Imperial and Commonwealth History*, Vol. 17, No. 1, October 1988, pp. 52–82

Kimball, W.F., 'Churchill and Roosevelt: The Personal Equation', *Prologue*, Vol. 6, pp. 169–82

Kirby, M.W. and Rose, Mary B., 'Whitehall and Industrial Decline: The Diary of Sir Raymond Streat', *Hist. Journal*, Vol. 32, No. 3, 1989, pp. 763–8

Kitchen, M., 'Winston Churchill and the Soviet Union during the Second World War', *Hist. Journal*, Vol. 30, No. 2, 1987, pp. 415–36

Krishnan, Y., 'Mountbatten and the Partition of India', *History*, Vol. 68, February 1983, pp. 22–38

Labedz, L., 'The Two Minds of George Kennan: How to Un-learn from Experience', *Survey*, Vol. 30, No. 1/2, March 1988, pp. 223–39

LaFeber, W., 'Roosevelt, Churchill and Indo-China, 1942–45', *American Hist. Rev.*, Vol. 80, 1975, pp. 1277–95

Lammers, D., 'Fascism, Communism, and the Foreign Office, 1937–9', *J. Cont. Hist.*, Vol. 6, No. 3, 1971, pp. 66–86

Lawford, V., 'Three Ministers', *The Cornhill Magazine*, Winter 1956–7, pp. 73–99

Leffler, M.P., 'The American Conception of National Security and the Beginnings of the Cold War, 1945–48', *American Hist. Rev.*, Vol. 89, No. 2, April 1984, pp. 346–81 (and comments to p. 390)

Leffler, M.P., 'Strategy, Diplomacy and the Cold War: The United States, Turkey, and NATO, 1945–1952', *J. American Hist.*, Vol. 71, No. 4, March 1985, pp. 807–25

Leffler, M.P., 'Was the Cold War Necessary?', *Diplomatic History*, Vol. 15, No. 2, Spring 1991, pp. 265–75

Lieberman, S.R., 'The Evacuation of Industry in the Soviet Union during World War II', *Soviet Studies*, Vol. 30, No. 1, January 1983, pp. 90–102

Linz, S., 'Measuring the Carryover Cost of World War II to the Soviet People: 1945–1953', *Explorations in Economic History*, Vol. 20, 1983, pp. 375–86

Lundestad, G., 'Empire by Invitation? The United States and Western Europe, 1945–1952', *J. Peace Studies*, Vol. 23, No. 3, 1986, pp. 263–77

Lundestad, G., 'Moralism, Presentism, Exceptionalism, Provincialism, and Other Extravagances in American Writings on the Early Cold War Years', *Diplomatic History*, Vol. 13, No. 4, Fall 1989, pp. 527–45

Macdonald, C.A., 'The Politics of Intervention: The United States and Argentina, 1941–1946', *J. Latin American History*, Vol. 12, 1980, pp. 365–96

McFarland, S., 'A Peripheral View of the Origins of the Cold War: The Crises in Iran, 1941–1947', *Diplomatic History*, Vol. 4, No. 4, Fall 1980, pp. 333–51

Mackenzie, S.P., 'Vox Populi: British Army Newspapers in the Second World War', *J. Cont. Hist.*, Vol. 24, No. 4, 1989, pp. 665–81

Maddox, R., 'Reparations and the Origins of the Cold War', *Mid-America: An Historical Review*, Vol. 67, October 1985, pp. 125–35

Mark, E., 'Charles E. Bohlen and the Acceptable Limits of Soviet Hegemony in Eastern Europe: A Memorandum of 18 October 1945', *Diplomatic History*, Vol. 3, No. 2, Spring 1979, pp. 201–13

Marsot, Alain-Gérard, 'The Crucial Year: Indochina, 1946', *J. Cont. Hist.*, Vol. 19, No. 2, 1984, pp. 337–54

Mayers, D., 'Young Kennan's Criticisms and Recommendations', *Biography*, Vol. 8, No. 3, 1985, pp. 227–47

Mayers, D., 'Soviet War Aims and the Grand Alliance: George Kennan's Views, 1944–1946', *J. Cont. Hist.*, Vol. 21, No. 1, 1986, pp. 57–79

Mayers, D., 'Ambassador Joseph Davies Reconsidered', *SHAFR Newsletter*, Vol. 23, No. 3, September 1992, pp. 1–16

Mayhew, C., 'British Foreign Policy since 1945', *International Affairs*, Vol. 26, No. 4, pp. 477–86

Merrick, R., 'The Russia Committee of the British Foreign Office and the Cold War, 1946–7', *J. Cont. Hist.*, Vol. 20, No. 3, 1985, pp. 453–68

Messer, R.L., 'Paths Not Taken: The United States Department of State and Alternatives to Containment, 1945–6', *Diplomatic History*, Vol. 1, No. 4, Fall 1977, pp. 297–319

Miliband, R., 'State Power and Class Interests', *New Left Review*, No. 138, March–April 1983, pp. 57–68

Millar, J.R. and Linz, S., 'The Cost of World War II to the Soviet People', *J. Economic History*, Vol. 38, No. 4, December 1978, pp. 959–62

Munting, R., 'Lend-Lease and the Soviet War Effort', *J. Cont. Hist.*, Vol. 19, No. 3, July 1984, pp. 495–510

Myers, F., 'Conscription and the Politics of Military Strategy in the Attlee Government', *J. Strategic Studies*, Vol. 7, No. 1, March 1984, pp. 55–73

Nachmani, A., ' "It is a matter of getting the mixture right": Britain's Post-war Relations with America in the Middle East', *J. Cont. Hist.*, Vol. 18, No. 1, January 1983, pp. 117–40

Nitz, K.K., 'Japanese Military Policy towards French Indo-China during the Second World War: The Road to the *Meigo Sakusen*, 9 March 1945', *J. South East Asian Studies*, Vol. 14, No. 2, September 1983, pp. 328–53

Nitz, K.K., 'Independence without Nationalists?: The Japanese and Vietnamese Nationalism during the Japanese Period, 1940–45', *J. South East Asian Studies*, Vol. 15, No. 1, March 1984, pp. 108–33

Ovendale, R., 'Britain, the United States, and the Cold War in South-East Asia, 1949–1950', *International Affairs*, Vol. 58, No. 3, Summer 1982, pp. 447–64

Patterson, T.G., 'The Abortive Loan to Russia and the Origins of the Cold War, 1943–1946', *J. American history*, Vol. 61, No. 1, June 1969, pp. 70–92

Patterson, T.G., 'Presidential Foreign Policy, Public Opinion and Congress: The Truman Years', *Diplomatic History*, Vol. 3, No. 1, Winter 1979, pp. 1–18

Popas, F.L., 'Creating a Hard Line towards Russia: The Training of State Department Soviet Experts, 1927–1937', *Diplomatic History*, Vol. 8, No. 3, Summer 1984, pp. 209–26

Reynolds, D., 'Roosevelt, the British Left, and the Appointment of John G. Winant as

United States Ambassador to Britain in 1941', *Internat. Hist. Rev.*, Vol. 4, No. 3, August 1982, pp. 393–413

Reynolds, D., 'The Origins of the Cold War: The European Dimension, 1944–1951', *Hist. Journal*, Vol. 28, No. 2, 1985, pp. 497–515

Reynolds, D., 'A Special Relationship?: America, Britain and the International Order since the Second World War', *International Affairs*, Vol. 68, No. 1, Winter 1985–86, pp. 1–20

Reynolds, D., 'Britain and the New Europe: The Search for Identity since 1940', *Hist. Journal*, Vol. 31, No. 1, March 1988, pp. 223–39

Reynolds, D., 'Eden the Diplomatist 1931–1956: Suicide of a Statesman?' *History*, Vol. 74, February 1989, pp. 65–84

Reynolds, D., 'Britain and the Cold War', *Hist. Journal*, Vol. 35, No. 2, 1992, pp. 501–3

Robbins, K., '1945: British Victory', *History*, Vol. 71, February 1986, pp. 61–8

Rose, Lisle A., Review of D. Yergin, *Shattered Peace*, in *Revue d'histoire du 2e guerre mondiale*, No. 122, 1981, pp. 98–102

Rosenberg, D.A., 'The Origins of Overkill: Nuclear Weapons and American Strategy, 1945–1960', *Internat. Security*, Vol. 7, No. 4, Spring 1983, pp. 3–71

Ross, G., 'Foreign Office Attitudes to the Soviet Union, 1941–5', *J. Cont. Hist.*, Vol. 16, No. 3, 1981, pp. 521–40

Ryan, H.B., 'A New Look at Churchill's "Iron Curtain" Speech', *Hist. Journal*, Vol. 22, No. 4, 1979, pp. 895–920

Sainsbury, K., 'British Policy and German Unity at the End of the Second World War', *English Hist. Review*, Vol. 94, October 1979, pp. 786–804

Sander, A.D., 'Truman and the National Security Council: 1945–1947', *J. American History*, Vol. 59, No. 2, September 1972, pp. 369–88

Saville, J., 'Labour and Income Redistribution', in R. Miliband and J. Saville, eds, *Socialist Register*, London, 1965, pp. 147–62

Saville, J., 'May Day, 1937', in A. Briggs and J. Saville, eds, *Essays in Labour History 1918–1939*, London, 1977, pp. 232–84

Saville, J., 'Britain: Internationalism and the Labour Movement between the Wars', in F. van Holthoon and M. van der Linden, eds, *Internationalism in the Labour Movement, 1830–1940*, Leiden, 1988, pp. 565–82

Sberga, J.J., 'The Anti-Colonial Policy of Franklin D. Roosevelt: A Re-appraisal', *Political Science Quarterly*, Vol. 101, No. 1, 1986, pp. 65–84

Schaffer, R., 'General Stanley D. Embick: Military Dissenter', *Military Affairs*, Vol. 37, October 1973, pp. 89–95

Singleton, J., 'Planning for Cotton, 1945–1951', *Econ. History Review*, 2nd Ser., Vol. 43, No. 1, 1990, pp. 62–78

Siracusa, J.M., 'Will the Real Author of Containment Stand Up: The Strange Case of George Kennan and Frank Roberts', *SHAFR Newsletter*, Vol. 22, No. 3, September 1991, pp. 1–27

Smith, L., 'Covert British Propaganda: The Information Research Department, 1944–7', *Millennium: Journal of International Studies*, Vol. 9, No. 1, 1980, pp. 67–83

Smith, R.B., 'The Japanese Period in Indo-China and the Coup of 9 March 1945', *J. South East Asian Studies*, Vol. 9, No. 2, September 1978, pp. 268–301

Smith, R., 'A Climate of Opinion: British Officials and the Development of British

Soviet Policy, 1945–7', *International Affairs*, Vol. 64, No. 4, Autumn 1988, pp. 631–47

Smith, R. and Zametica, J., 'The Cold Warrior: Clement Attlee Reconsidered, 1945–7', *International Affairs*, Vol. 61, No. 2, Spring 1985, pp. 237–52

Stoler, M.A., 'From Continentalism to Globalism: General Stanley D. Embick, the Joint Strategic Survey Committee, and the Military View of American National Policy during the Second World War', *Diplomatic History*, Vol. 6, No. 3, Summer 1982, pp. 303–21

Thomas, B., 'Cold War Origins, II', *J. Cont. Hist.*, Vol. 3, No. 1, January 1968, pp. 183–98

Thorne, C., 'Indo-China and Anglo-American Relations, 1942–1945', *Pacific Hist. Rev.*, Vol. 45, February 1976, pp. 73–96

Tomlinson, J., 'The Attlee Government and the Balance of Payments, 1945–1951', *Twentieth-Century British History*, Vol. 2, No. 1, 1991, pp. 47–66

Tomlinson, J., 'Mr Attlee's Supply-Side Socialism: Survey and Speculations', *Discussion Papers in Economics*, Brunel University, No. 9101, 1992, 43 pp.

Urban, G., 'From Containment . . . to Self-Containment: A Conversation with George F. Kennan', *Encounter*, September 1976, pp. 10–43

Walker, J.S., 'The Origins of the Cold War: Reviving and Revising an Old Debate', *The Public Historian*, Vol. 8, No. 4, Fall 1986, pp. 81–6

Warner, G., 'The Anglo-American Special Relationship', *Diplomatic History*, Vol. 13, No. 4, Fall 1989, pp. 479–99

Weiler, P., 'British Labour and the Cold War: The Foreign Policy of the Labour Governments, 1945–51', *J. British Studies*, Vol. 26, January 1987, pp. 54–82

Wright, K.M., 'Dollar Pooling in the Sterling Area, 1939–1952', *American Econ. Review*, Vol. 44, September 1954, pp. 559–77

Zeeman, B., 'Britain and the Cold War: An Alternative Approach. The Treaty of Dunkirk Example', *European Hist. Quarterly*, Vol. 16, No. 3, July 1986, pp. 343–67

5. Theses and Dissertations

Albert, J.G., 'Attlee, the Chiefs of Staff and the Re-structuring of Commonwealth Defence between VJ Day and the Outbreak of the Korean War', D. Phil., Oxford, 1986

Amaratunga, C.S., 'The British Presence and the Nationalist Challenge: Anglo-Iranian Relations, 1941–1953', Ph.D., London, 1986

Chester, A., 'Planning, the Labour Governments and British Economic Policy, 1943–1951', Ph.D., Bristol, 1983

Converse, E.V., III, 'United States Plans for a Post-War Overseas Military Base System, 1942–1948', Ph.D., Princeton, 1984

Holly, S.K., 'Multinational Oil, Anglo-American Defence Policy and National Security in the Persian Gulf, 1943–1953', Ph.D., Essex, 1987

Howe, S., 'Anti-Colonialism in British Politics: The Left and the End of Empire, 1939–1964', D.Phil., Oxford, 1984

Kemp, L., 'The Left and the Debate over Labour Party Policy, 1943–1950', Ph.D., Cambridge, 1985

Langley, H.M.L., 'The Foreign Office and the Preparation of Post-War Policy', M.Phil., London, 1978

Moxham, K.I., 'The Labour Party and the Soviet Union, 1945–1951', Ph.D., Cambridge, 1986

Qasim bin Ahmed, 'The British Government and the Franco Dictatorship, 1945–1950', Ph.D., London, 1987

Saravanamutta, P., 'The Influence of an Idea in Foreign Policy: The Case of the Domino Theory in American Foreign Policy in Indo-China, 1945–1956', Ph.D., London, 1986

Index

Acheson, Dean 106, 154
Addison, Christopher, 1st Viscount 53
Advisory Committee on Post-War Policy
    (US) 181–2
Alamein, battles, 1942 182
Alamogordo 149
Alba, Duke of 38
Albania 95
Alexander, A. V. 120, 143
Amery, L. S. 21, 66
Amulree Committee 83
Anderson, Sir John 84
Anglo-American Council on
    Productivity 170
Anglo-Iranian Oil Company 44
Anglo-Russian Trade Union
    Committee 99
Arab nationalism 58, 131, 138, 146–7
Arab States Confederation 126, 127,
    132–3
Arcos Raid (1927) 40, 99
Argentina 64
Arnold, Matthew 163
Aron, Raymond 155
Atlantic Charter 21, 65, 184
Atom Bomb 74, 75, 76, 79, 102, 128,
    149, 178
Atomic Energy 64, 134
Attlee, Clement 25, 40, 86, 89, 105,
    106, 124, 131, 134, 138, 143,
    144, 147
  early life 112–3
  general political ideas 5, 113; *Labour
    Party in Perspective*, 115, 116–7
  Coalition Government (1940–45)
    115, 117–18, 119, 120, 121
  attitudes towards Soviet Union

119–20, 123–4, 125, 126,
    138–9, 140–41
  and Indian independence 3, 90, 98,
    118, 136
  Middle East and differences with
    Ernest Bevin 5, 32, 43, 59–
    60, 92, 99, 120, 121–4, 125–
    7, 129, 131, 134–5, 136, 137,
    138–43, 146–8
  see also: Cabinet, Defence
    Committee; United Kingdom
Attlee, Tom 113
Attlee, Mrs Violet 114
Auchlinleck, Field Marshall Sir Claude
    168
Australia 2, 26, 50, 84, 95, 121, 136,
    197
Austria 30, 31, 145

Bacon, Alice MP 56
Balliol College, Oxford University 13,
    214, 223
Baldwin, Stanley 41
Balfour, John 67, 154
Bao Dai 178
Barclay, Sir Roderick 91, 103, 104, 106
Barnett, Correlli 168
Barry, Gerald 154
Beaverbrook, Max 119
Bentinck, V. F. W. Cavendish: *see:*
    Cavendish-Bentinck, V. F. W.
Bergson, A. 209
Berle, A. A. 70
Bevan, Aneurin 15, 54, 115, 129
Bevin, Ernest 2, 5, 6, 25, 32, 44, 47, 55,
    59 ff., 72, 94, 100, 123, 137–8,
    201–2

285